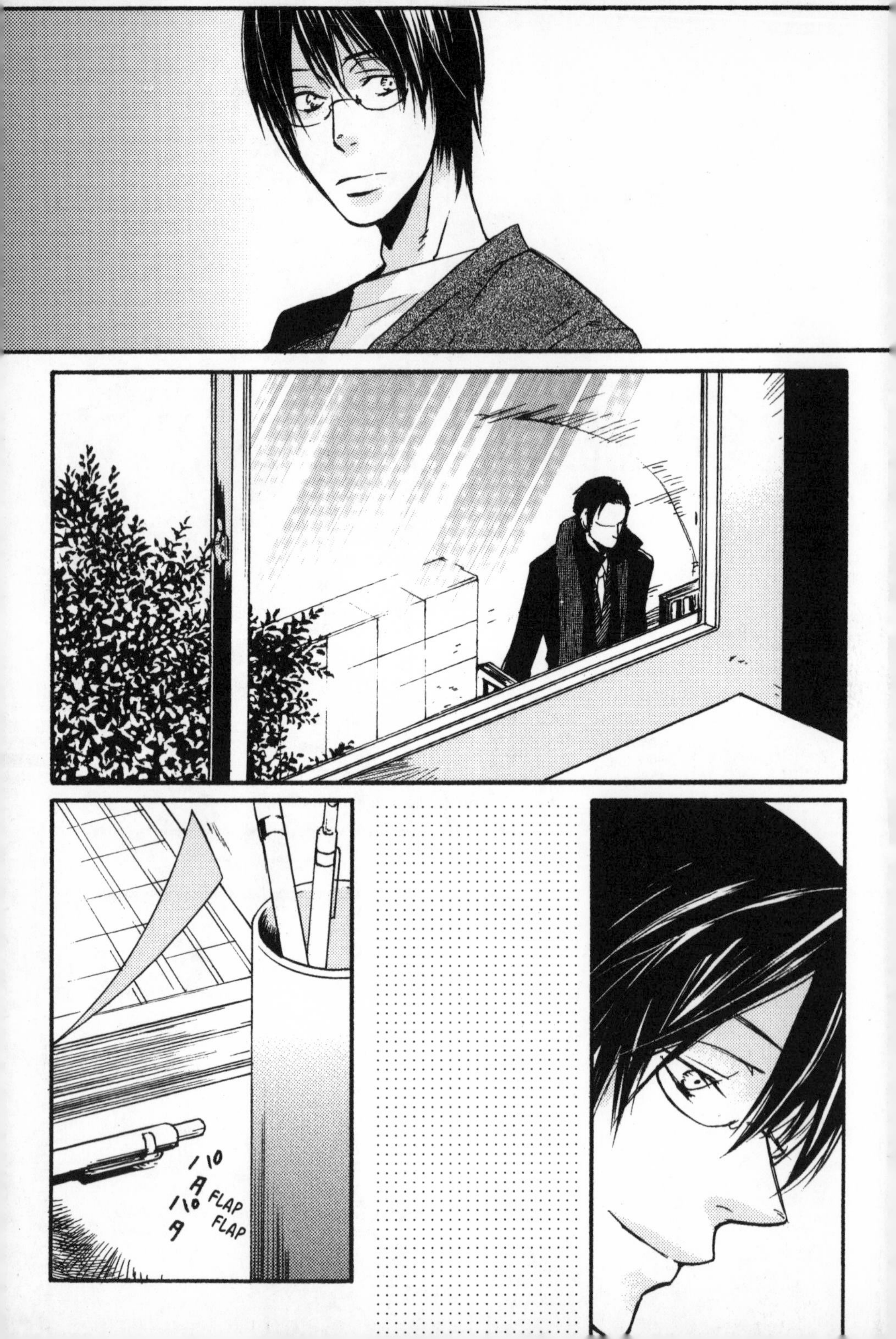
FLAP
FLAP

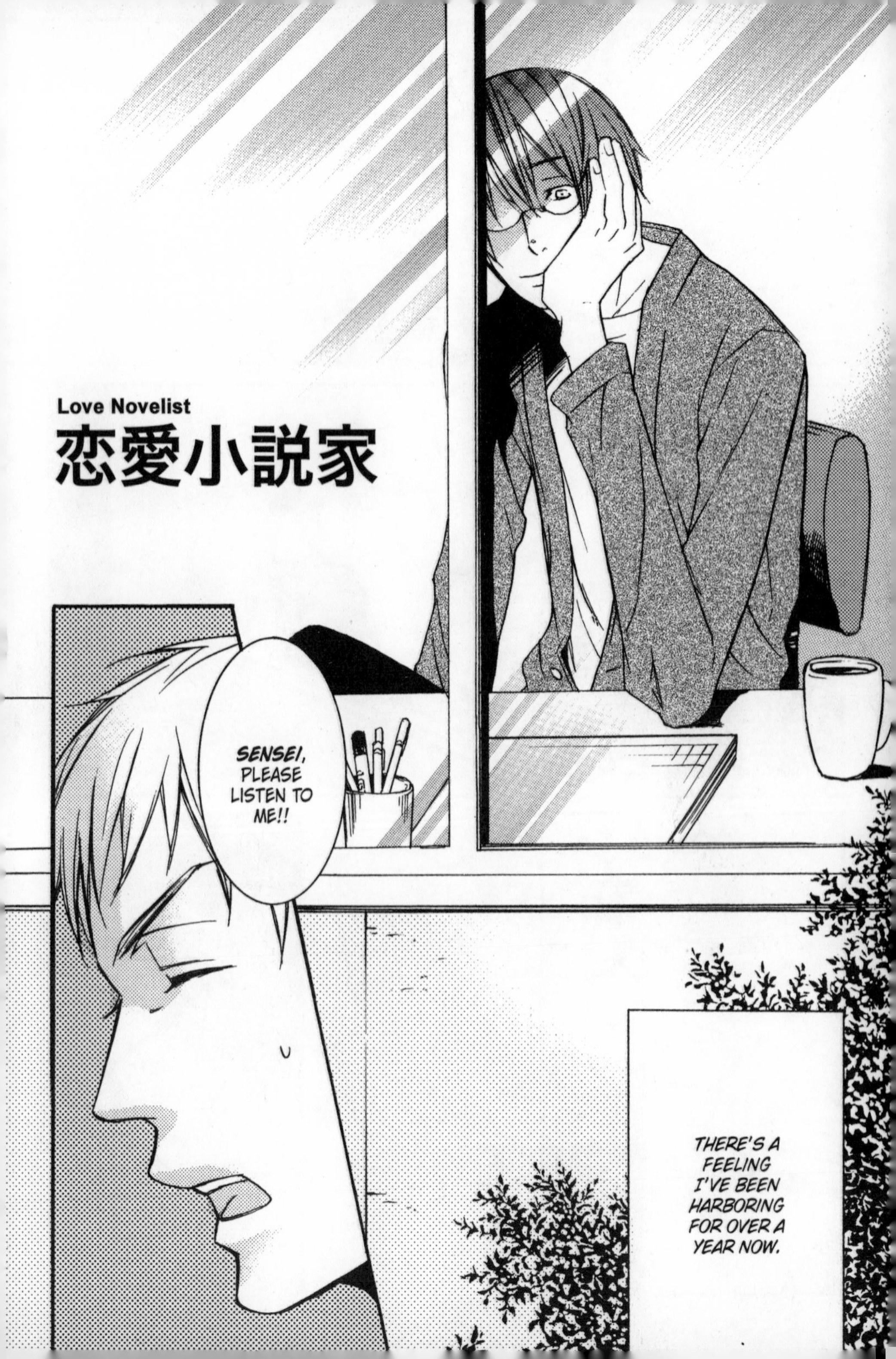
Love Novelist
恋愛小説家
SENSEI, PLEASE LISTEN TO ME!!
THERE'S A FEELING I'VE BEEN HARBORING FOR OVER A YEAR NOW.

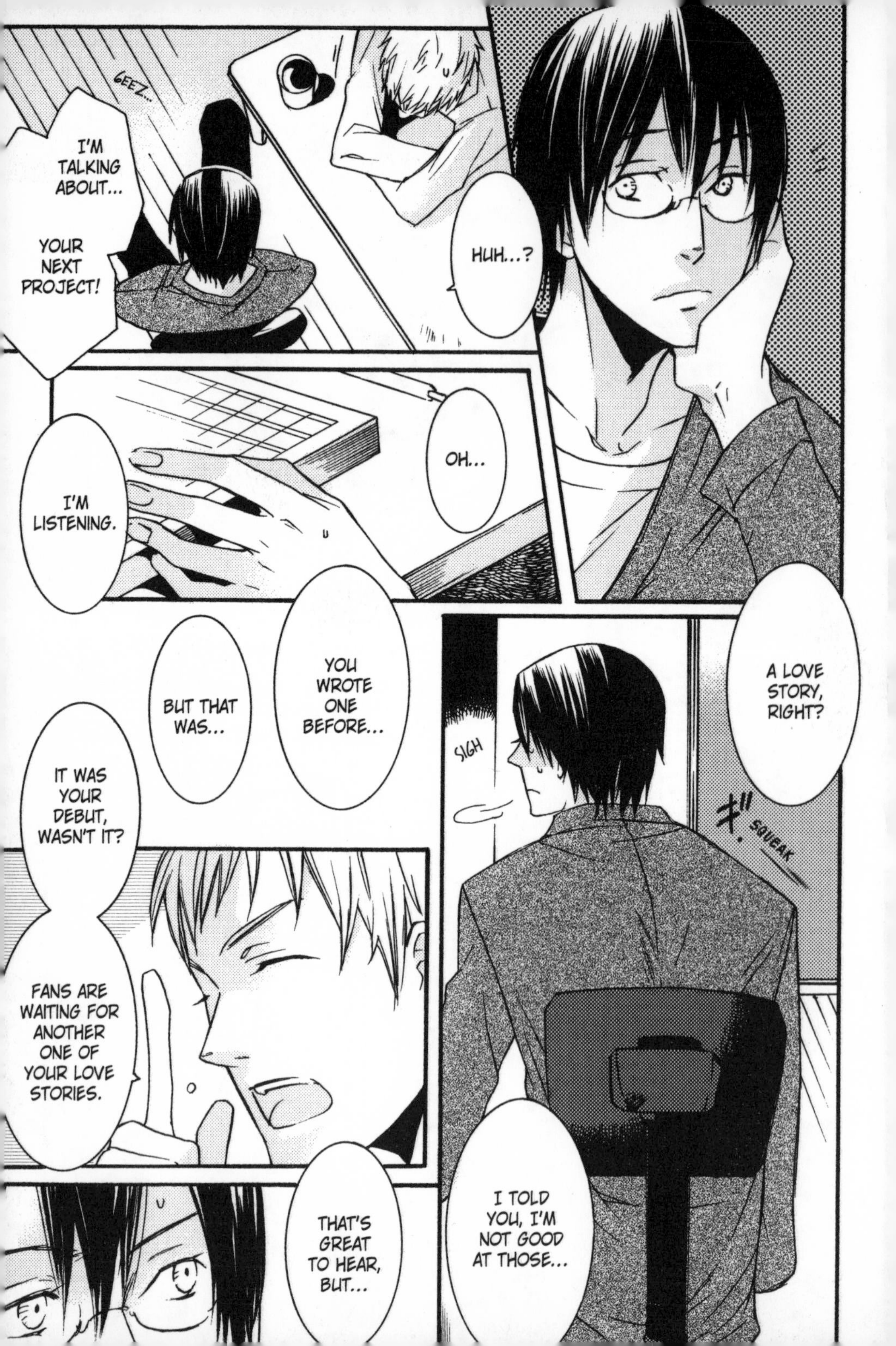
HUH...?
GEEZ...
I'M TALKING ABOUT...
YOUR NEXT PROJECT!
OH...
I'M LISTENING.
A LOVE STORY, RIGHT?
ギ SQUEAK
SIGH
I TOLD YOU, I'M NOT GOOD AT THOSE...
YOU WROTE ONE BEFORE...
BUT THAT WAS...
IT WAS YOUR DEBUT, WASN'T IT?
FANS ARE WAITING FOR ANOTHER ONE OF YOUR LOVE STORIES.
THAT'S GREAT TO HEAR, BUT...

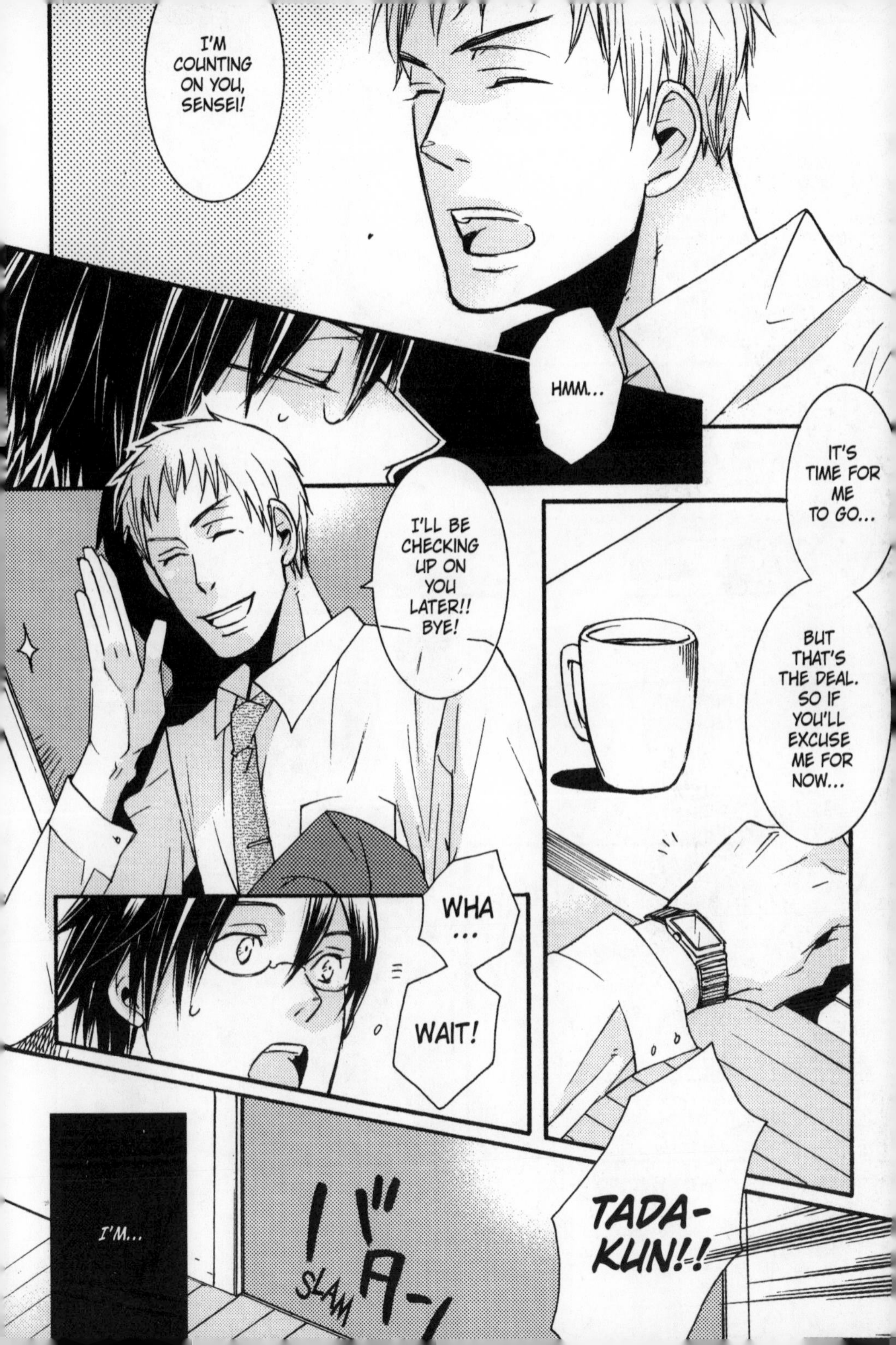
I'M COUNTING ON YOU, SENSEI!
HMM...
IT'S TIME FOR ME TO GO...
BUT THAT'S THE DEAL. SO IF YOU'LL EXCUSE ME FOR NOW...
I'LL BE CHECKING UP ON YOU LATER!! BYE!
WHA...
WAIT!
TADA-KUN!!
SLAM
I'M...

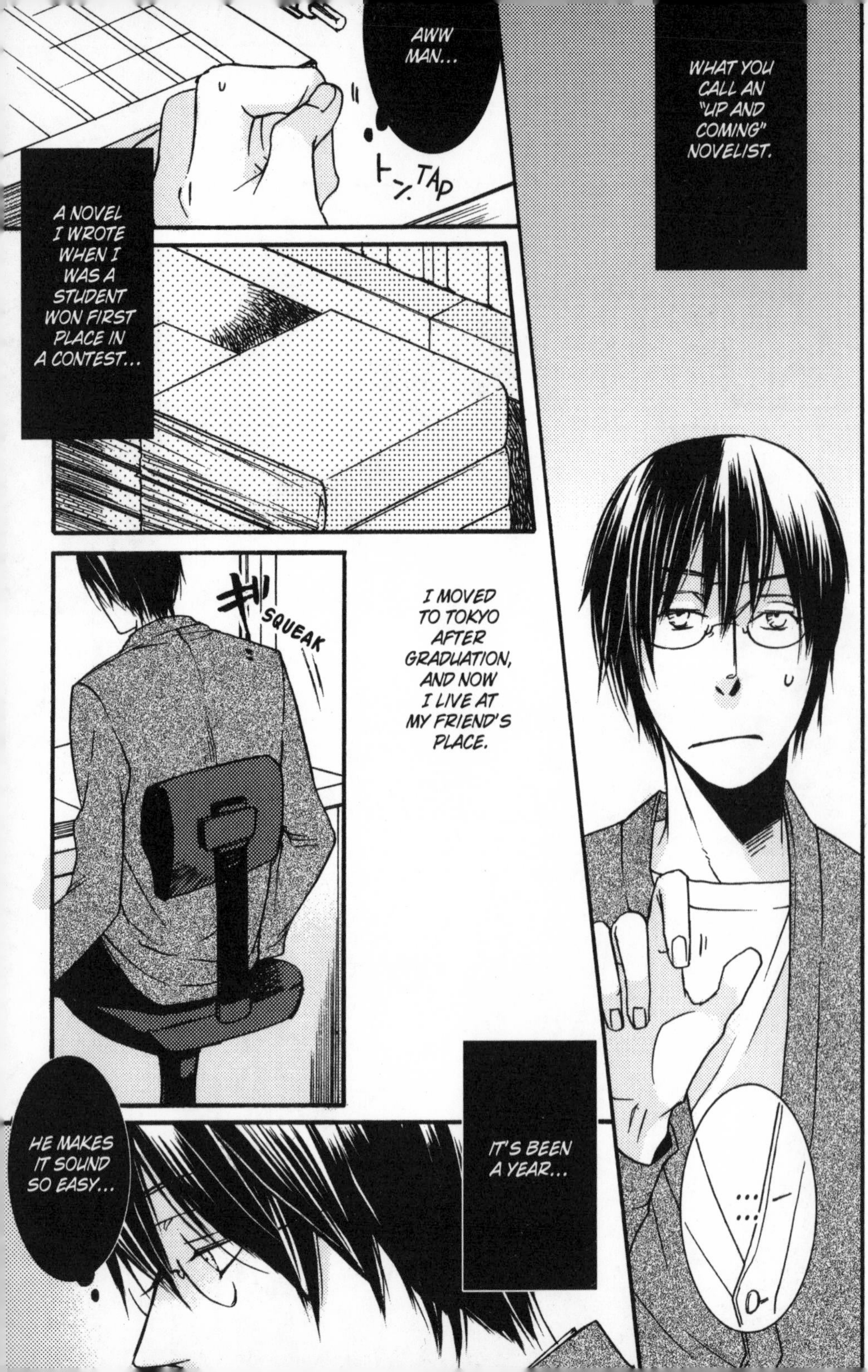
AWW MAN...
トン TAP
A NOVEL I WROTE WHEN I WAS A STUDENT WON FIRST PLACE IN A CONTEST...
WHAT YOU CALL AN "UP AND COMING" NOVELIST.
I MOVED TO TOKYO AFTER GRADUATION, AND NOW I LIVE AT MY FRIEND'S PLACE.
ギッ SQUEAK
IT'S BEEN A YEAR...
......
HE MAKES IT SOUND SO EASY...

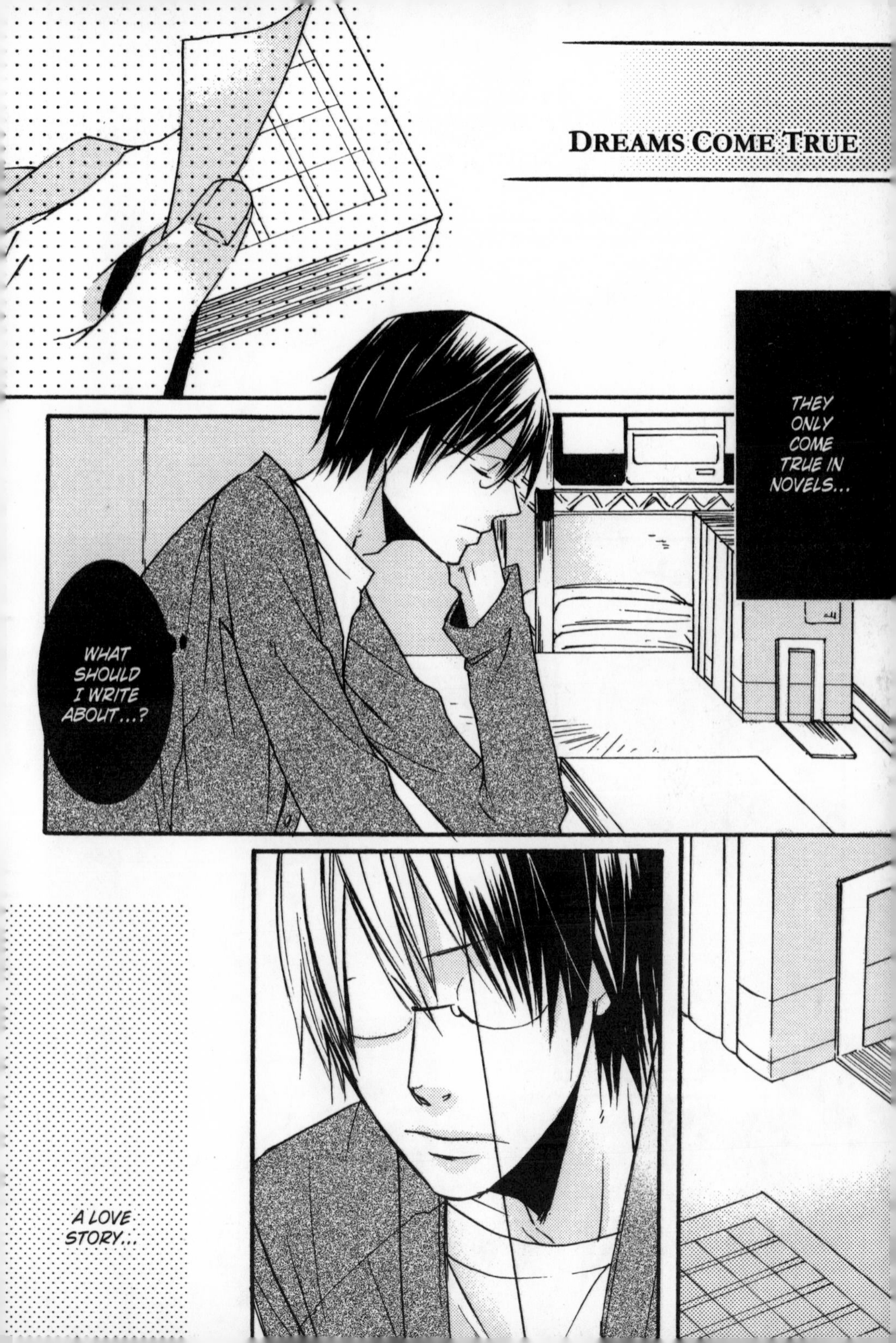
DREAMS COME TRUE
THEY ONLY COME TRUE IN NOVELS...
WHAT SHOULD I WRITE ABOUT...?
A LOVE STORY...

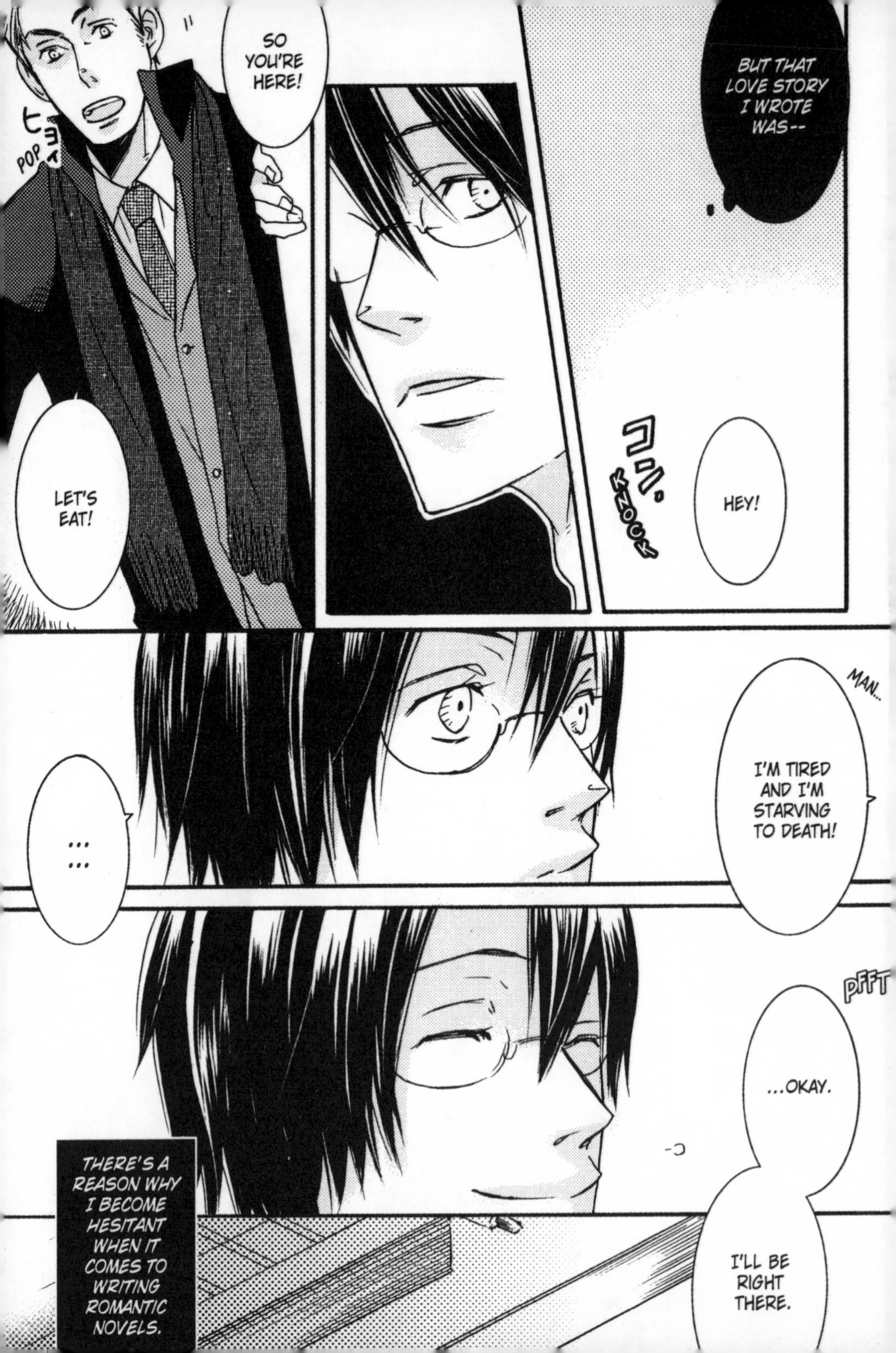
BUT THAT LOVE STORY I WROTE WAS--
KNOCK
HEY!
SO YOU'RE HERE!
POP
LET'S EAT!
MAN...
I'M TIRED AND I'M STARVING TO DEATH!
... ...
pFFT
...OKAY.
I'LL BE RIGHT THERE.
THERE'S A REASON WHY I BECOME HESITANT WHEN IT COMES TO WRITING ROMANTIC NOVELS.

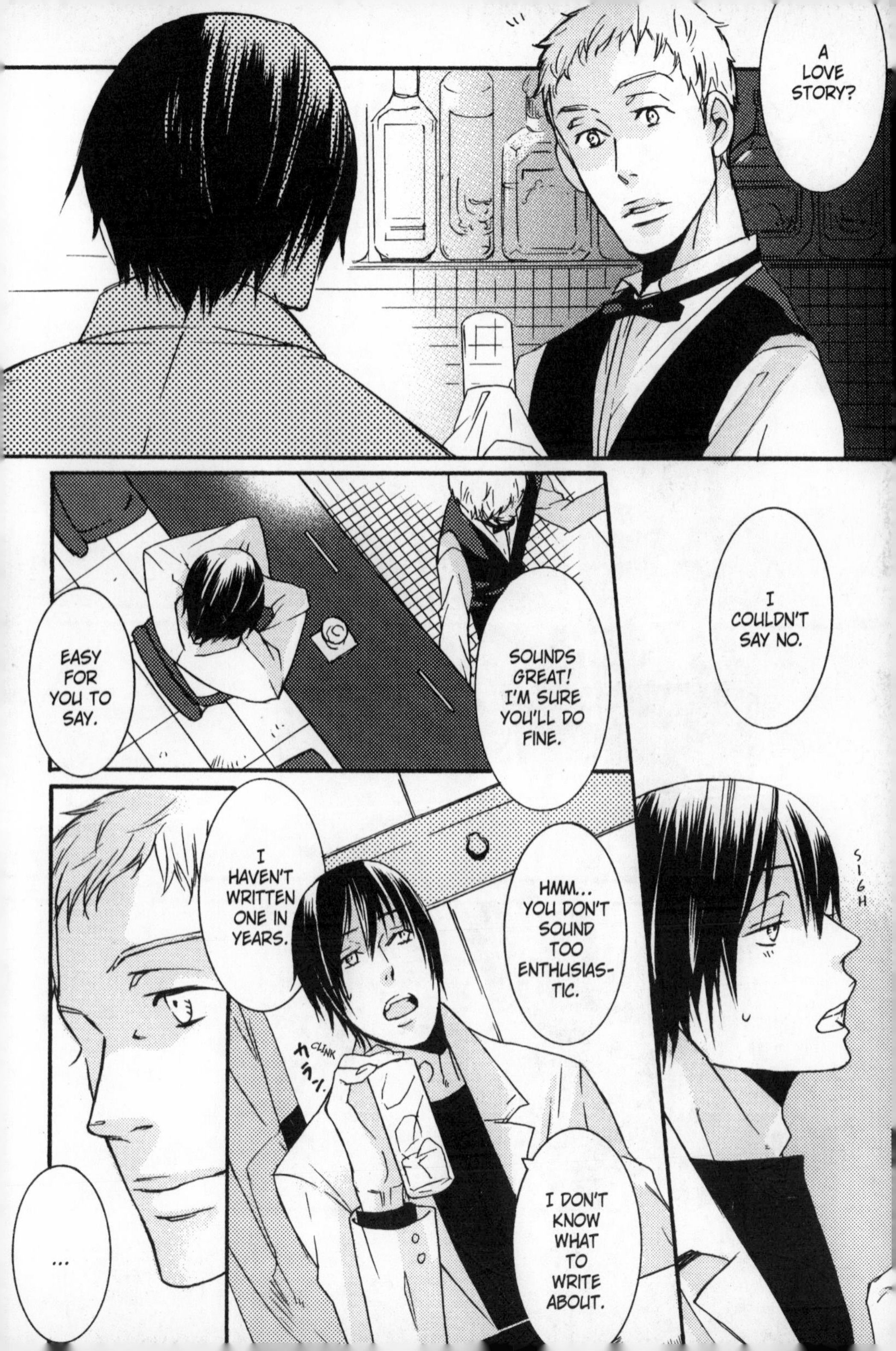
A LOVE STORY?
I COULDN'T SAY NO.
SOUNDS GREAT! I'M SURE YOU'LL DO FINE.
EASY FOR YOU TO SAY.
SIGH
HMM... YOU DON'T SOUND TOO ENTHUSIAS-TIC.
I HAVEN'T WRITTEN ONE IN YEARS.
CLINK
I DON'T KNOW WHAT TO WRITE ABOUT.
...

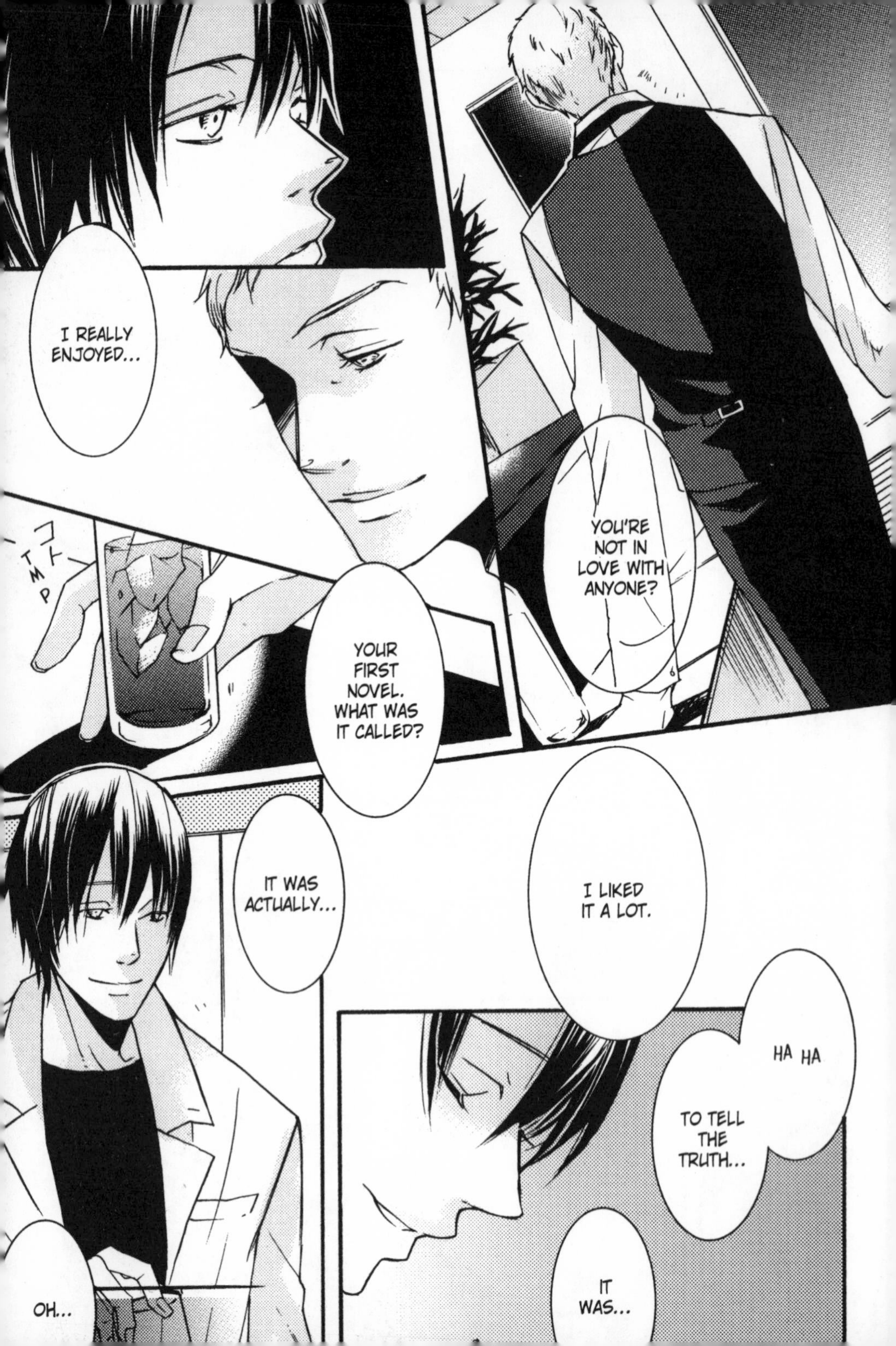
YOU'RE NOT IN LOVE WITH ANYONE?
I REALLY ENJOYED...
YOUR FIRST NOVEL. WHAT WAS IT CALLED?
コト
TMP
I LIKED IT A LOT.
HA HA
TO TELL THE TRUTH...
IT WAS...
IT WAS ACTUALLY...
OH...

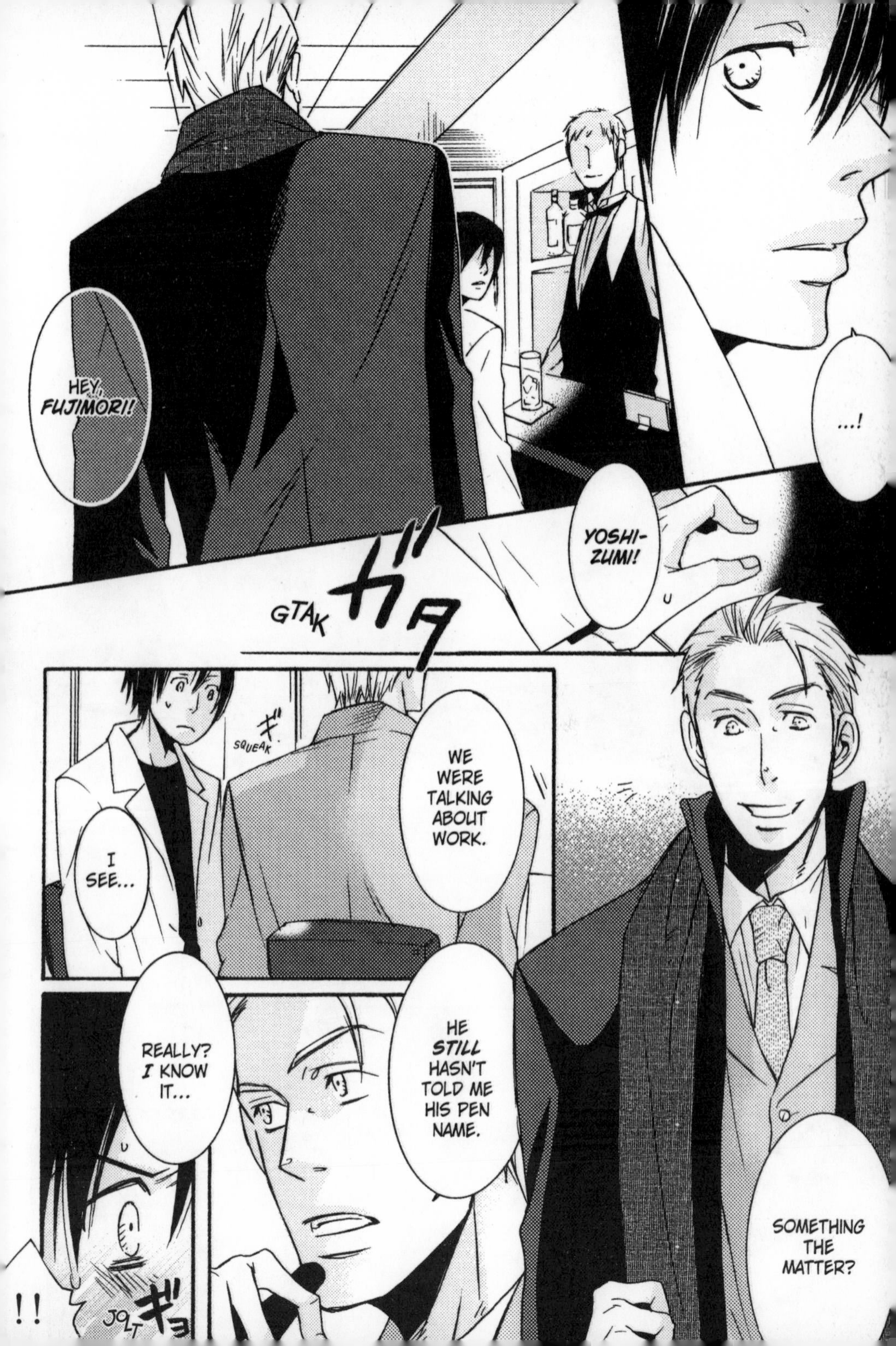

...!
HEY, FUJIMORI!
YOSHI-ZUMI!
GTAK
SOMETHING THE MATTER?
SQUEAK
WE WERE TALKING ABOUT WORK.
I SEE...
HE STILL HASN'T TOLD ME HIS PEN NAME.
REALLY? I KNOW IT...
JOLT
!!

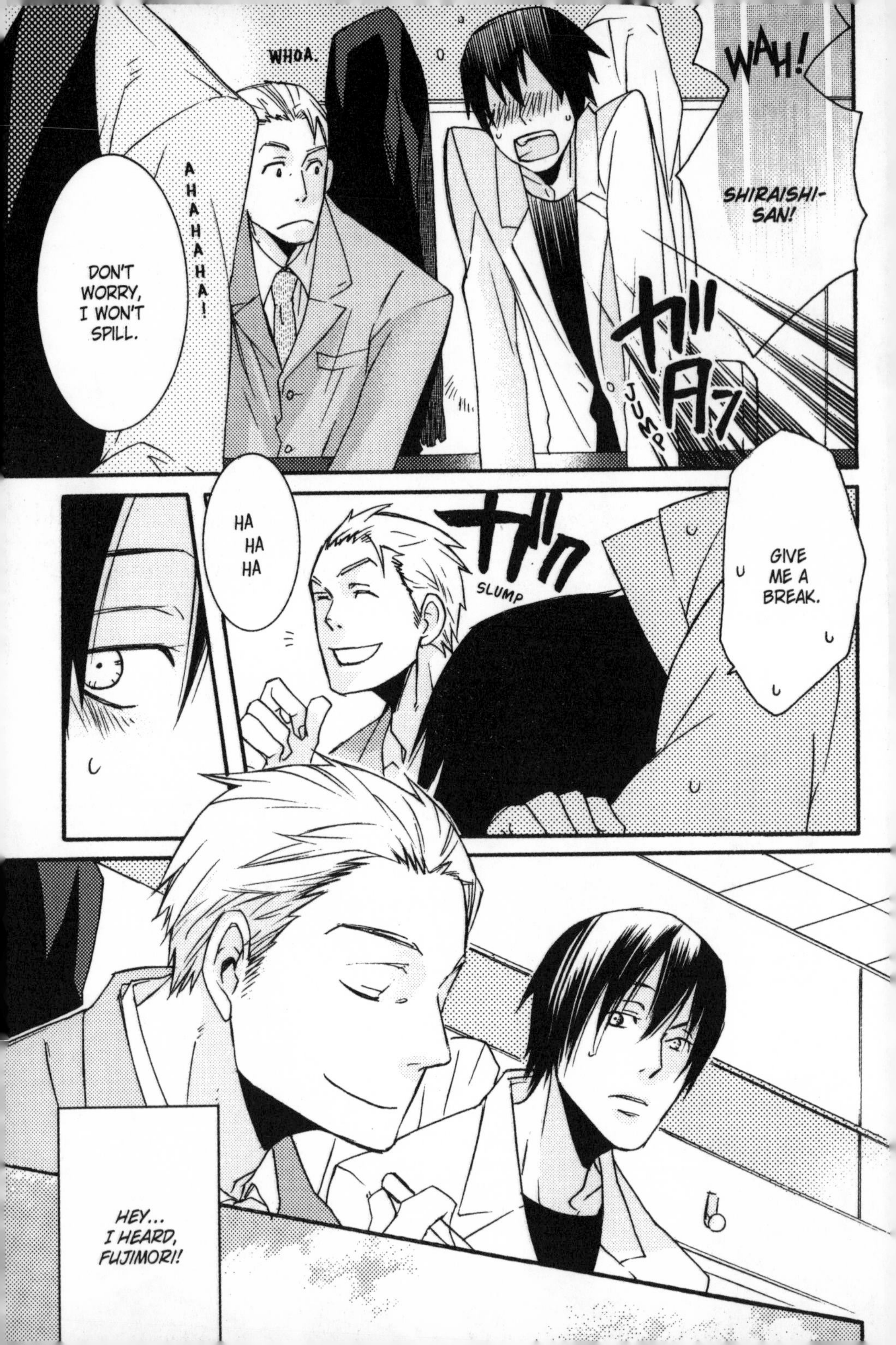
WAH!
SHIRAISHI-SAN!
ガタッ
JUMP
WHOA.
AHAHAHA!
DON'T WORRY, I WON'T SPILL.
GIVE ME A BREAK.
ガクッ
SLUMP
HA HA HA
HEY... I HEARD, FUJIMORI!

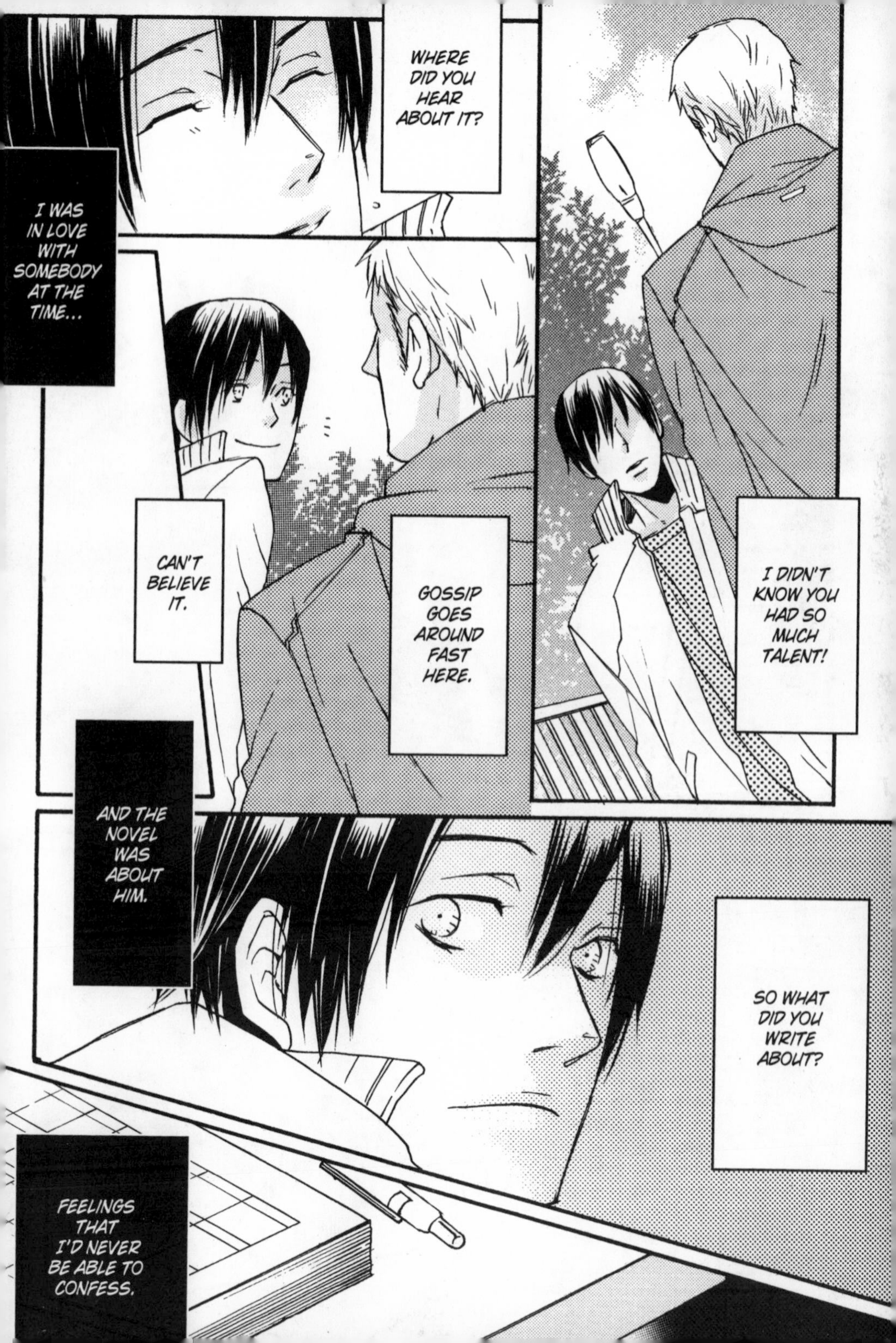
I DIDN'T KNOW YOU HAD SO MUCH TALENT!
WHERE DID YOU HEAR ABOUT IT?
I WAS IN LOVE WITH SOMEBODY AT THE TIME...
GOSSIP GOES AROUND FAST HERE.
CAN'T BELIEVE IT.
SO WHAT DID YOU WRITE ABOUT?
AND THE NOVEL WAS ABOUT HIM.
FEELINGS THAT I'D NEVER BE ABLE TO CONFESS.

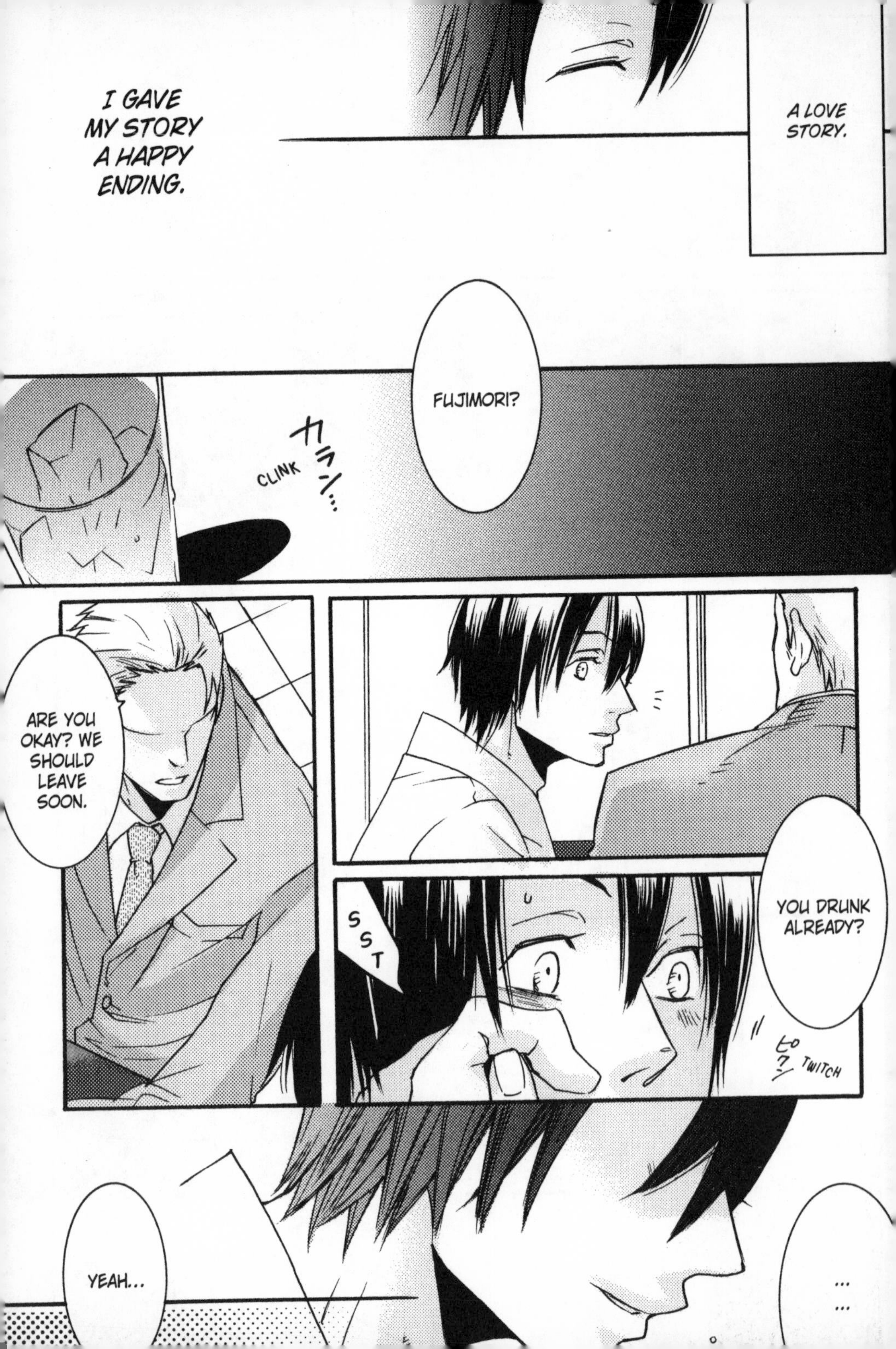
A LOVE STORY.
I GAVE MY STORY A HAPPY ENDING.
FUJIMORI?
カラン…
CLINK
YOU DRUNK ALREADY?
ピクッ
TWITCH
SST
ARE YOU OKAY? WE SHOULD LEAVE SOON.
…
…
YEAH…

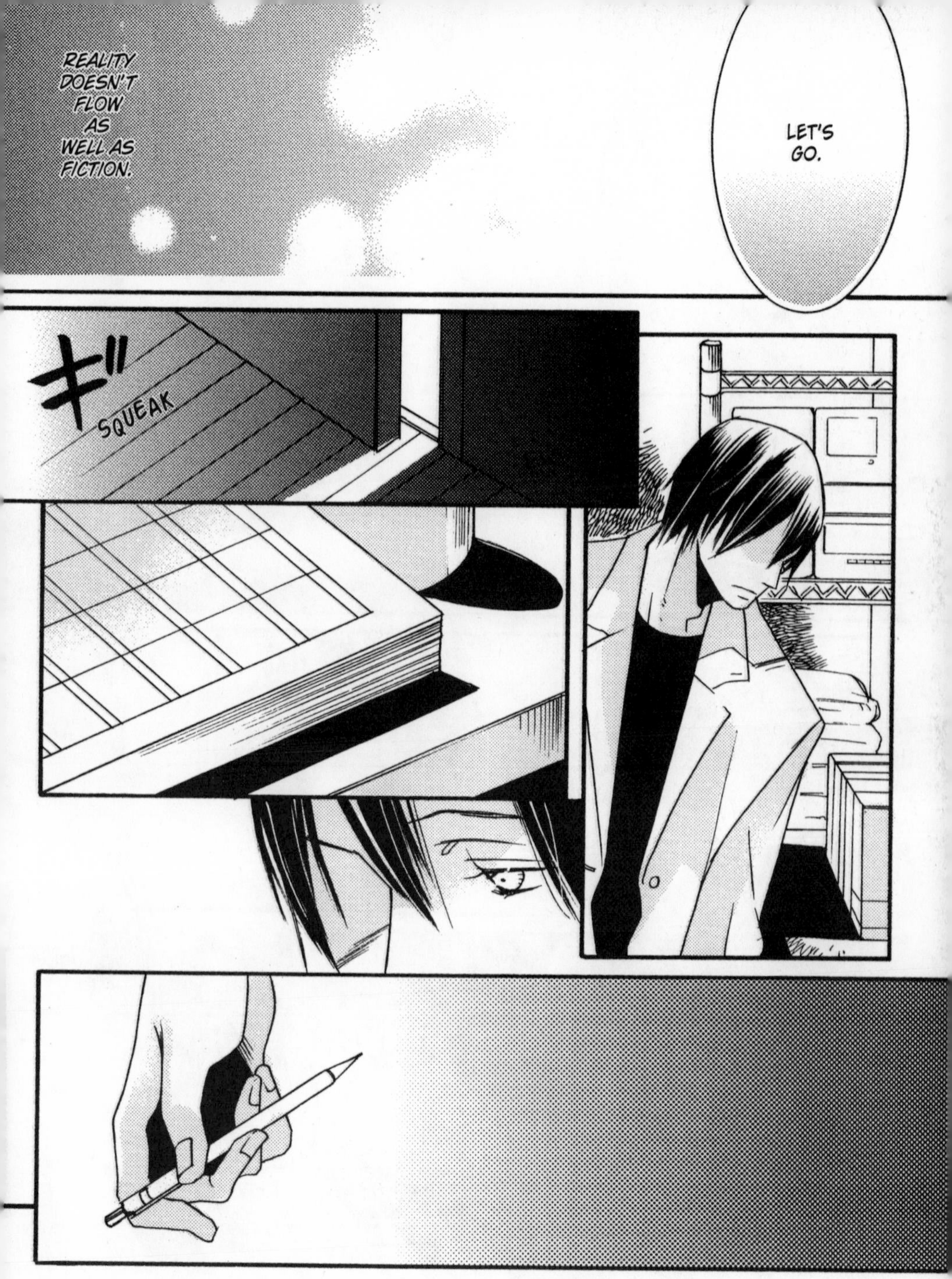
LET'S GO.
REALITY DOESN'T FLOW AS WELL AS FICTION.
ギ
SQUEAK

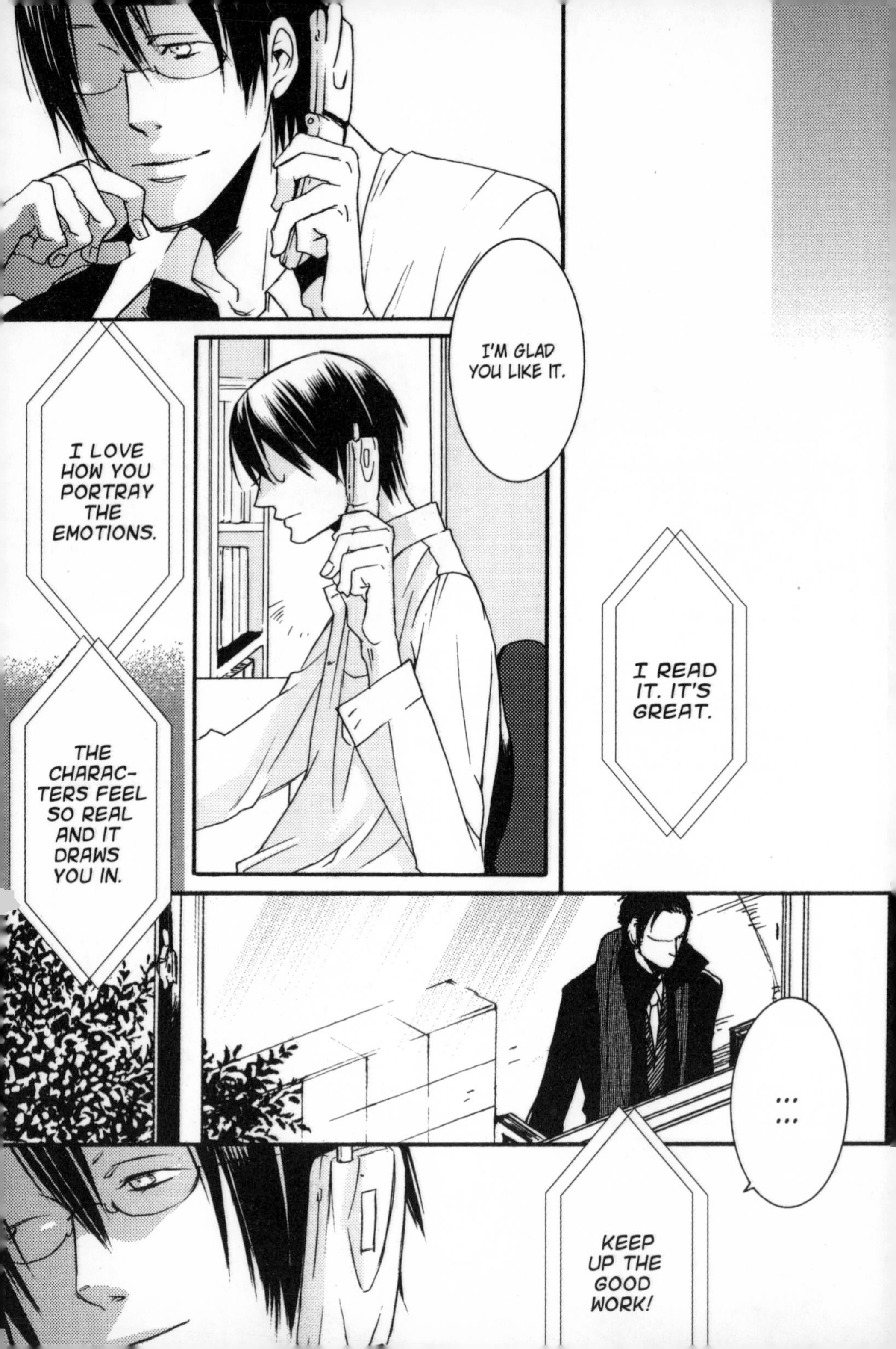

I'M GLAD YOU LIKE IT.
I READ IT. IT'S GREAT.
I LOVE HOW YOU PORTRAY THE EMOTIONS.
THE CHARAC-TERS FEEL SO REAL AND IT DRAWS YOU IN.
... ...
KEEP UP THE GOOD WORK!

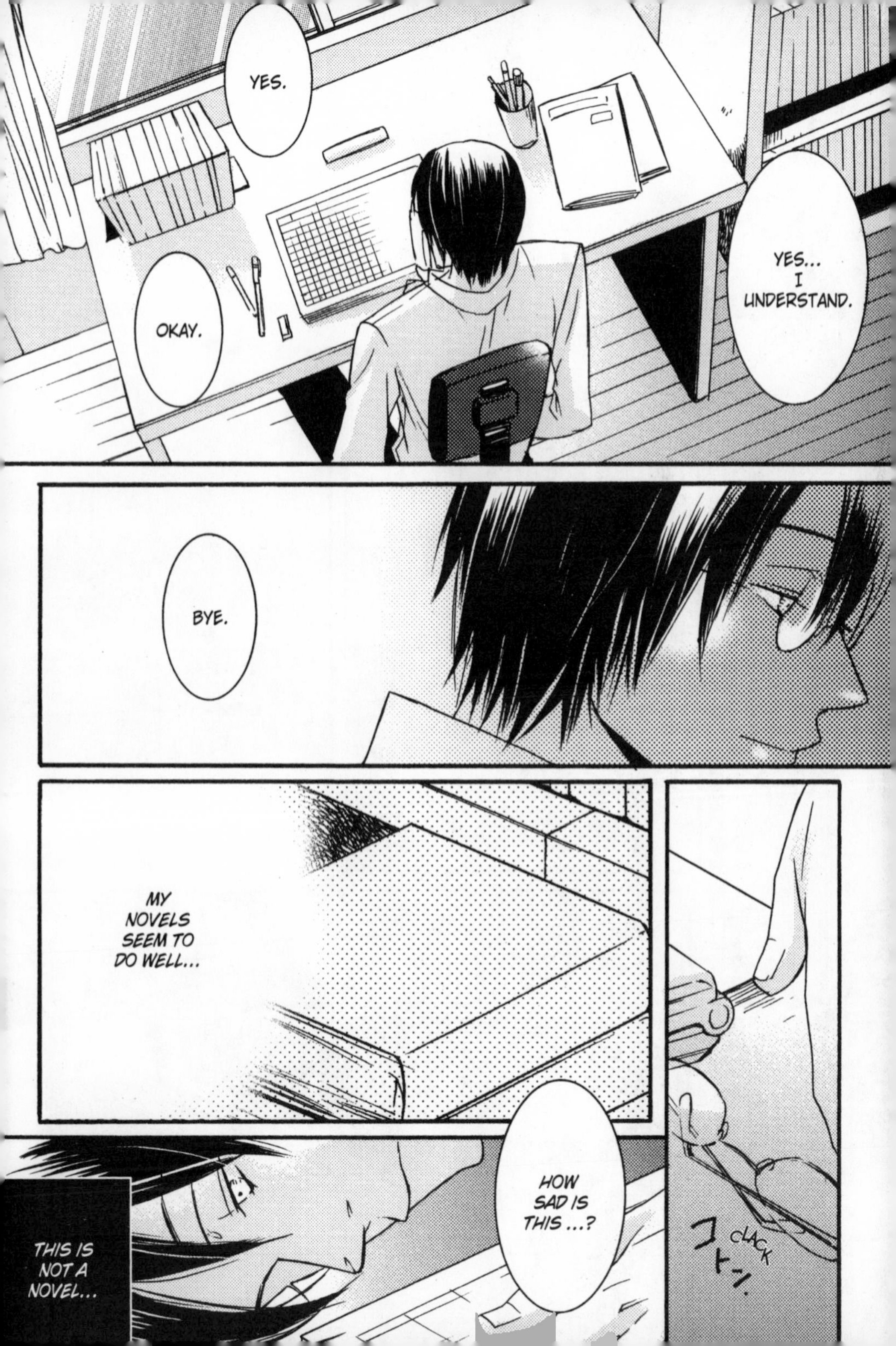
YES... I UNDERSTAND.
YES.
OKAY.
BYE.
コトン
CLACK
MY NOVELS SEEM TO DO WELL...
HOW SAD IS THIS ...?
THIS IS NOT A NOVEL...

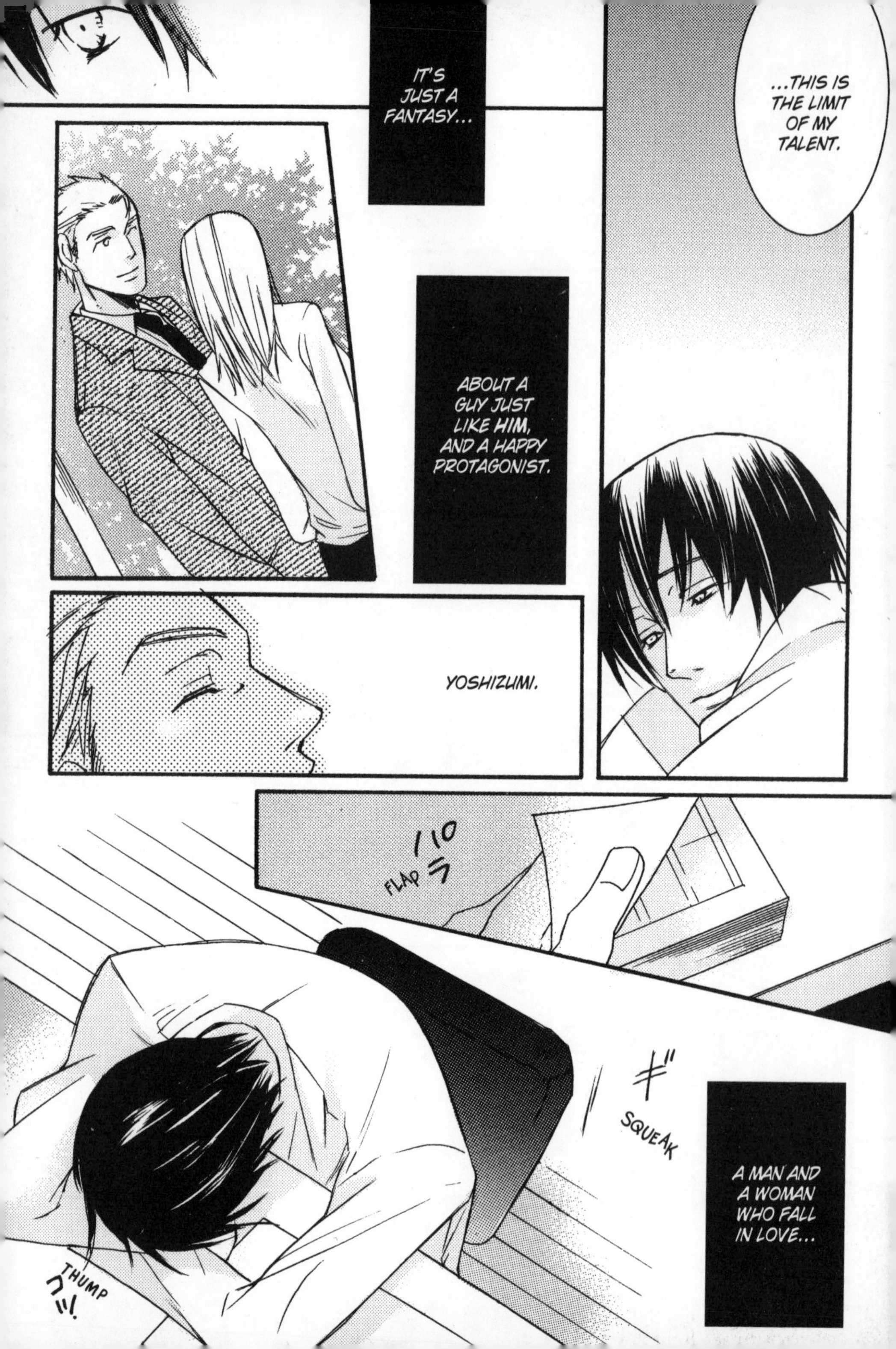
...THIS IS THE LIMIT OF MY TALENT.
IT'S JUST A FANTASY...
ABOUT A GUY JUST LIKE HIM, AND A HAPPY PROTAGONIST.
YOSHIZUMI.
FLAP
SQUEAK
A MAN AND A WOMAN WHO FALL IN LOVE...
THUMP

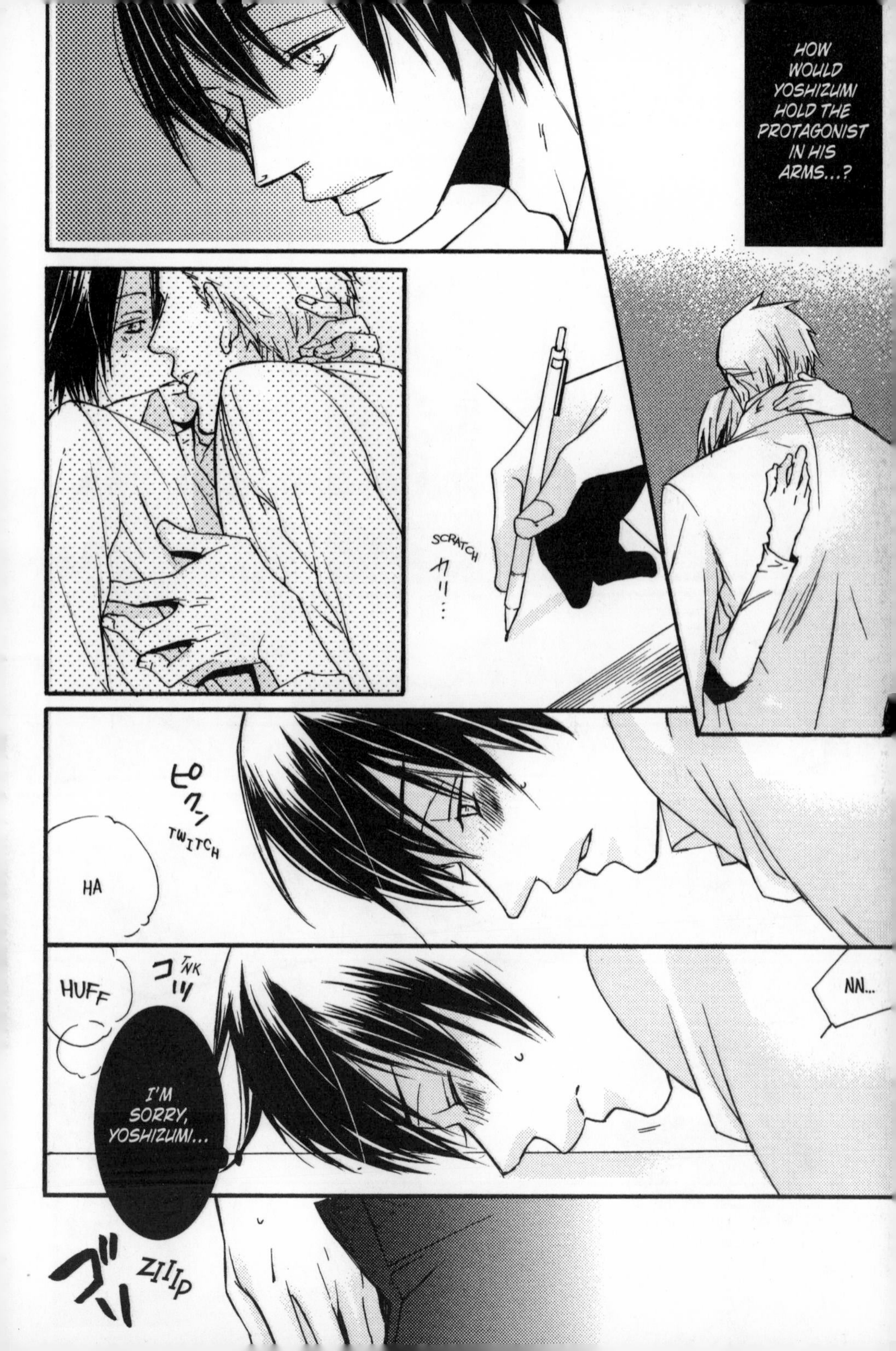
HOW WOULD YOSHIZUMI HOLD THE PROTAGONIST IN HIS ARMS...?
SCRATCH
TWITCH
HA
NN...
TNK
HUFF
I'M SORRY, YOSHIZUMI...
ZIIIP

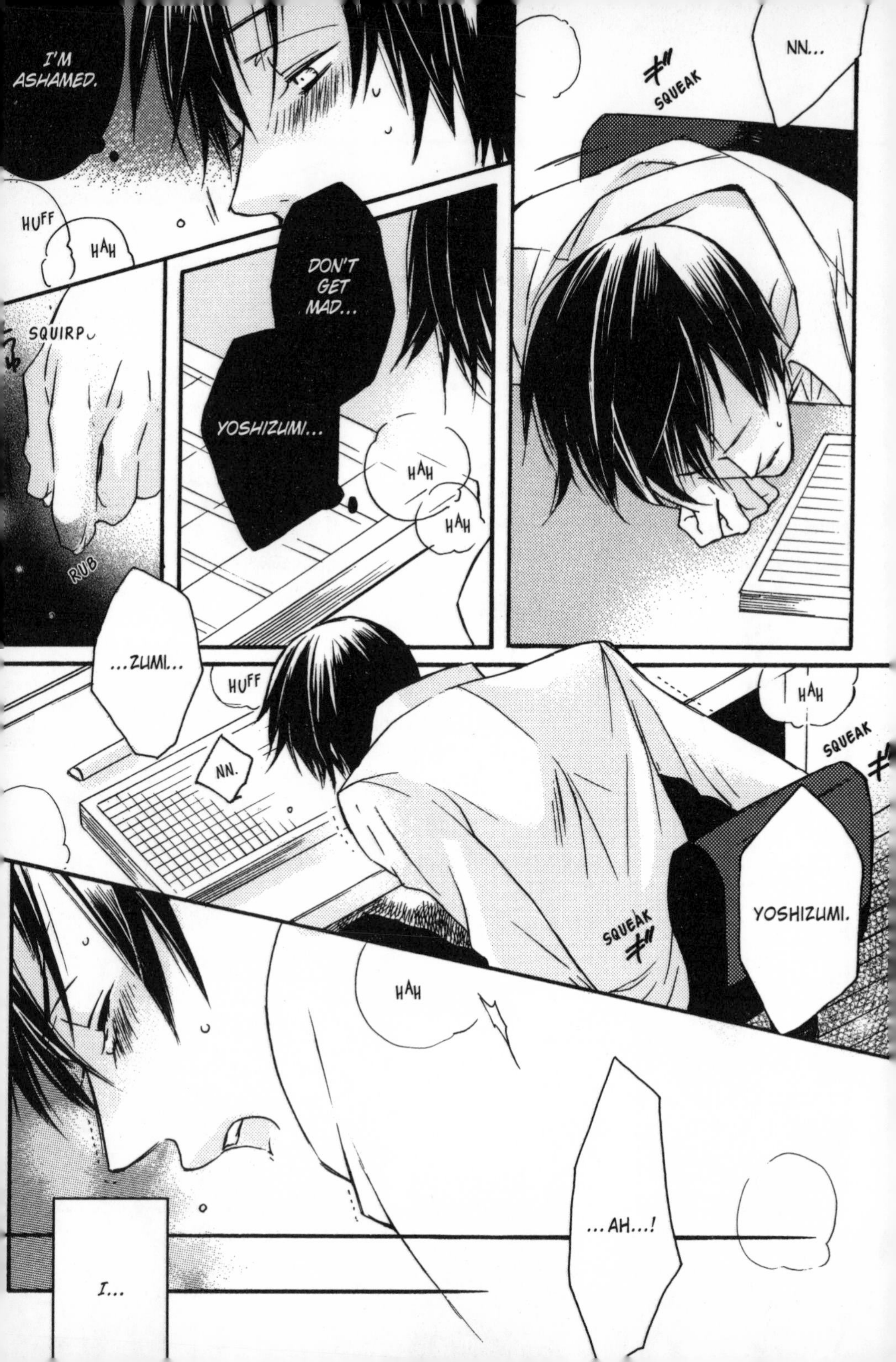

NN...
SQUEAK
I'M ASHAMED.
DON'T GET MAD...
YOSHIZUMI...
HAH
HAH
HUFF
HAH
SQUIRP
RUB
...ZUMI...
HAH
SQUEAK
YOSHIZUMI.
SQUEAK
NN.
HUFF
HAH
...AH...!
I...

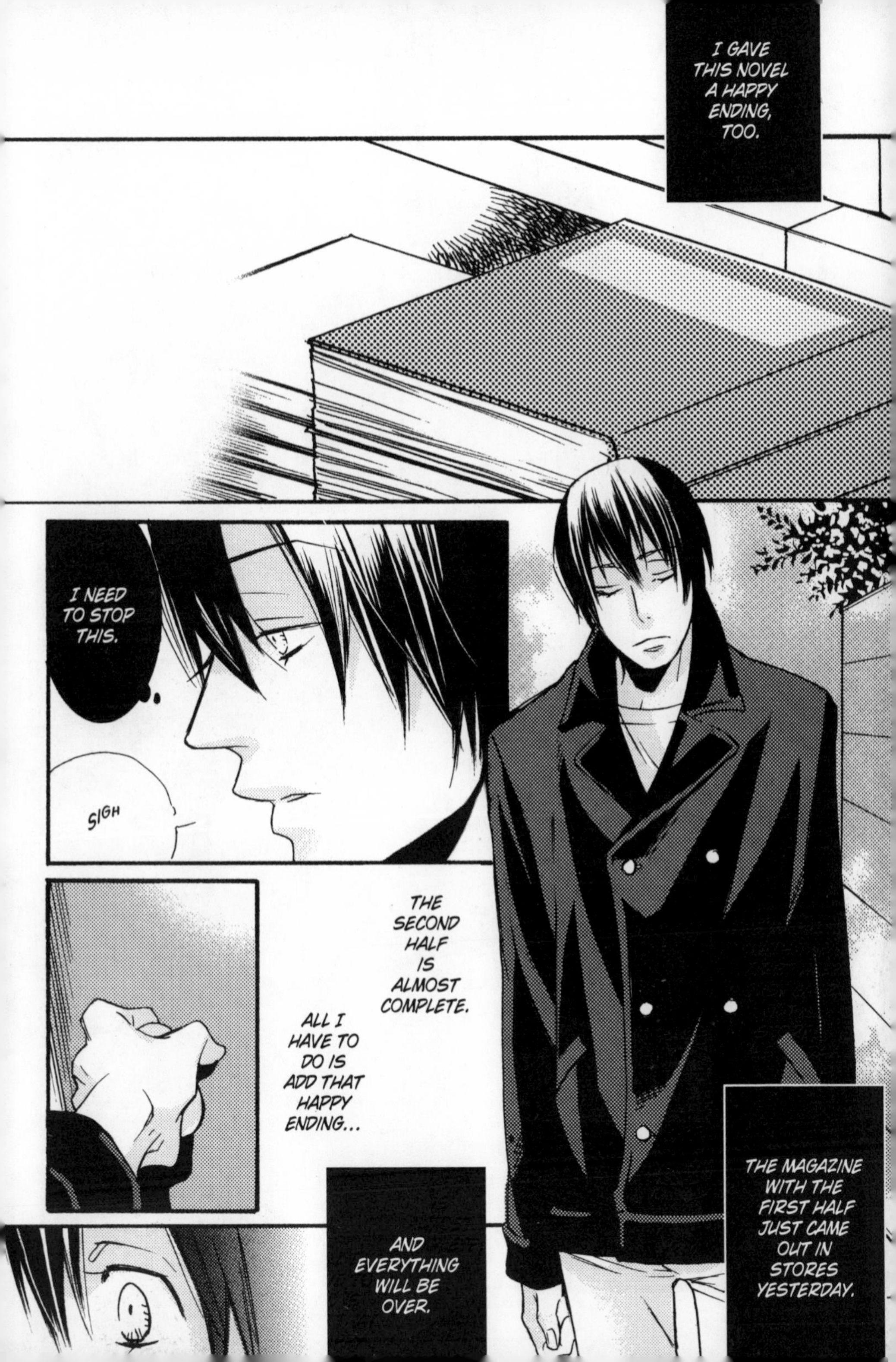

I GAVE THIS NOVEL A HAPPY ENDING, TOO.
THE MAGAZINE WITH THE FIRST HALF JUST CAME OUT IN STORES YESTERDAY.
I NEED TO STOP THIS.
SIGH
THE SECOND HALF IS ALMOST COMPLETE.
ALL I HAVE TO DO IS ADD THAT HAPPY ENDING...
AND EVERYTHING WILL BE OVER.

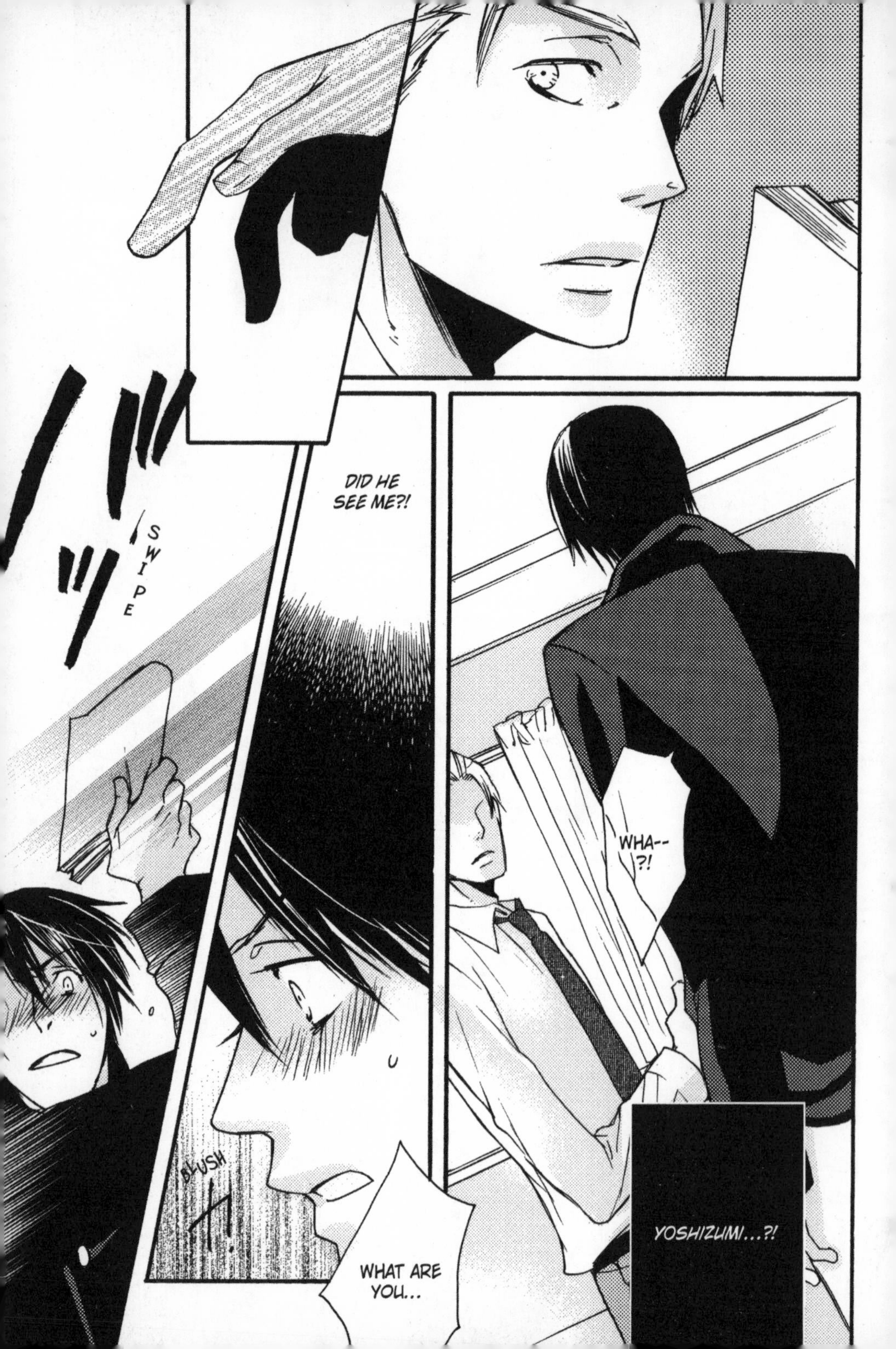
WHA-- ?!
YOSHIZUMI...?!
DID HE SEE ME?!
BLUSH
WHAT ARE YOU...
SWIPE

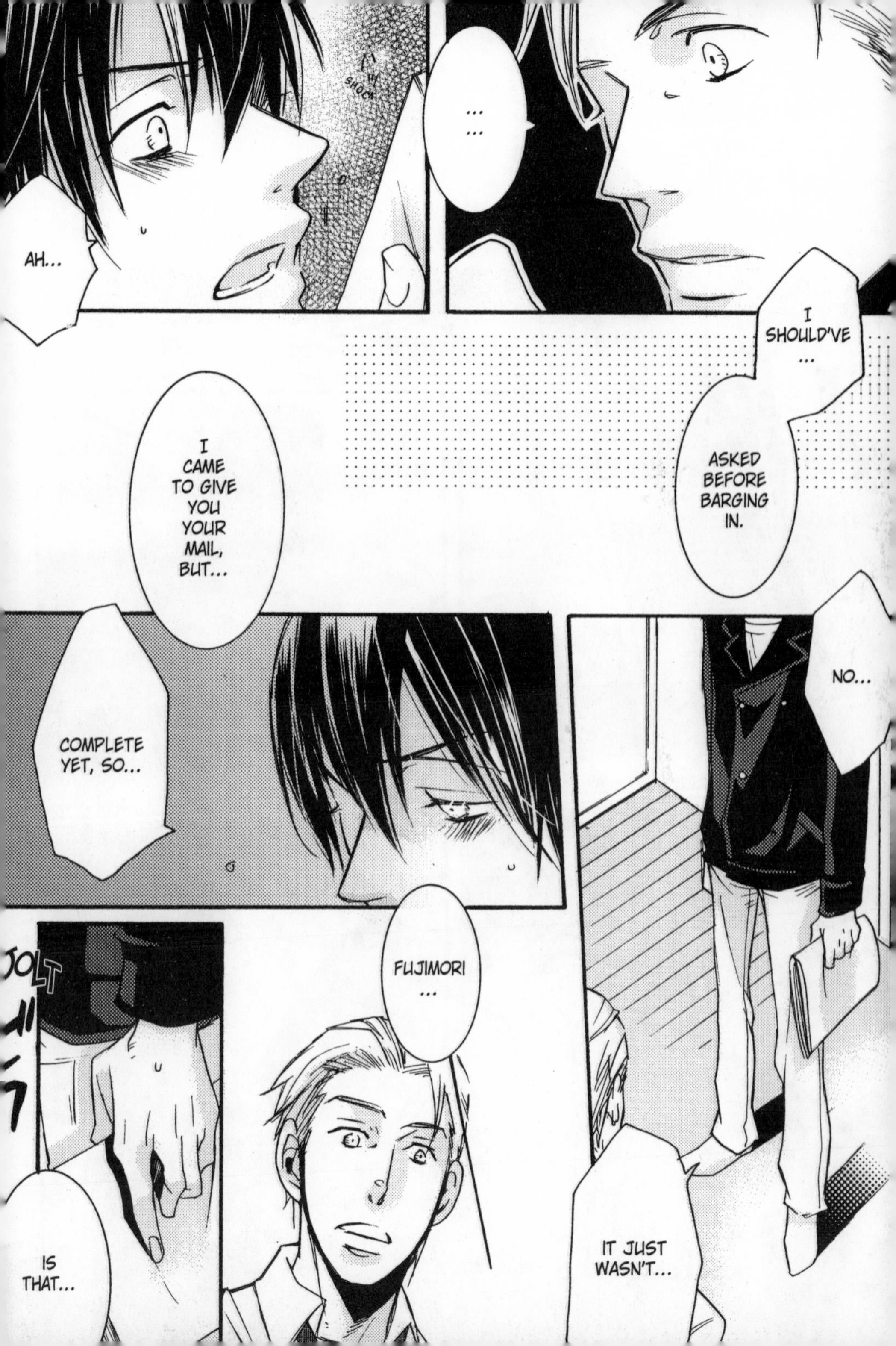

... ...
SHOCK
AH...
I SHOULD'VE ...
ASKED BEFORE BARGING IN.
I CAME TO GIVE YOU YOUR MAIL, BUT...
NO...
IT JUST WASN'T...
COMPLETE YET, SO...
FUJIMORI ...
JOLT
IS THAT...

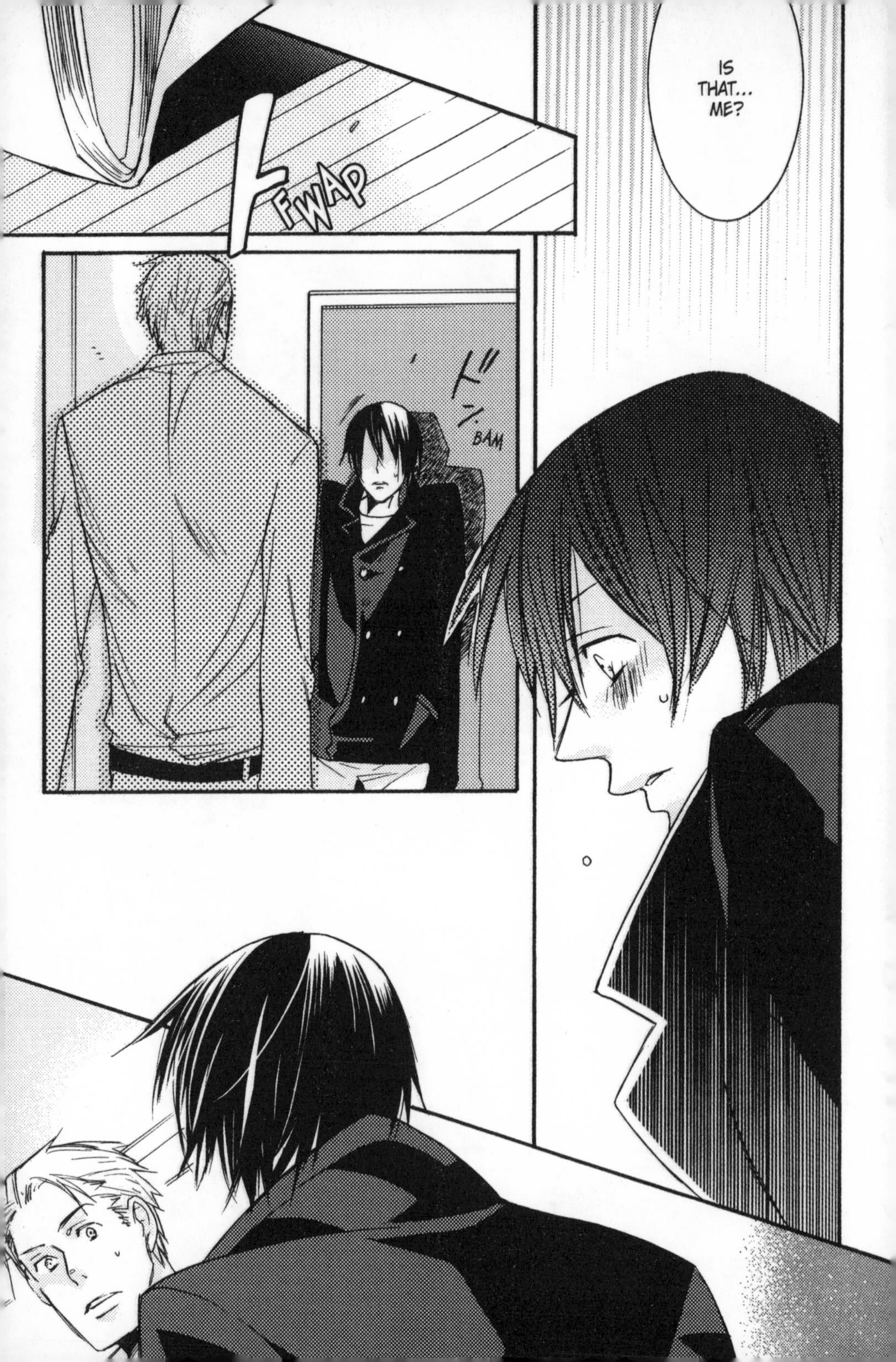
IS THAT... ME?
FWAP
ドン
BAM

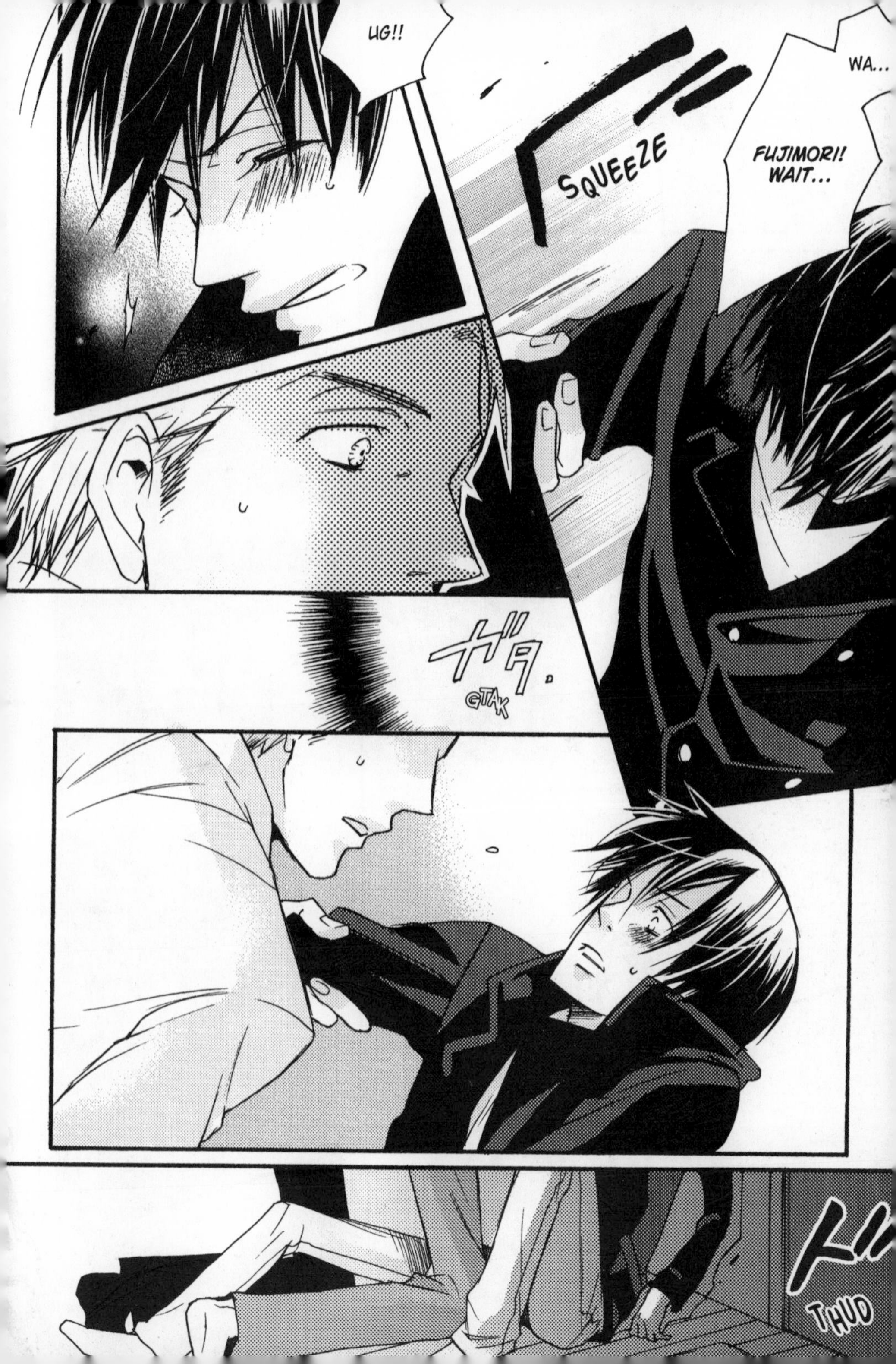
WA...
FUJIMORI! WAIT...
SQUEEZE
UG!!
ガタ
GTAK
THUD

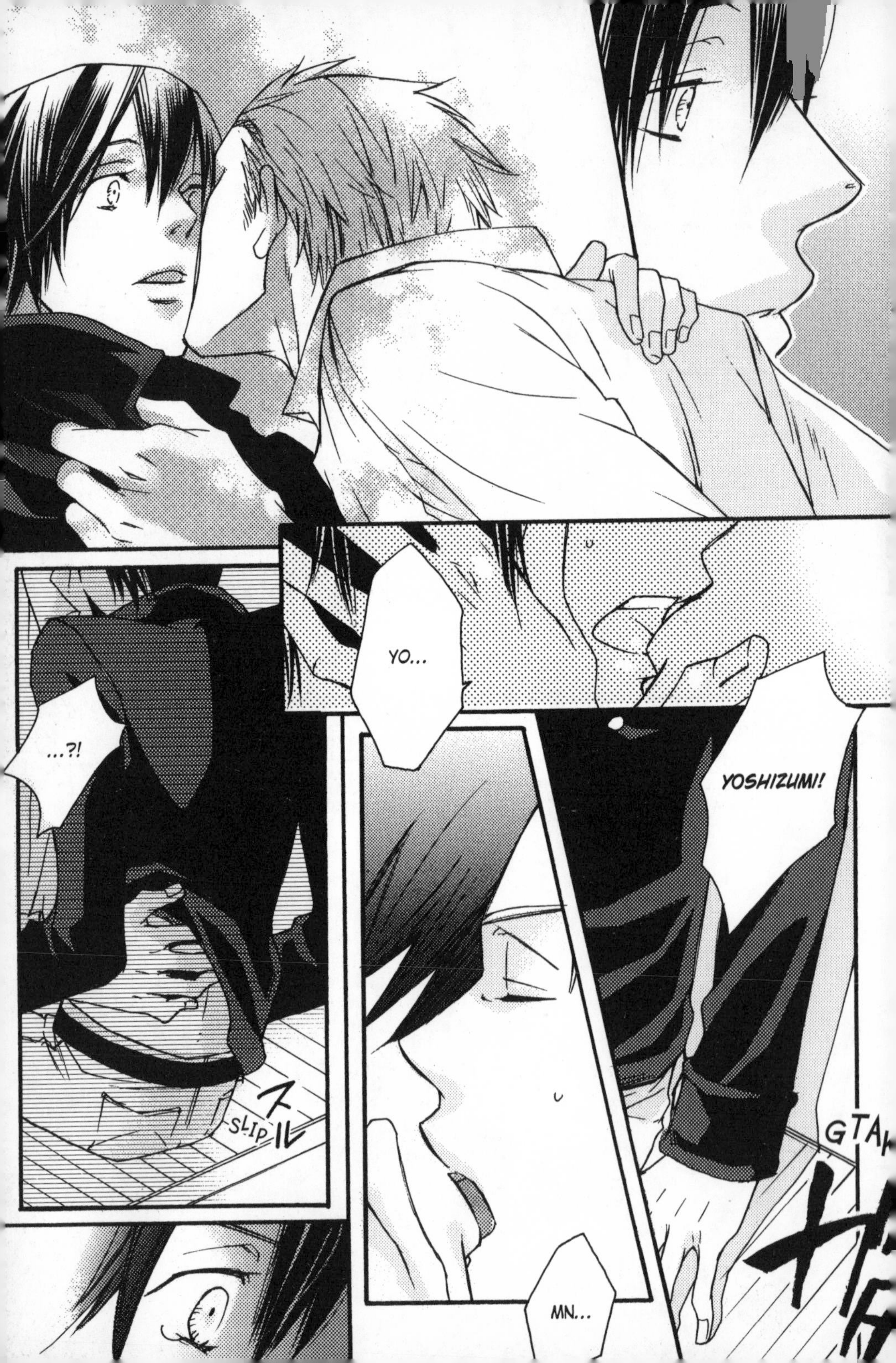

YO...
YOSHIZUMI!
GTAK
MN...
...?!
スル
SLIP

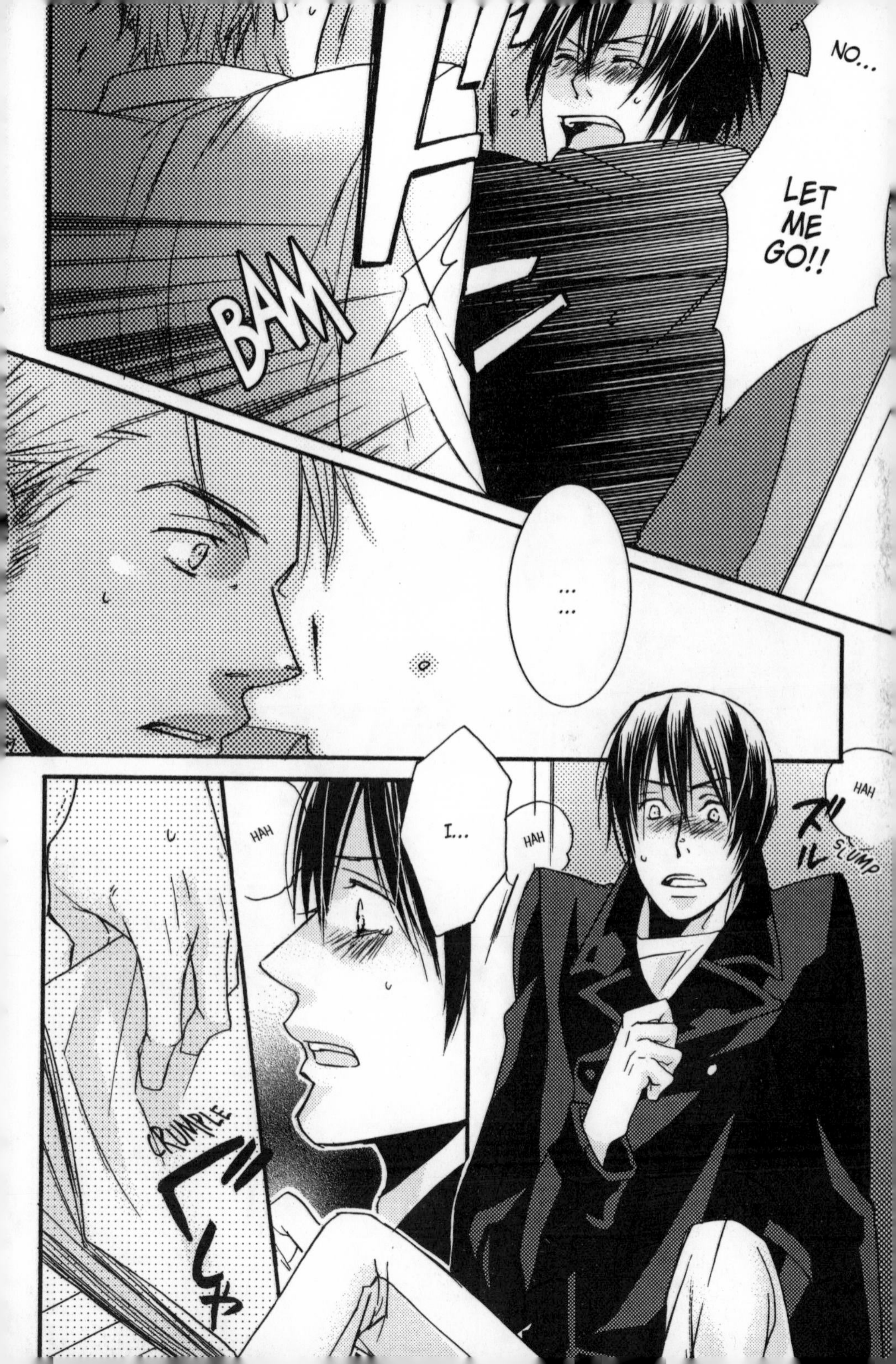
NO...
LET ME GO!!
BAM
......
HAH
ズル
SLUMP
HAH
I...
HAH
CRUMPLE
ぐしゃ

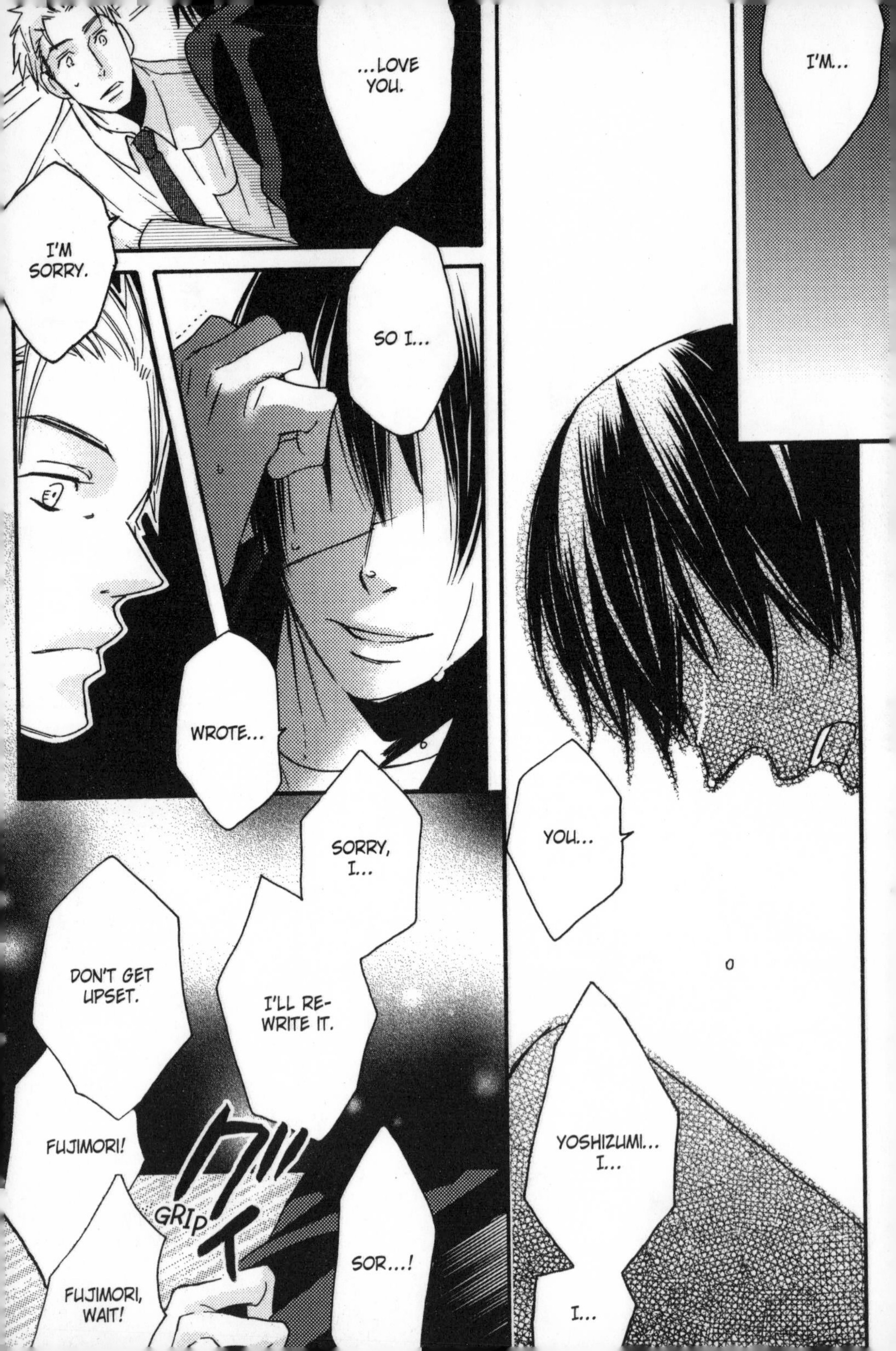
I'M...
YOU...
YOSHIZUMI... I...
I...
...LOVE YOU.
I'M SORRY.
SO I...
WROTE...
SORRY, I...
I'LL RE-WRITE IT.
DON'T GET UPSET.
SOR...!
GRIP
FUJIMORI!
FUJIMORI, WAIT!

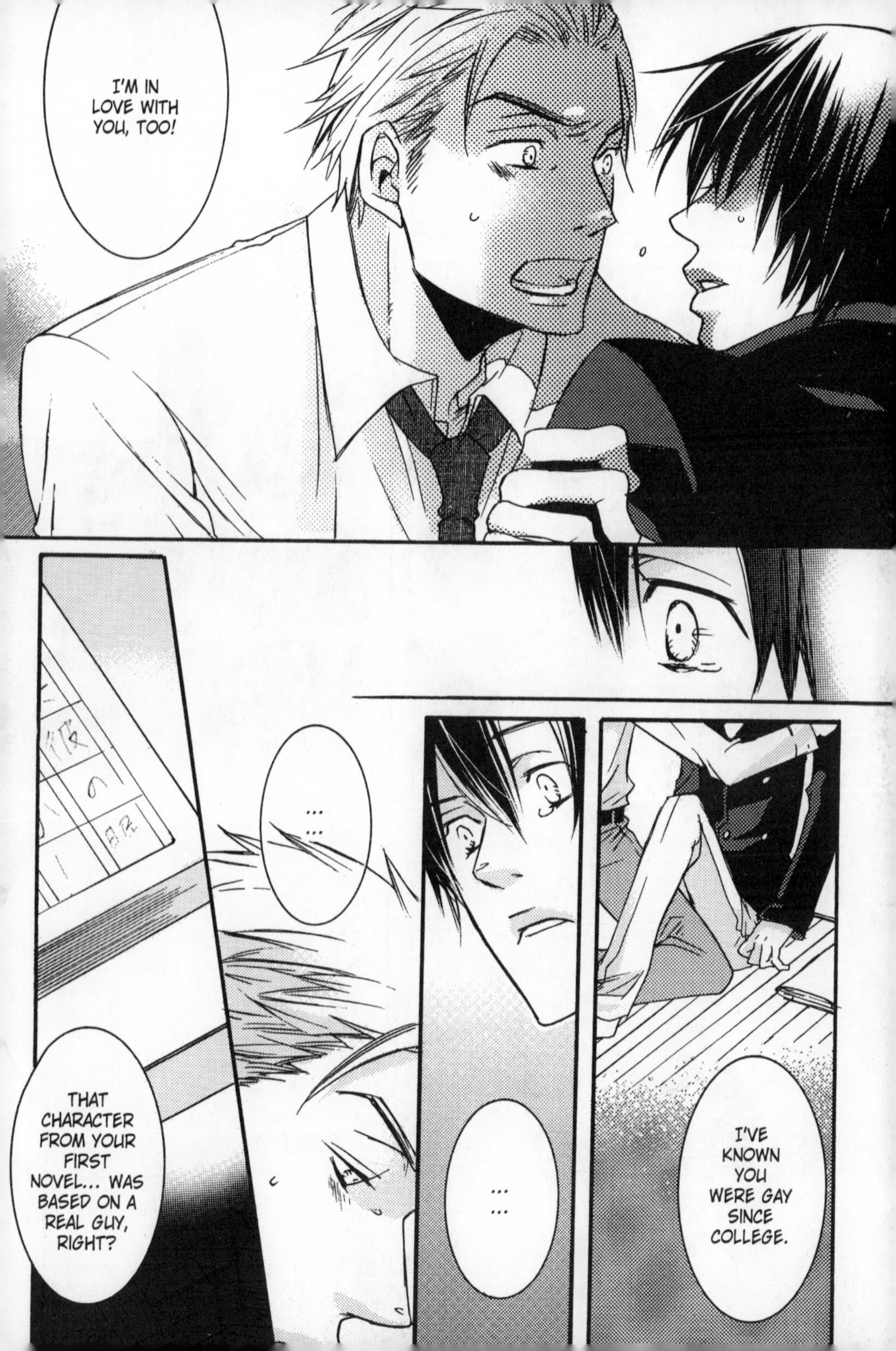
I'M IN LOVE WITH YOU, TOO!
I'VE KNOWN YOU WERE GAY SINCE COLLEGE.
... ...
... ...
THAT CHARACTER FROM YOUR FIRST NOVEL... WAS BASED ON A REAL GUY, RIGHT?

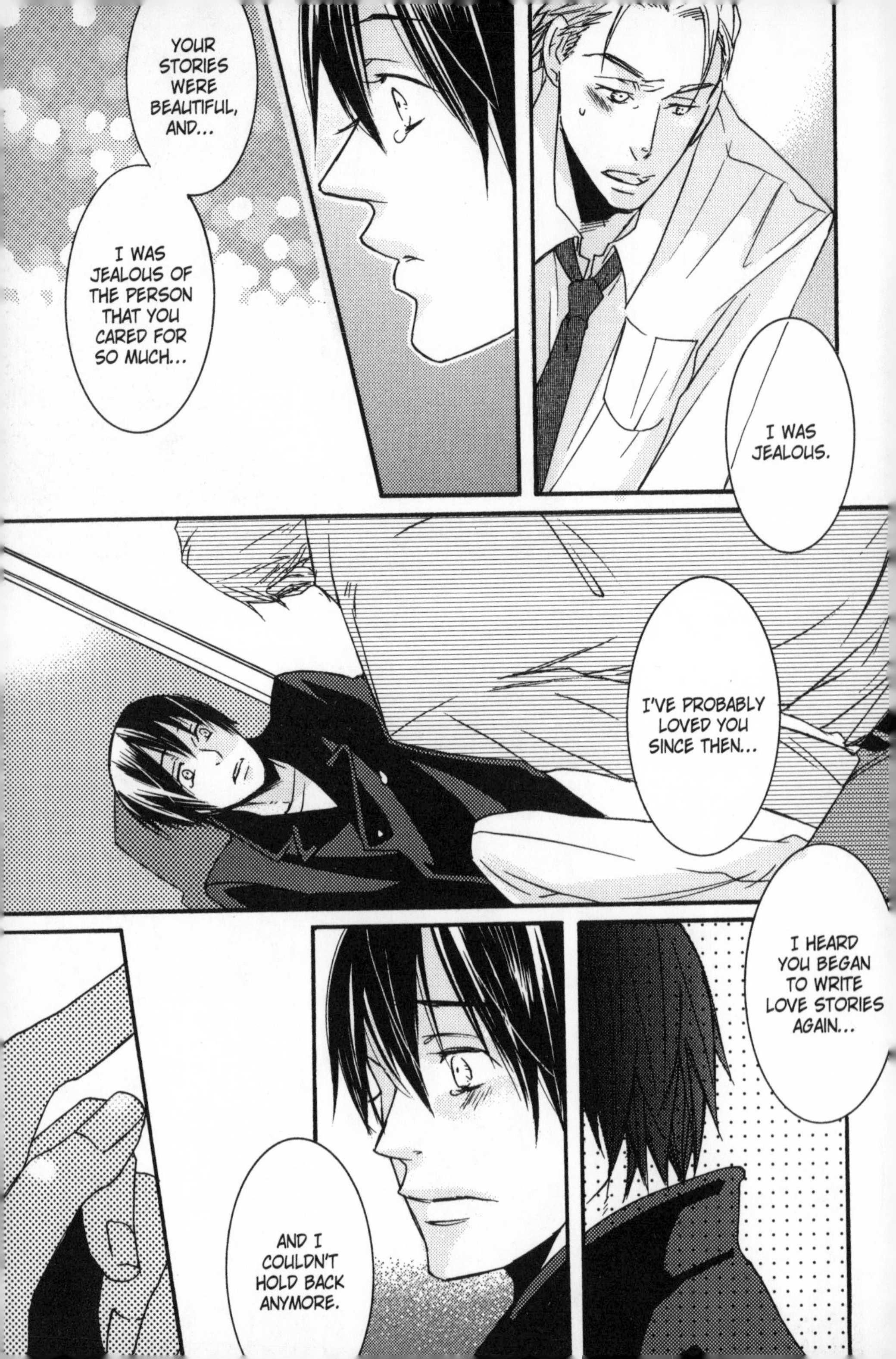

I WAS JEALOUS.
YOUR STORIES WERE BEAUTIFUL, AND...
I WAS JEALOUS OF THE PERSON THAT YOU CARED FOR SO MUCH...
I'VE PROBABLY LOVED YOU SINCE THEN...
I HEARD YOU BEGAN TO WRITE LOVE STORIES AGAIN...
AND I COULDN'T HOLD BACK ANYMORE.

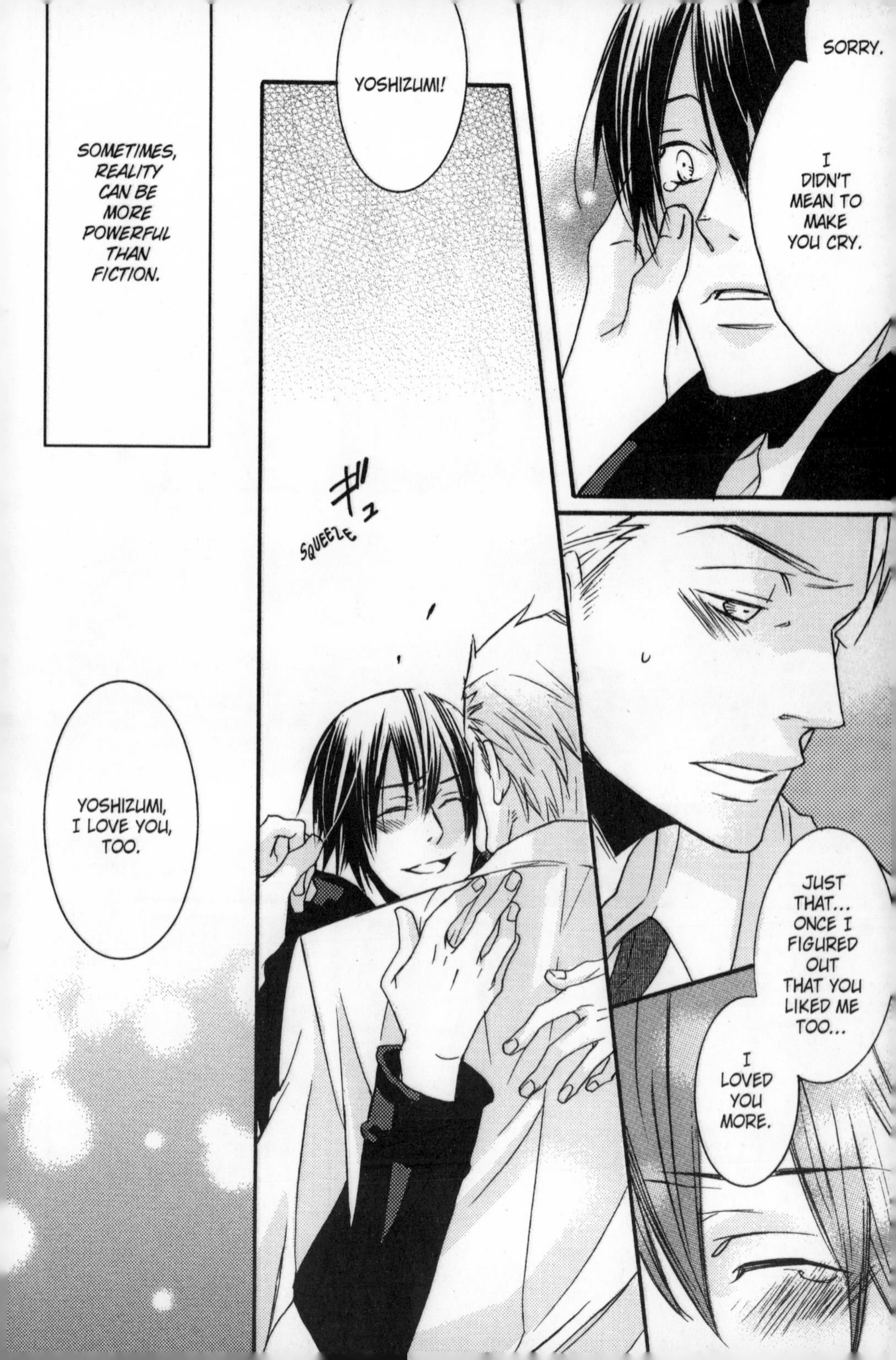
SORRY.
I DIDN'T MEAN TO MAKE YOU CRY.
JUST THAT... ONCE I FIGURED OUT THAT YOU LIKED ME TOO...
I LOVED YOU MORE.
YOSHIZUMI!
ギュ
SQUEEZE
SOMETIMES, REALITY CAN BE MORE POWERFUL THAN FICTION.
YOSHIZUMI, I LOVE YOU, TOO.

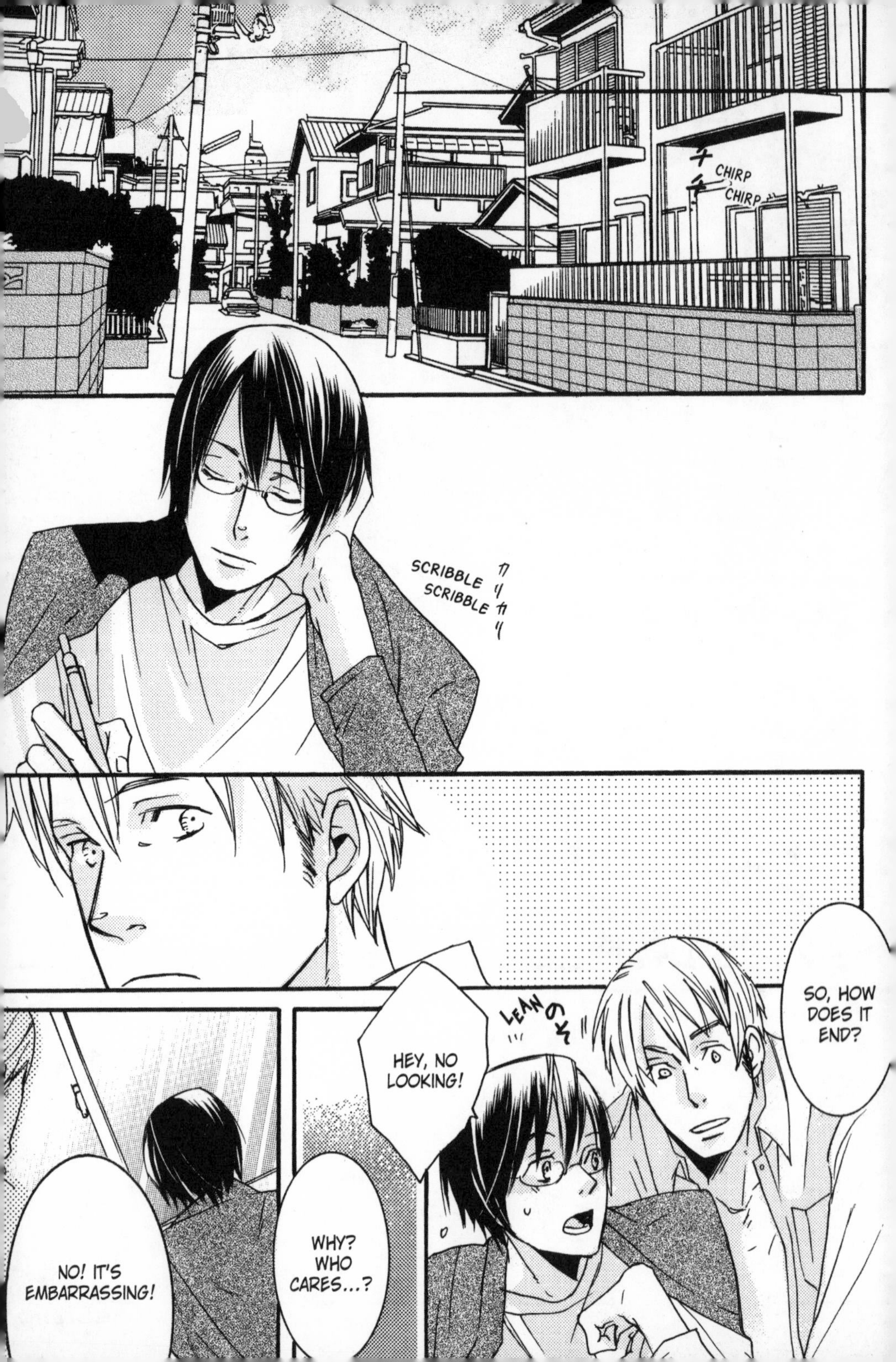
CHIRP
CHIRP
SCRIBBLE
SCRIBBLE
SO, HOW DOES IT END?
LEAN
HEY, NO LOOKING!
WHY? WHO CARES...?
NO! IT'S EMBARRASSING!

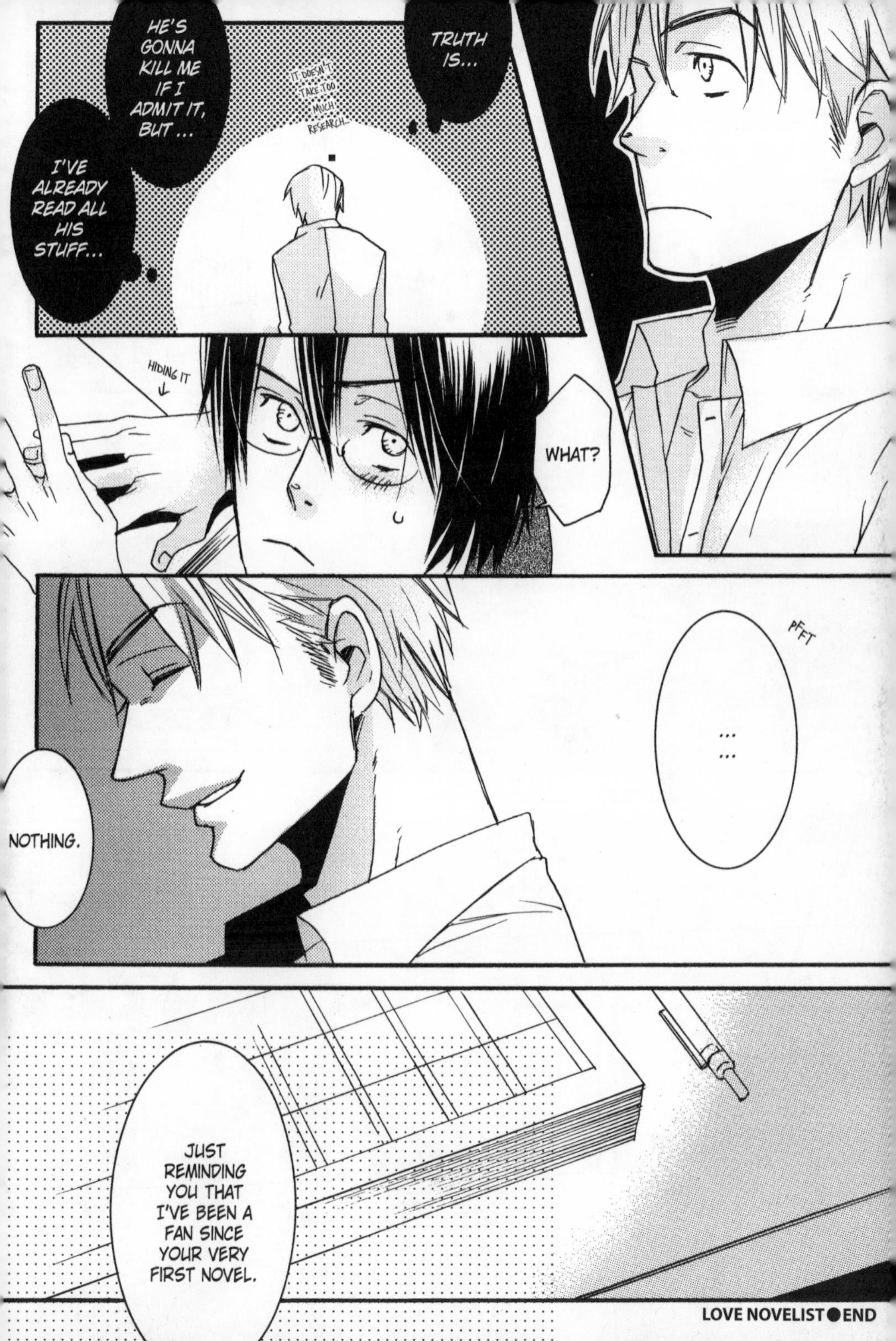
TRUTH IS...
HE'S GONNA KILL ME IF I ADMIT IT, BUT...
I'VE ALREADY READ ALL HIS STUFF...
IT DOESN'T TAKE TOO MUCH RESEARCH...
WHAT?
HIDING IT
......
PFFT
NOTHING.
JUST REMINDING YOU THAT I'VE BEEN A FAN SINCE YOUR VERY FIRST NOVEL.

LOVE NOVELIST ● END

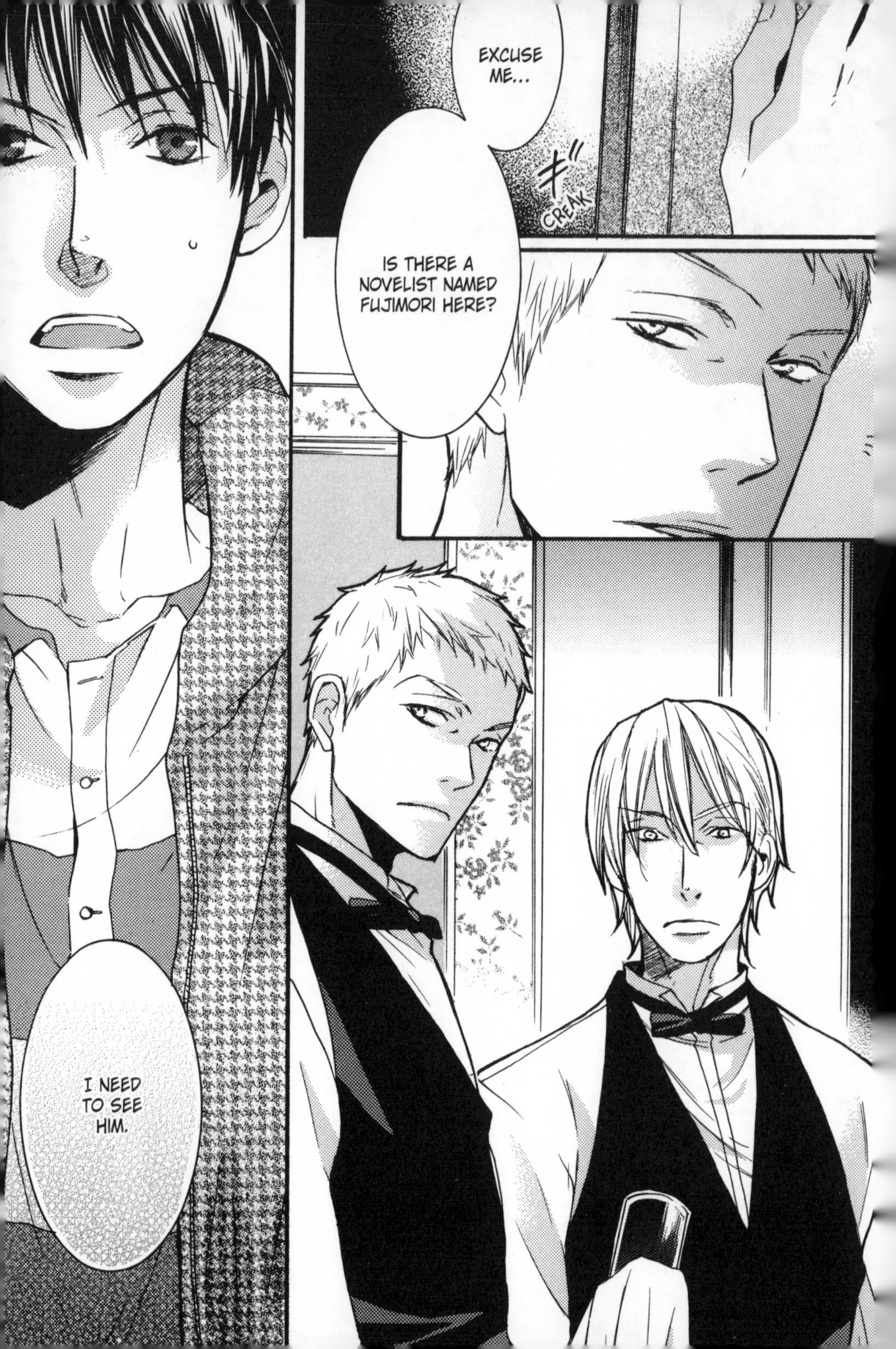
EXCUSE ME...
ギ
CREAK
IS THERE A NOVELIST NAMED FUJIMORI HERE?
I NEED TO SEE HIM.

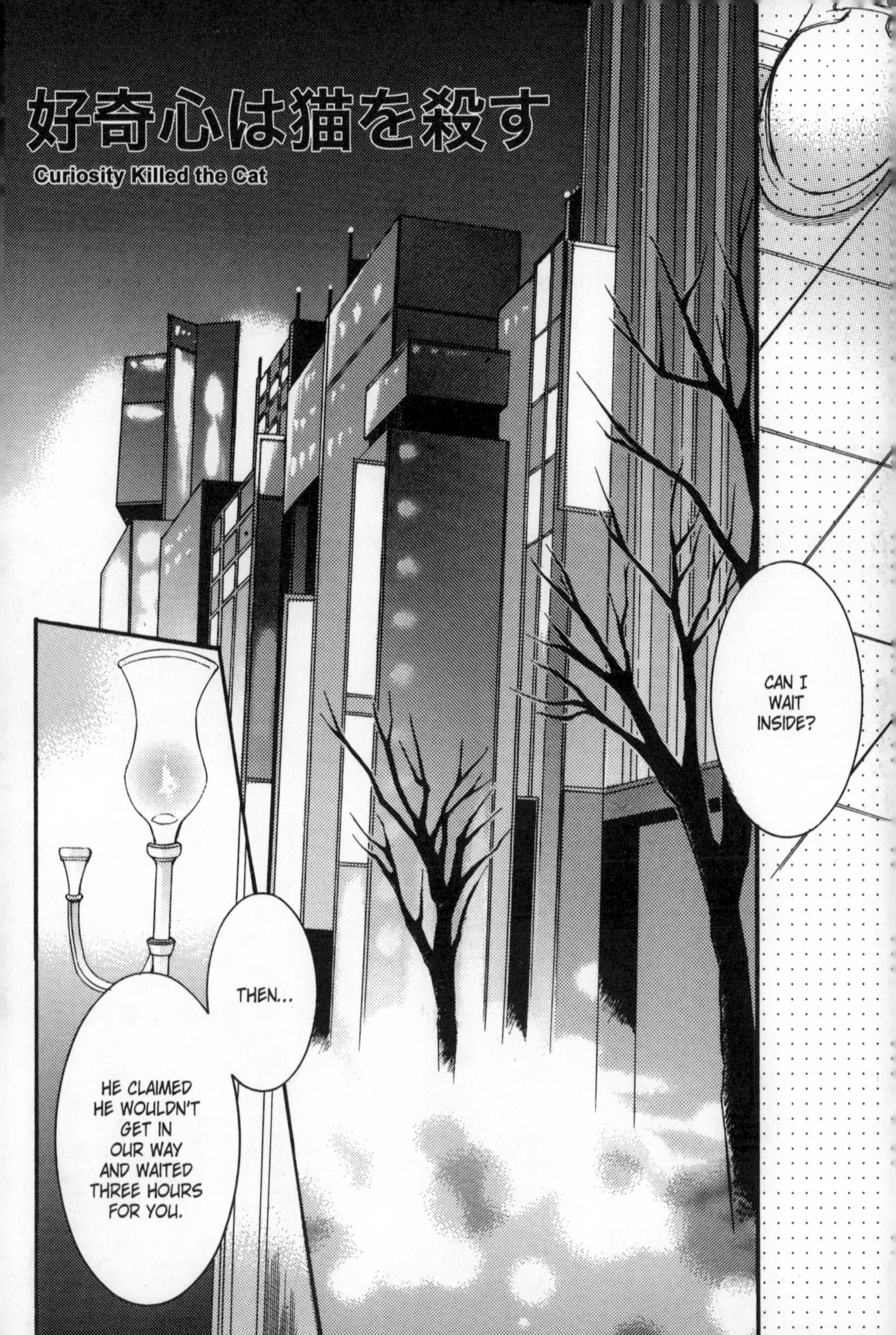
好奇心は猫を殺す
Curiosity Killed the Cat
CAN I WAIT INSIDE?
THEN...
HE CLAIMED HE WOULDN'T GET IN OUR WAY AND WAITED THREE HOURS FOR YOU.

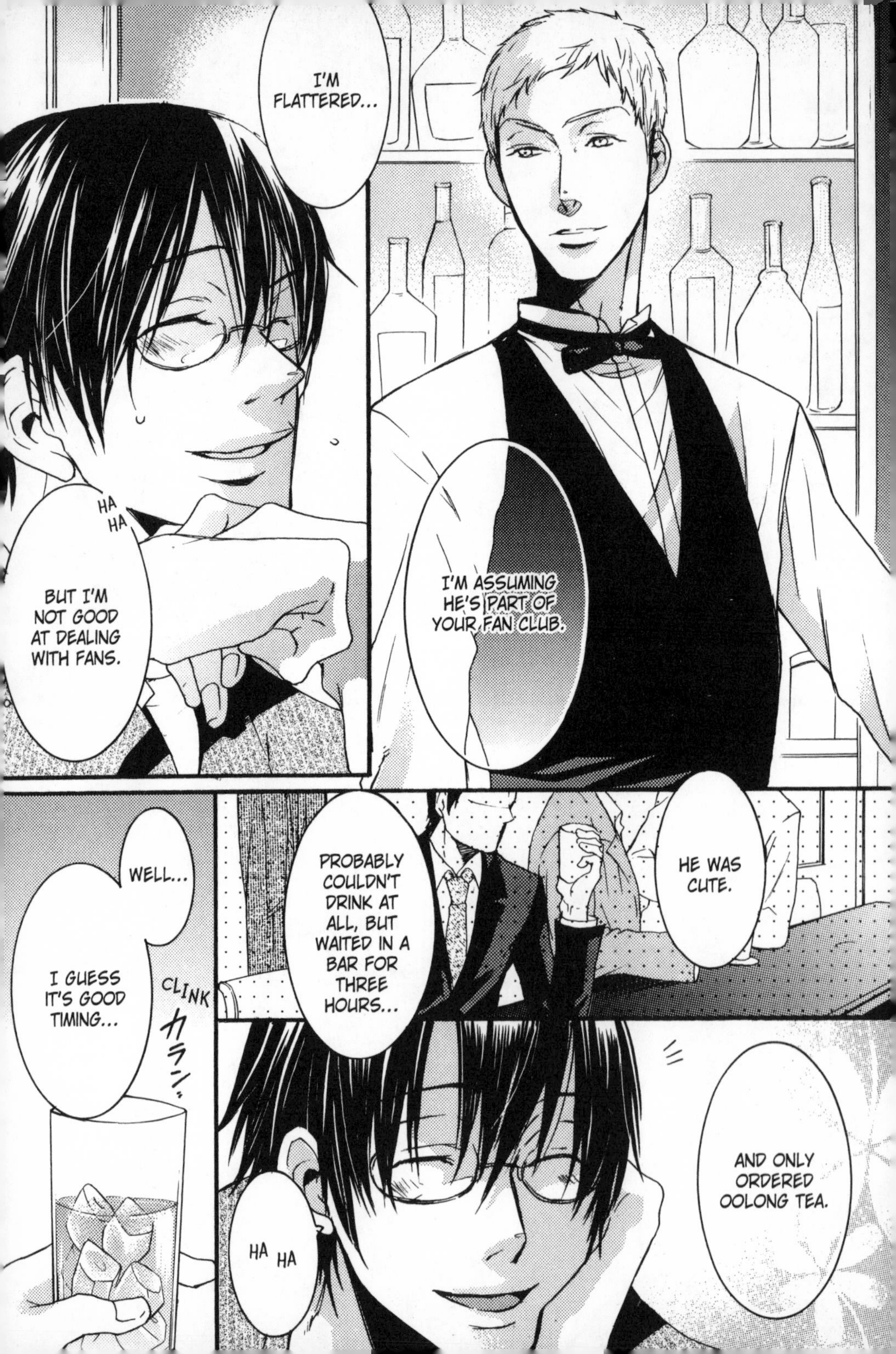
I'M ASSUMING HE'S PART OF YOUR FAN CLUB.
I'M FLATTERED...
HA HA
BUT I'M NOT GOOD AT DEALING WITH FANS.
HE WAS CUTE.
PROBABLY COULDN'T DRINK AT ALL, BUT WAITED IN A BAR FOR THREE HOURS...
AND ONLY ORDERED OOLONG TEA.
HA HA
WELL...
I GUESS IT'S GOOD TIMING...
CLINK
カラン

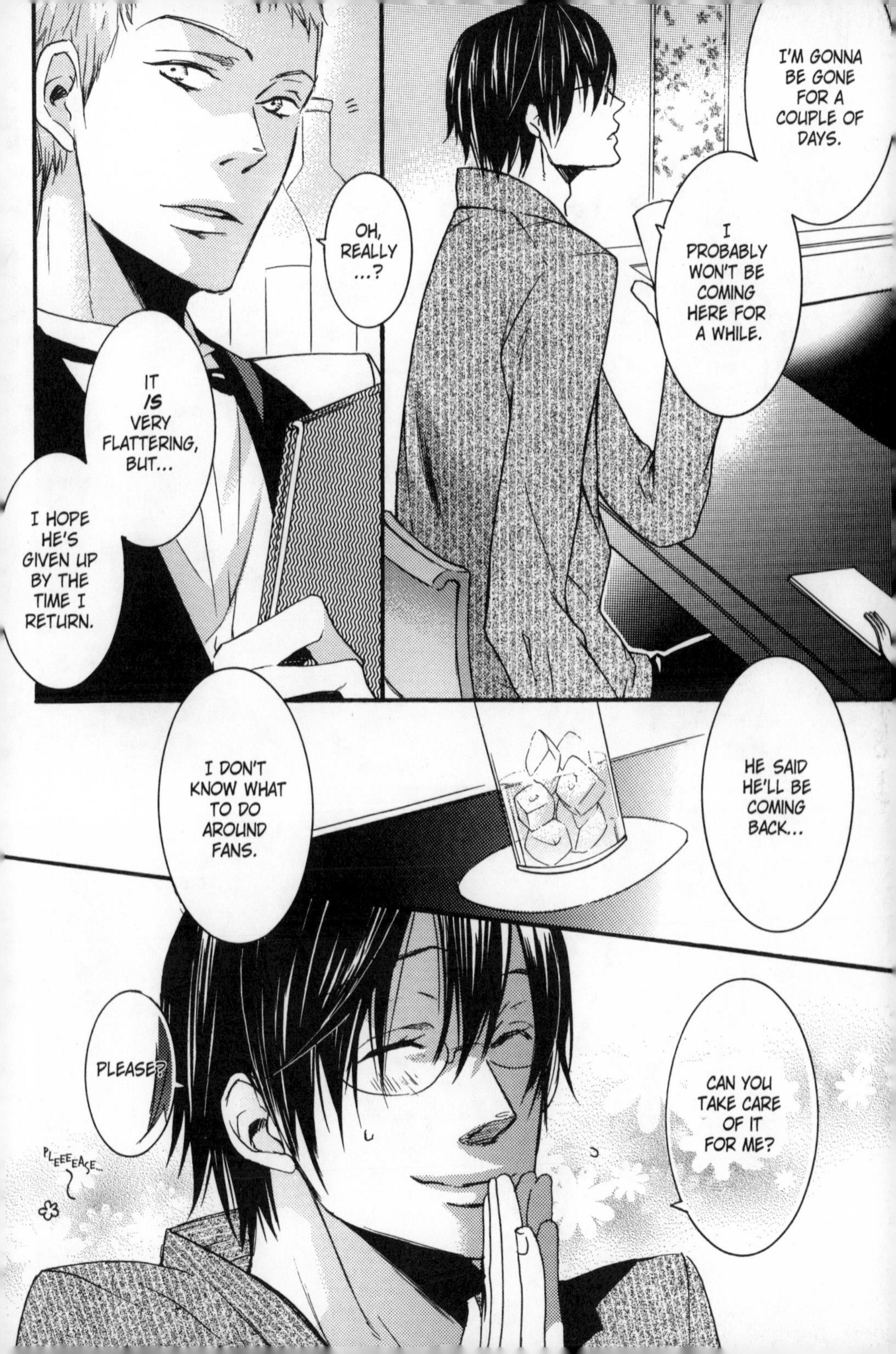
I'M GONNA BE GONE FOR A COUPLE OF DAYS.
I PROBABLY WON'T BE COMING HERE FOR A WHILE.
OH, REALLY ...?
IT *IS* VERY FLATTERING, BUT...
I HOPE HE'S GIVEN UP BY THE TIME I RETURN.
HE SAID HE'LL BE COMING BACK...
I DON'T KNOW WHAT TO DO AROUND FANS.
CAN YOU TAKE CARE OF IT FOR ME?
PLEASE?
PLEEEEASE...

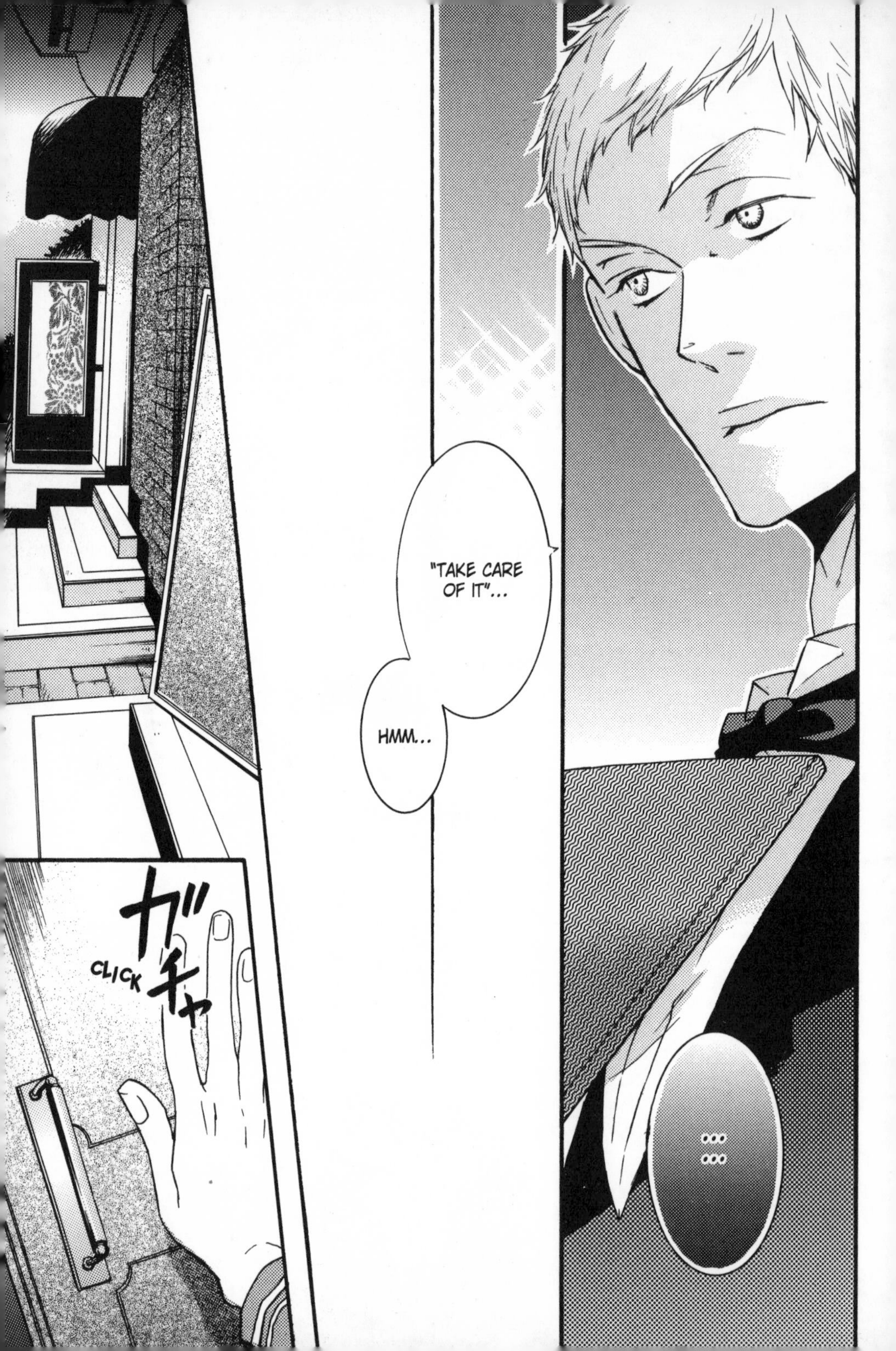
......
"TAKE CARE OF IT"...
HMM...
CLICK
ガチャ

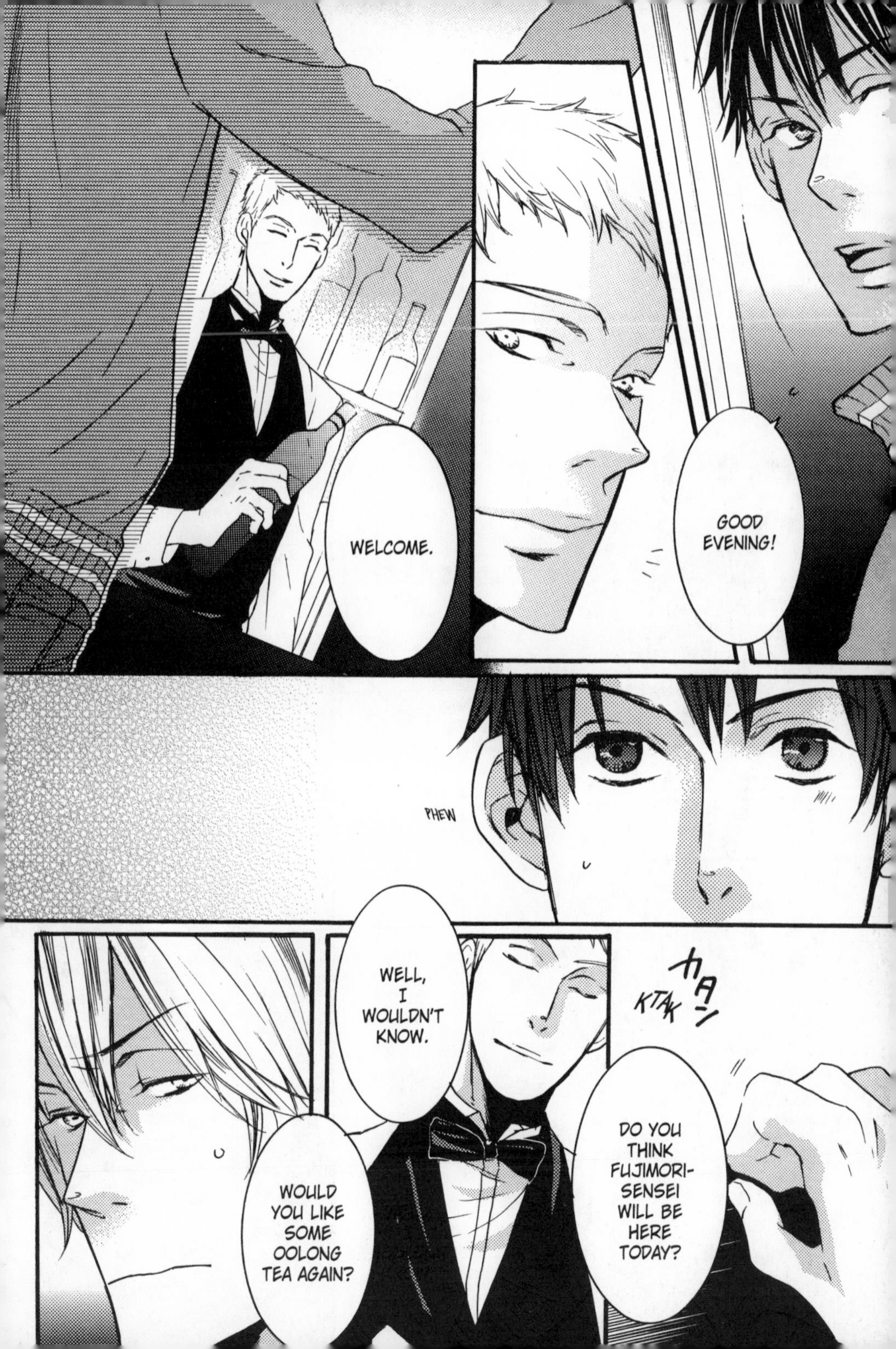
GOOD EVENING!
WELCOME.
PHEW
KTAK
DO YOU THINK FUJIMORI-SENSEI WILL BE HERE TODAY?
WELL, I WOULDN'T KNOW.
WOULD YOU LIKE SOME OOLONG TEA AGAIN?

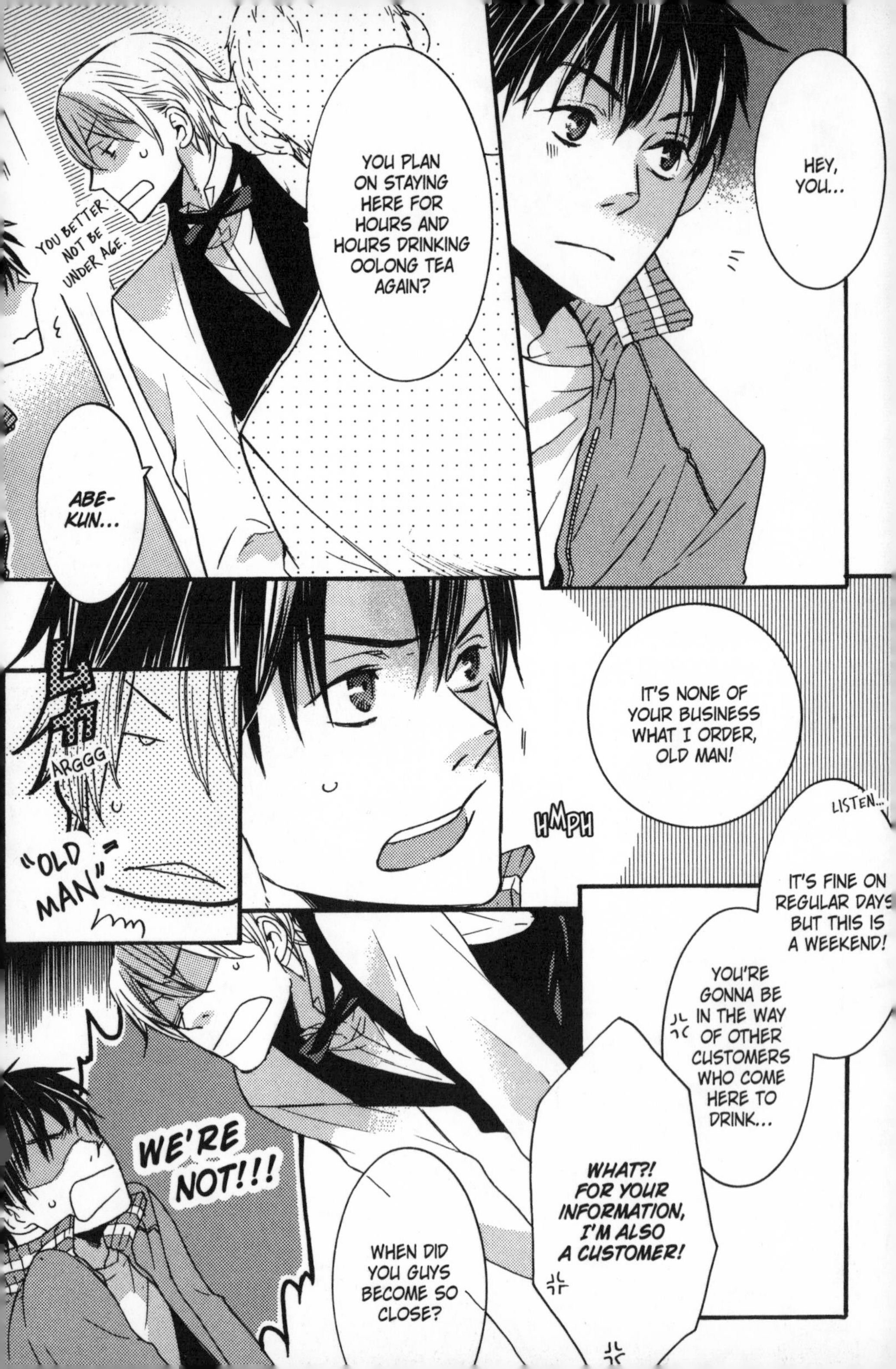
HEY, YOU...
YOU PLAN ON STAYING HERE FOR HOURS AND HOURS DRINKING OOLONG TEA AGAIN?
YOU BETTER NOT BE UNDER AGE.
ABE-KUN...
IT'S NONE OF YOUR BUSINESS WHAT I ORDER, OLD MAN!
HMPH
ARGGG
"OLD MAN"
LISTEN...
IT'S FINE ON REGULAR DAYS BUT THIS IS A WEEKEND!
YOU'RE GONNA BE IN THE WAY OF OTHER CUSTOMERS WHO COME HERE TO DRINK...
WHAT?! FOR YOUR INFORMATION, I'M ALSO A CUSTOMER!
WHEN DID YOU GUYS BECOME SO CLOSE?
WE'RE NOT!!!

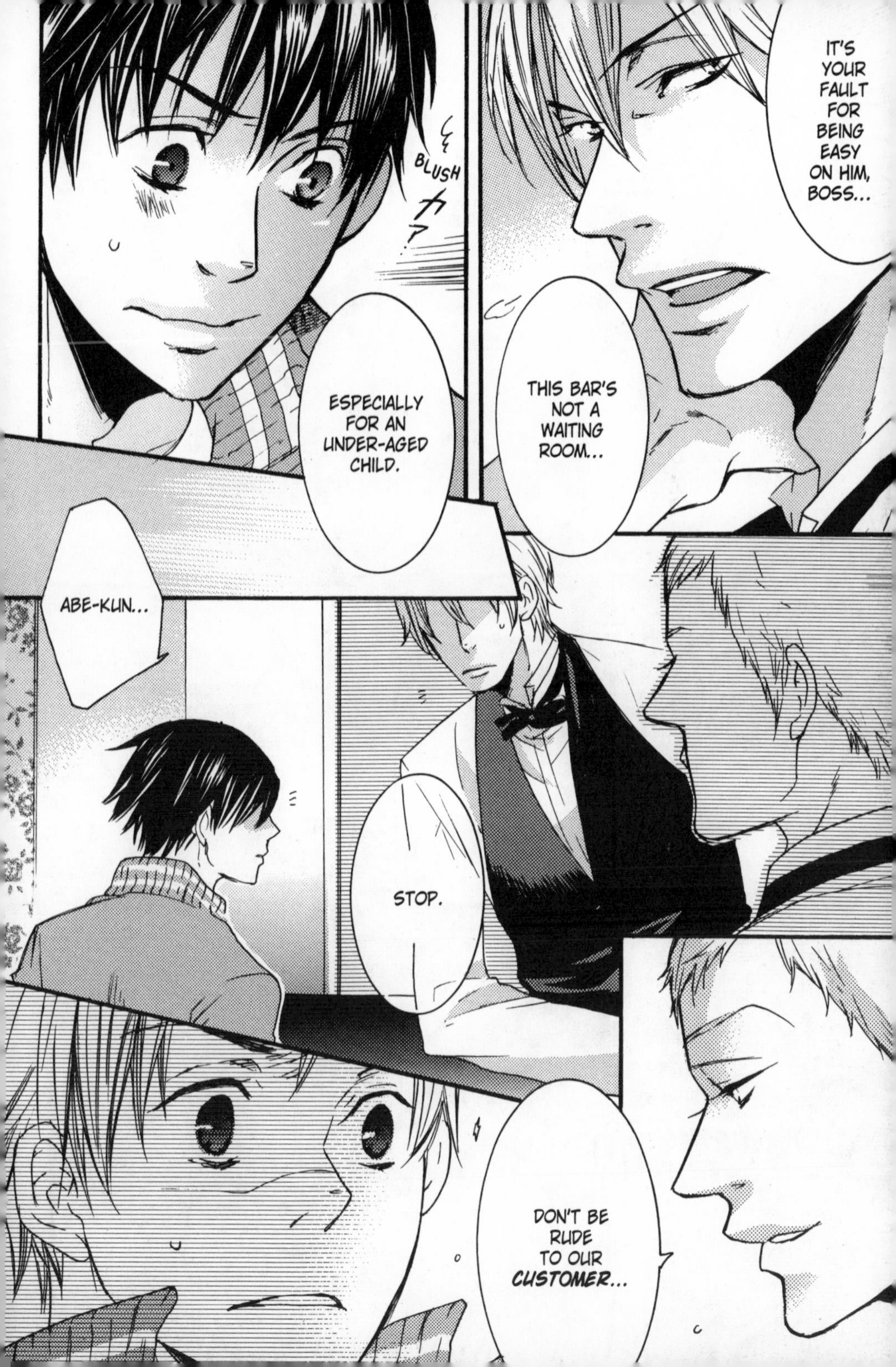
IT'S YOUR FAULT FOR BEING EASY ON HIM, BOSS...
THIS BAR'S NOT A WAITING ROOM...
BLUSH
ESPECIALLY FOR AN UNDER-AGED CHILD.
STOP.
ABE-KUN...
DON'T BE RUDE TO OUR CUSTOMER...

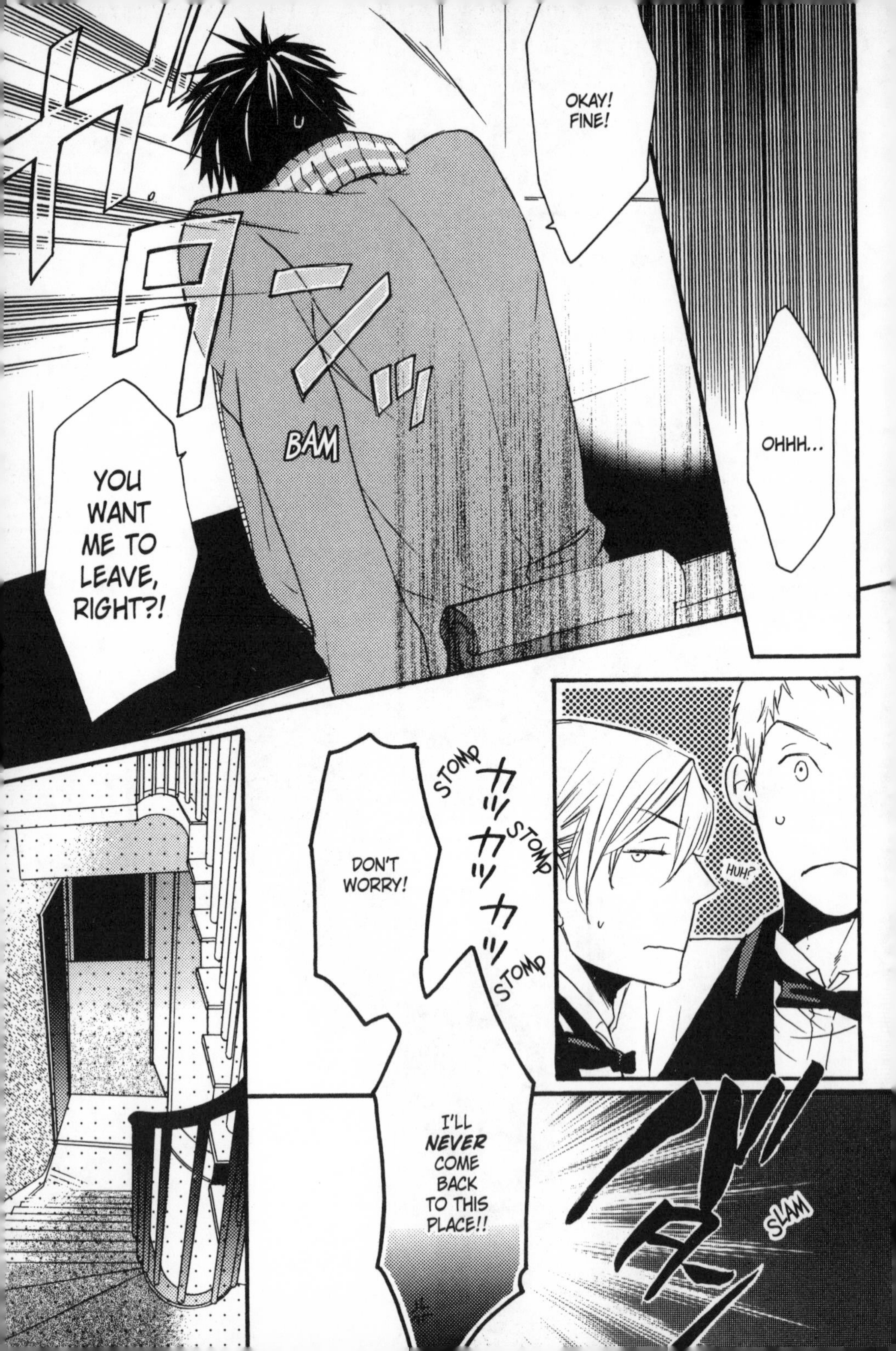
OKAY! FINE!
OHHH...
BAM
YOU WANT ME TO LEAVE, RIGHT?!
HUH?
STOMP
STOMP
STOMP
DON'T WORRY!
I'LL NEVER COME BACK TO THIS PLACE!!
SLAM

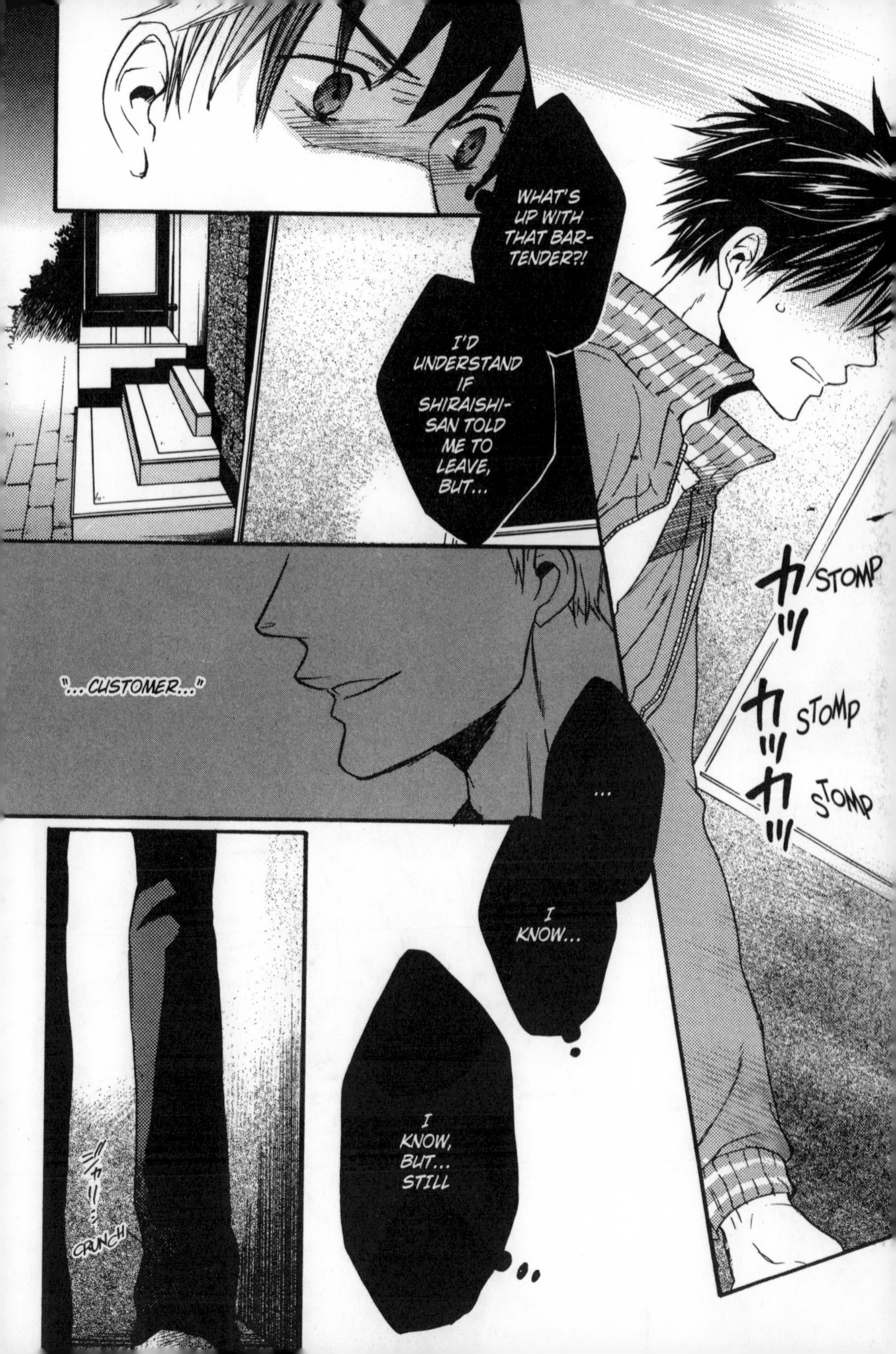
WHAT'S UP WITH THAT BAR-TENDER?!
I'D UNDERSTAND IF SHIRAISHI-SAN TOLD ME TO LEAVE, BUT...
STOMP
STOMP
STOMP
"...CUSTOMER..."
...
I KNOW...
I KNOW, BUT... STILL
CRUNCH

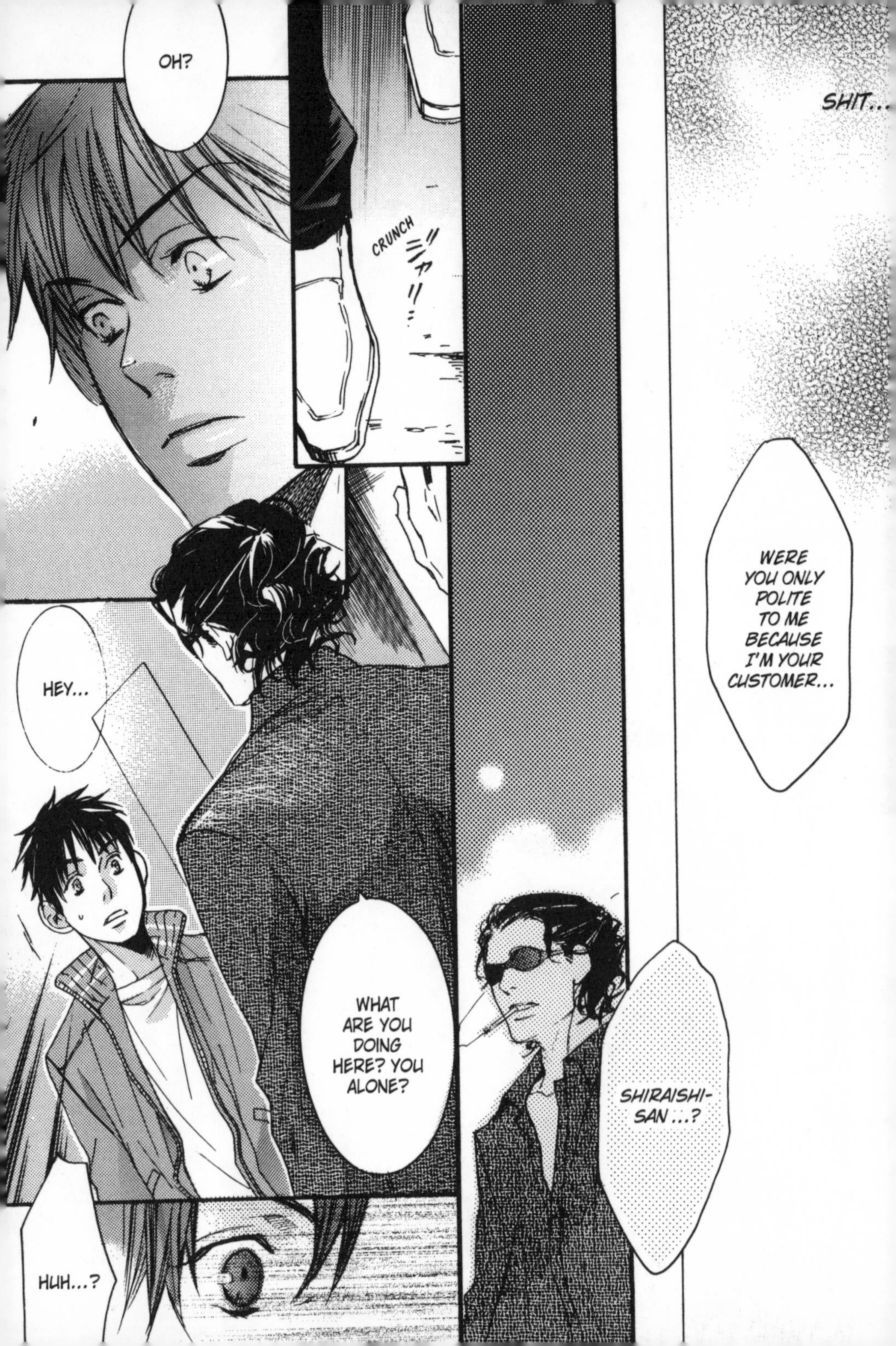
SHIT...
WERE YOU ONLY POLITE TO ME BECAUSE I'M YOUR CUSTOMER...
CRUNCH
SHIRAISHI-SAN...?
OH?
HEY...
WHAT ARE YOU DOING HERE? YOU ALONE?
HUH...?

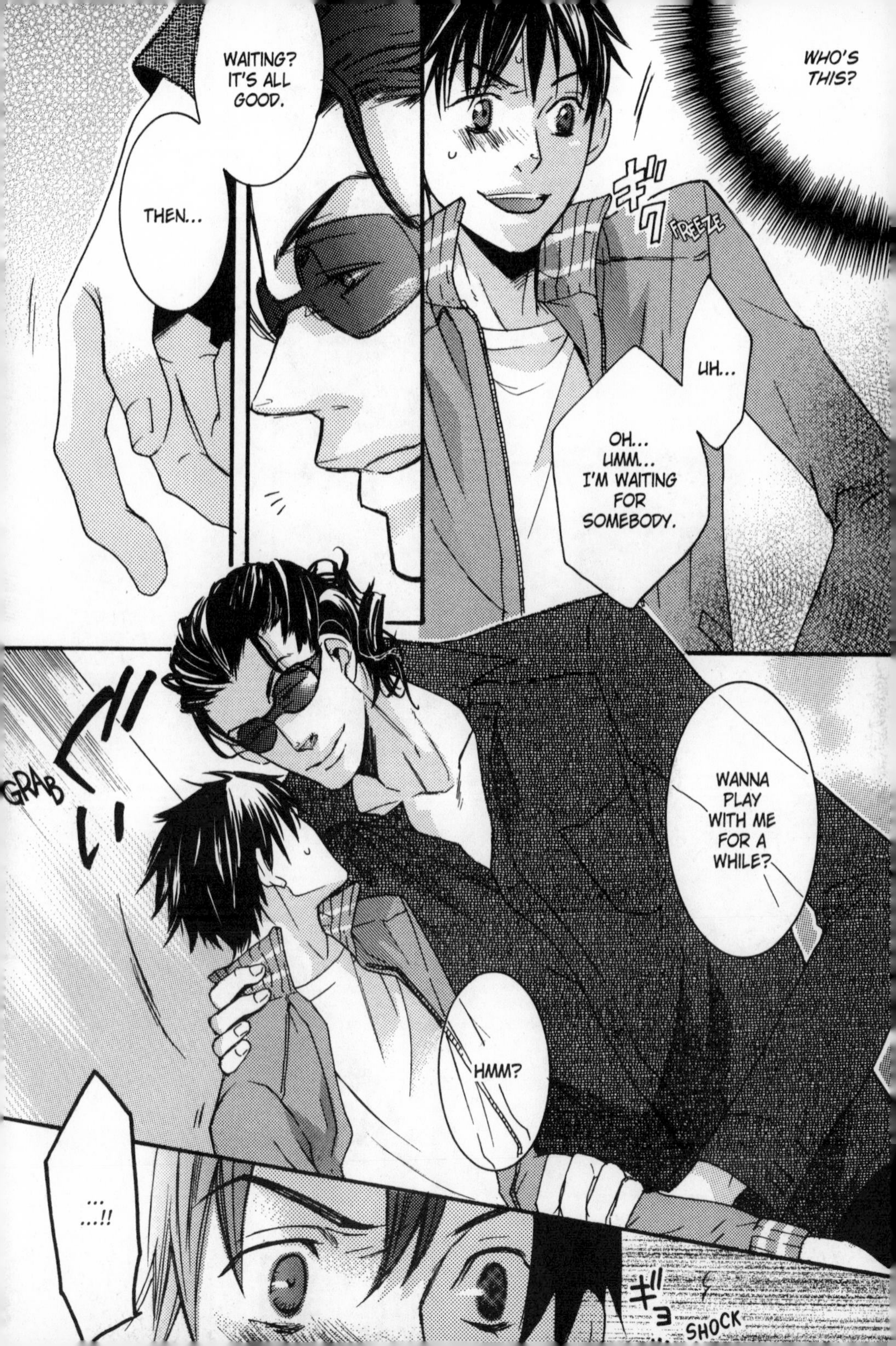
WHO'S THIS?
FREEZE
UH...
OH... UMM... I'M WAITING FOR SOMEBODY.
WAITING? IT'S ALL GOOD.
THEN...
WANNA PLAY WITH ME FOR A WHILE?
GRAB
HMM?
SHOCK
... ...!!

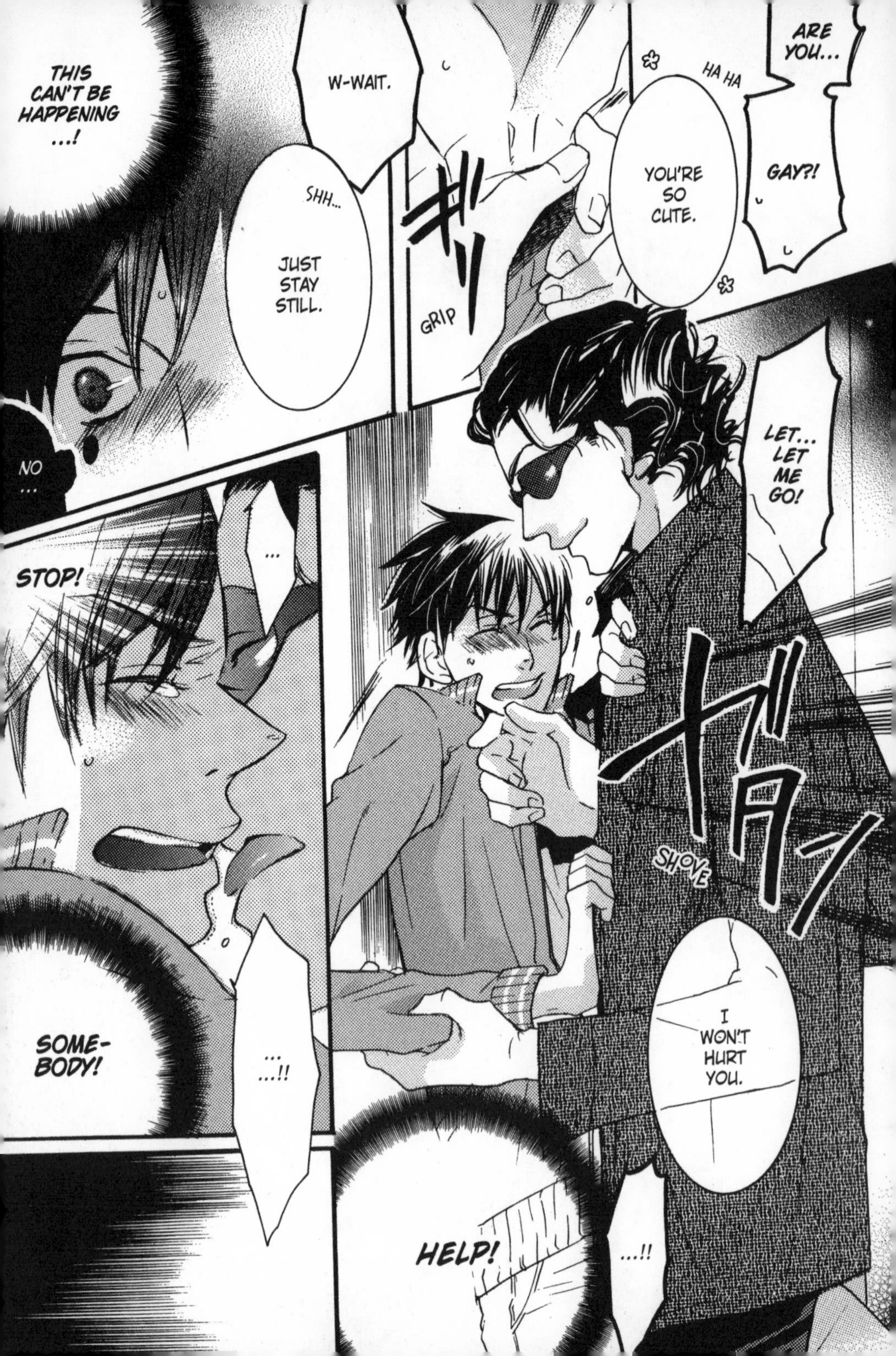
ARE YOU... GAY?!
HA HA
YOU'RE SO CUTE.
W-WAIT.
GRIP
SHH... JUST STAY STILL.
THIS CAN'T BE HAPPENING ...!
NO ...
LET... LET ME GO!
SHOVE
I WON'T HURT YOU.
...
STOP!
SOME-BODY!
... ...!!
HELP!
...!!

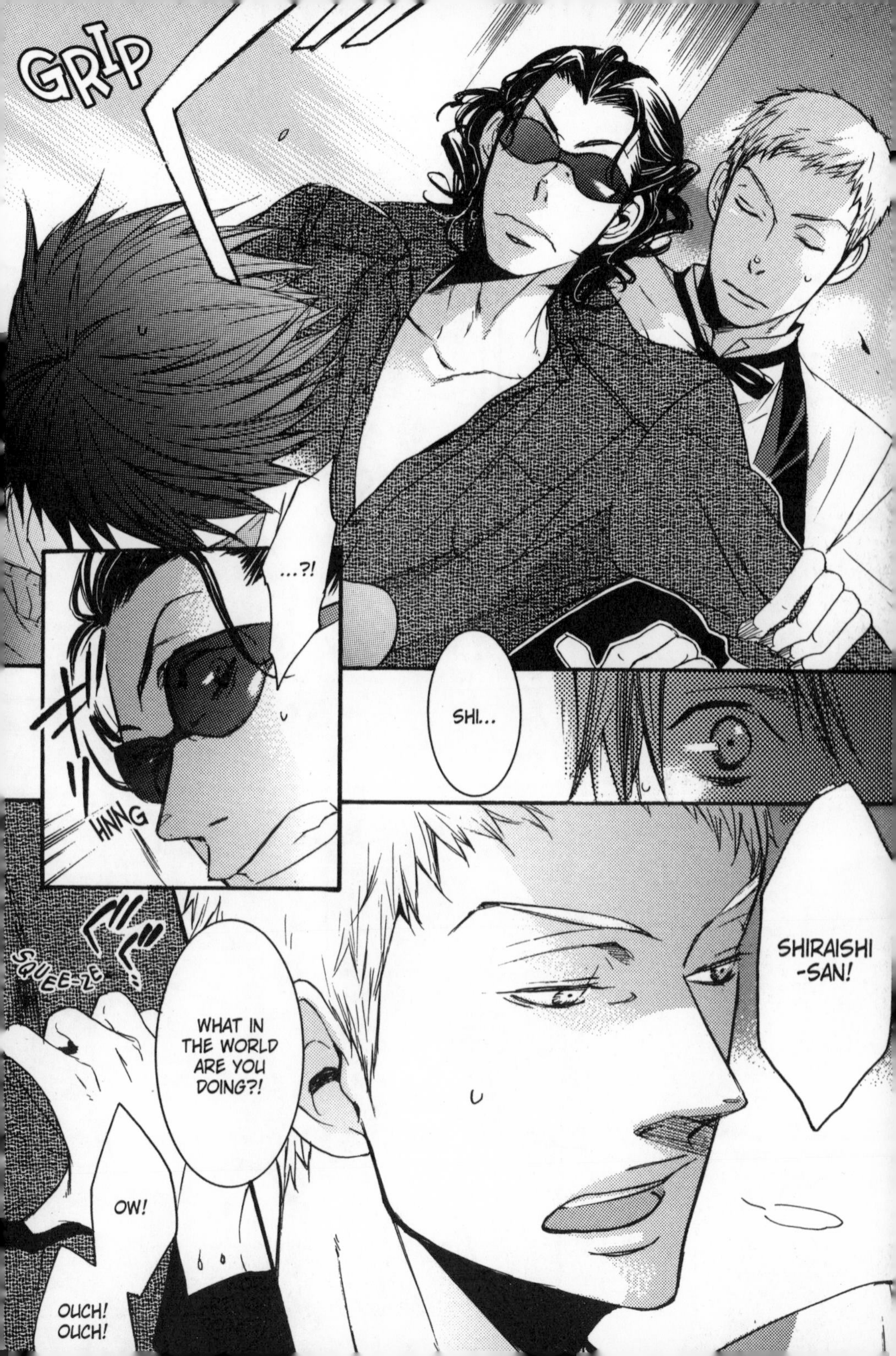
GRIP
...?!
HNNG
SHI...
SHIRAISHI-SAN!
WHAT IN THE WORLD ARE YOU DOING?!
SQUEE-ZE
OW!
OUCH! OUCH!

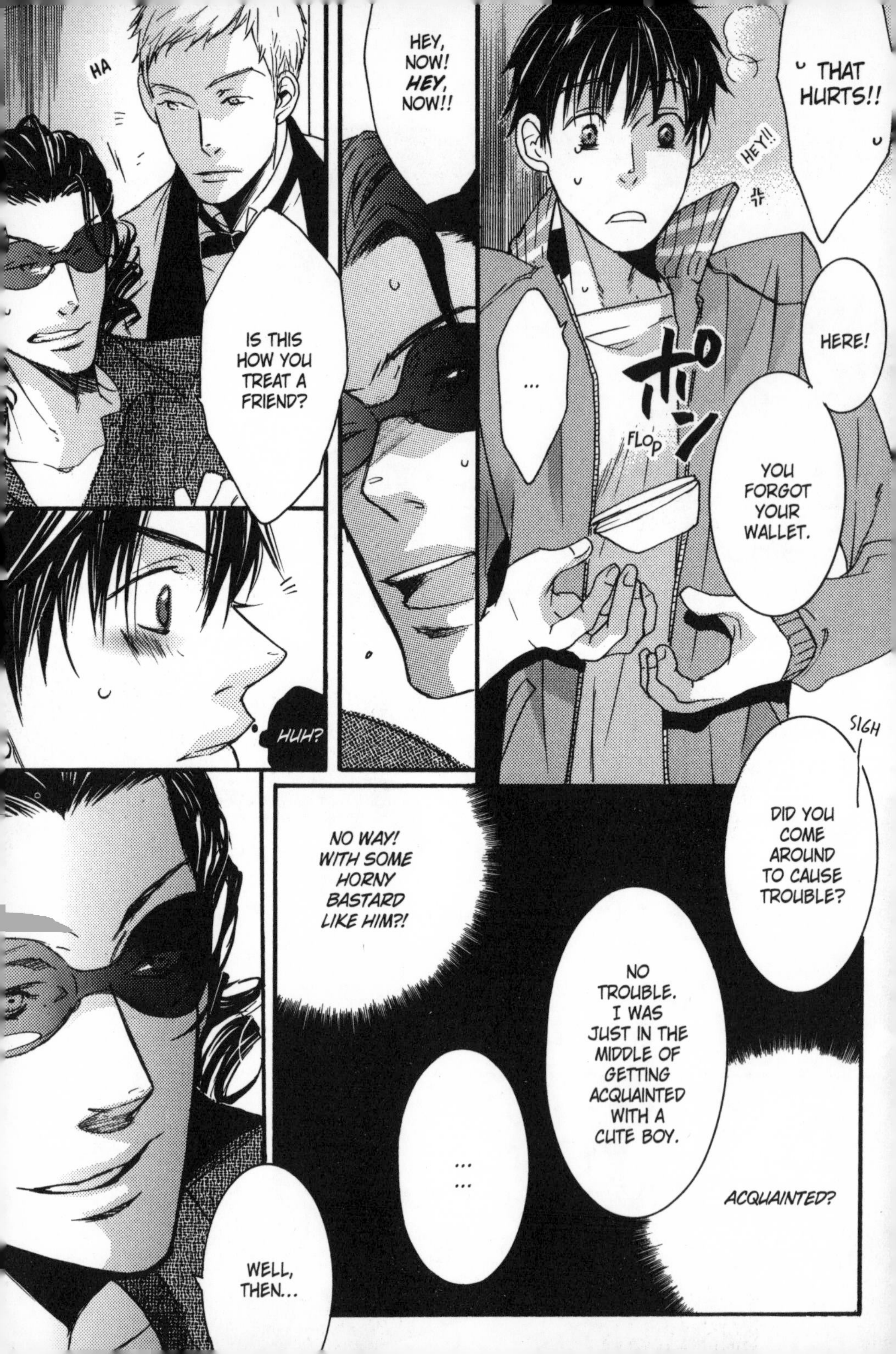

THAT HURTS!!
HEY!!
HERE!
...
YOU FORGOT YOUR WALLET.
ポン
FLOP
HEY, NOW! HEY, NOW!!
HA
IS THIS HOW YOU TREAT A FRIEND?
HUH?
SIGH
DID YOU COME AROUND TO CAUSE TROUBLE?
NO TROUBLE. I WAS JUST IN THE MIDDLE OF GETTING ACQUAINTED WITH A CUTE BOY.
ACQUAINTED?
... ...
NO WAY! WITH SOME HORNY BASTARD LIKE HIM?!
WELL, THEN...

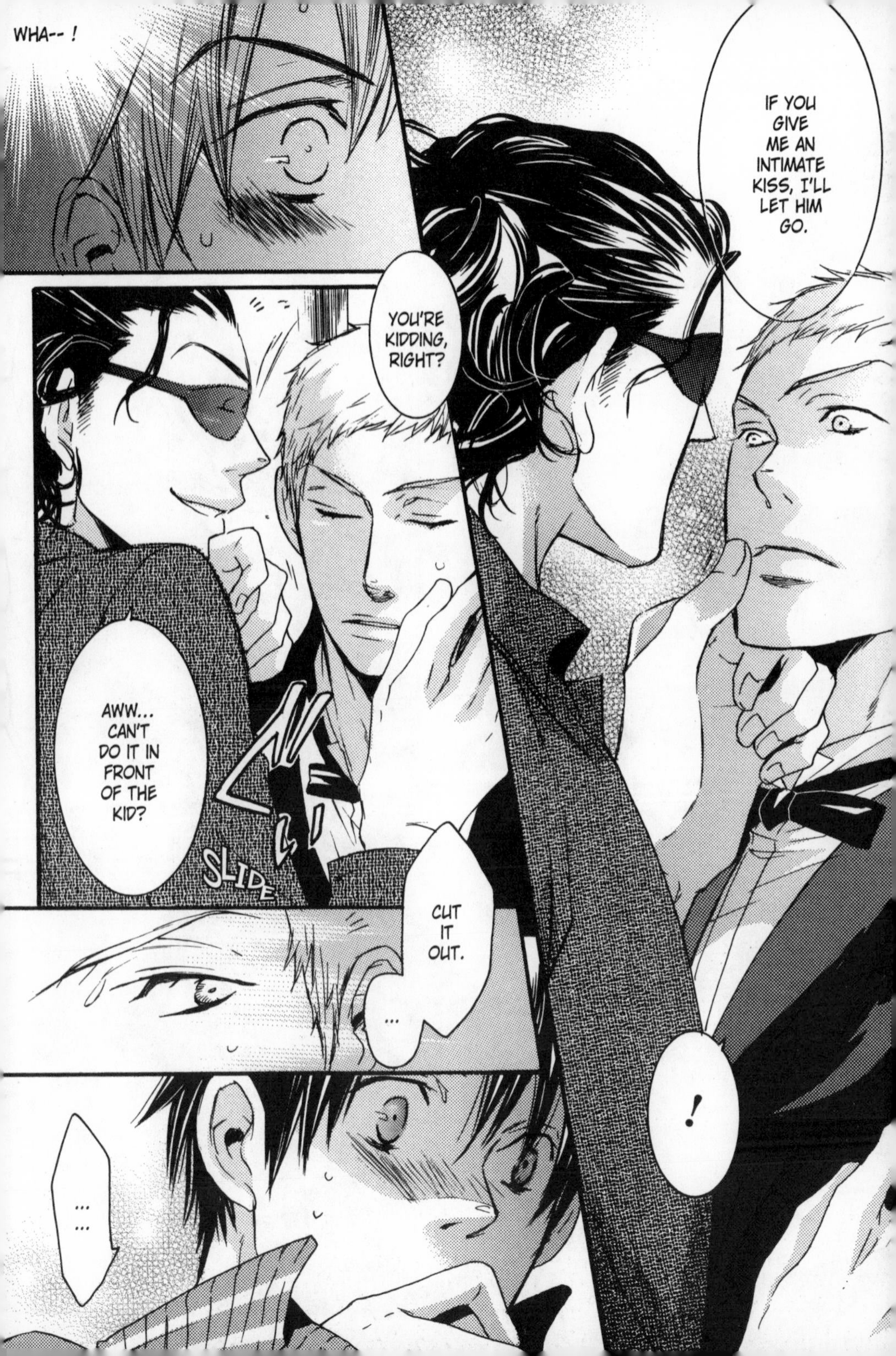

IF YOU GIVE ME AN INTIMATE KISS, I'LL LET HIM GO.
WHA-- !
YOU'RE KIDDING, RIGHT?
AWW... CAN'T DO IT IN FRONT OF THE KID?
SLIDE
CUT IT OUT.
...
!
... ...

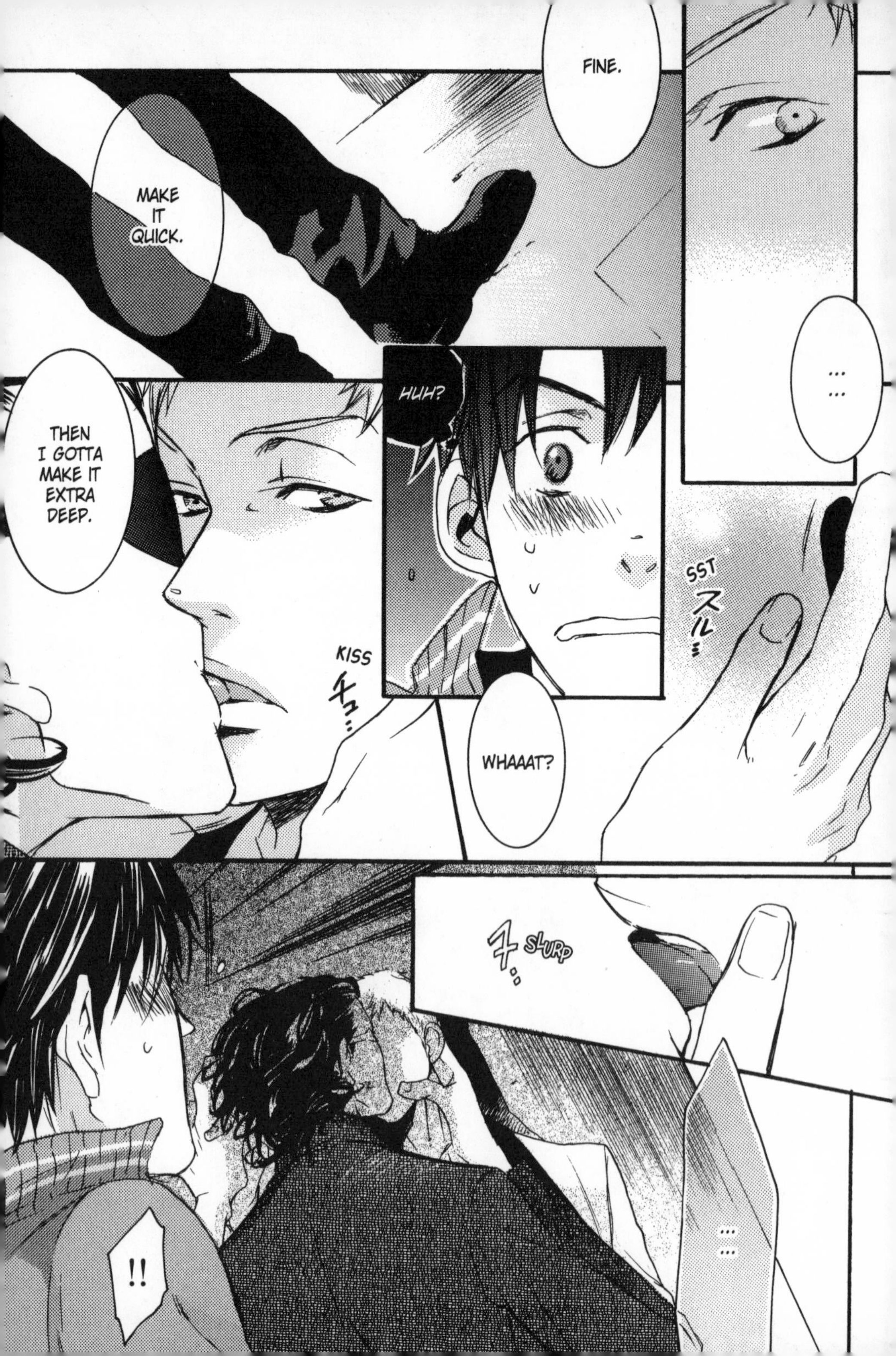
FINE.
……
MAKE IT QUICK.
SST
スル
HUH?
WHAAAT?
THEN I GOTTA MAKE IT EXTRA DEEP.
KISS
チュ
チ
SLURP
……
!!

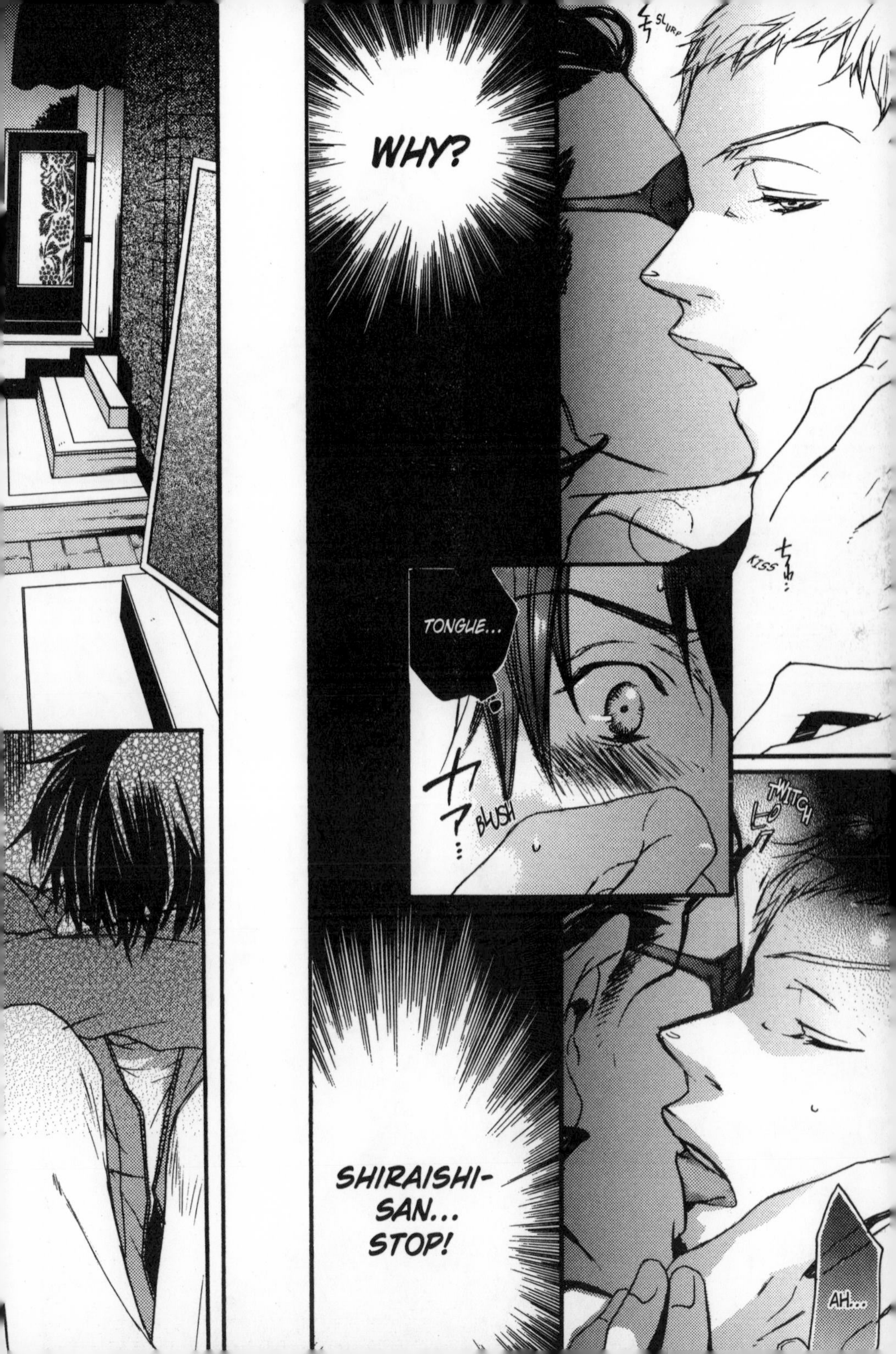
SLURP
WHY?
KISS
TONGUE...
BLUSH
TWITCH
AH...
SHIRAISHI-SAN... STOP!

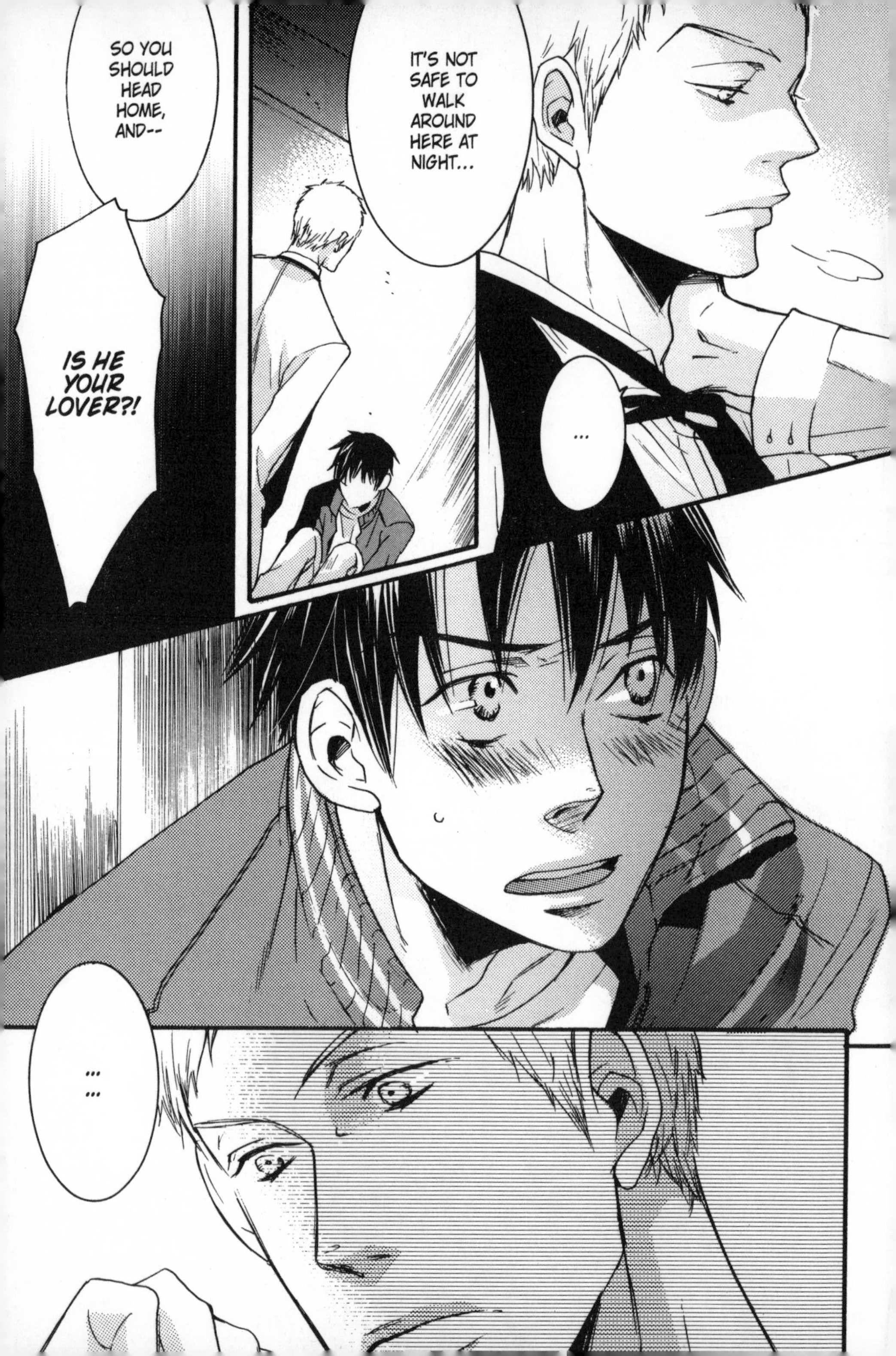
IT'S NOT SAFE TO WALK AROUND HERE AT NIGHT...
...
SO YOU SHOULD HEAD HOME, AND--
IS HE YOUR LOVER?!
... ...

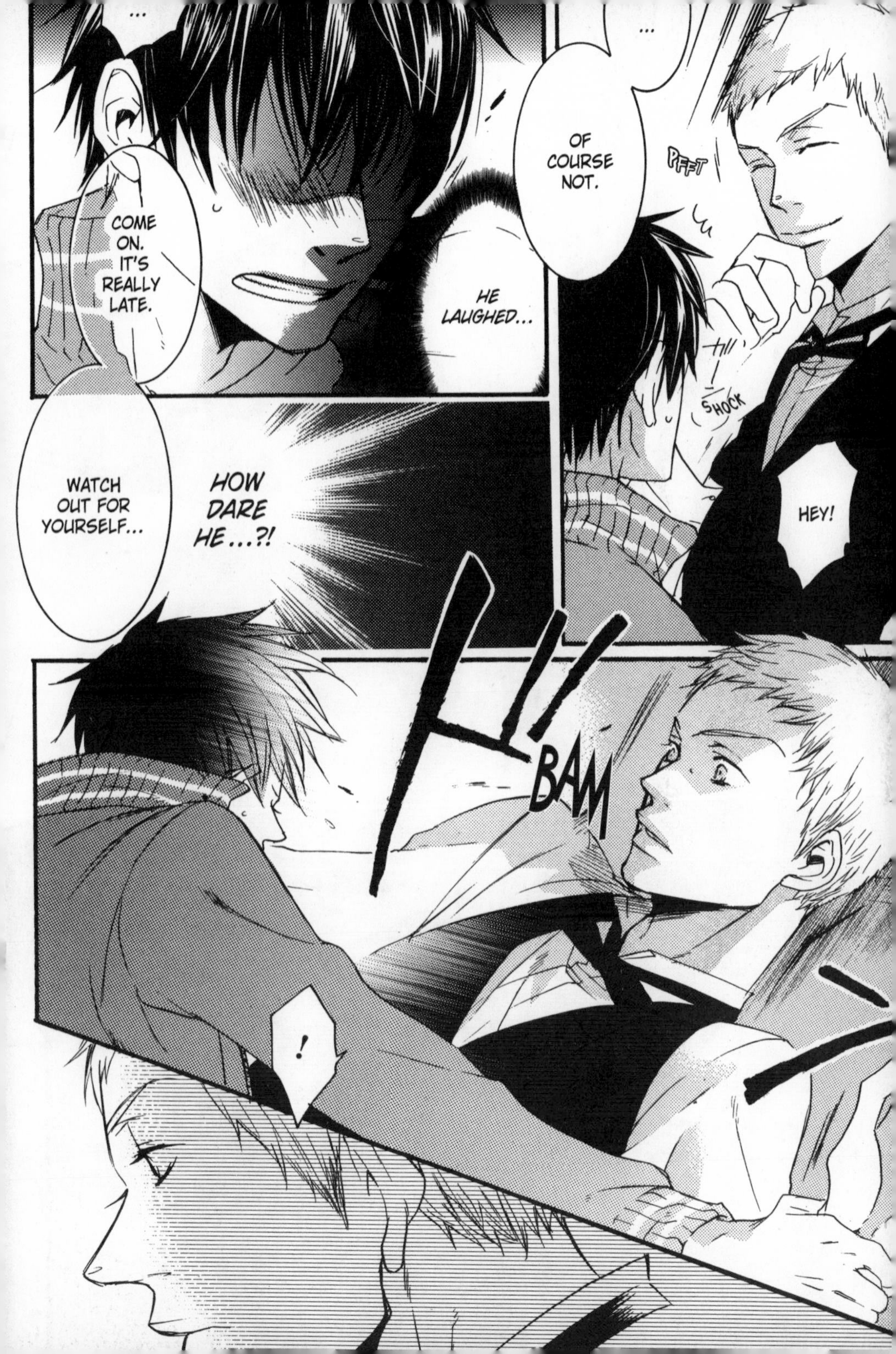
...
OF COURSE NOT.
PFFT
SHOCK
HEY!
...
COME ON. IT'S REALLY LATE.
HE LAUGHED...
HOW DARE HE...?!
WATCH OUT FOR YOURSELF...
BAM
!

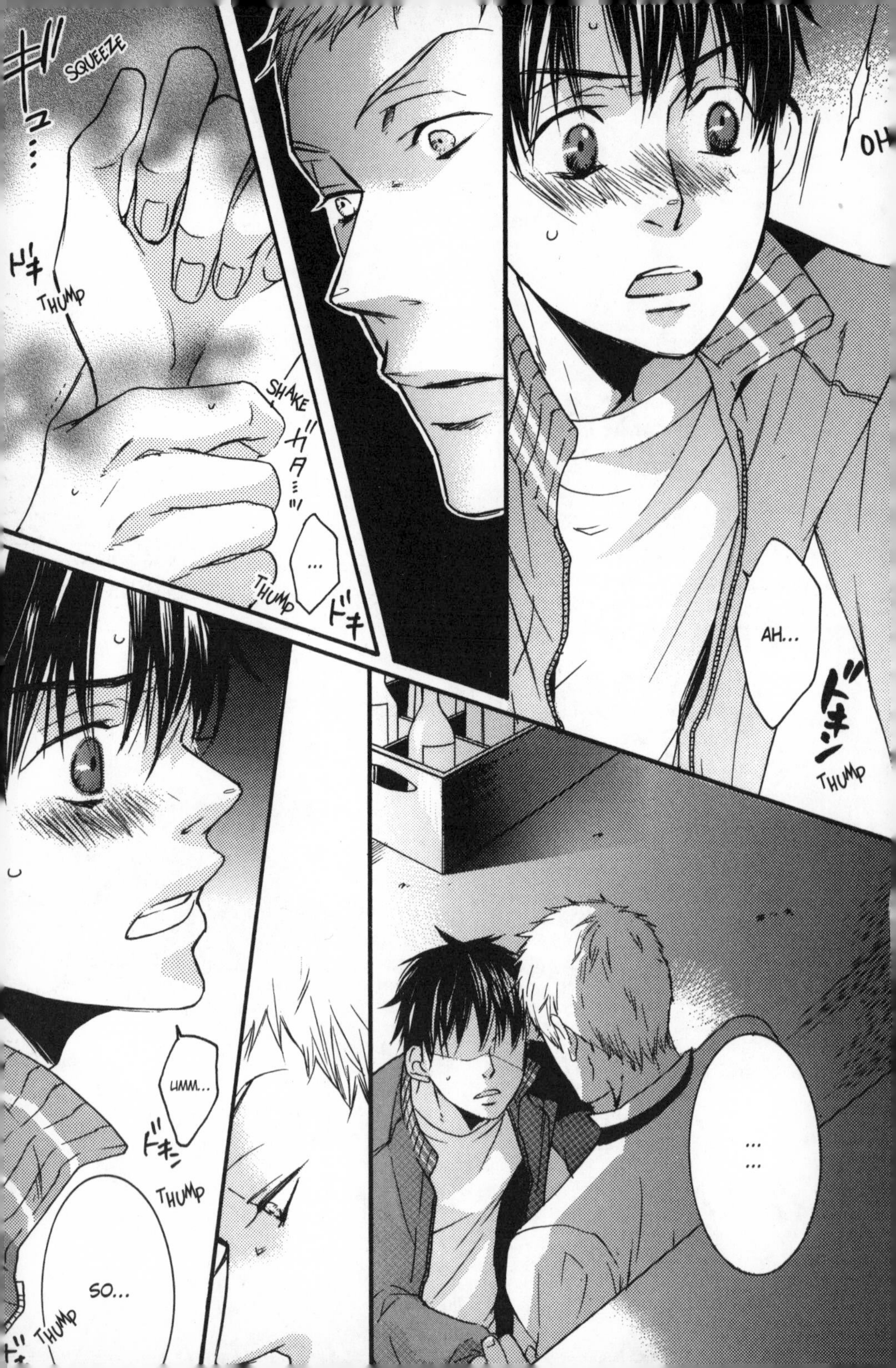

OH
AH...
ドキン
THUMP
ギュ…
SQUEEZE
ドキ
THUMP
SHAKE
ガタッ
...
THUMP
ドキ
... ...
UMM...
ドキン
THUMP
SO...
THUMP

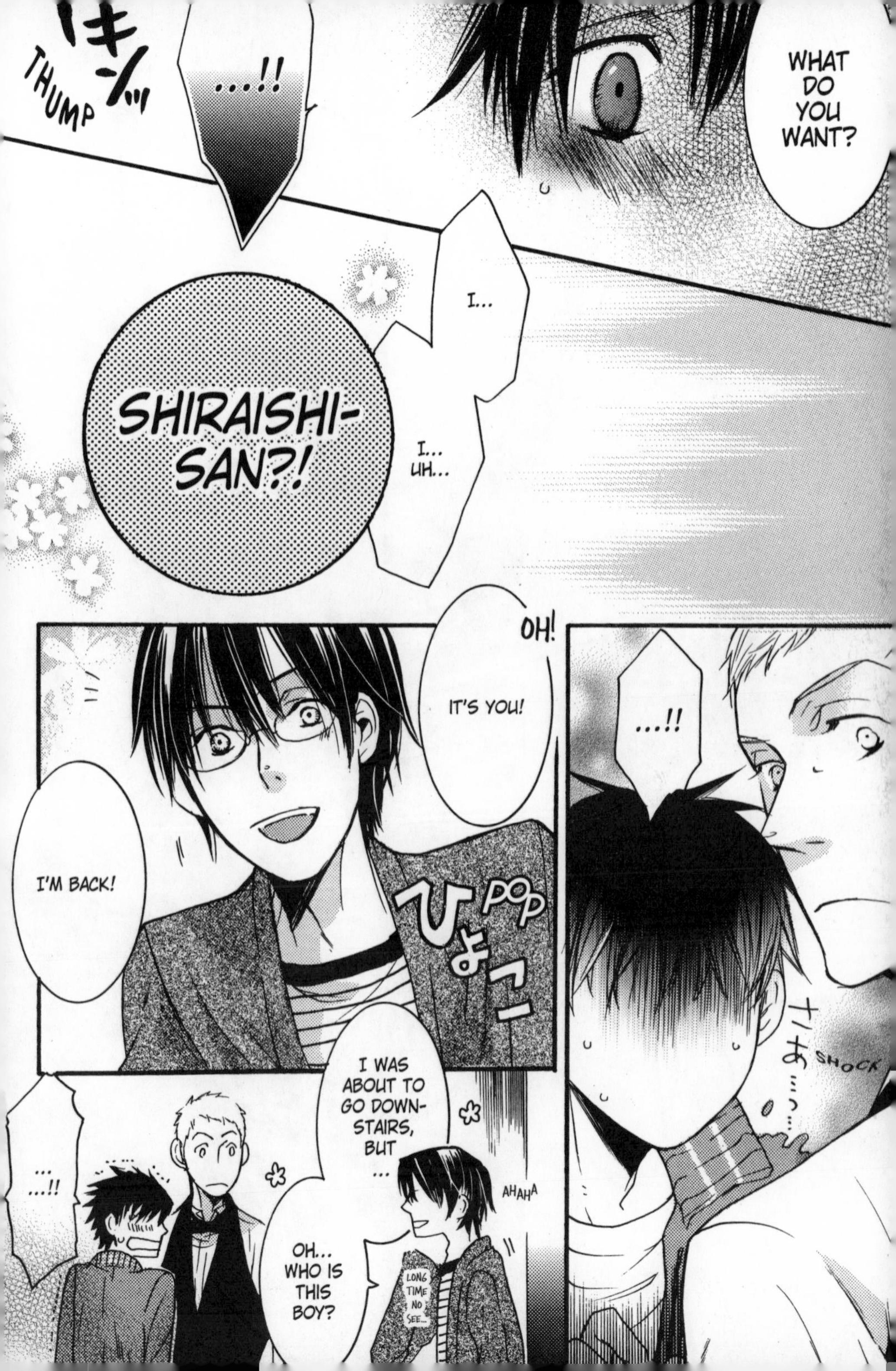

WHAT DO YOU WANT?
...!!
THUMP
I...
I... UH...
SHIRAISHI-SAN?!
...!!
SHOCK
OH!
IT'S YOU!
POP
I'M BACK!
I WAS ABOUT TO GO DOWN-STAIRS, BUT ...
AHAHA
LONG TIME NO SEE...
OH... WHO IS THIS BOY?
... ...!!

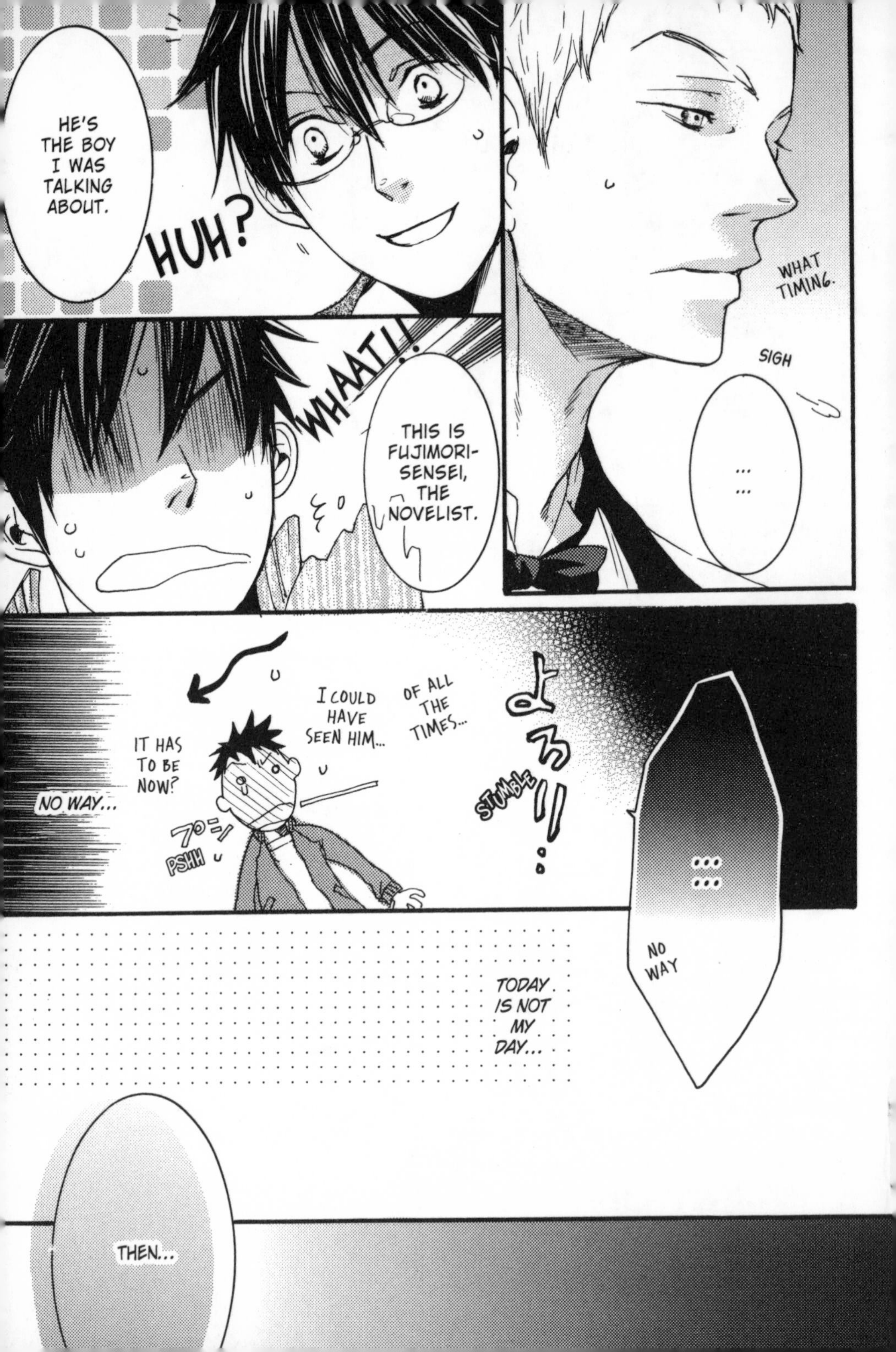

WHAT TIMING.
SIGH
......
HE'S THE BOY I WAS TALKING ABOUT.
HUH?
WHAAT!!
THIS IS FUJIMORI-SENSEI, THE NOVELIST.
......
STUMBLE
OF ALL THE TIMES...
I COULD HAVE SEEN HIM...
IT HAS TO BE NOW?
NO WAY...
PSHH
NO WAY
TODAY IS NOT MY DAY...
THEN...

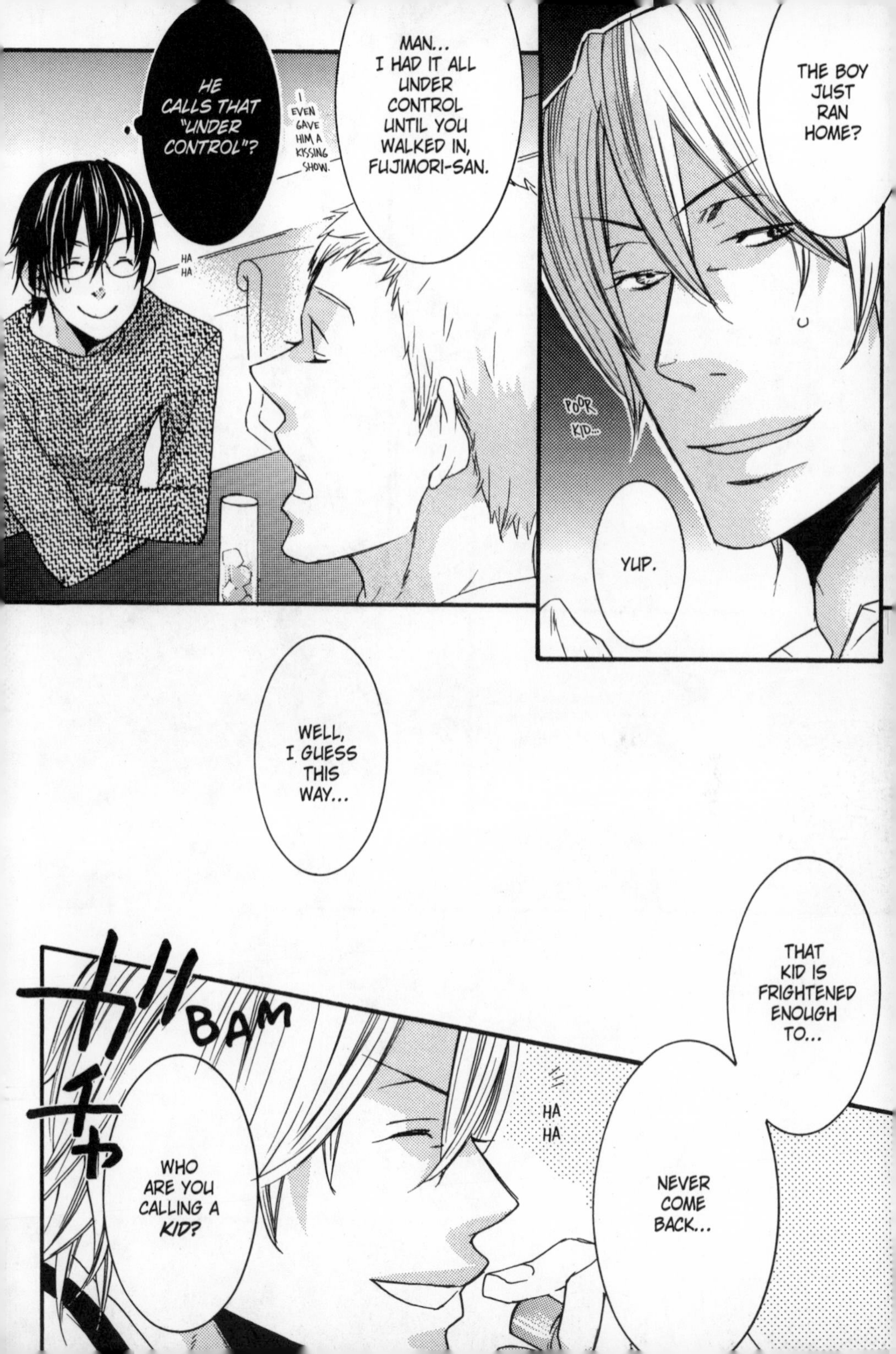
THE BOY JUST RAN HOME?
POOR KID...
YUP.
MAN... I HAD IT ALL UNDER CONTROL UNTIL YOU WALKED IN, FUJIMORI-SAN.
I EVEN GAVE HIM A KISSING SHOW.
HE CALLS THAT "UNDER CONTROL"?
HA HA
WELL, I GUESS THIS WAY...
THAT KID IS FRIGHTENED ENOUGH TO...
NEVER COME BACK...
HA HA
ガチャ
BAM
WHO ARE YOU CALLING A *KID*?

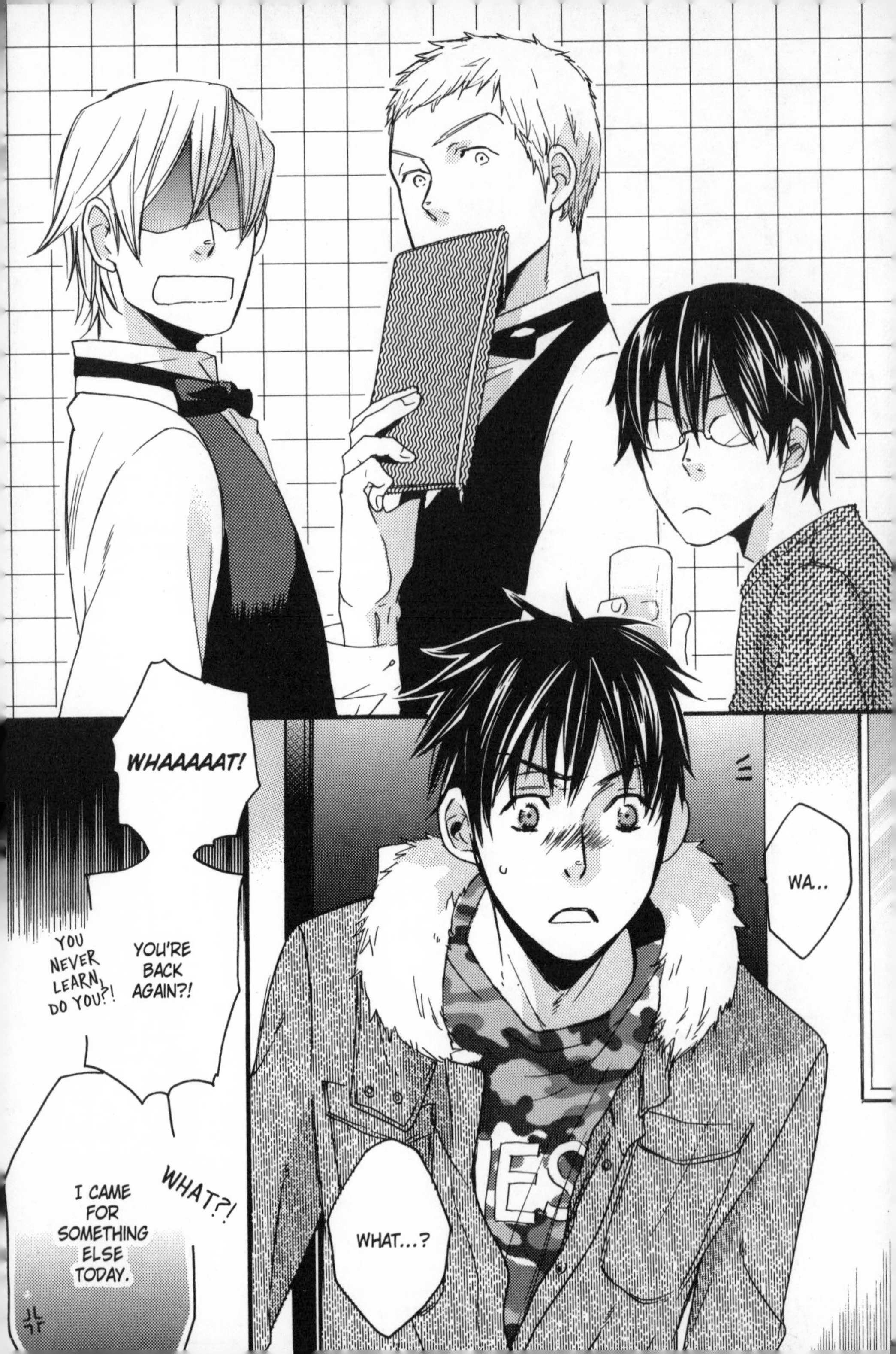
WA...
WHAAAAAT!
YOU'RE BACK AGAIN?!
YOU NEVER LEARN, DO YOU?!
WHAT...?
WHAT?!
I CAME FOR SOMETHING ELSE TODAY.

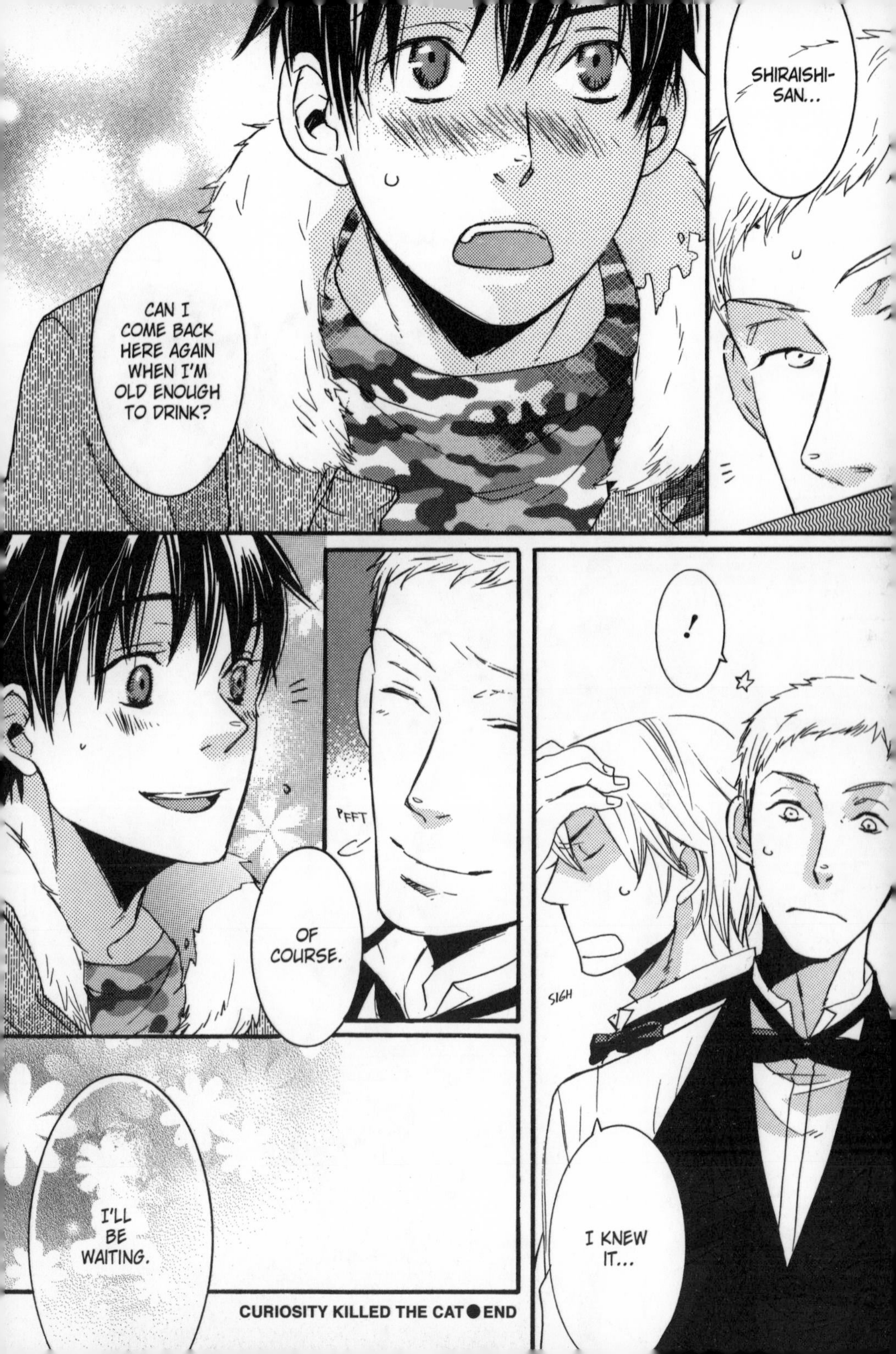
SHIRAISHI-SAN...
CAN I COME BACK HERE AGAIN WHEN I'M OLD ENOUGH TO DRINK?
!
SIGH
I KNEW IT...
PFFT
OF COURSE.
I'LL BE WAITING.
CURIOSITY KILLED THE CAT●END

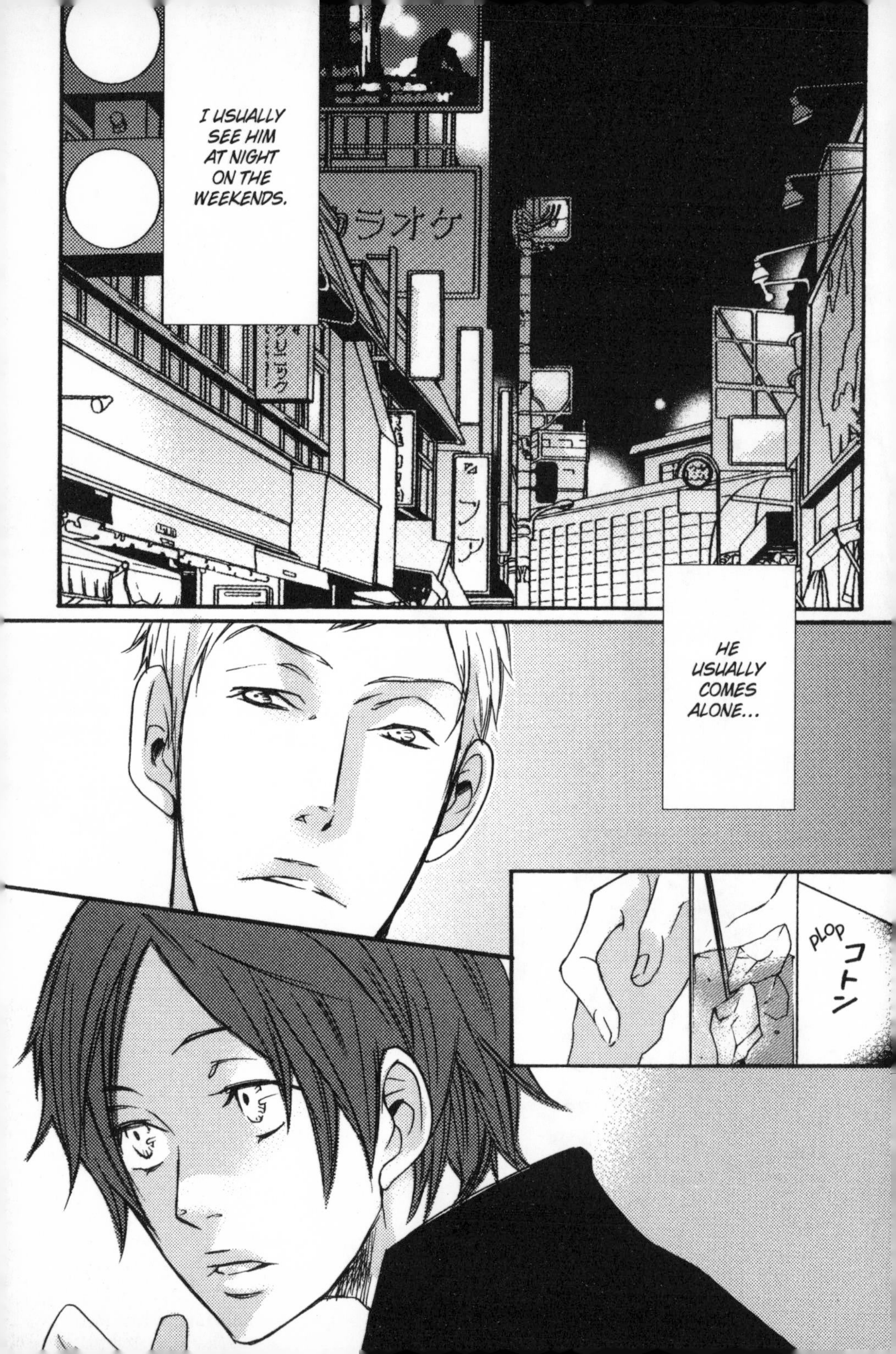
I USUALLY SEE HIM AT NIGHT ON THE WEEKENDS.
HE USUALLY COMES ALONE...
PLOP
コトン

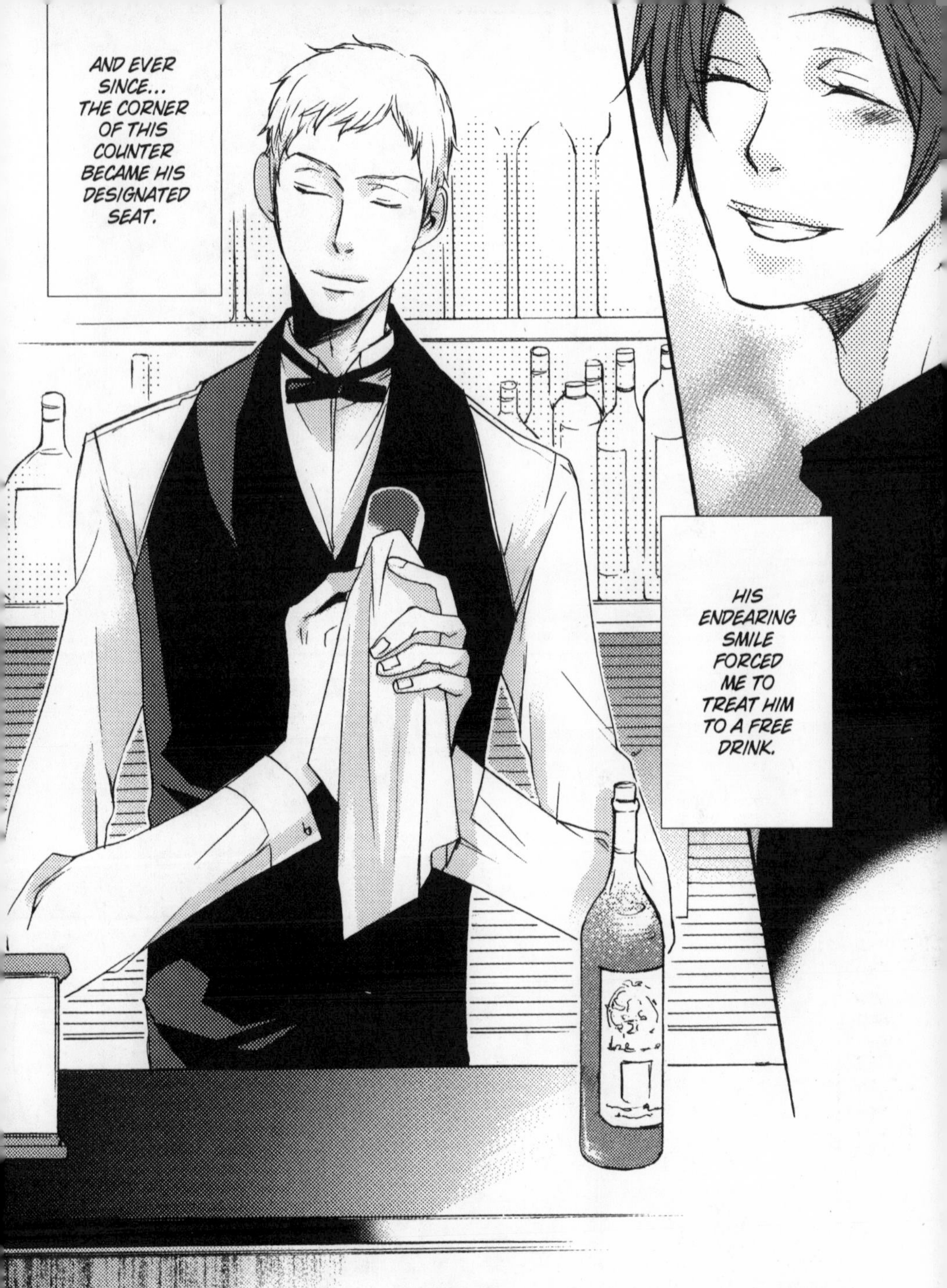
HIS ENDEARING SMILE FORCED ME TO TREAT HIM TO A FREE DRINK.
AND EVER SINCE... THE CORNER OF THIS COUNTER BECAME HIS DESIGNATED SEAT.

終末の近い週末

The Weekend Near the End...

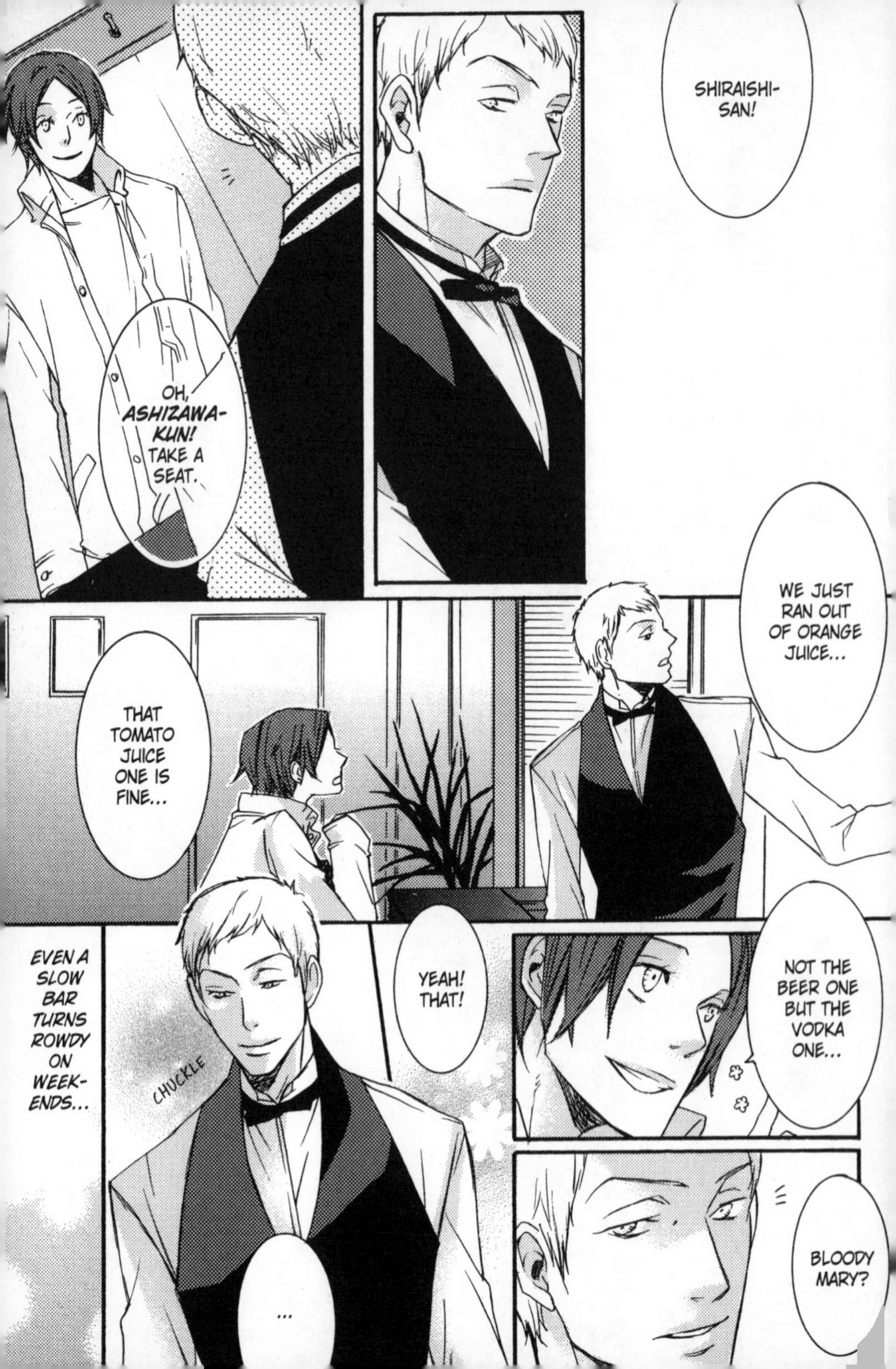
SHIRAISHI-SAN!
OH, ASHIZAWA-KUN! TAKE A SEAT.
WE JUST RAN OUT OF ORANGE JUICE...
THAT TOMATO JUICE ONE IS FINE...
NOT THE BEER ONE BUT THE VODKA ONE...
BLOODY MARY?
YEAH! THAT!
EVEN A SLOW BAR TURNS ROWDY ON WEEK-ENDS...
CHUCKLE
...

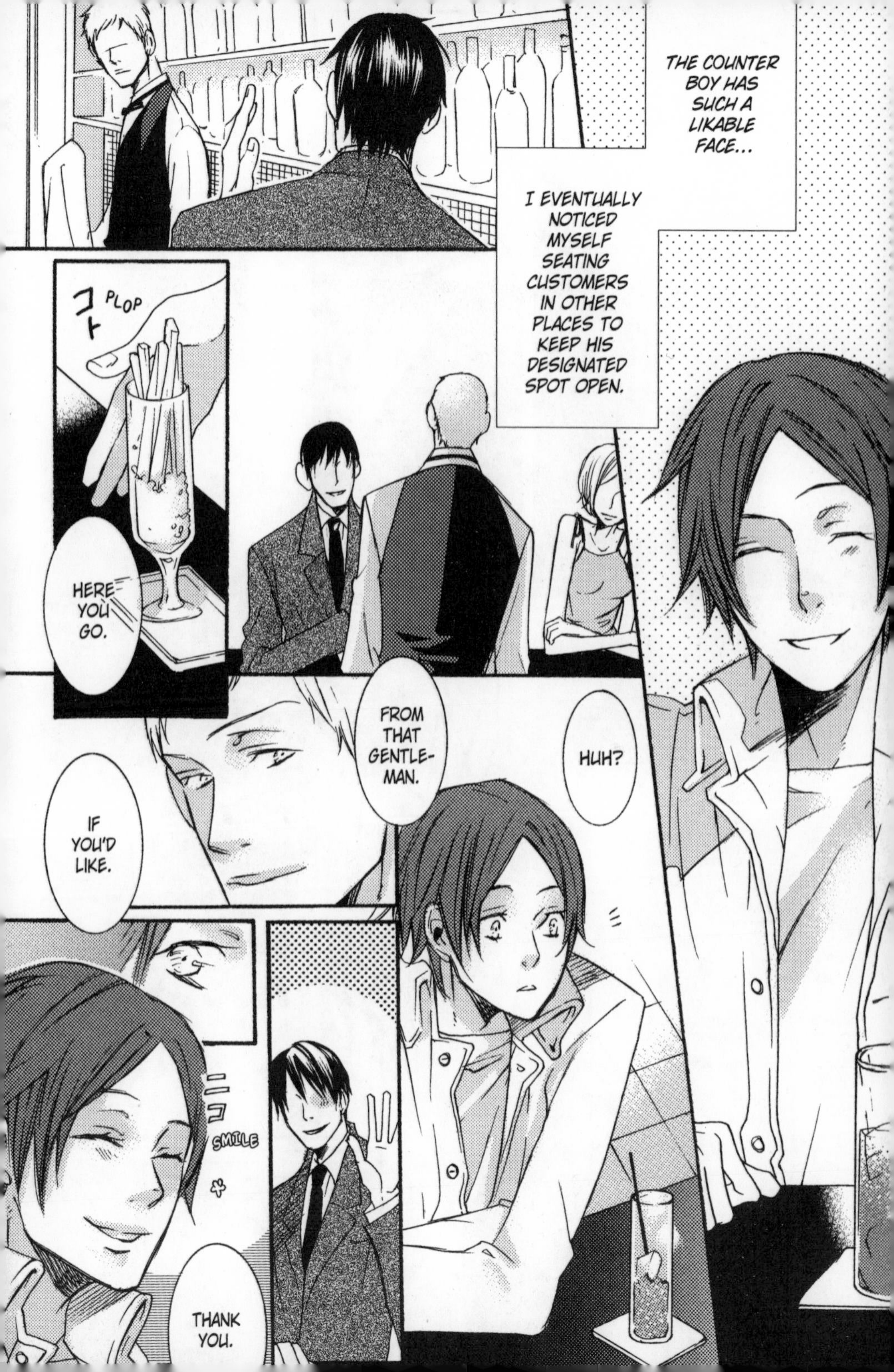
THE COUNTER BOY HAS SUCH A LIKABLE FACE...
I EVENTUALLY NOTICED MYSELF SEATING CUSTOMERS IN OTHER PLACES TO KEEP HIS DESIGNATED SPOT OPEN.
コト
PLOP
HERE YOU GO.
HUH?
FROM THAT GENTLE-MAN.
IF YOU'D LIKE.
SMILE
THANK YOU.

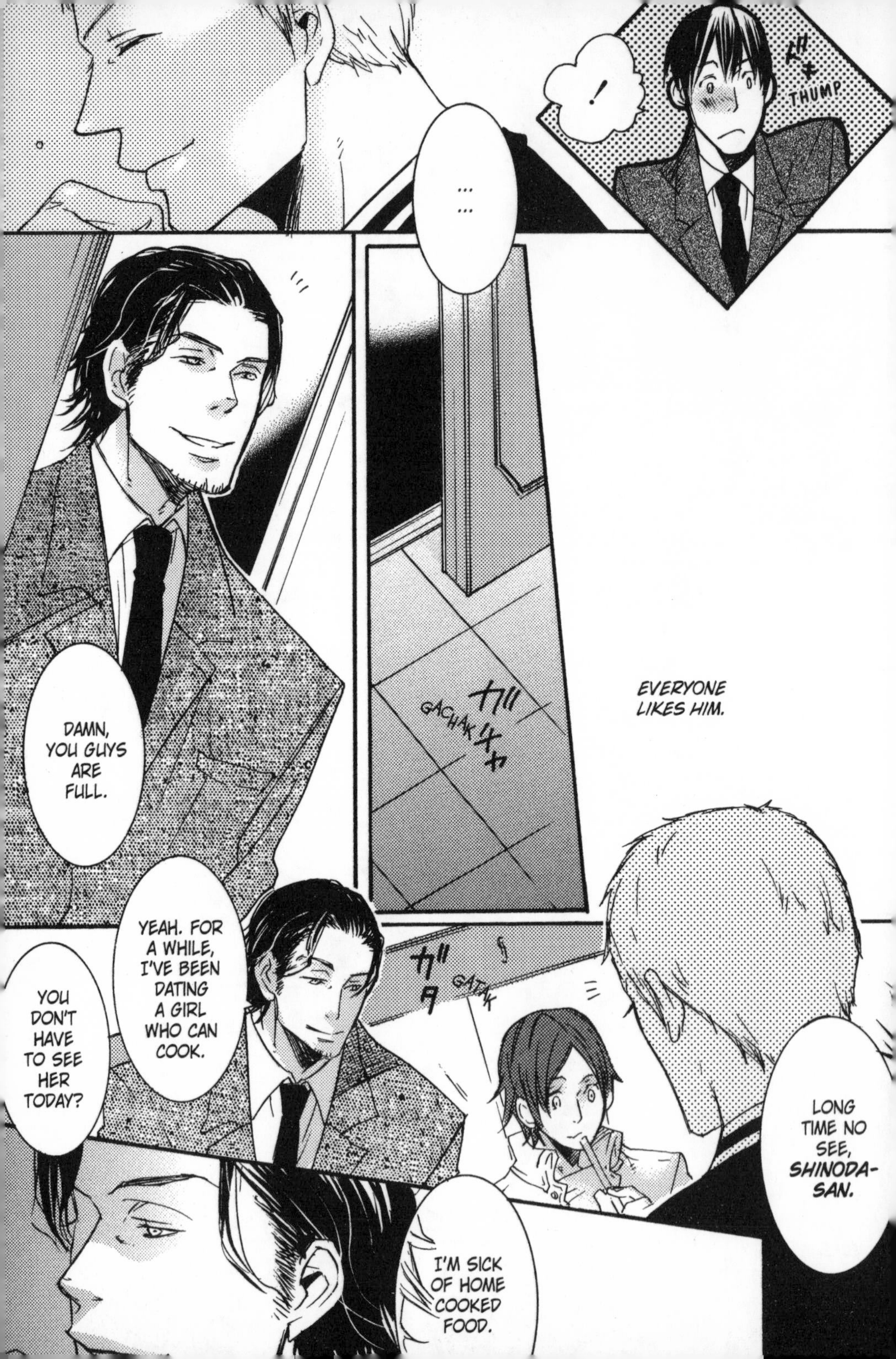
!
THUMP
... ...
EVERYONE LIKES HIM.
GACHAK
DAMN, YOU GUYS ARE FULL.
LONG TIME NO SEE, SHINODA-SAN.
GATAK
YEAH. FOR A WHILE, I'VE BEEN DATING A GIRL WHO CAN COOK.
YOU DON'T HAVE TO SEE HER TODAY?
I'M SICK OF HOME COOKED FOOD.

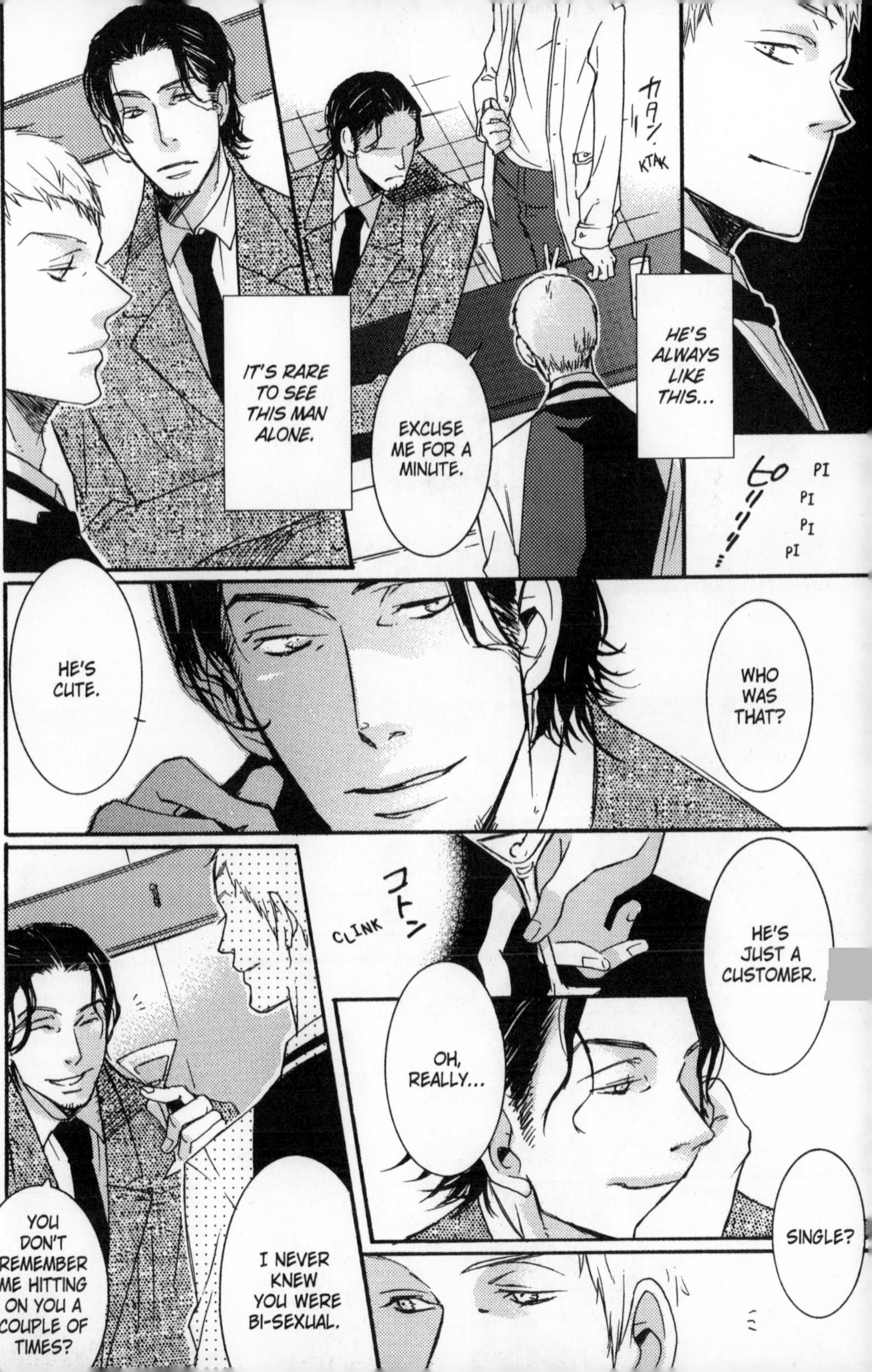

HE'S ALWAYS LIKE THIS...
PI PI PI PI
カタン
KTAK
EXCUSE ME FOR A MINUTE.
IT'S RARE TO SEE THIS MAN ALONE.
WHO WAS THAT?
HE'S CUTE.
HE'S JUST A CUSTOMER.
コトン
CLINK
OH, REALLY...
SINGLE?
I NEVER KNEW YOU WERE BI-SEXUAL.
YOU DON'T REMEMBER ME HITTING ON YOU A COUPLE OF TIMES?

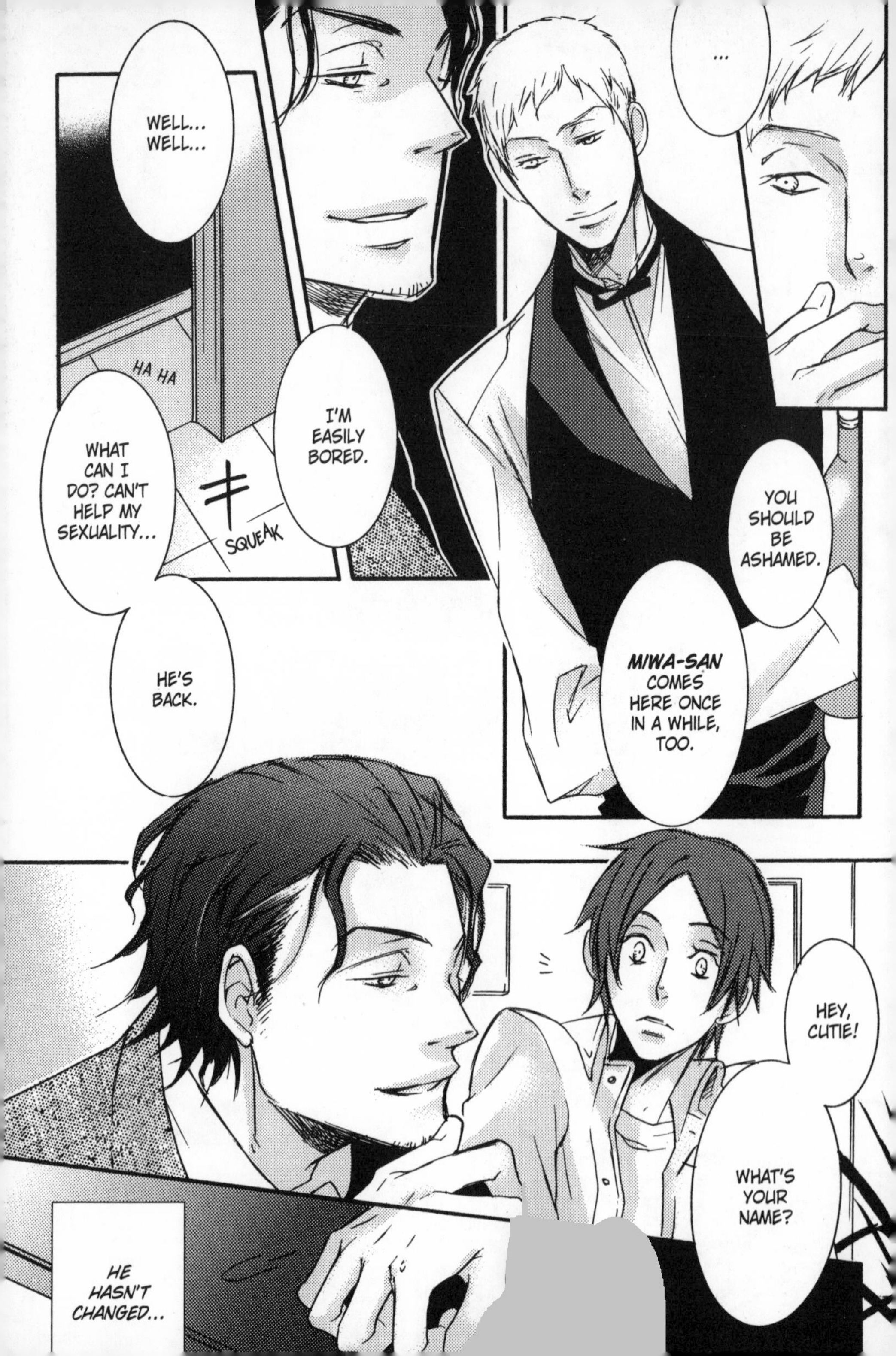
...
YOU SHOULD BE ASHAMED.
MIWA-SAN COMES HERE ONCE IN A WHILE, TOO.
WELL... WELL...
I'M EASILY BORED.
HA HA
SQUEAK
WHAT CAN I DO? CAN'T HELP MY SEXUALITY...
HE'S BACK.
HEY, CUTIE!
WHAT'S YOUR NAME?
HE HASN'T CHANGED...

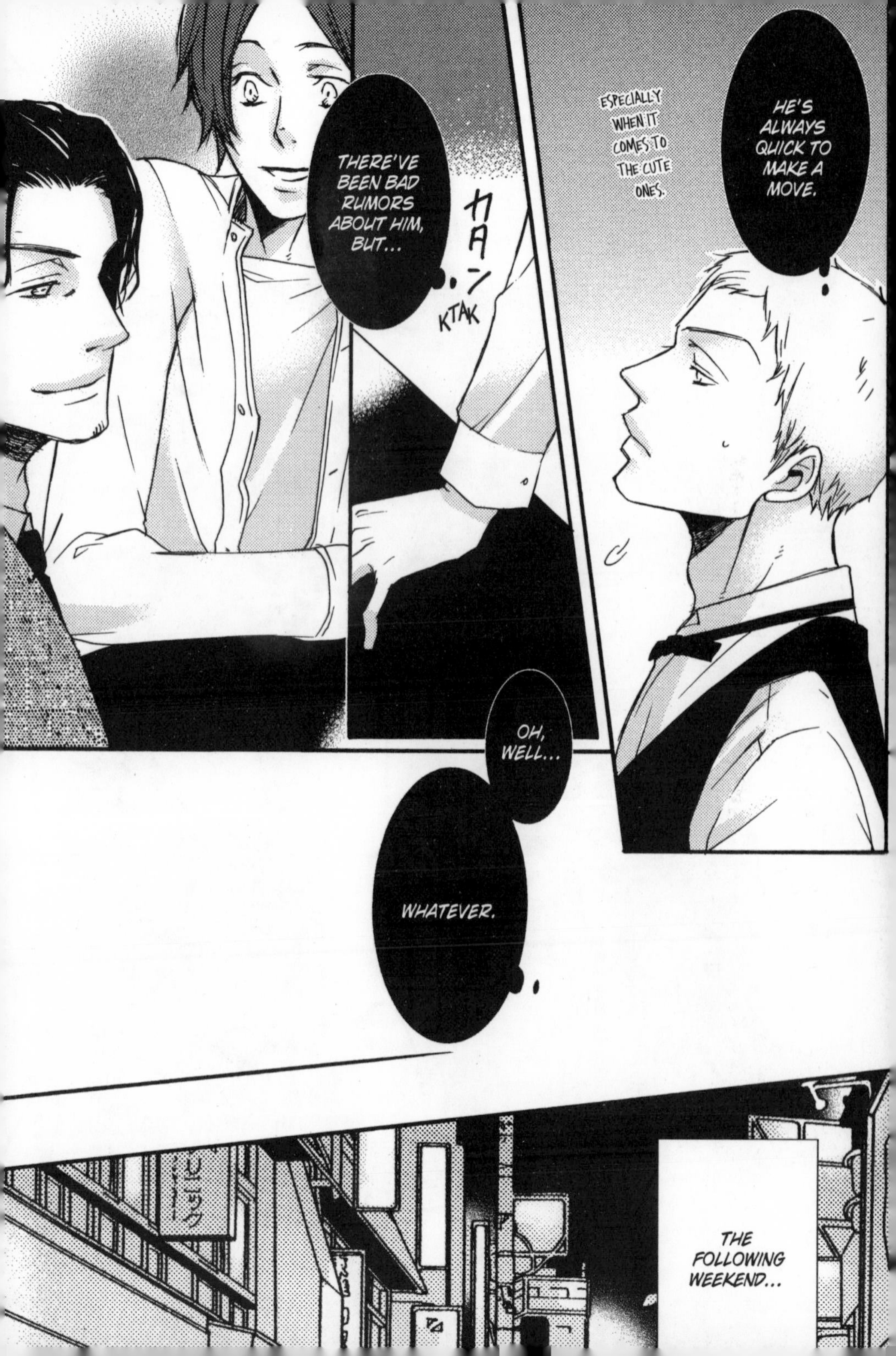

HE'S ALWAYS QUICK TO MAKE A MOVE.
ESPECIALLY WHEN IT COMES TO THE CUTE ONES.
THERE'VE BEEN BAD RUMORS ABOUT HIM, BUT...
カタン
KTAK
OH, WELL...
WHATEVER.
THE FOLLOWING WEEKEND...

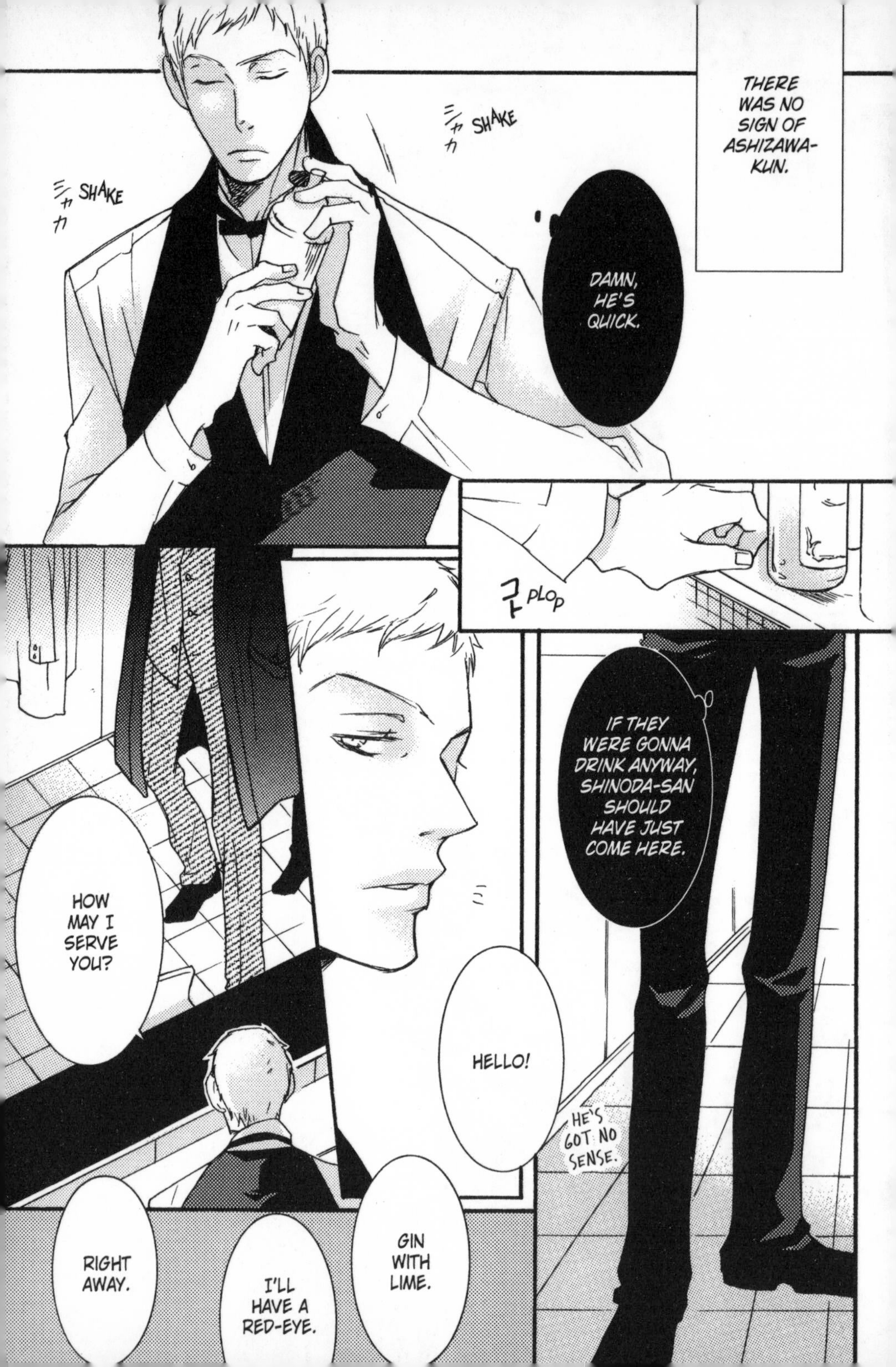
THERE WAS NO SIGN OF ASHIZAWA-KUN.
DAMN, HE'S QUICK.
SHAKE
SHAKE
PLOP
IF THEY WERE GONNA DRINK ANYWAY, SHINODA-SAN SHOULD HAVE JUST COME HERE.
HELLO!
HE'S GOT NO SENSE.
HOW MAY I SERVE YOU?
GIN WITH LIME.
I'LL HAVE A RED-EYE.
RIGHT AWAY.

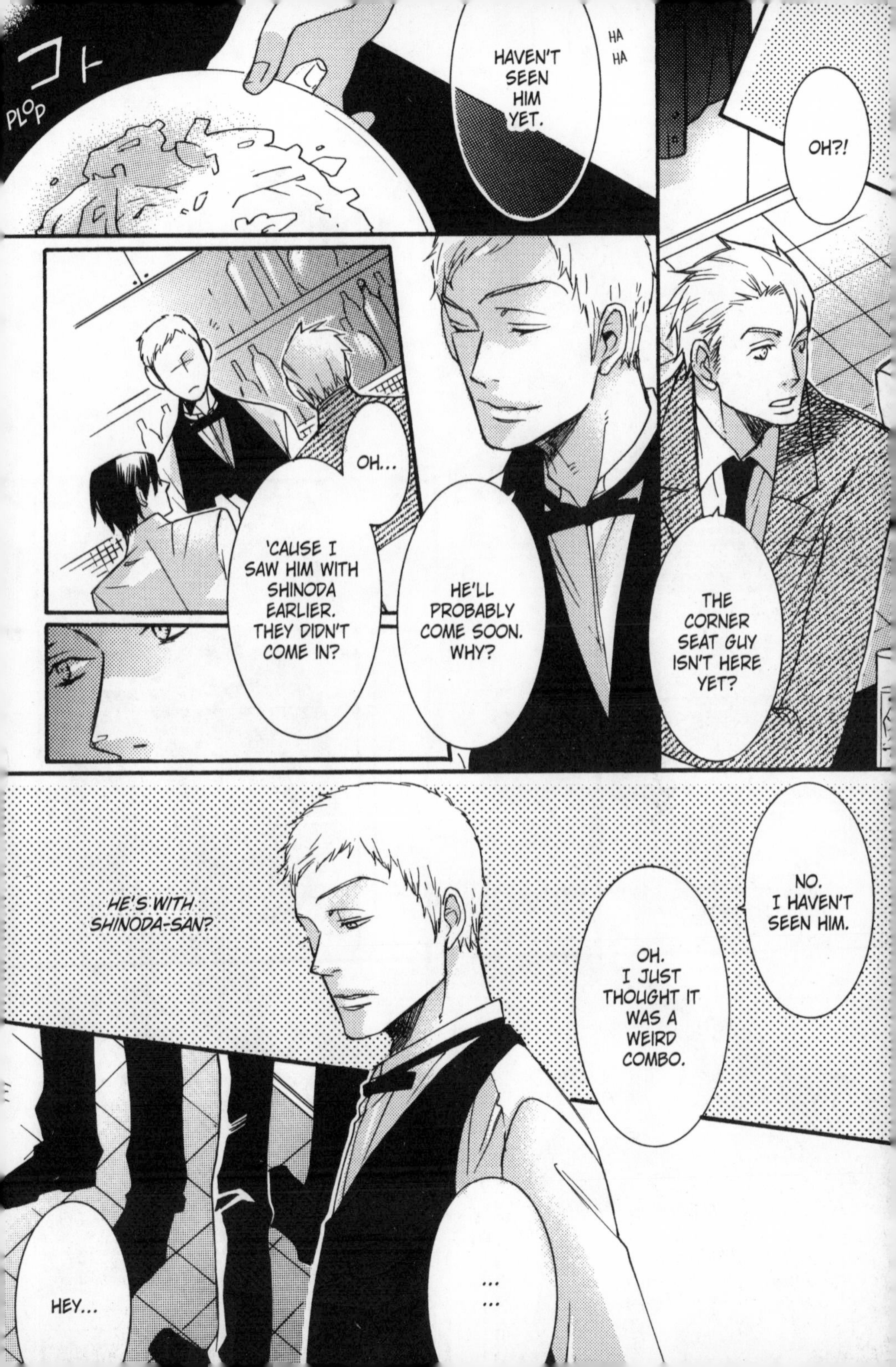
OH?!
HAVEN'T SEEN HIM YET.
HA HA
コト
PLOP
THE CORNER SEAT GUY ISN'T HERE YET?
HE'LL PROBABLY COME SOON. WHY?
OH...
'CAUSE I SAW HIM WITH SHINODA EARLIER. THEY DIDN'T COME IN?
NO. I HAVEN'T SEEN HIM.
OH. I JUST THOUGHT IT WAS A WEIRD COMBO.
HE'S WITH SHINODA-SAN?
......
HEY...

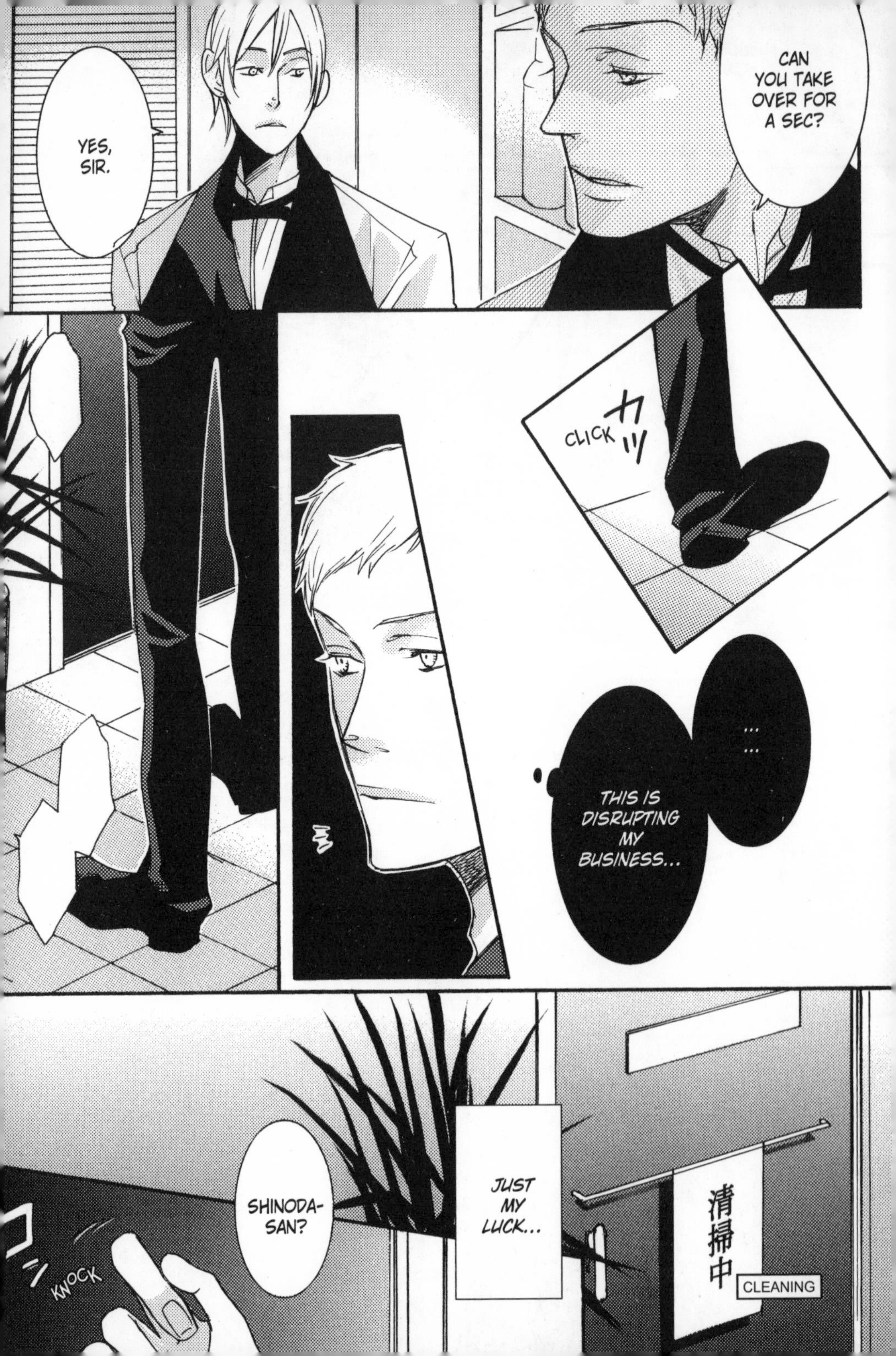
CAN YOU TAKE OVER FOR A SEC?
YES, SIR.
CLICK
カッ
......
THIS IS DISRUPTING MY BUSINESS...
清掃中
CLEANING
JUST MY LUCK...
SHINODA-SAN?
KNOCK

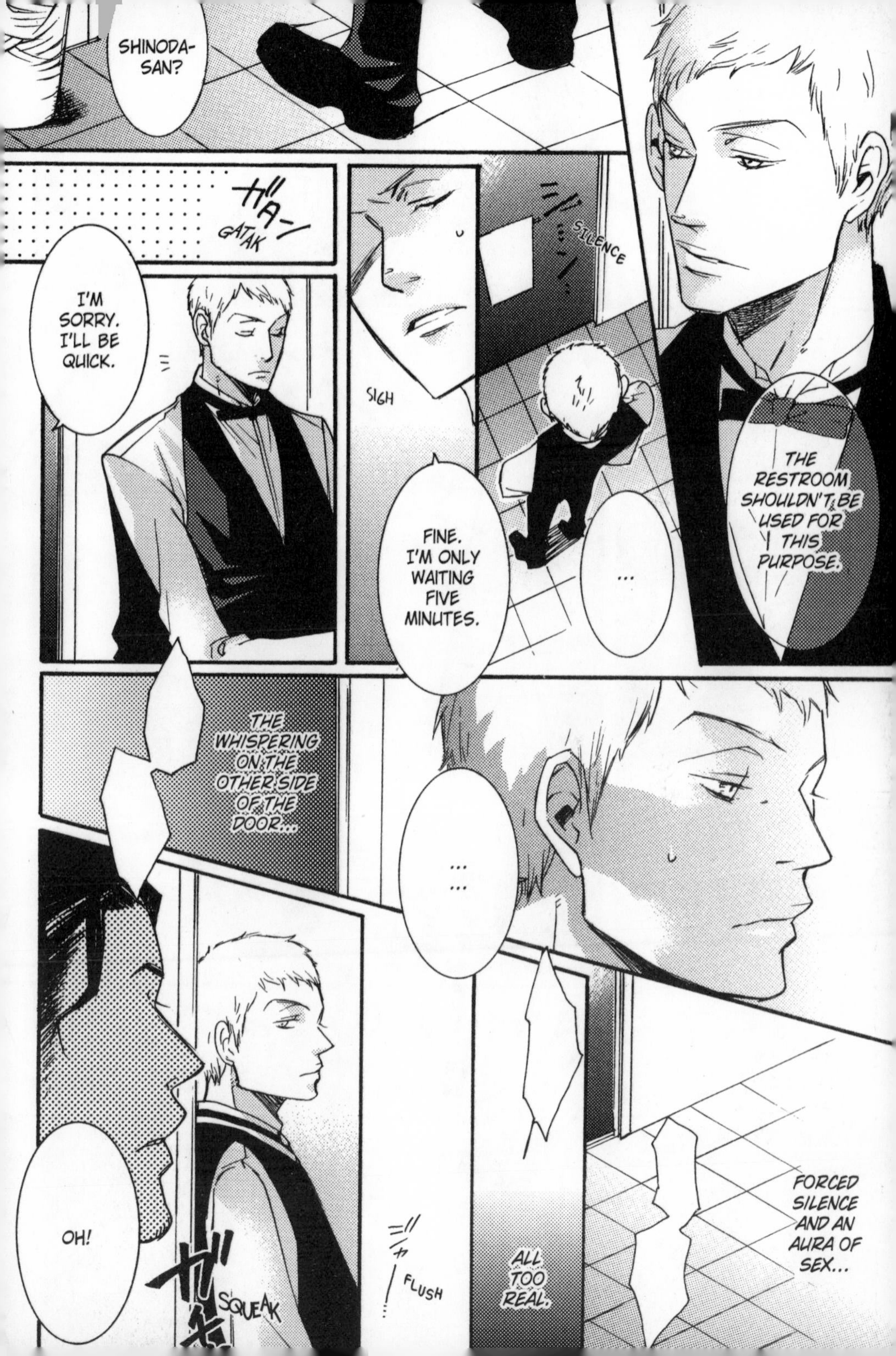
THE RESTROOM SHOULDN'T BE USED FOR THIS PURPOSE.
SHINODA-SAN?
SILENCE
...
SIGH
FINE. I'M ONLY WAITING FIVE MINUTES.
GATAK
I'M SORRY. I'LL BE QUICK.
... ...
THE WHISPERING ON THE OTHER SIDE OF THE DOOR...
FORCED SILENCE AND AN AURA OF SEX...
ALL TOO REAL.
FLUSH
OH!
SQUEAK

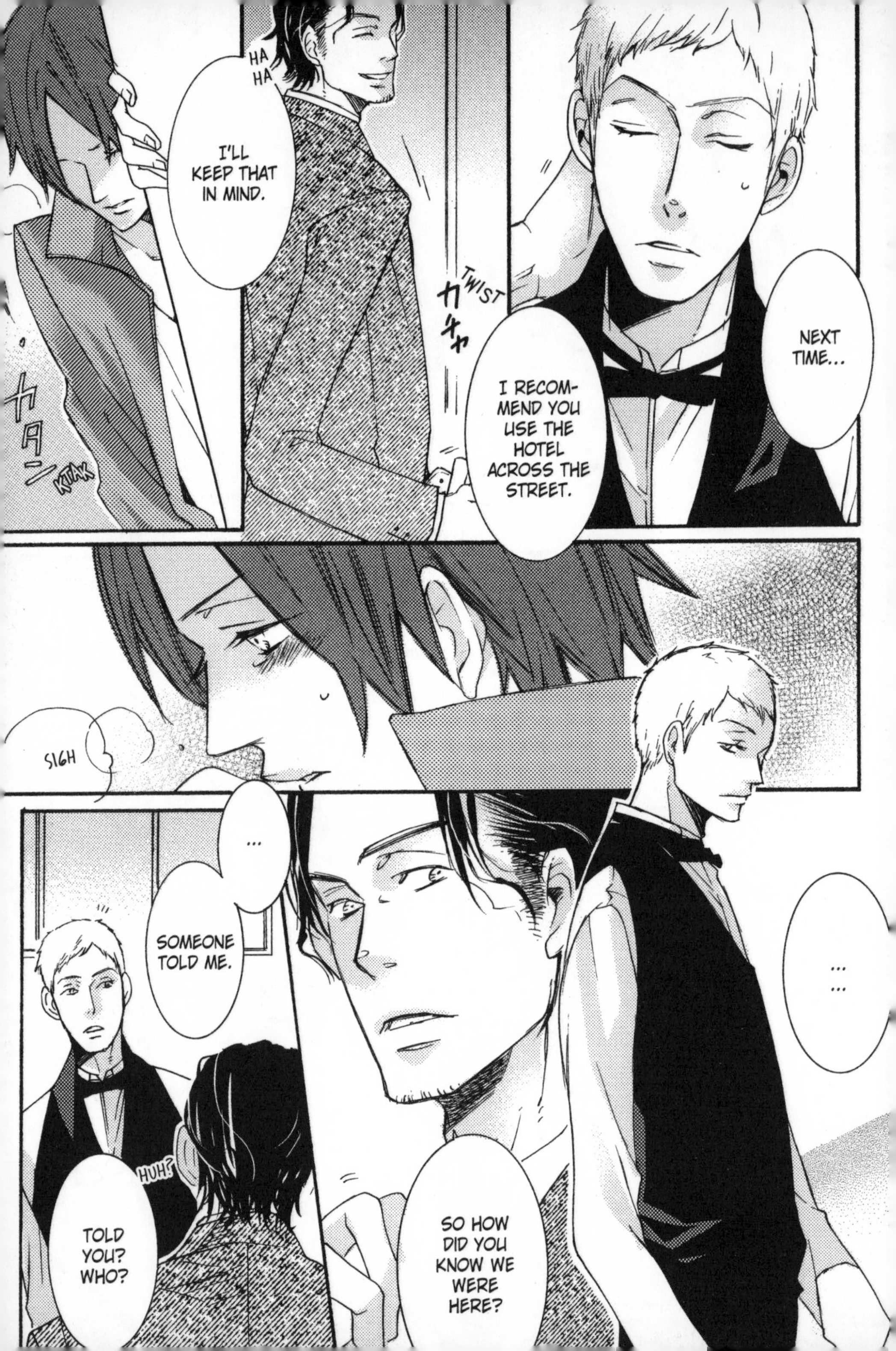
NEXT TIME...
I RECOMMEND YOU USE THE HOTEL ACROSS THE STREET.
ガチャ TWIST
HA HA
I'LL KEEP THAT IN MIND.
カタン KTAK
SIGH
......
SO HOW DID YOU KNOW WE WERE HERE?
...
SOMEONE TOLD ME.
HUH?
TOLD YOU? WHO?

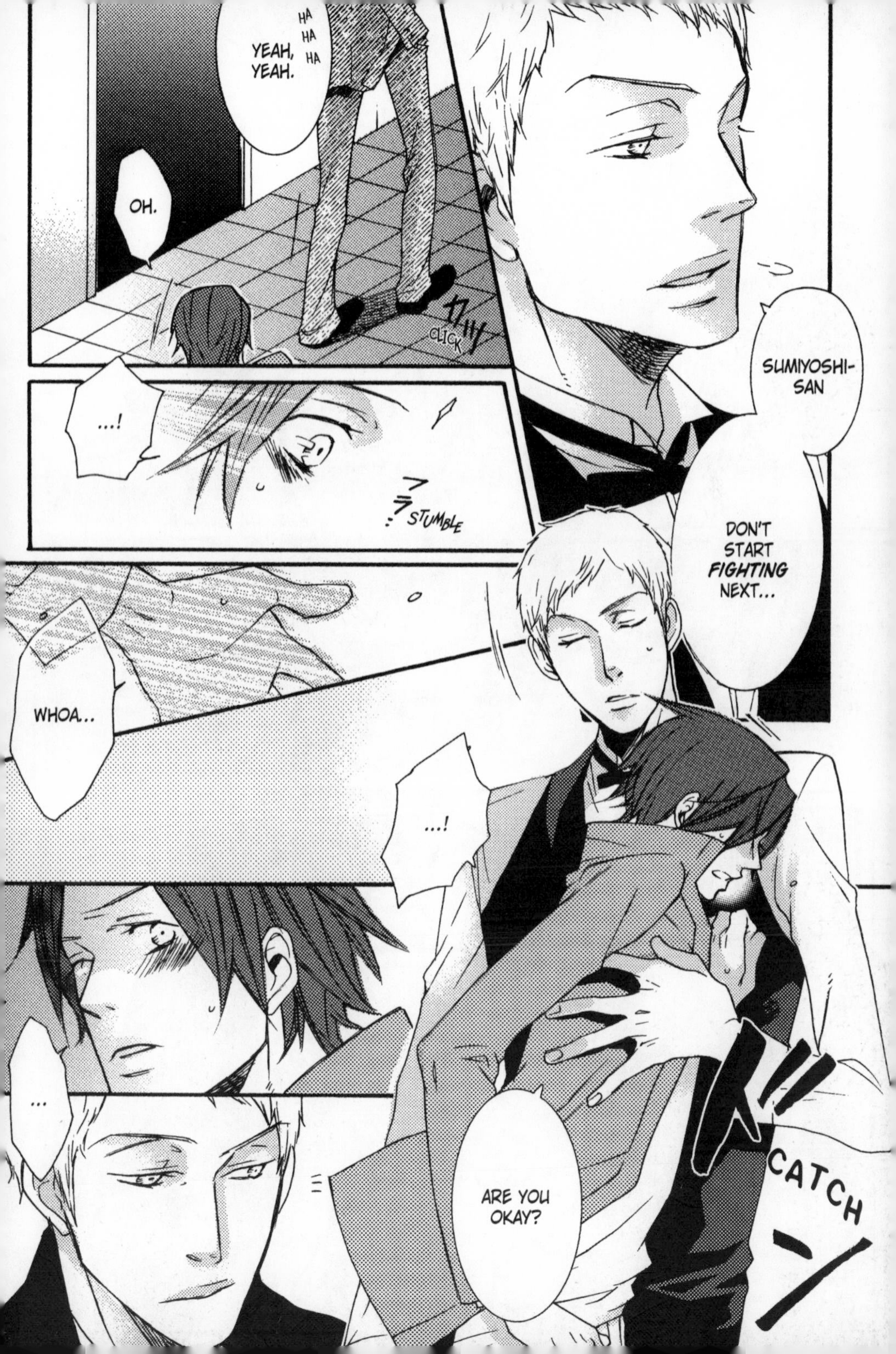
SUMIYOSHI-SAN
DON'T START FIGHTING NEXT...
YEAH, YEAH.
HA HA HA
OH.
CLICK
...!
STUMBLE
...!
CATCH
ARE YOU OKAY?
WHOA...
...

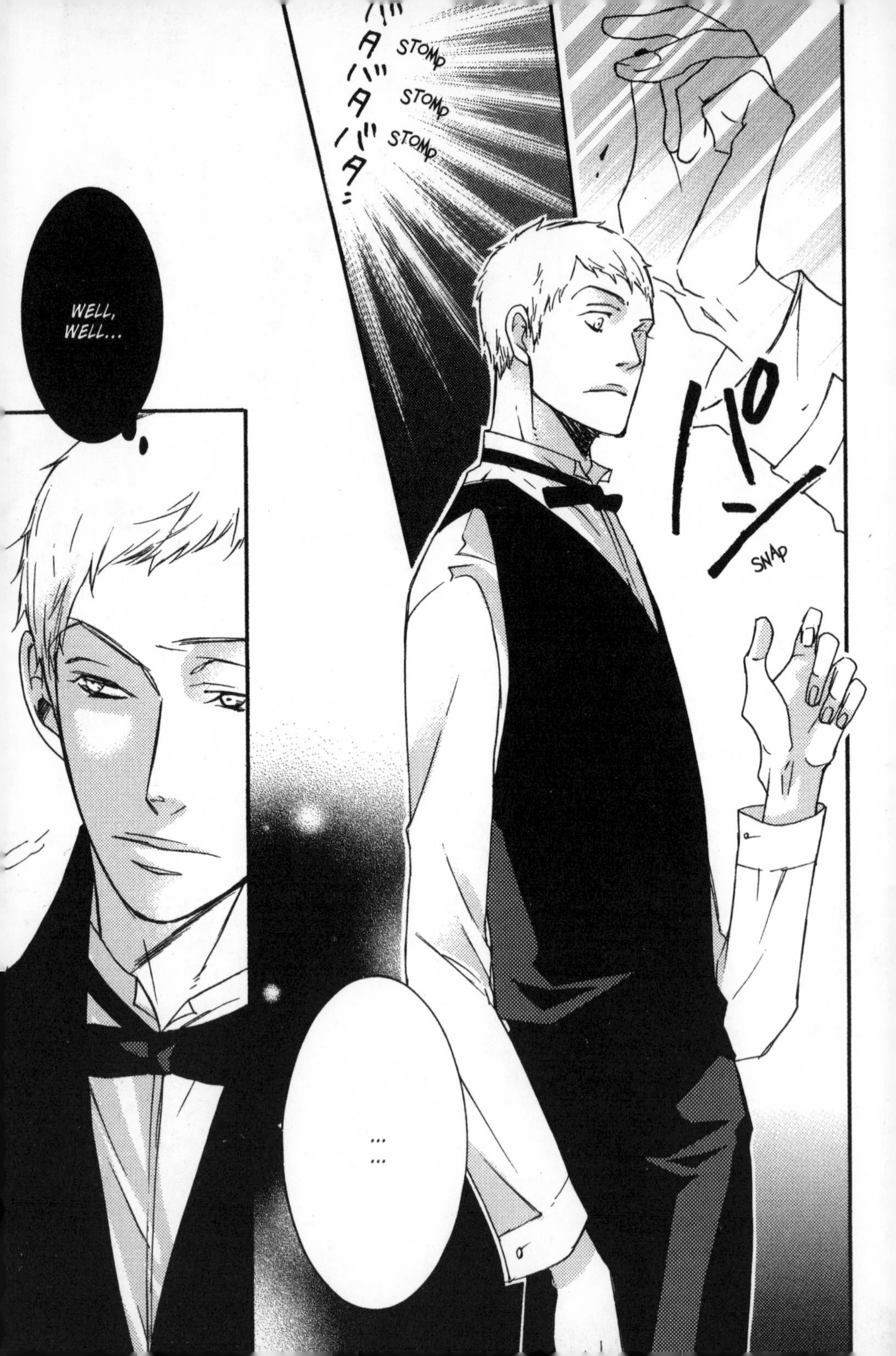
STOMP
STOMP
STOMP
SNAP
...
...
WELL, WELL...

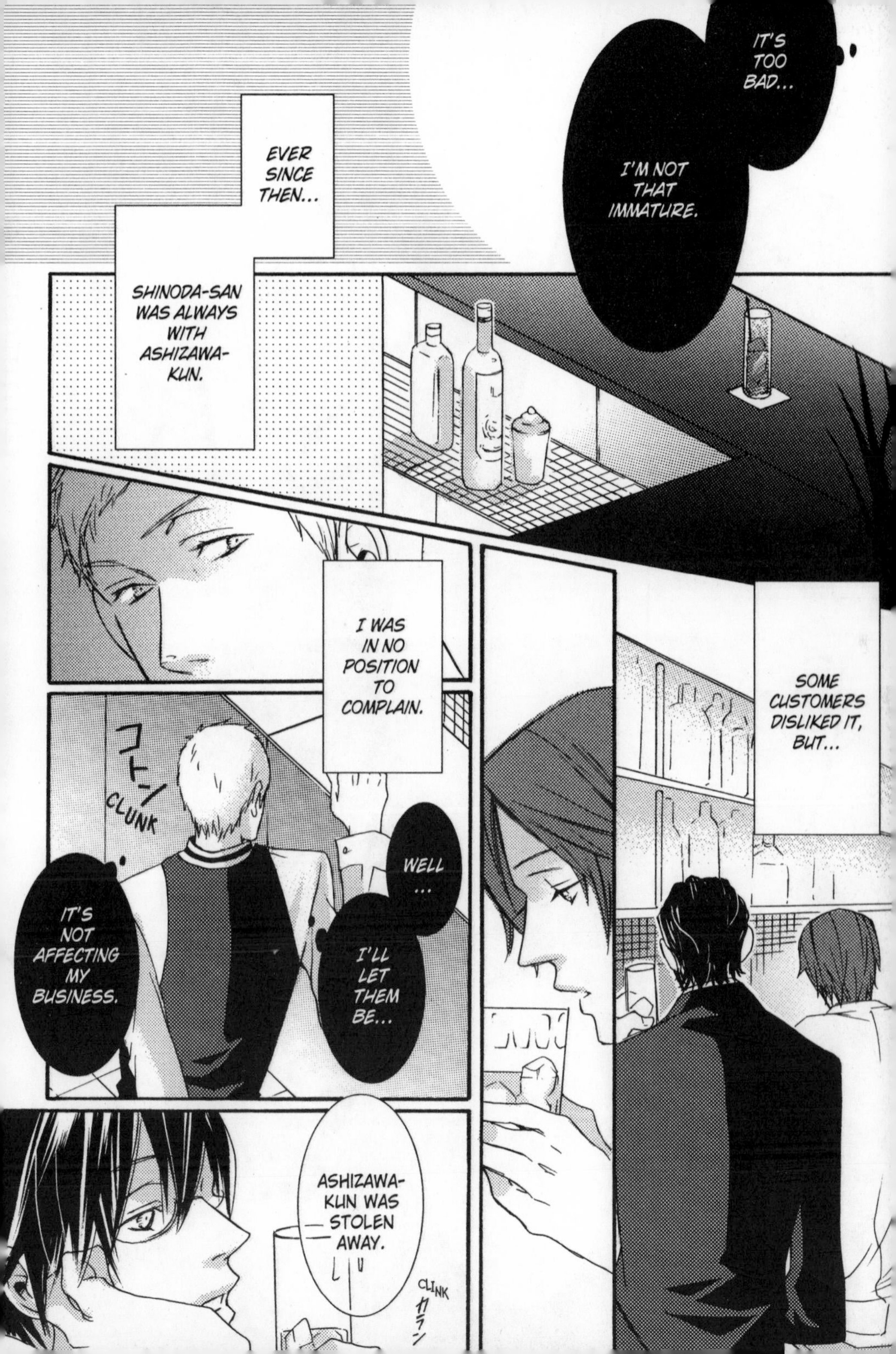
IT'S TOO BAD...
I'M NOT THAT IMMATURE.
EVER SINCE THEN...
SHINODA-SAN WAS ALWAYS WITH ASHIZAWA-KUN.
SOME CUSTOMERS DISLIKED IT, BUT...
I WAS IN NO POSITION TO COMPLAIN.
CLUNK
WELL...
I'LL LET THEM BE...
IT'S NOT AFFECTING MY BUSINESS.
ASHIZAWA-KUN WAS STOLEN AWAY.
CLINK

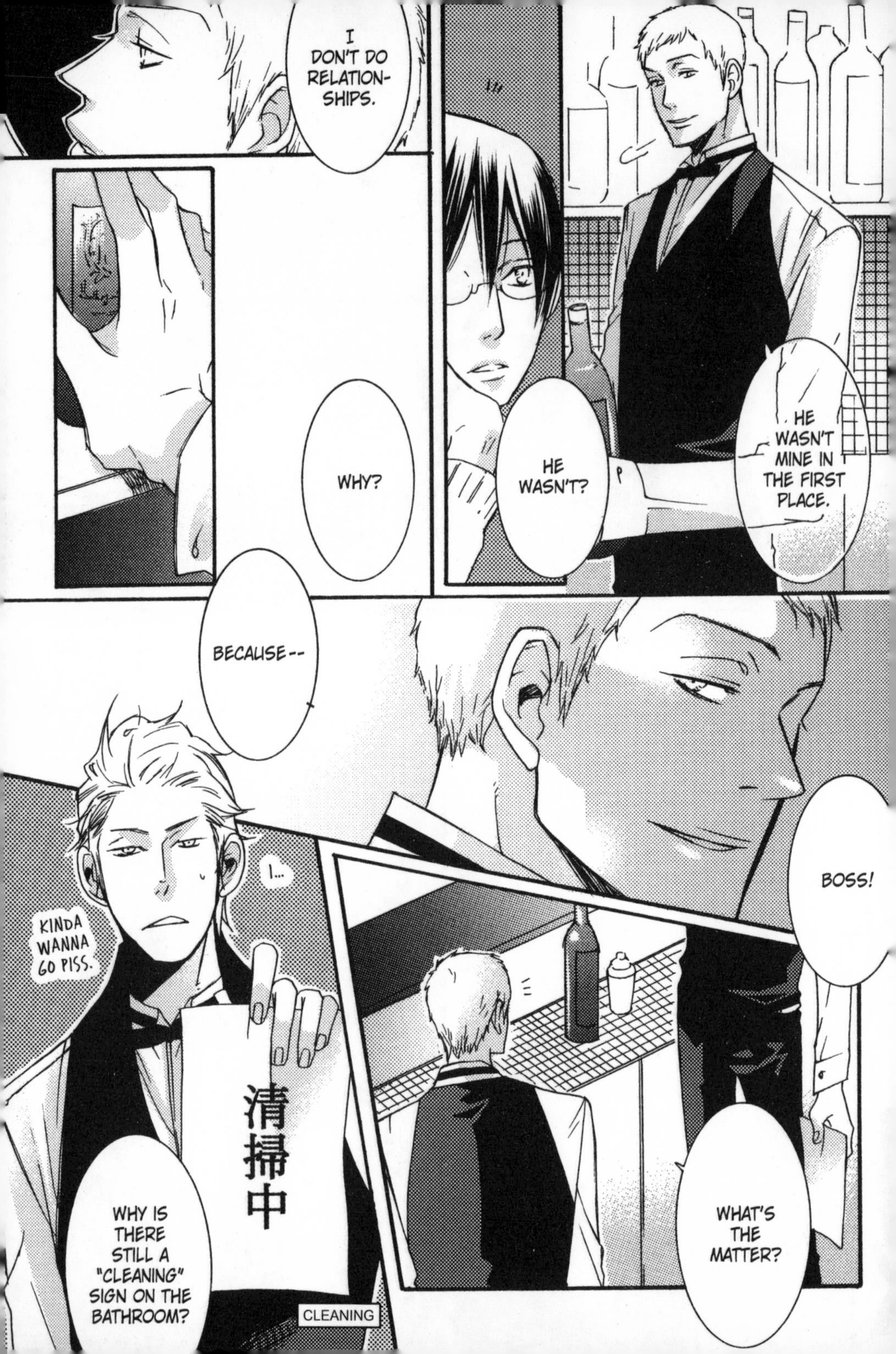
HE WASN'T MINE IN THE FIRST PLACE.
HE WASN'T?
I DON'T DO RELATIONSHIPS.
WHY?
BECAUSE--
BOSS!
WHAT'S THE MATTER?
I...
KINDA WANNA GO PISS.
清掃中
WHY IS THERE STILL A "CLEANING" SIGN ON THE BATHROOM?
CLEANING

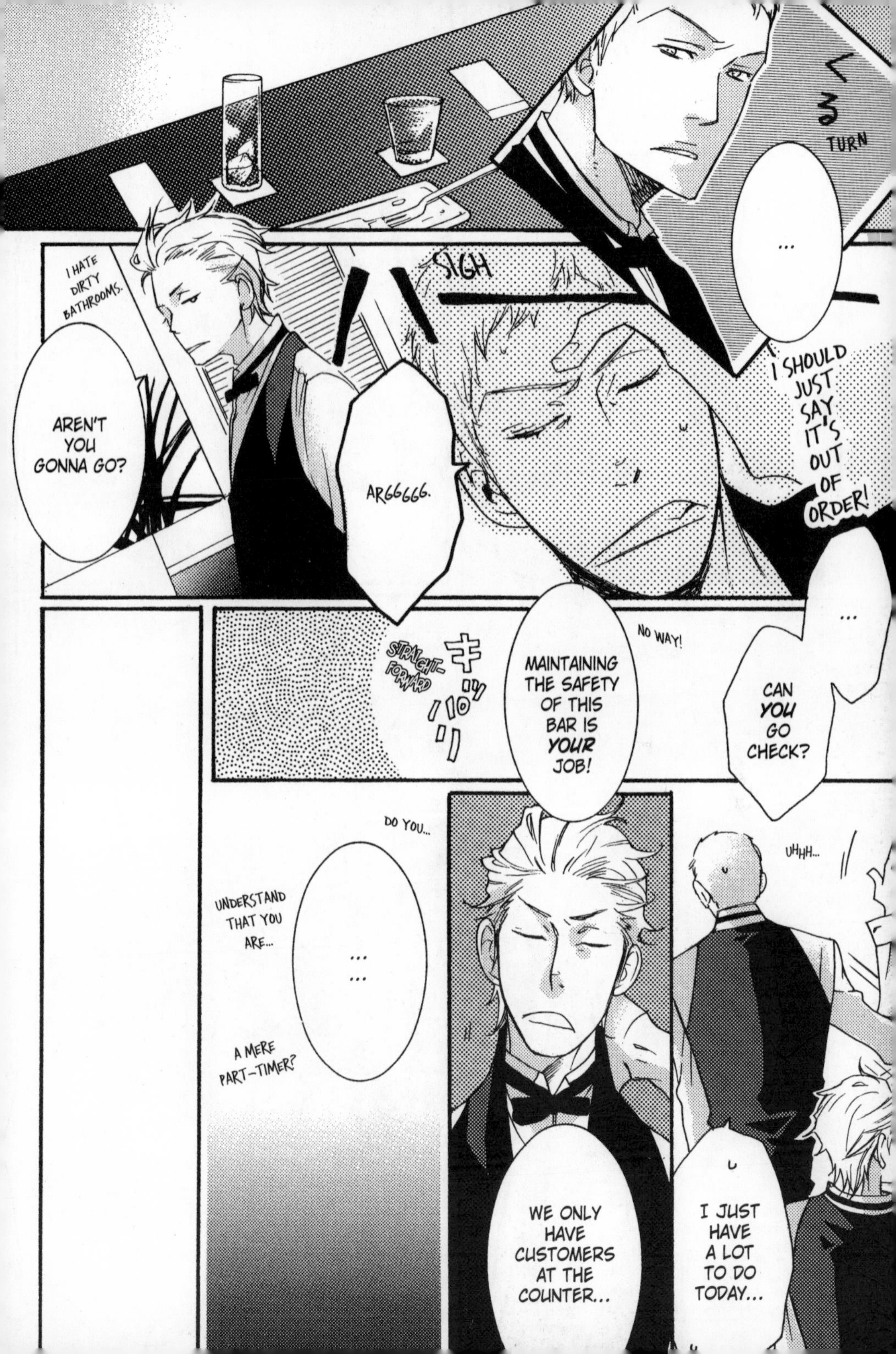
くる
TURN
...
I SHOULD JUST SAY IT'S OUT OF ORDER!
SIGH
ARGGGGG.
I HATE DIRTY BATHROOMS.
AREN'T YOU GONNA GO?
...
CAN YOU GO CHECK?
NO WAY!
MAINTAINING THE SAFETY OF THIS BAR IS YOUR JOB!
キッパリ
STRAIGHT-FORWARD
UHHH...
I JUST HAVE A LOT TO DO TODAY...
WE ONLY HAVE CUSTOMERS AT THE COUNTER...
DO YOU...
UNDERSTAND THAT YOU ARE...
......
A MERE PART-TIMER?

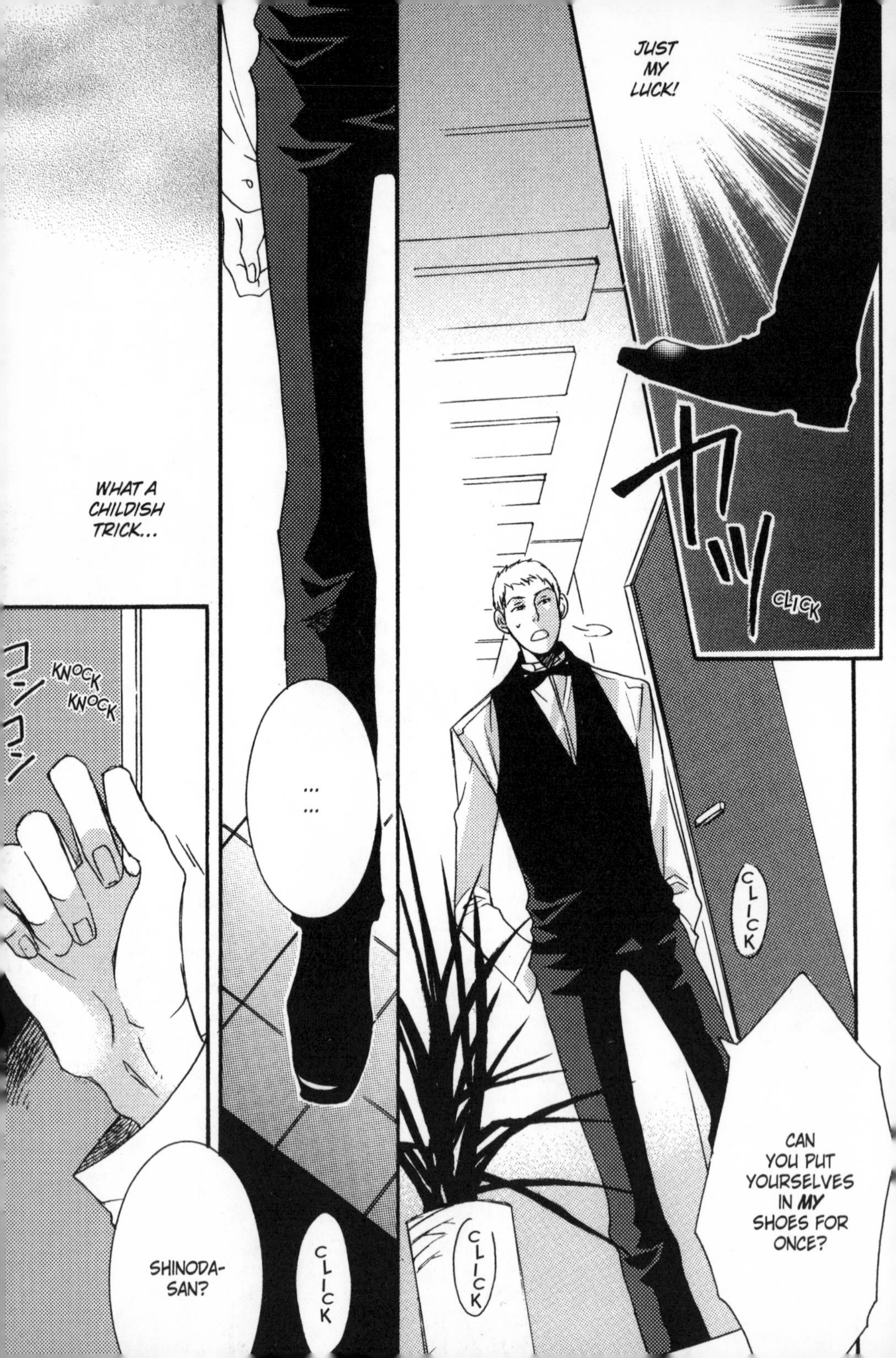
JUST MY LUCK!
ヤッ
CLICK
CLICK
CAN YOU PUT YOURSELVES IN *MY* SHOES FOR ONCE?
CLICK
......
CLICK
WHAT A CHILDISH TRICK...
コンコン
KNOCK KNOCK
SHINODA-SAN?

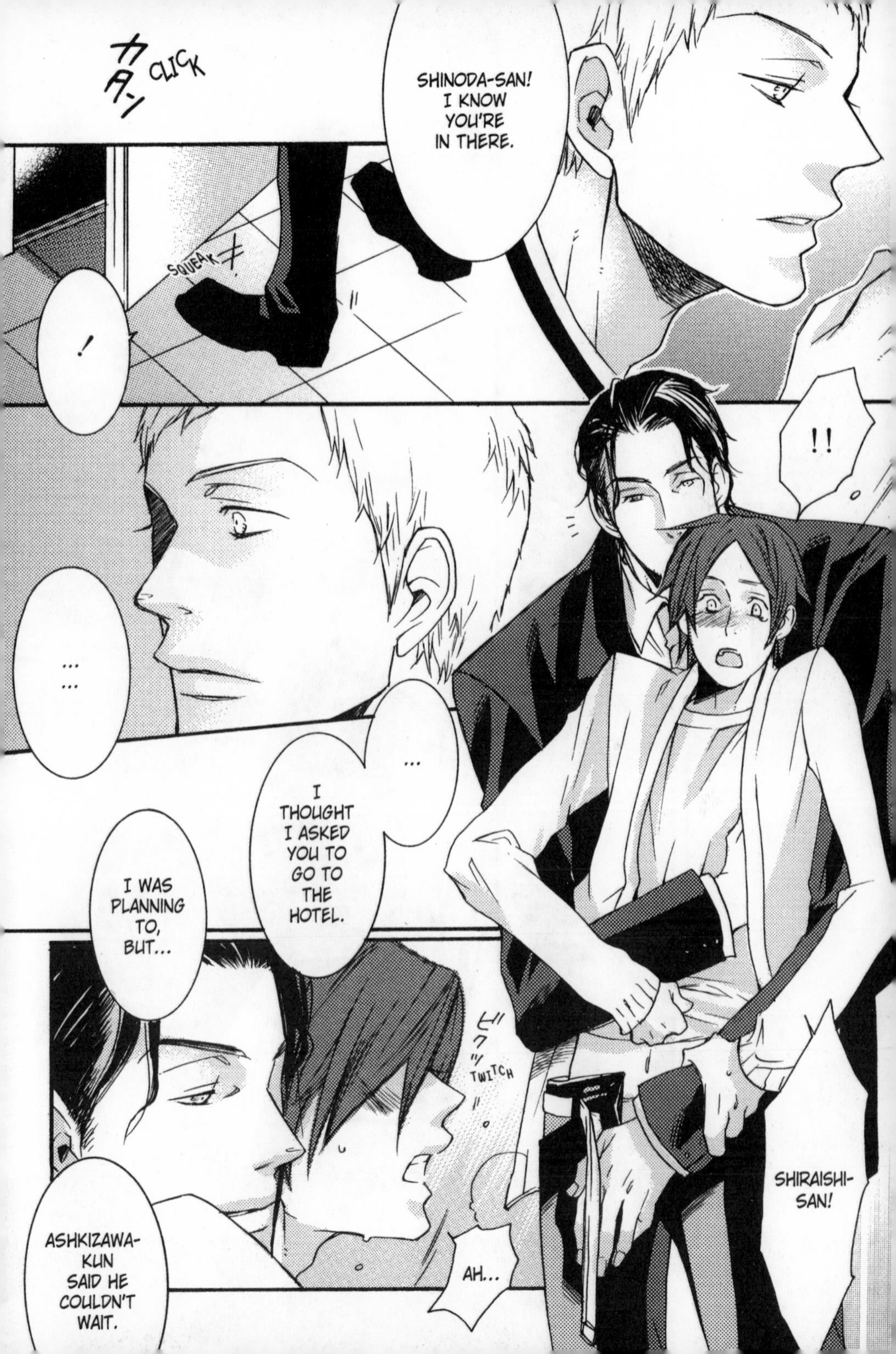
SHINODA-SAN! I KNOW YOU'RE IN THERE.
カタン CLICK
SQUEAK
!
!!
......
...
I THOUGHT I ASKED YOU TO GO TO THE HOTEL.
I WAS PLANNING TO, BUT...
SHIRAISHI-SAN!
TWITCH
AH...
ASHKIZAWA-KUN SAID HE COULDN'T WAIT.

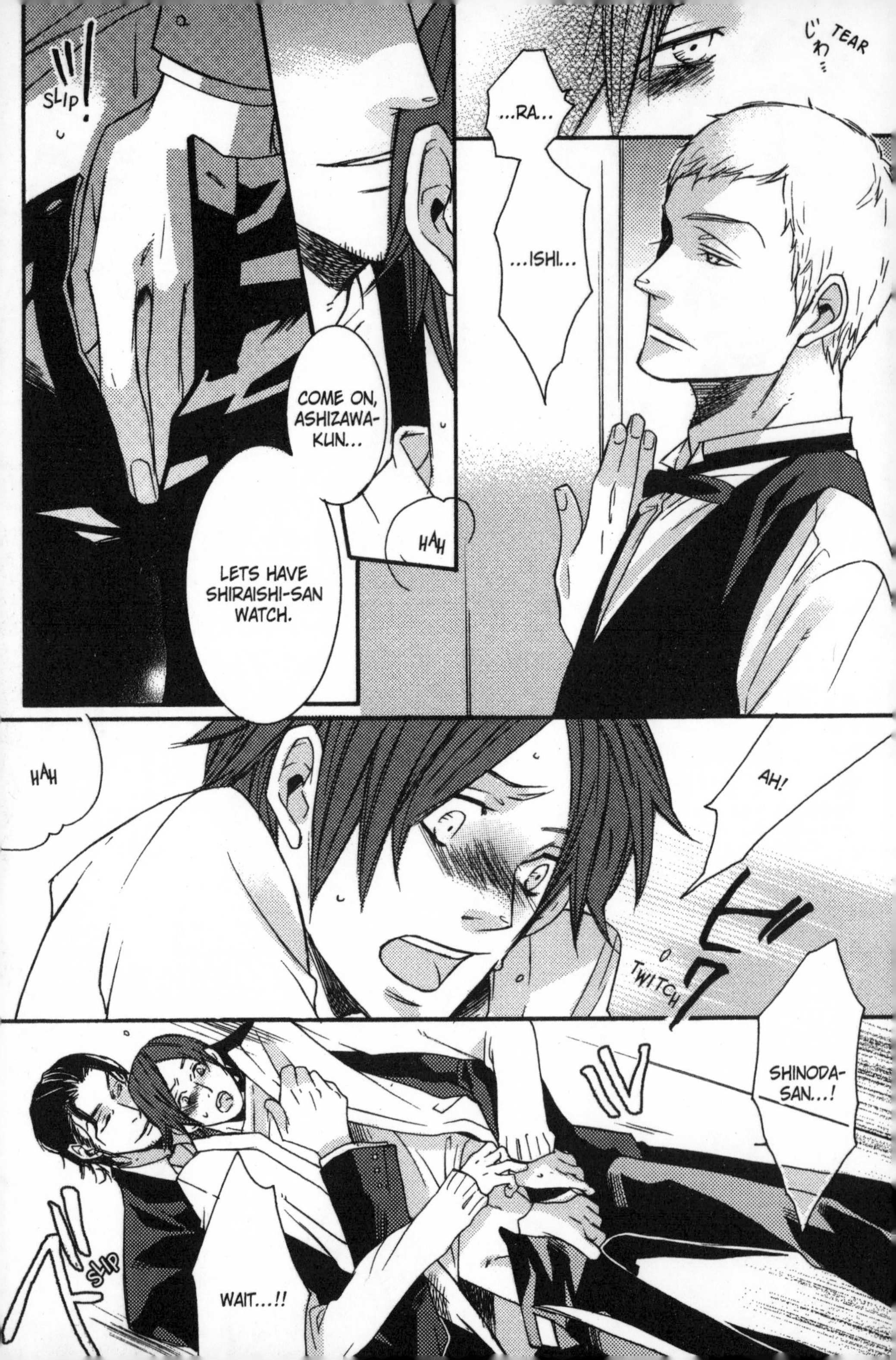
じわ
TEAR
...RA...
...ISHI...
SLIP!
COME ON, ASHIZAWA-KUN...
HAH
LETS HAVE SHIRAISHI-SAN WATCH.
AH!
TWITCH
HAH
SHINODA-SAN...!
WAIT...!!
SLIP

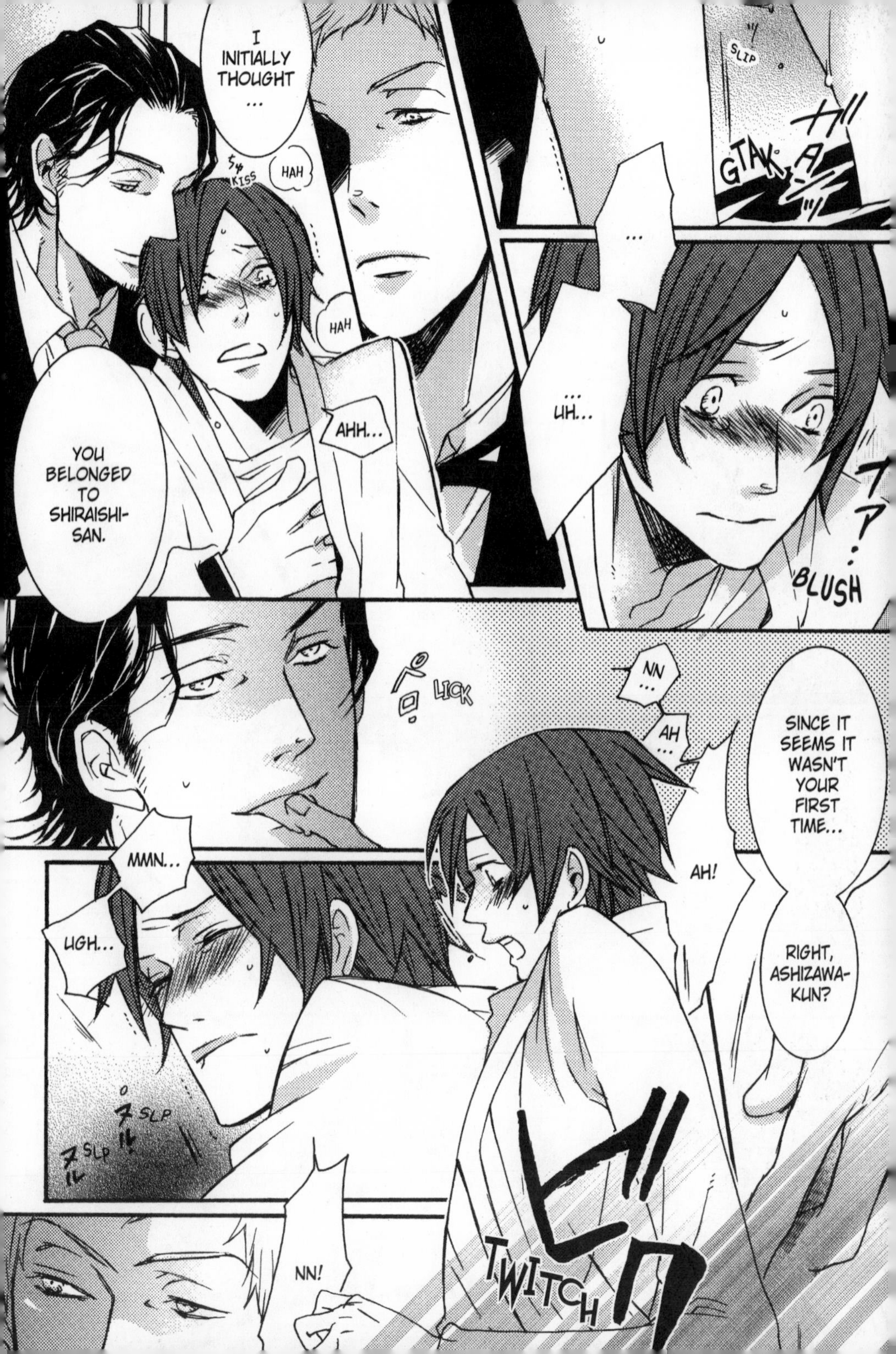
SLIP
GTAK
...
... UH...
BLUSH
AHH...
I INITIALLY THOUGHT ...
KISS
HAH
HAH
YOU BELONGED TO SHIRAISHI-SAN.
SINCE IT SEEMS IT WASN'T YOUR FIRST TIME...
RIGHT, ASHIZAWA-KUN?
NN ...
AH ...
AH!
LICK
MMN...
UGH...
SLP
SLP
TWITCH
NN!

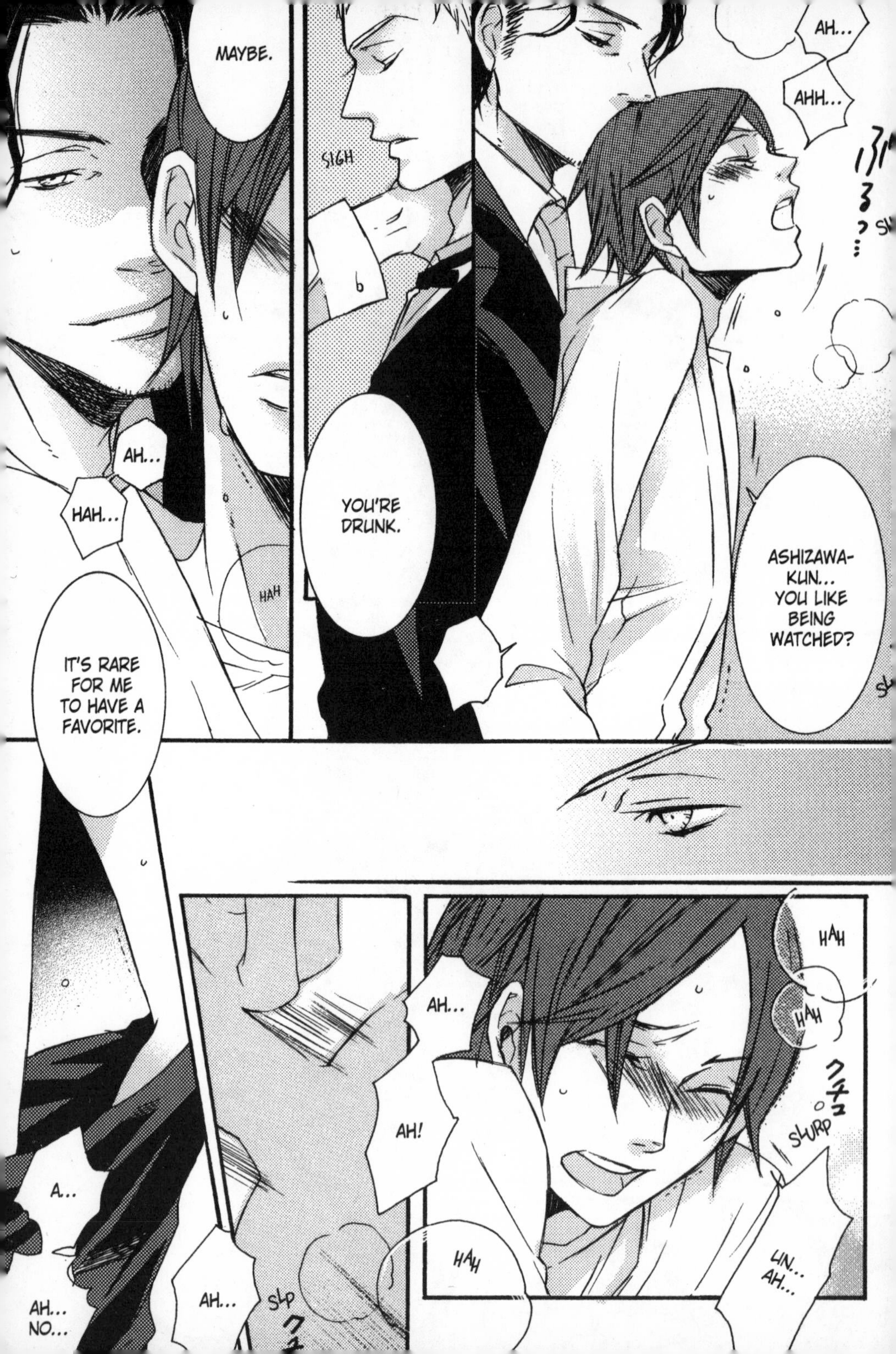
AH...
AHH...
ASHIZAWA-KUN... YOU LIKE BEING WATCHED?
SIGH
YOU'RE DRUNK.
HAH
HAH
SLURP
UN... AH...
AH...
AH!
AH...
SLP
MAYBE.
AH...
HAH...
HAH
IT'S RARE FOR ME TO HAVE A FAVORITE.
A...
AH... NO...

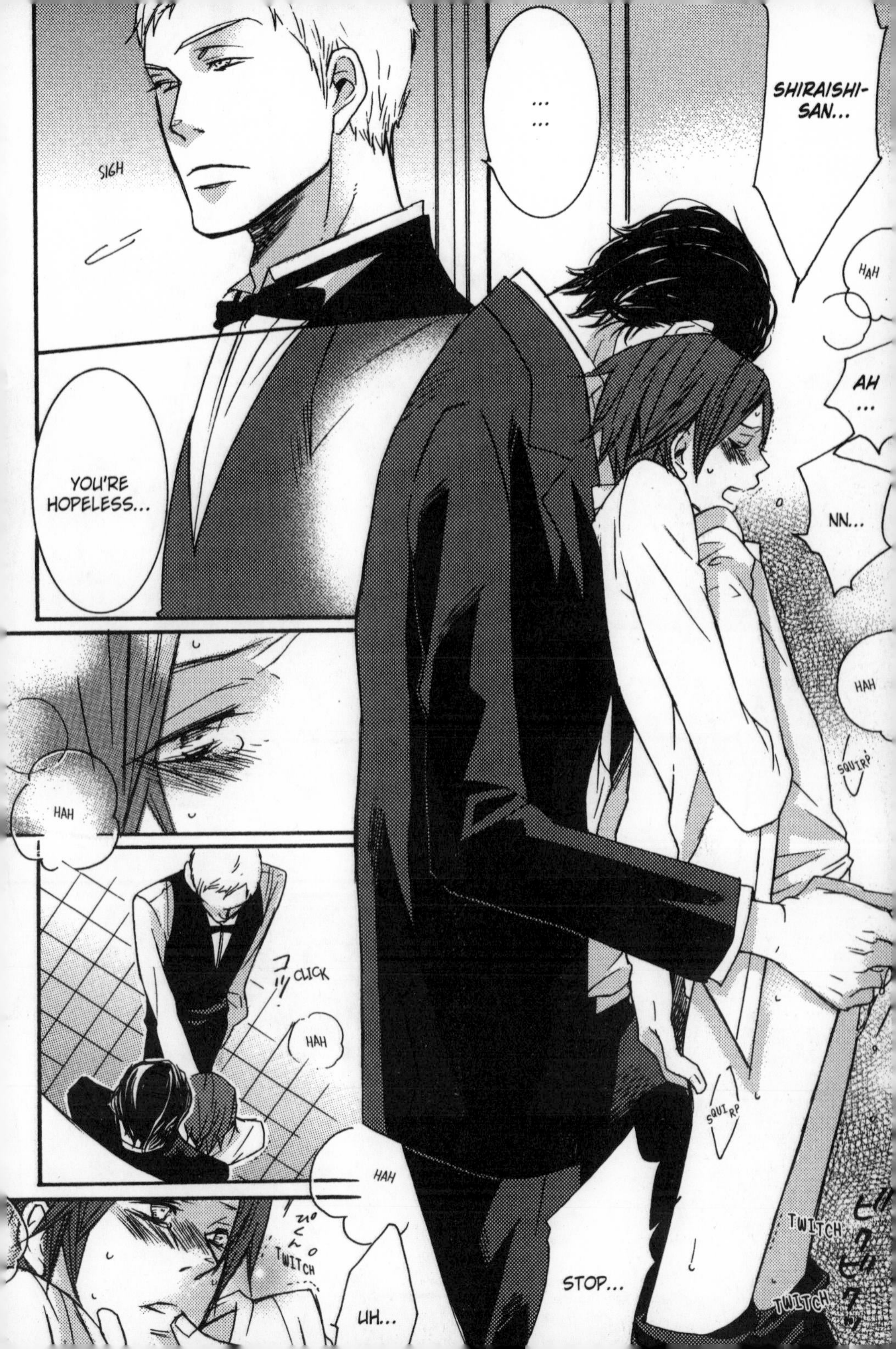

SHIRAISHI-SAN...
... ...
HAH
AH ...
NN...
HAH
SQUIRP
SQUIRP
TWITCH
TWITCH
STOP...
SIGH
YOU'RE HOPELESS...
HAH
CLICK
HAH
HAH
TWITCH
UH...

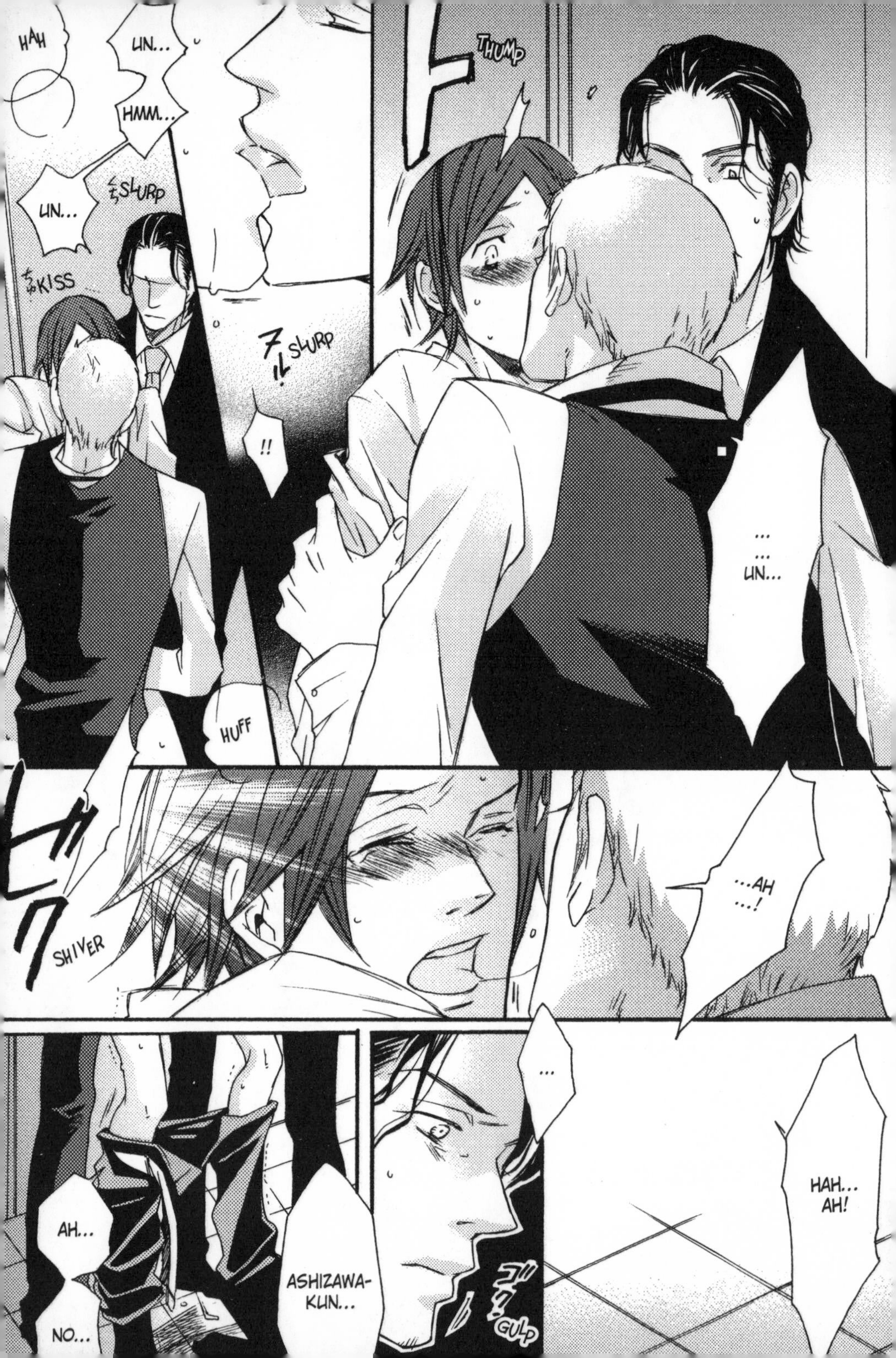
THUMP
...
...
UN...
SLURP
!!
HUFF
UN...
HMM...
HAH
SLURP
UN...
KISS
...AH
...!
SHIVER
HAH...
AH!
...
ASHIZAWA-
KUN...
GULP
AH...
NO...

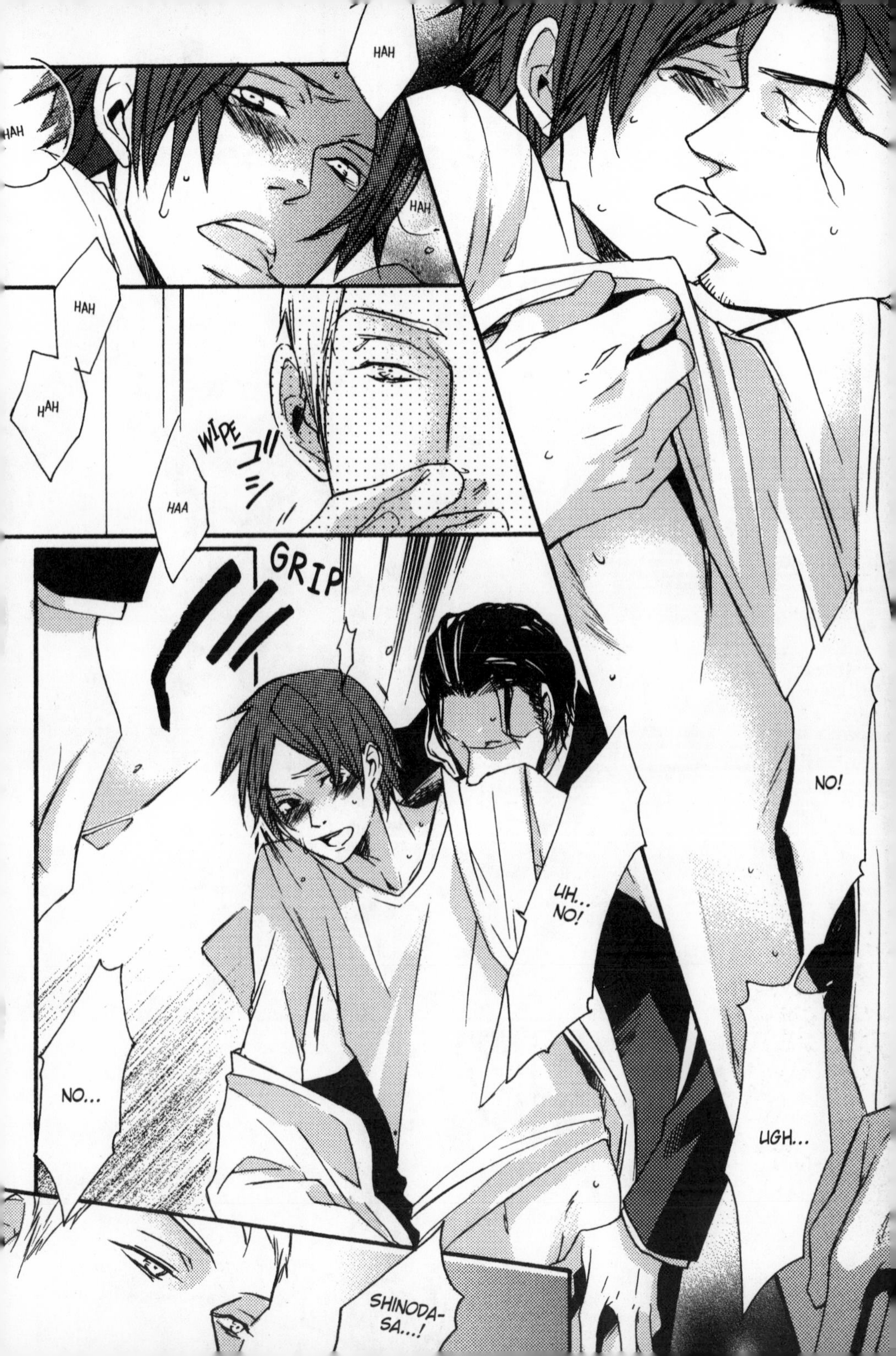
HAH
HAH
HAH
HAH
HAH
WIPE
HAA
GRIP
NO!
UH... NO!
UGH...
NO...
SHINODA-SA...!

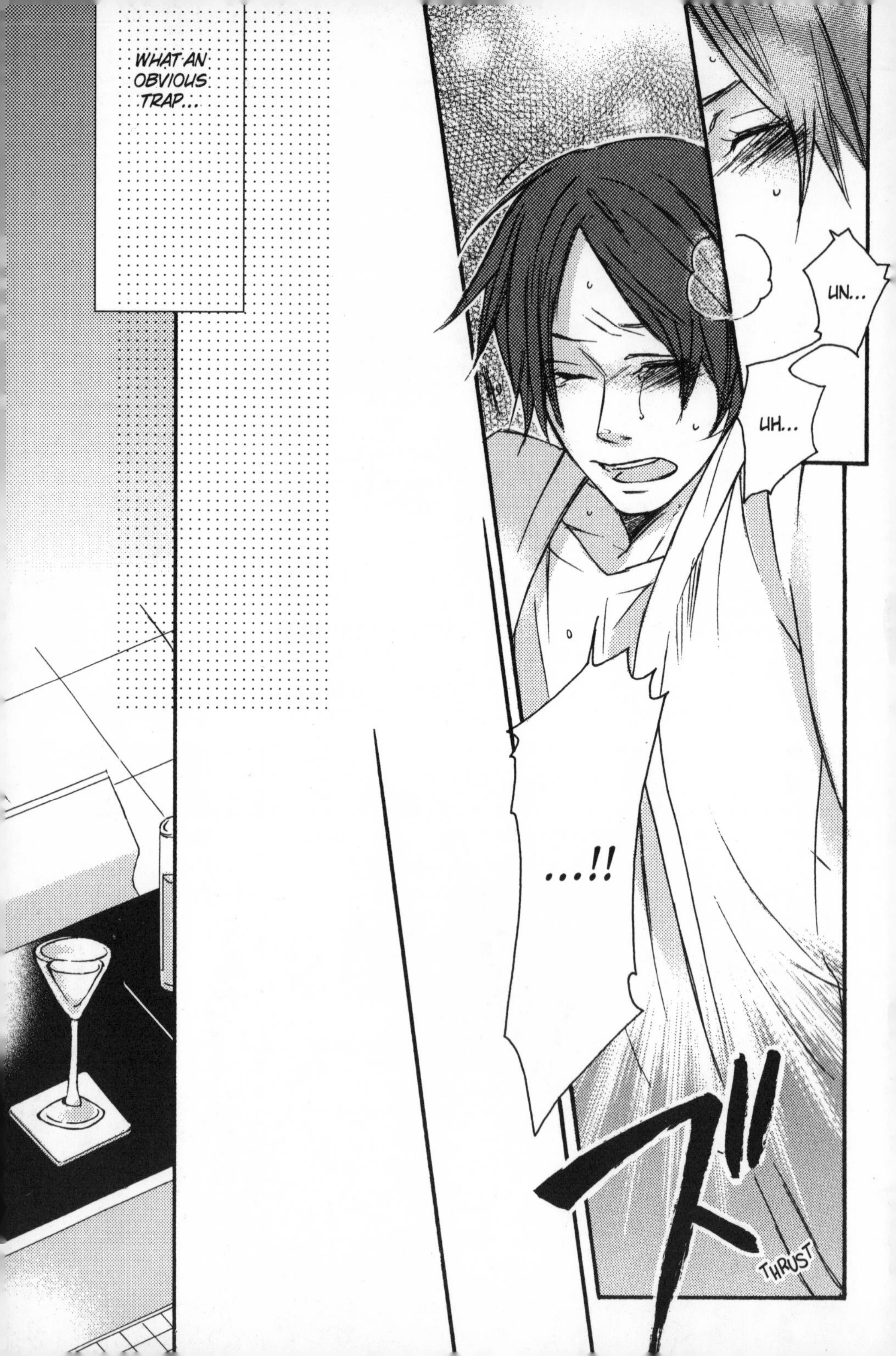
UN...
UH...
...!!
ズ
THRUST
WHAT AN OBVIOUS TRAP...

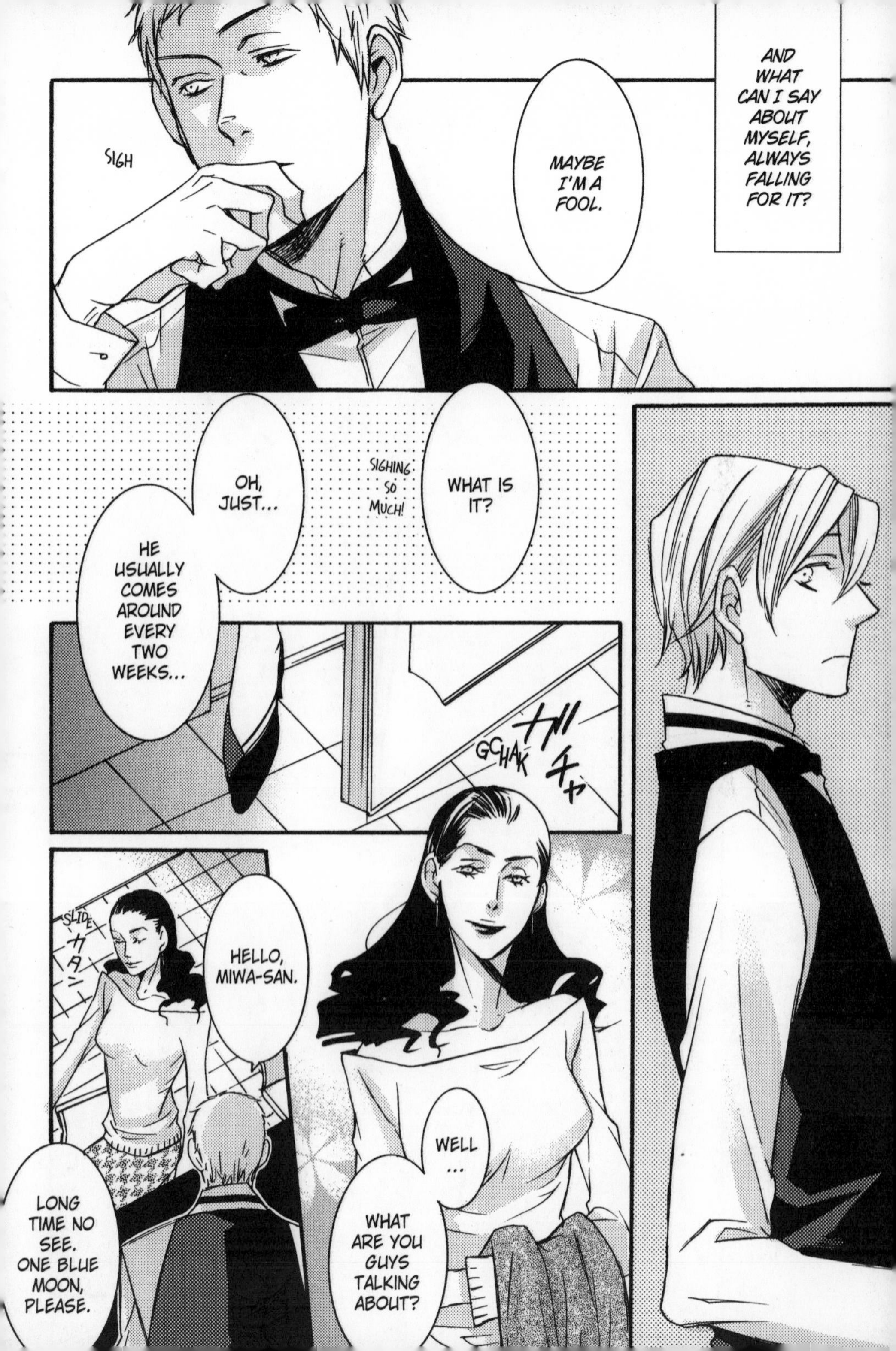
AND WHAT CAN I SAY ABOUT MYSELF, ALWAYS FALLING FOR IT?
MAYBE I'M A FOOL.
SIGH
WHAT IS IT?
SIGHING SO MUCH!
OH, JUST...
HE USUALLY COMES AROUND EVERY TWO WEEKS...
GCHAK
HELLO, MIWA-SAN.
SLIDE
WELL ...
WHAT ARE YOU GUYS TALKING ABOUT?
LONG TIME NO SEE. ONE BLUE MOON, PLEASE.

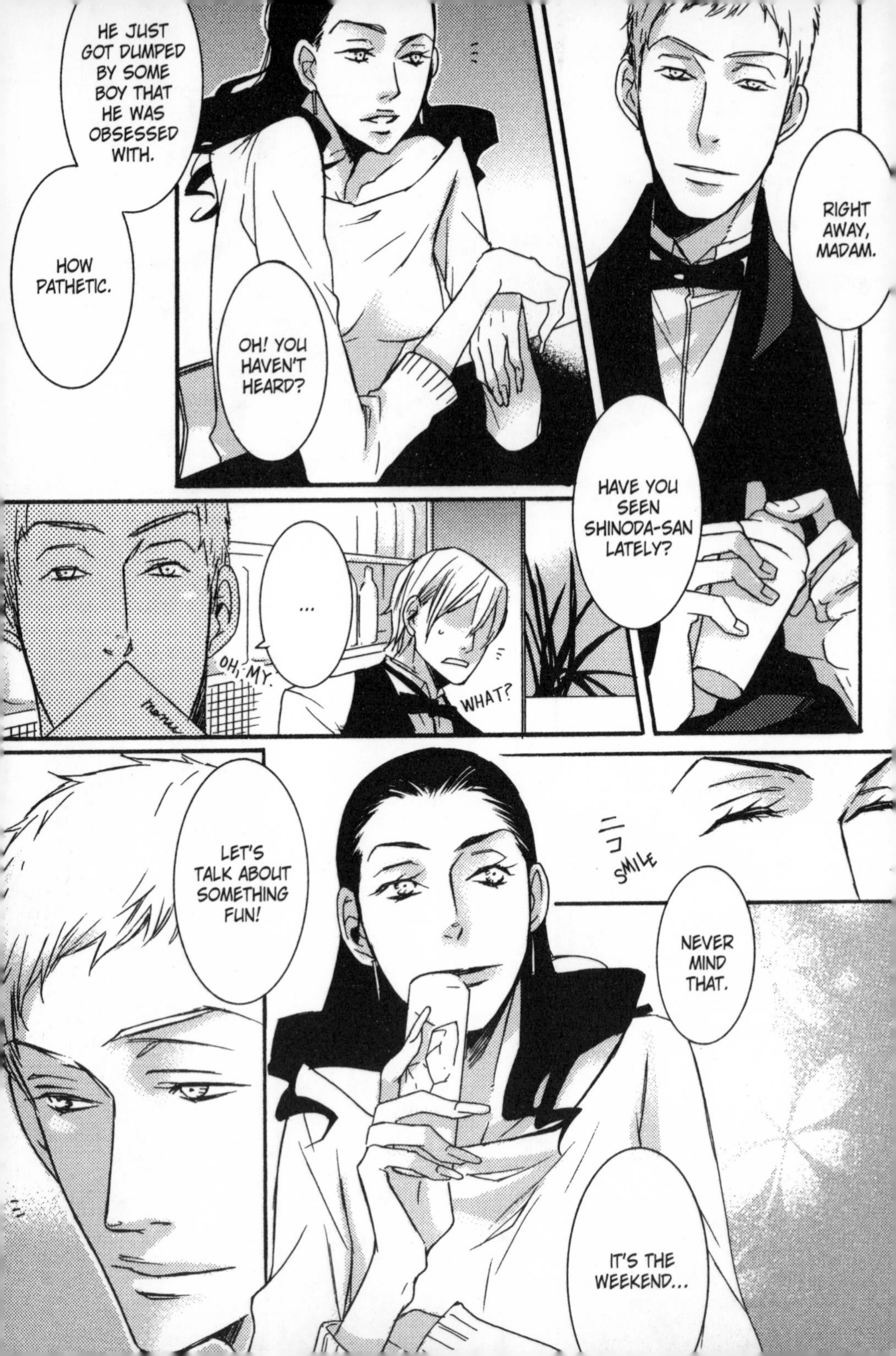
RIGHT AWAY, MADAM.
HAVE YOU SEEN SHINODA-SAN LATELY?
OH! YOU HAVEN'T HEARD?
HE JUST GOT DUMPED BY SOME BOY THAT HE WAS OBSESSED WITH.
HOW PATHETIC.
WHAT?
...
OH, MY.
SMILE
NEVER MIND THAT.
IT'S THE WEEKEND...
LET'S TALK ABOUT SOMETHING FUN!

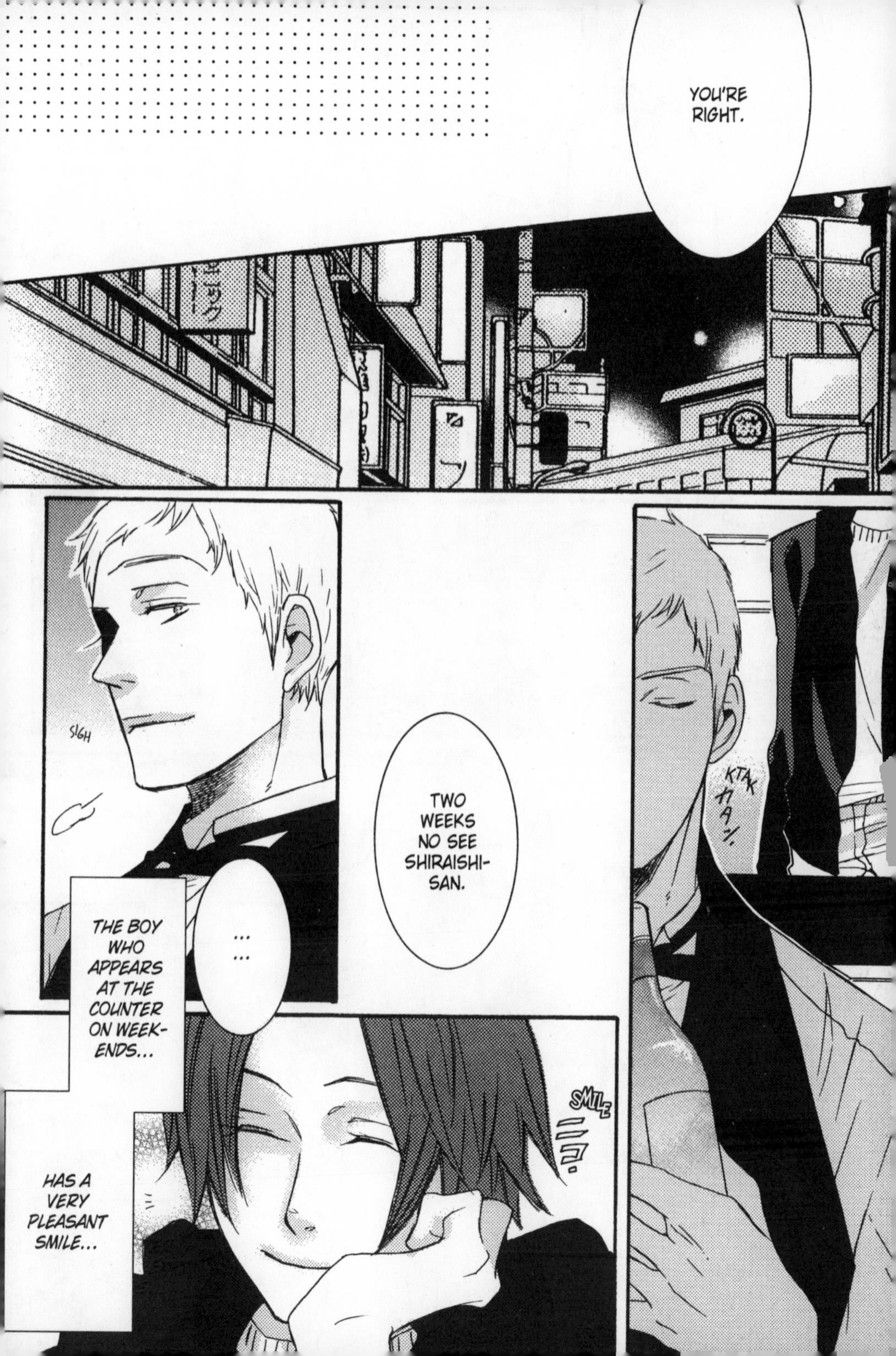

YOU'RE RIGHT.
KTAK
TWO WEEKS NO SEE SHIRAISHI-SAN.
SIGH
... ...
THE BOY WHO APPEARS AT THE COUNTER ON WEEK-ENDS...
SMILE
HAS A VERY PLEASANT SMILE...

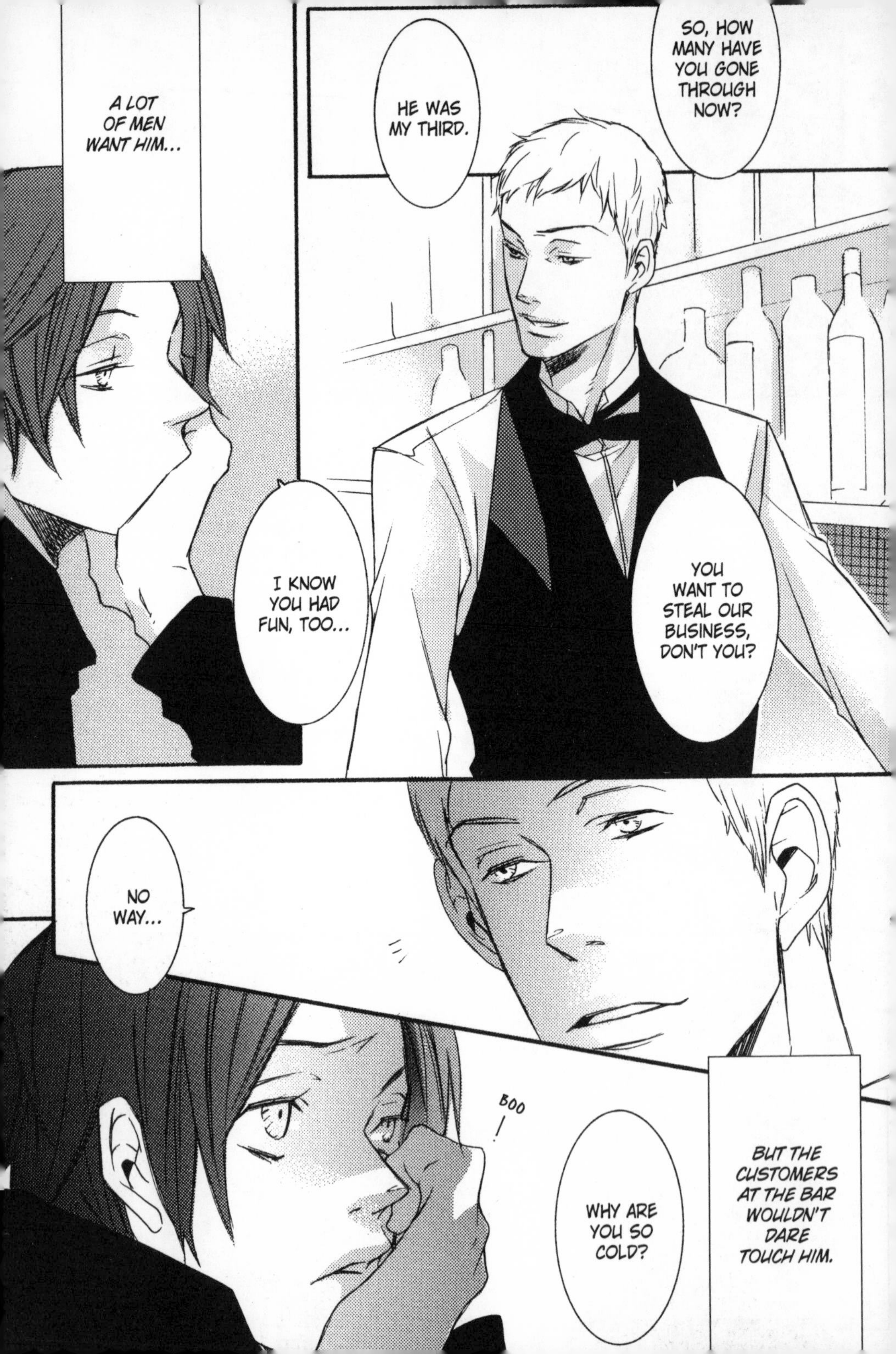

SO, HOW MANY HAVE YOU GONE THROUGH NOW?
HE WAS MY THIRD.
YOU WANT TO STEAL OUR BUSINESS, DON'T YOU?
I KNOW YOU HAD FUN, TOO...
A LOT OF MEN WANT HIM...
NO WAY...
BUT THE CUSTOMERS AT THE BAR WOULDN'T DARE TOUCH HIM.
WHY ARE YOU SO COLD?
BOO!

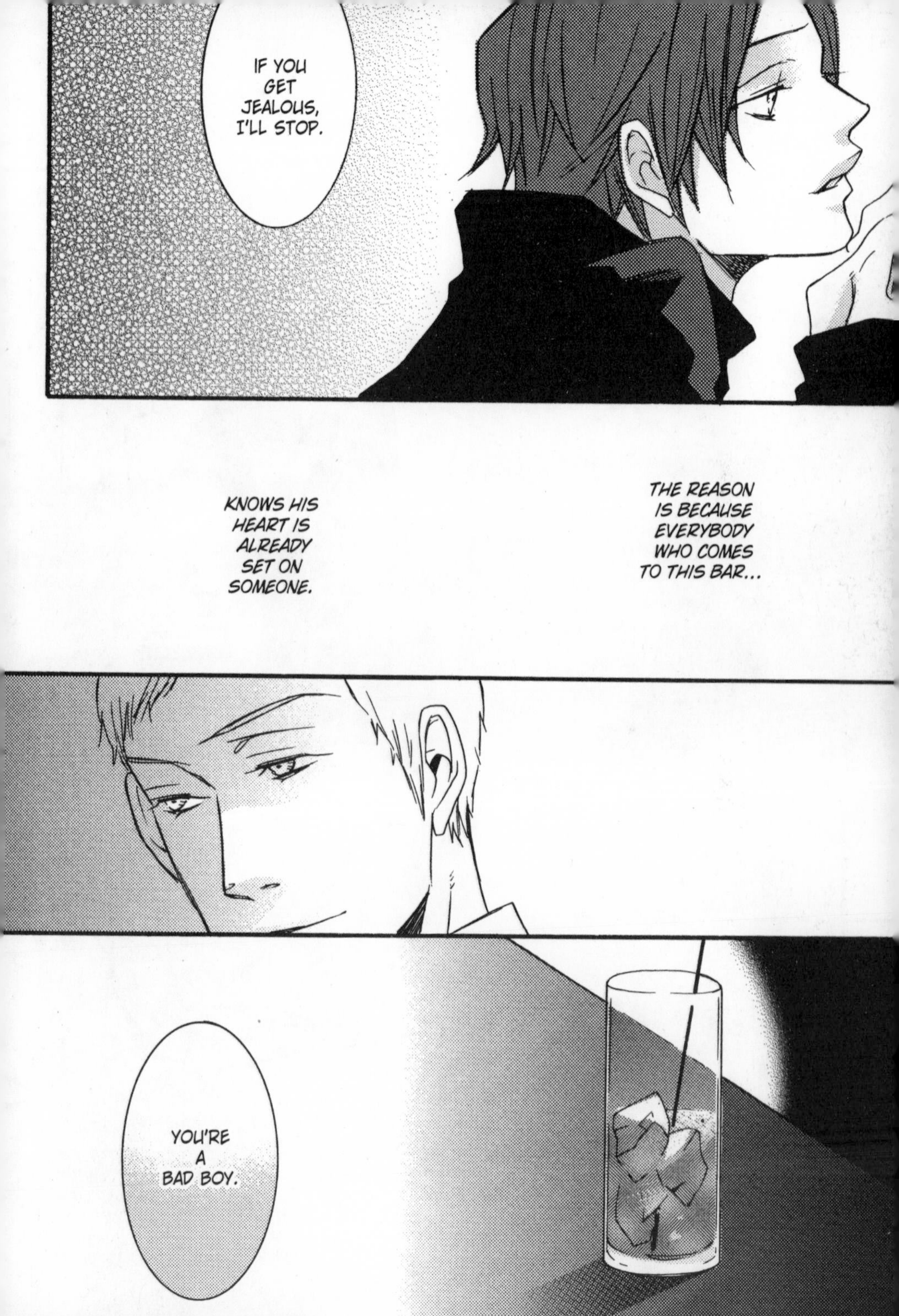
IF YOU GET JEALOUS, I'LL STOP.
THE REASON IS BECAUSE EVERYBODY WHO COMES TO THIS BAR...
KNOWS HIS HEART IS ALREADY SET ON SOMEONE.
YOU'RE A BAD BOY.

THE WEEKEND NEAR THE END ● END

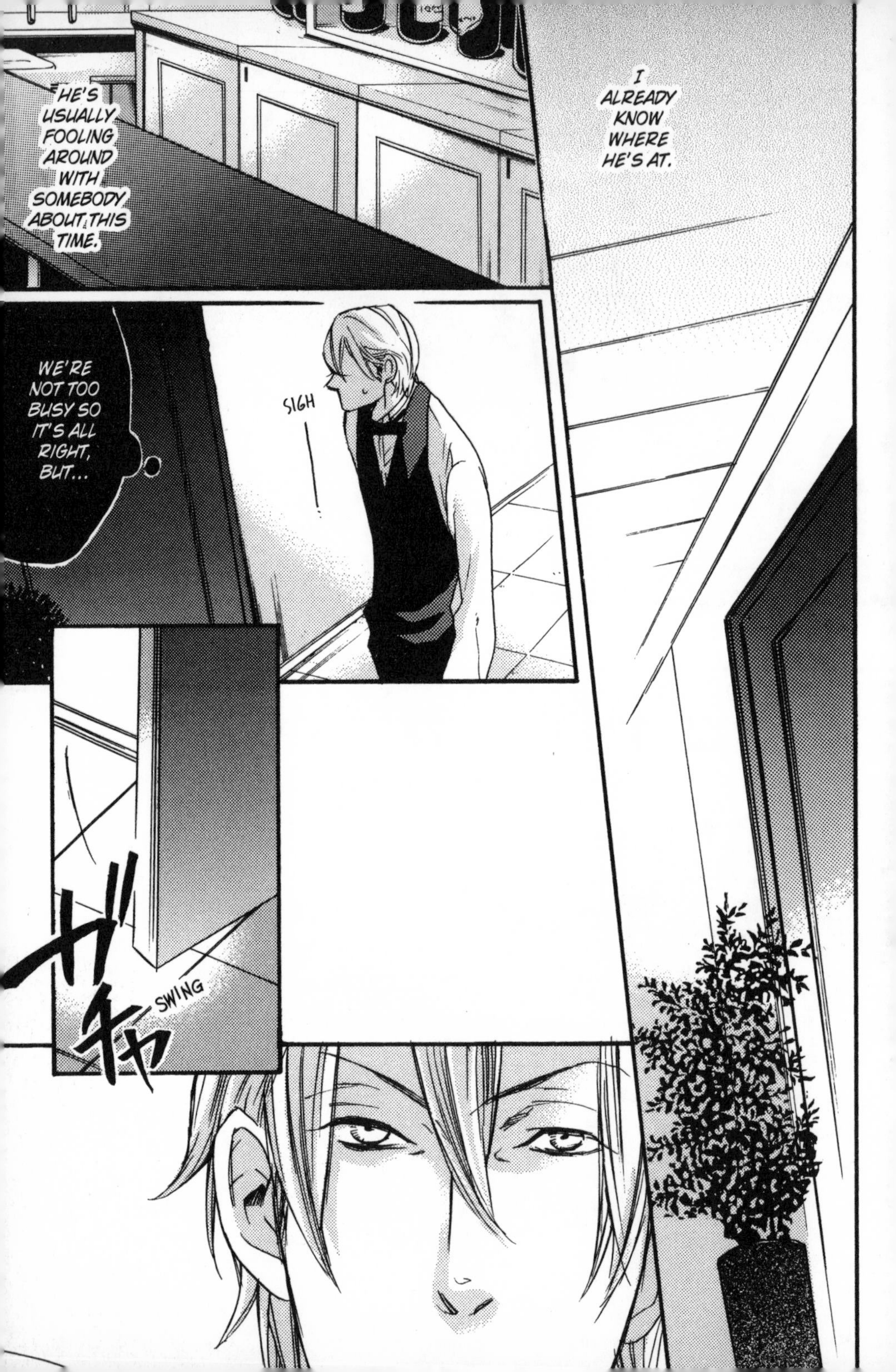
I ALREADY KNOW WHERE HE'S AT.
HE'S USUALLY FOOLING AROUND WITH SOMEBODY ABOUT THIS TIME.
WE'RE NOT TOO BUSY SO IT'S ALL RIGHT, BUT...
SIGH
ガチャ
SWING

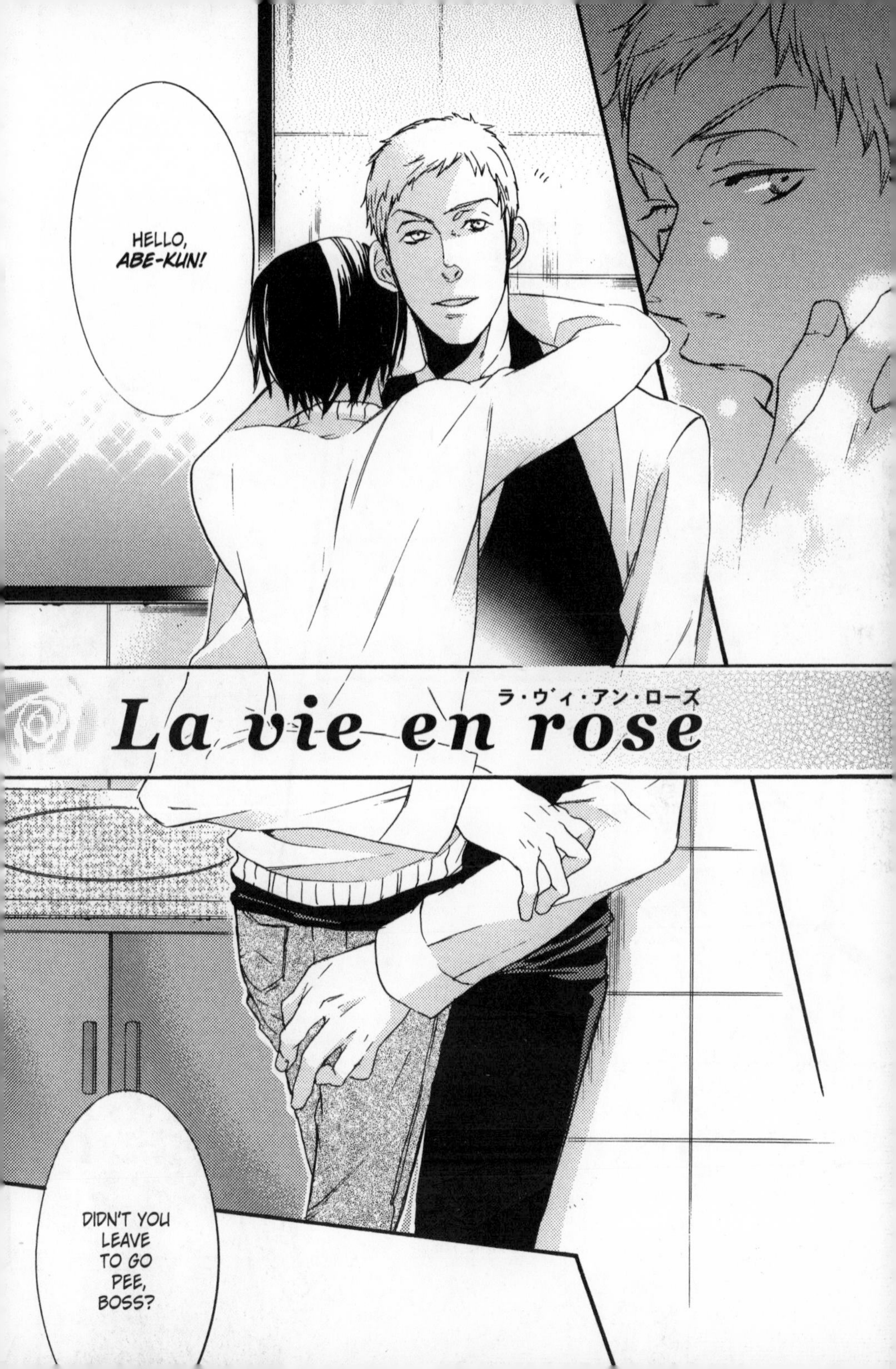
HELLO, ABE-KUN!
ラ・ヴィ・アン・ローズ
La vie en rose
DIDN'T YOU LEAVE TO GO PEE, BOSS?

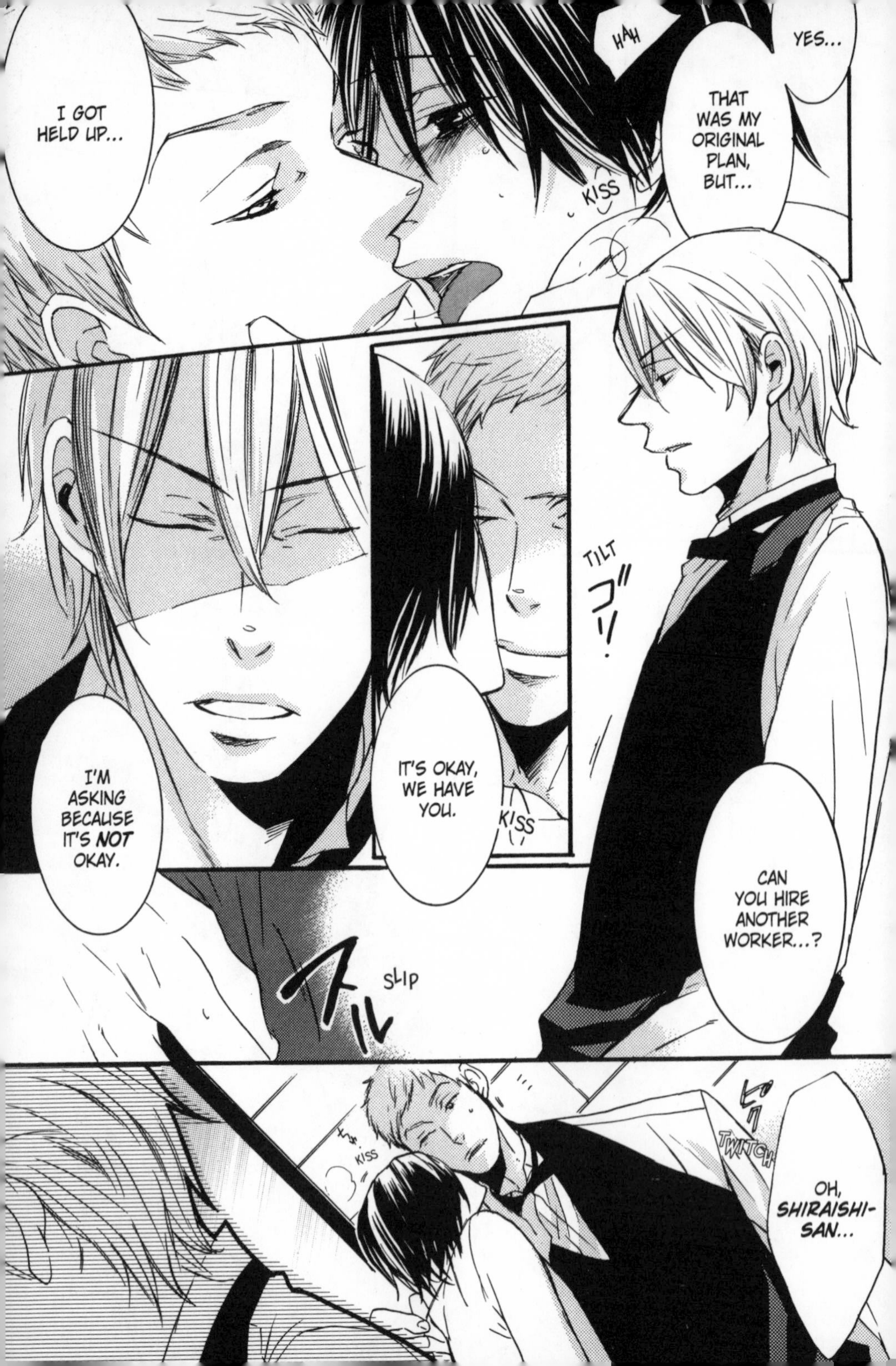
HAH
YES...
THAT WAS MY ORIGINAL PLAN, BUT...
KISS
I GOT HELD UP...
TILT
CAN YOU HIRE ANOTHER WORKER...?
IT'S OKAY, WE HAVE YOU.
KISS
I'M ASKING BECAUSE IT'S NOT OKAY.
SLIP
TWITCH
OH, SHIRAISHI-SAN...
KISS

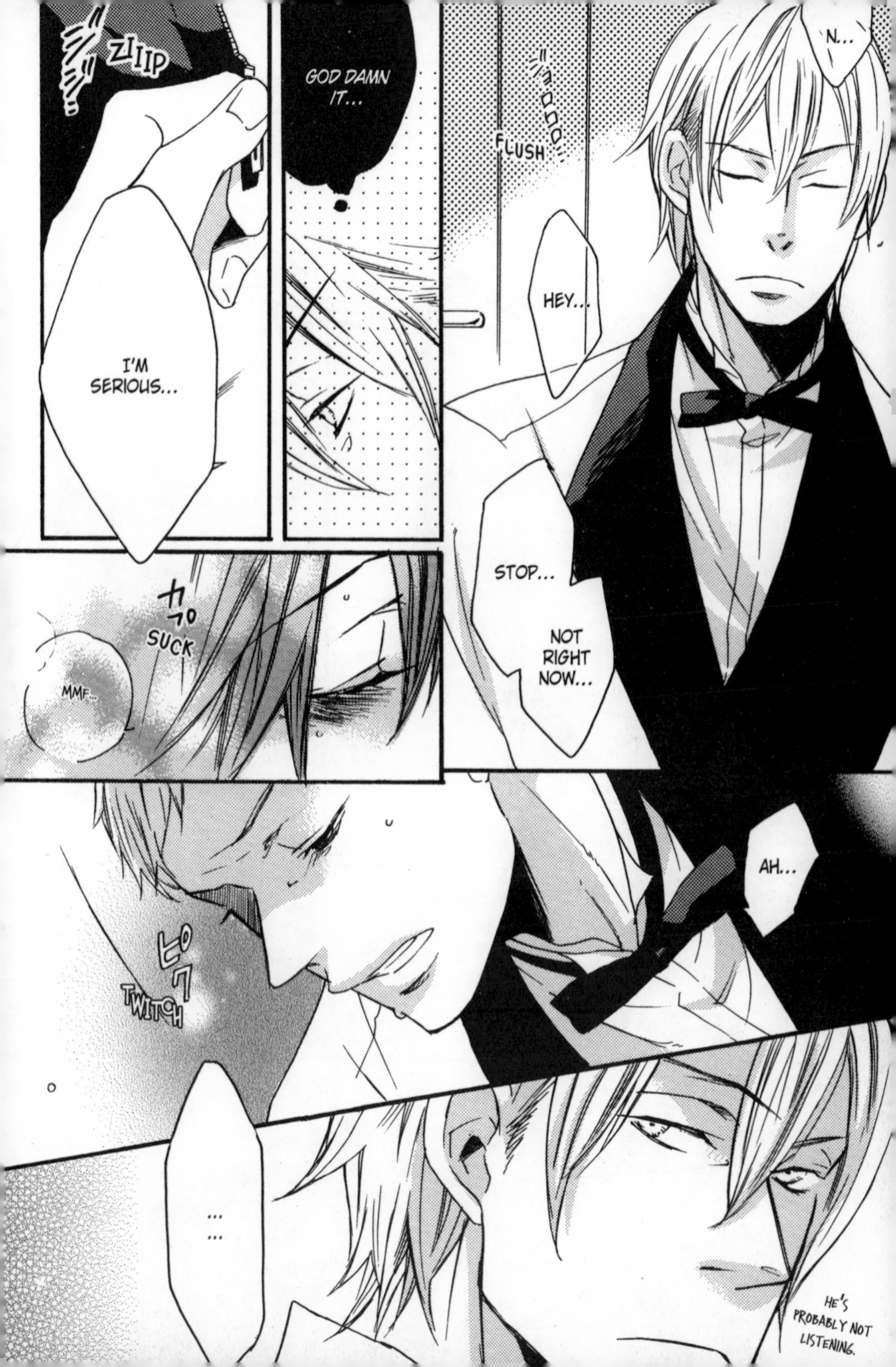
N...
FLUSH
HEY...
STOP...
NOT RIGHT NOW...
GOD DAMN IT...
ZIIP
I'M SERIOUS...
SUCK
MMF...
AH...
TWITCH
...
...
HE'S PROBABLY NOT LISTENING.

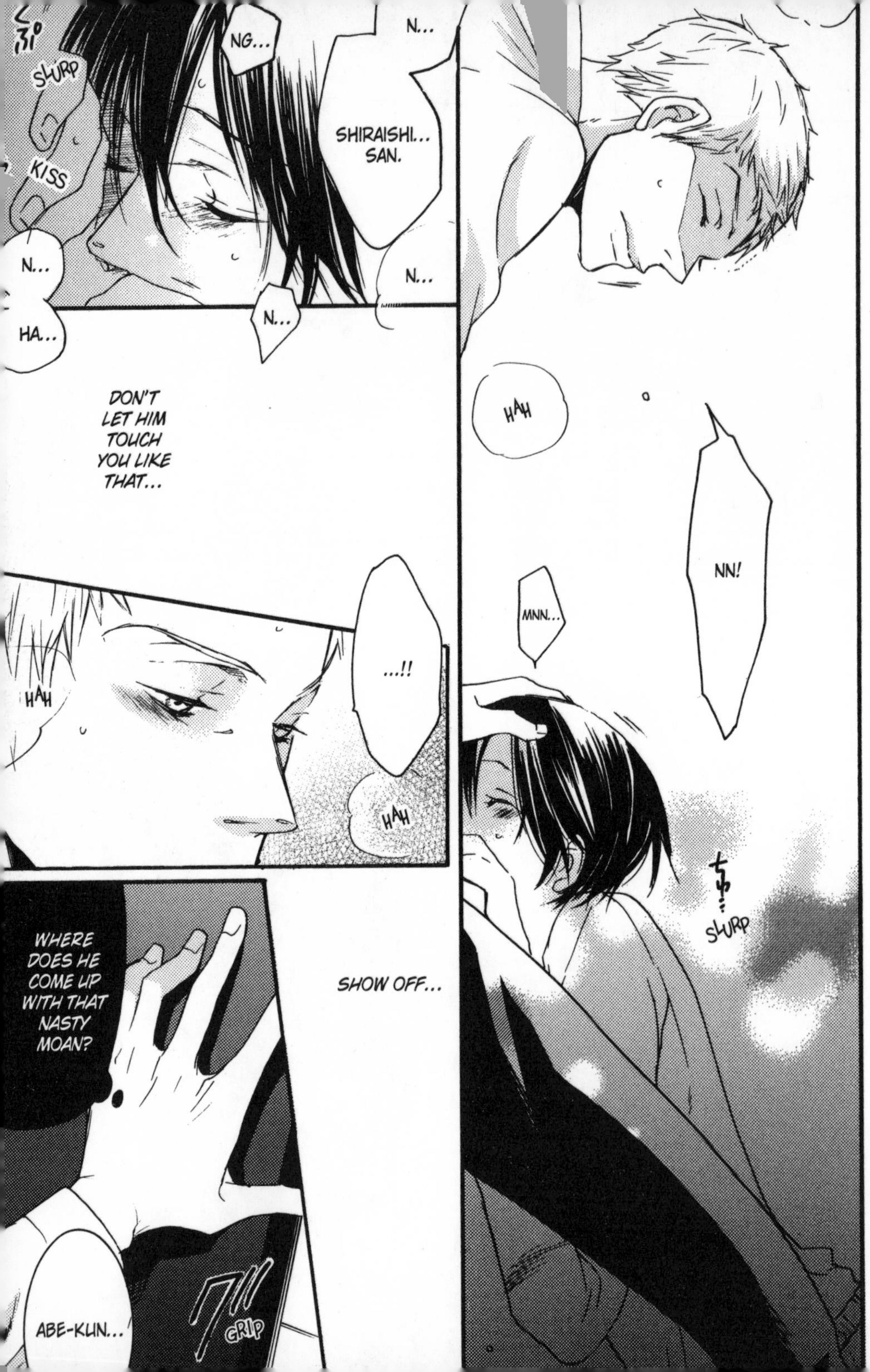
HAH
NN!
MNN...
SLURP
NG...
N...
SHIRAISHI... SAN.
SLURP
KISS
N...
N...
N...
HA...
DON'T LET HIM TOUCH YOU LIKE THAT...
...!!
HAH
HAH
SHOW OFF...
WHERE DOES HE COME UP WITH THAT NASTY MOAN?
ABE-KUN...
GRIP

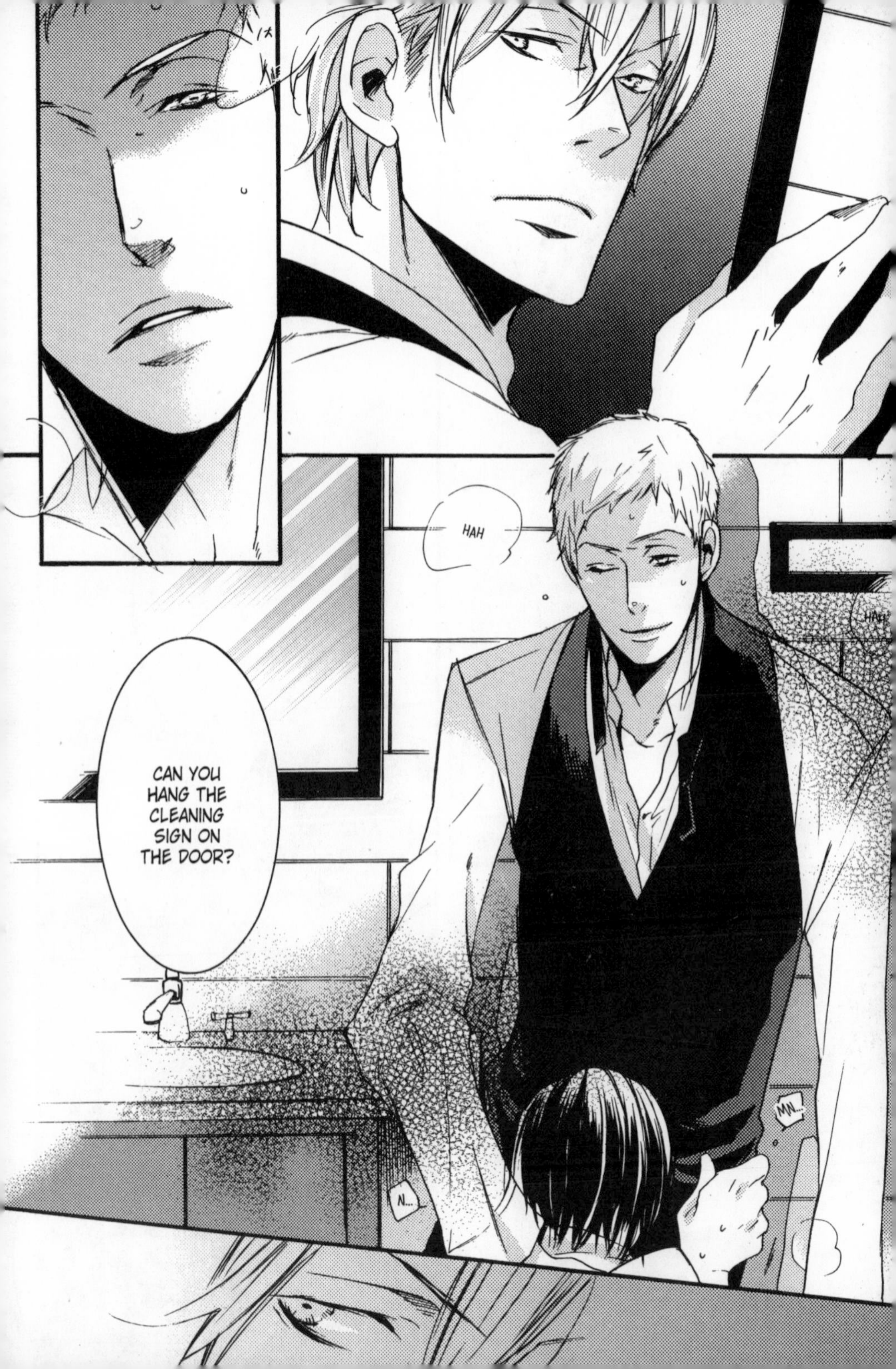
HAH
HAH
CAN YOU HANG THE CLEANING SIGN ON THE DOOR?
MN...
N...

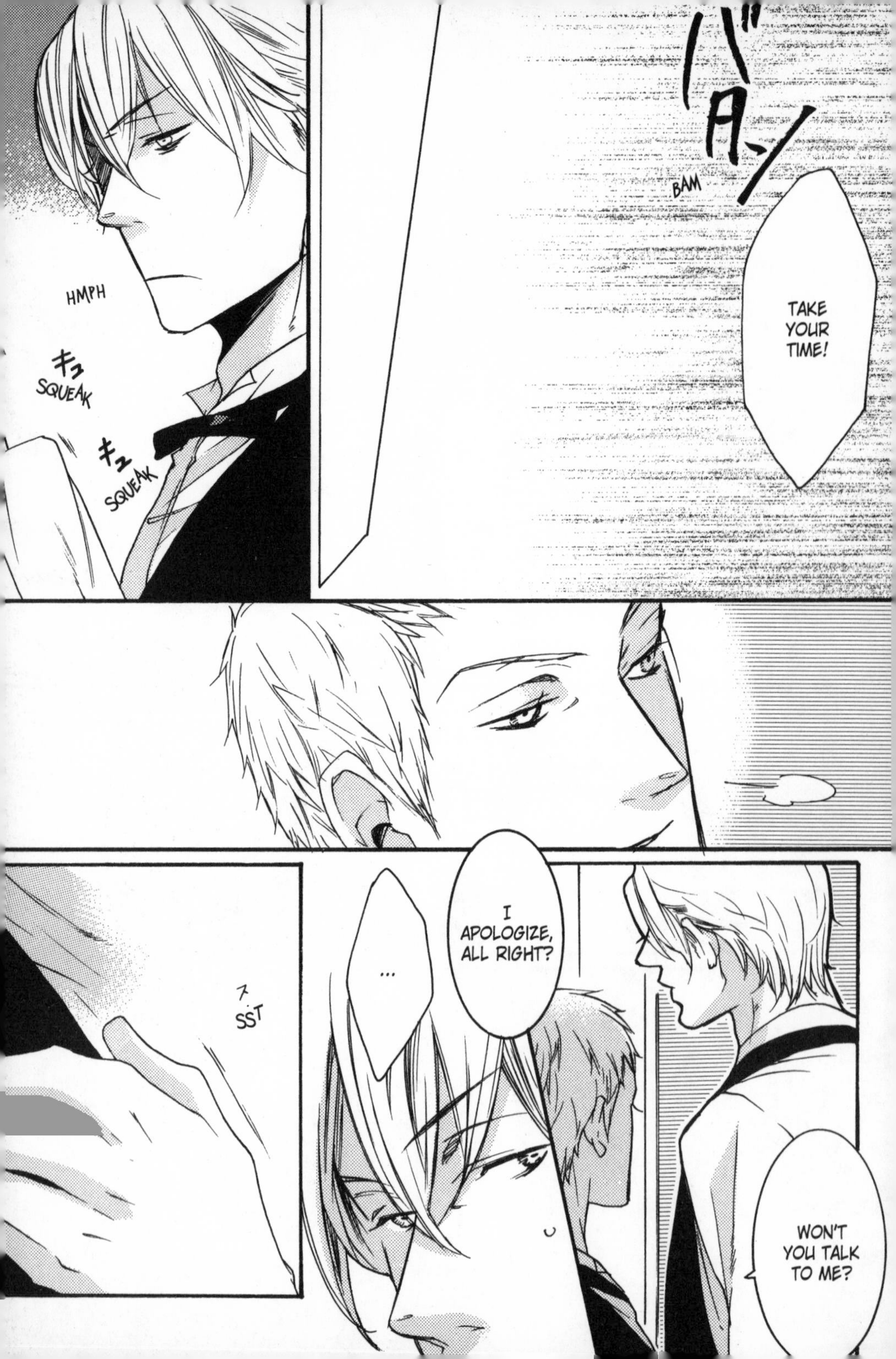
バタン
BAM
TAKE YOUR TIME!
HMPH
キュ
SQUEAK
キュ
SQUEAK
I APOLOGIZE, ALL RIGHT?
...
WON'T YOU TALK TO ME?
ス
SST

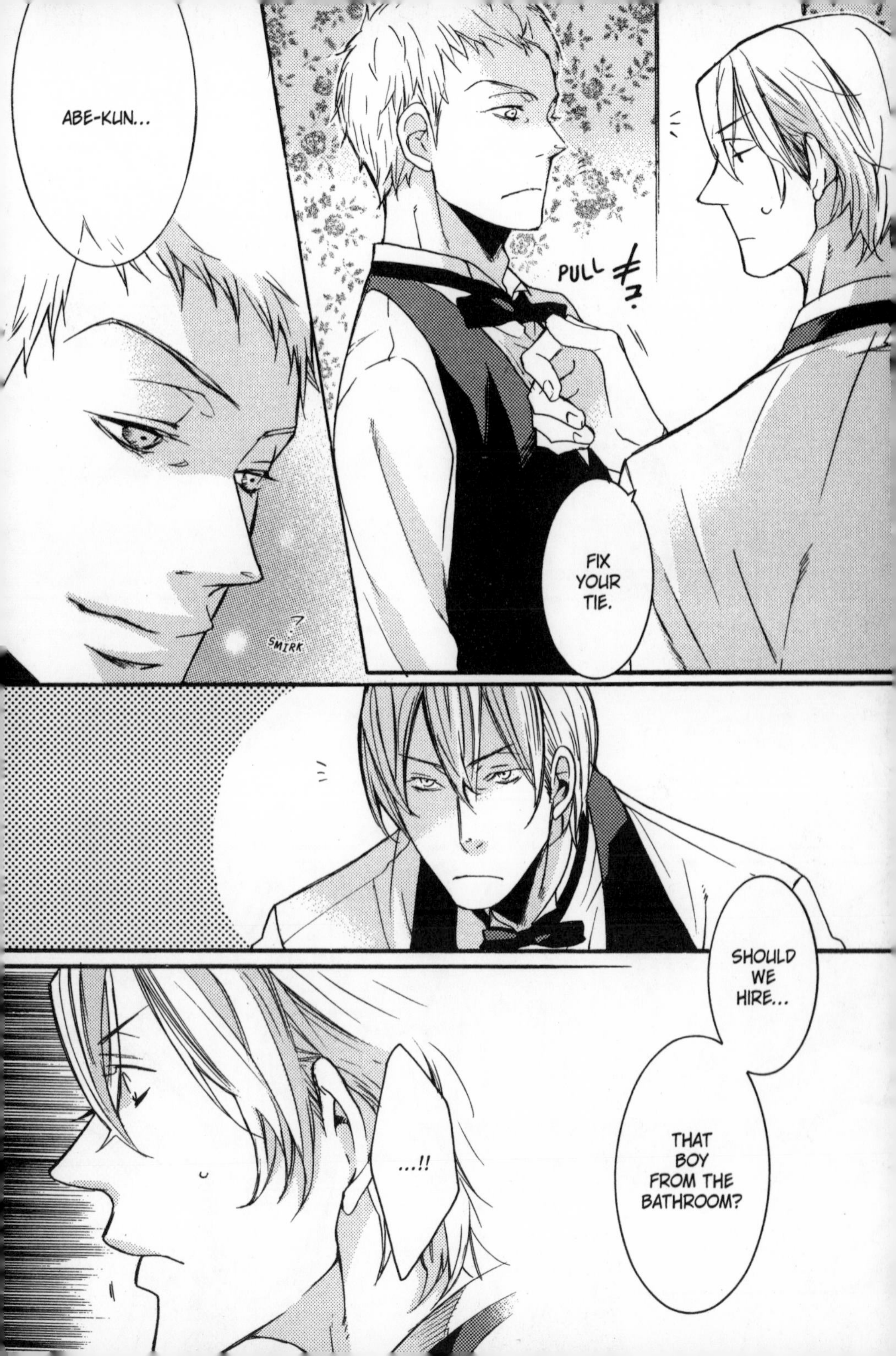
PULL
FIX YOUR TIE.
ABE-KUN...
SMIRK
SHOULD WE HIRE...
THAT BOY FROM THE BATHROOM?
...!!

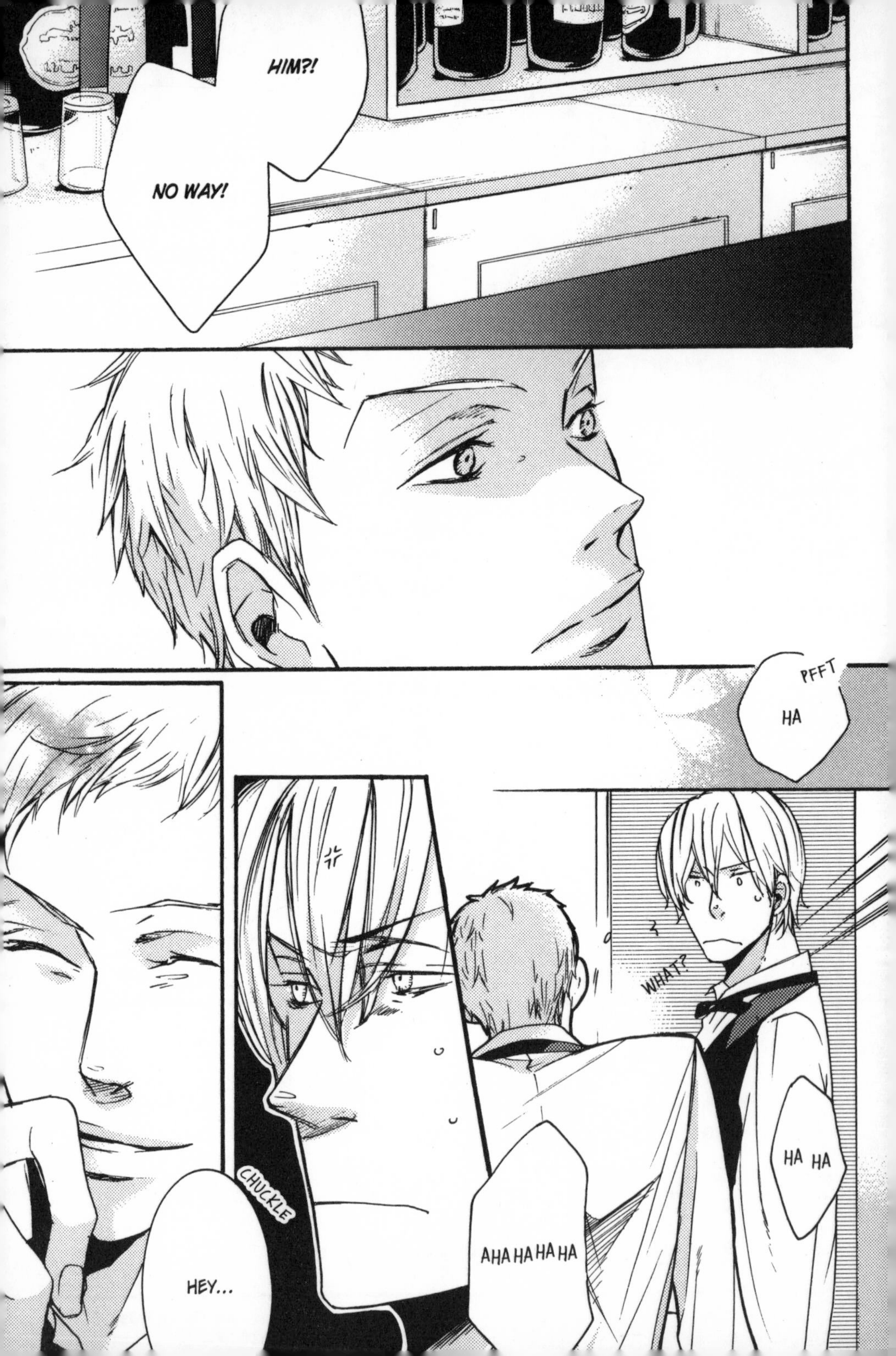
HIM?!
NO WAY!
PFFT
HA
WHAT?
HA HA
AHAHAHAHA
CHUCKLE
HEY...

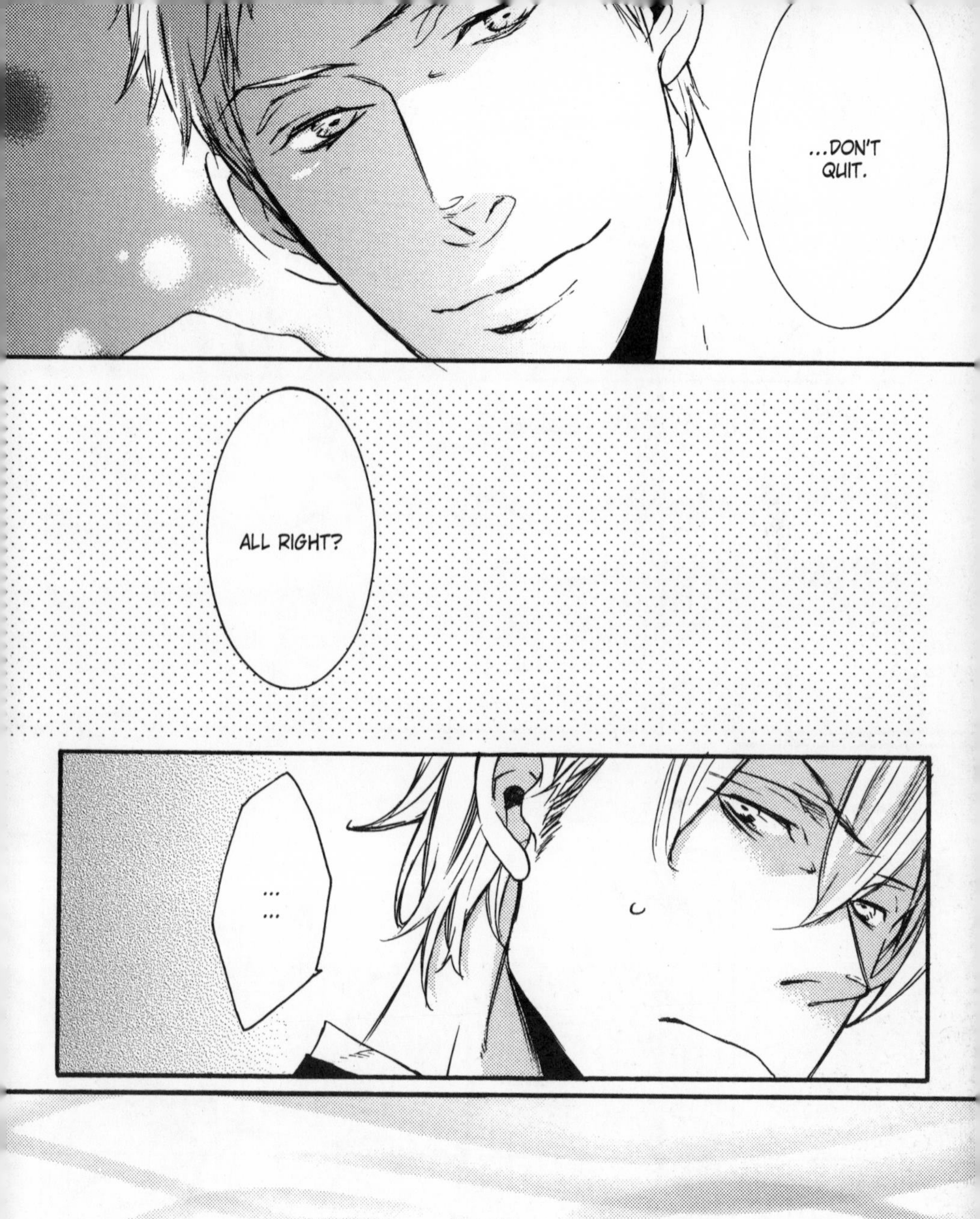
...DON'T QUIT.
ALL RIGHT?
......
La vie en rose

LA VIE EN ROSE●END

BabyBlue

ベイビー・ブルー

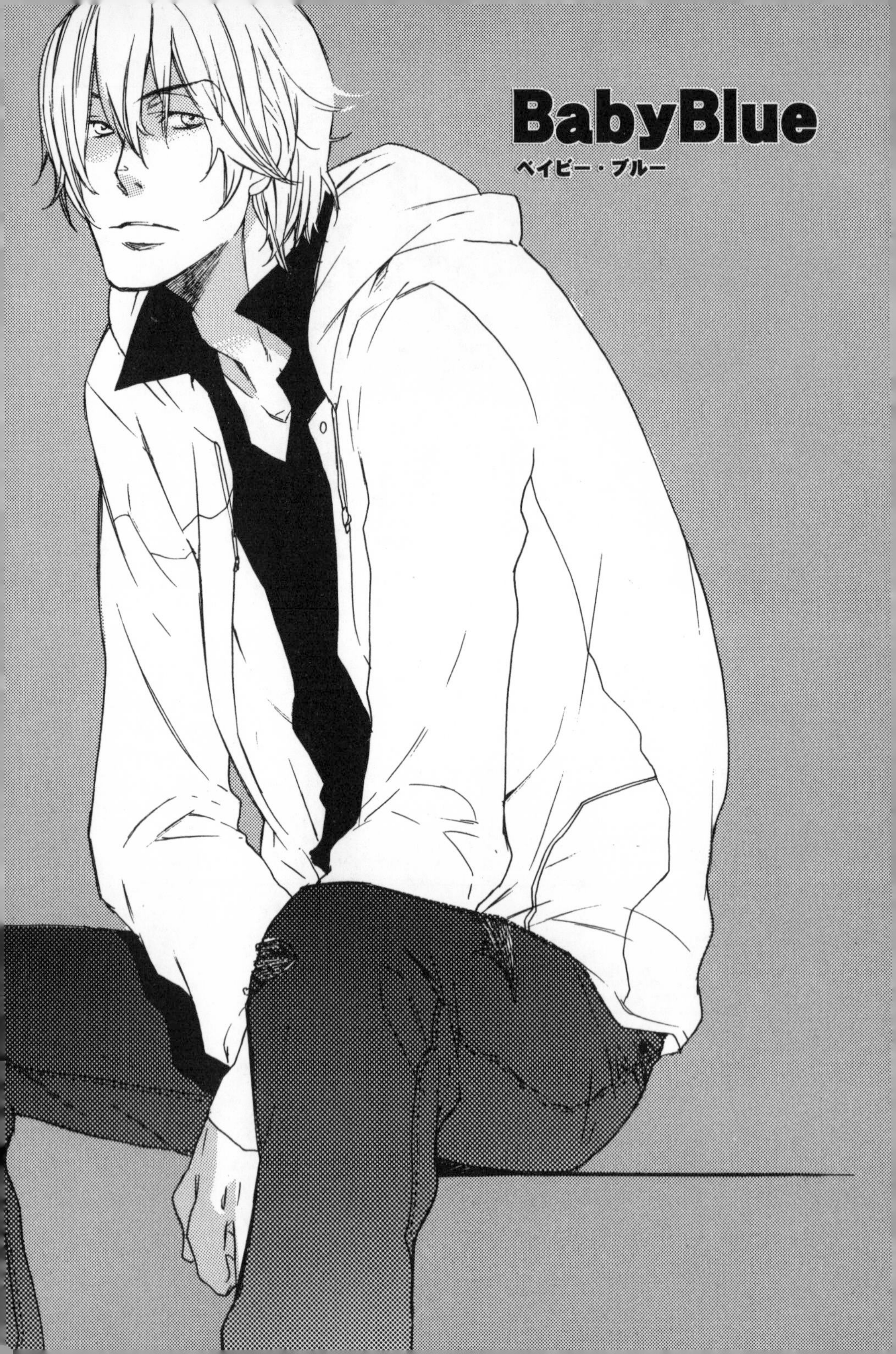

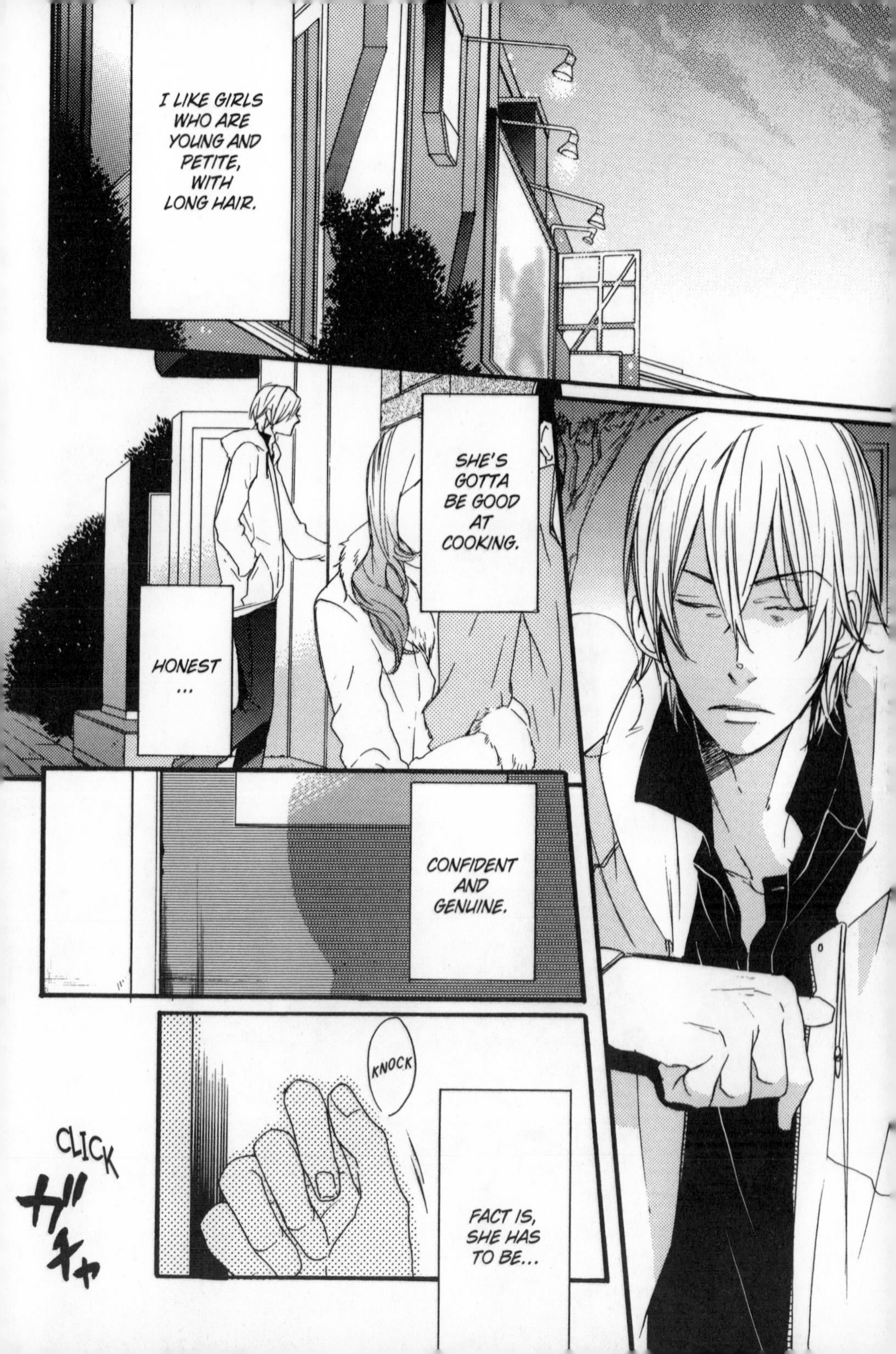
I LIKE GIRLS WHO ARE YOUNG AND PETITE, WITH LONG HAIR.
SHE'S GOTTA BE GOOD AT COOKING.
HONEST ...
CONFIDENT AND GENUINE.
KNOCK
CLICK
FACT IS, SHE HAS TO BE...

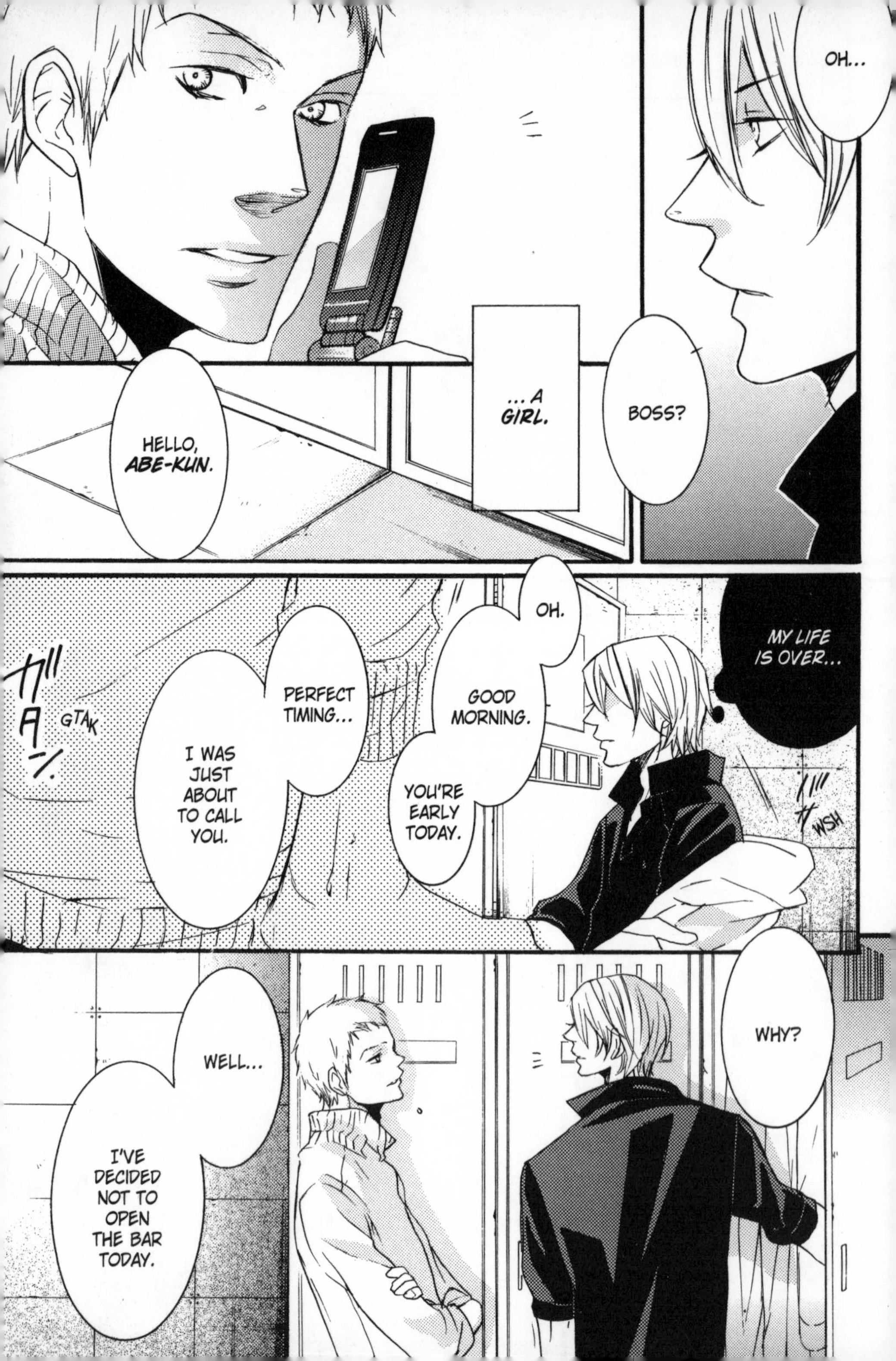
OH...
BOSS?
... A GIRL.
HELLO, ABE-KUN.
MY LIFE IS OVER...
WSH
OH.
GOOD MORNING.
YOU'RE EARLY TODAY.
PERFECT TIMING...
I WAS JUST ABOUT TO CALL YOU.
GTAK
WHY?
WELL...
I'VE DECIDED NOT TO OPEN THE BAR TODAY.

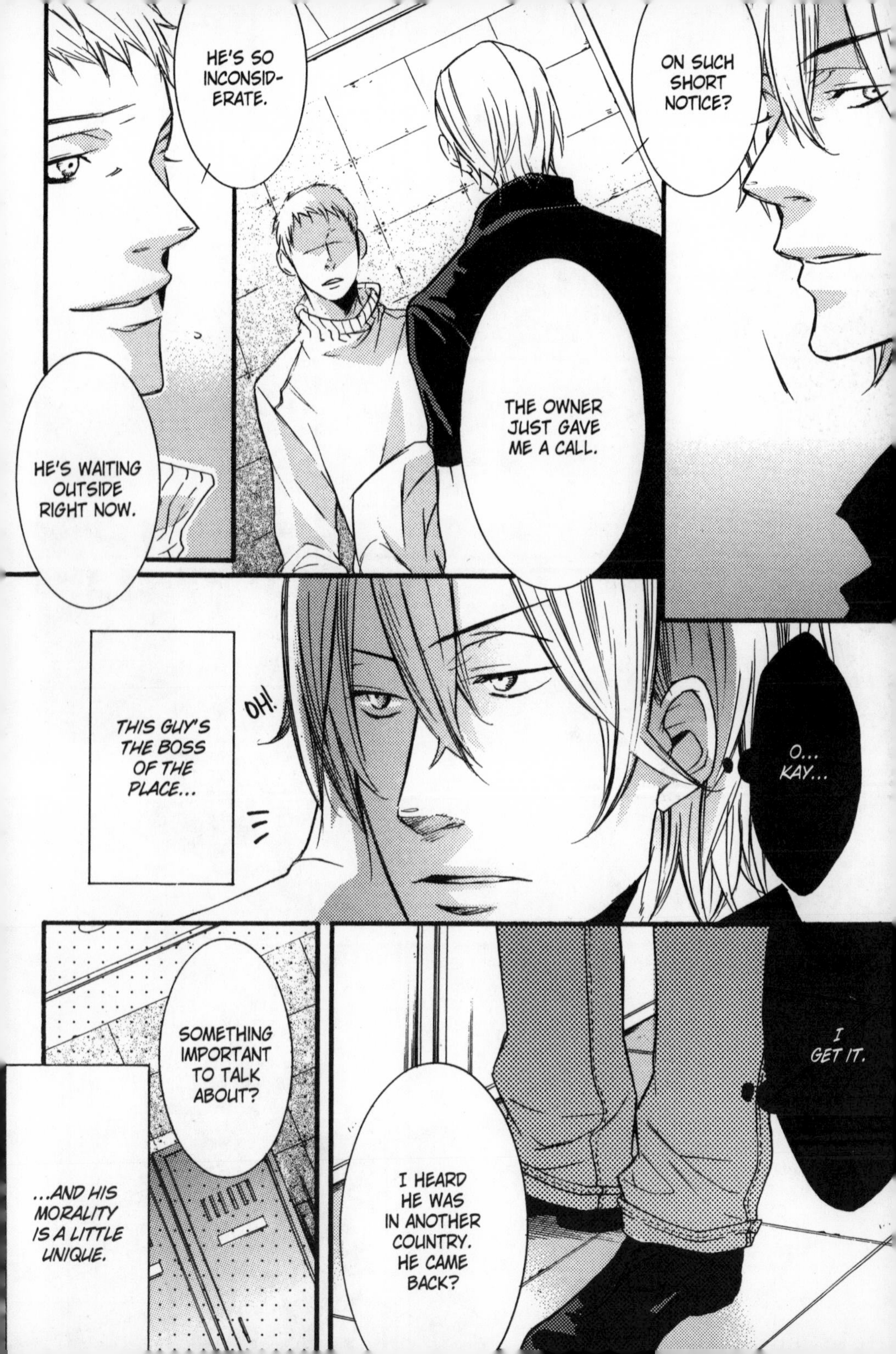
ON SUCH SHORT NOTICE?
THE OWNER JUST GAVE ME A CALL.
HE'S SO INCONSIDERATE.
HE'S WAITING OUTSIDE RIGHT NOW.
O... KAY...
OH!
THIS GUY'S THE BOSS OF THE PLACE...
I GET IT.
I HEARD HE WAS IN ANOTHER COUNTRY. HE CAME BACK?
SOMETHING IMPORTANT TO TALK ABOUT?
...AND HIS MORALITY IS A LITTLE UNIQUE.

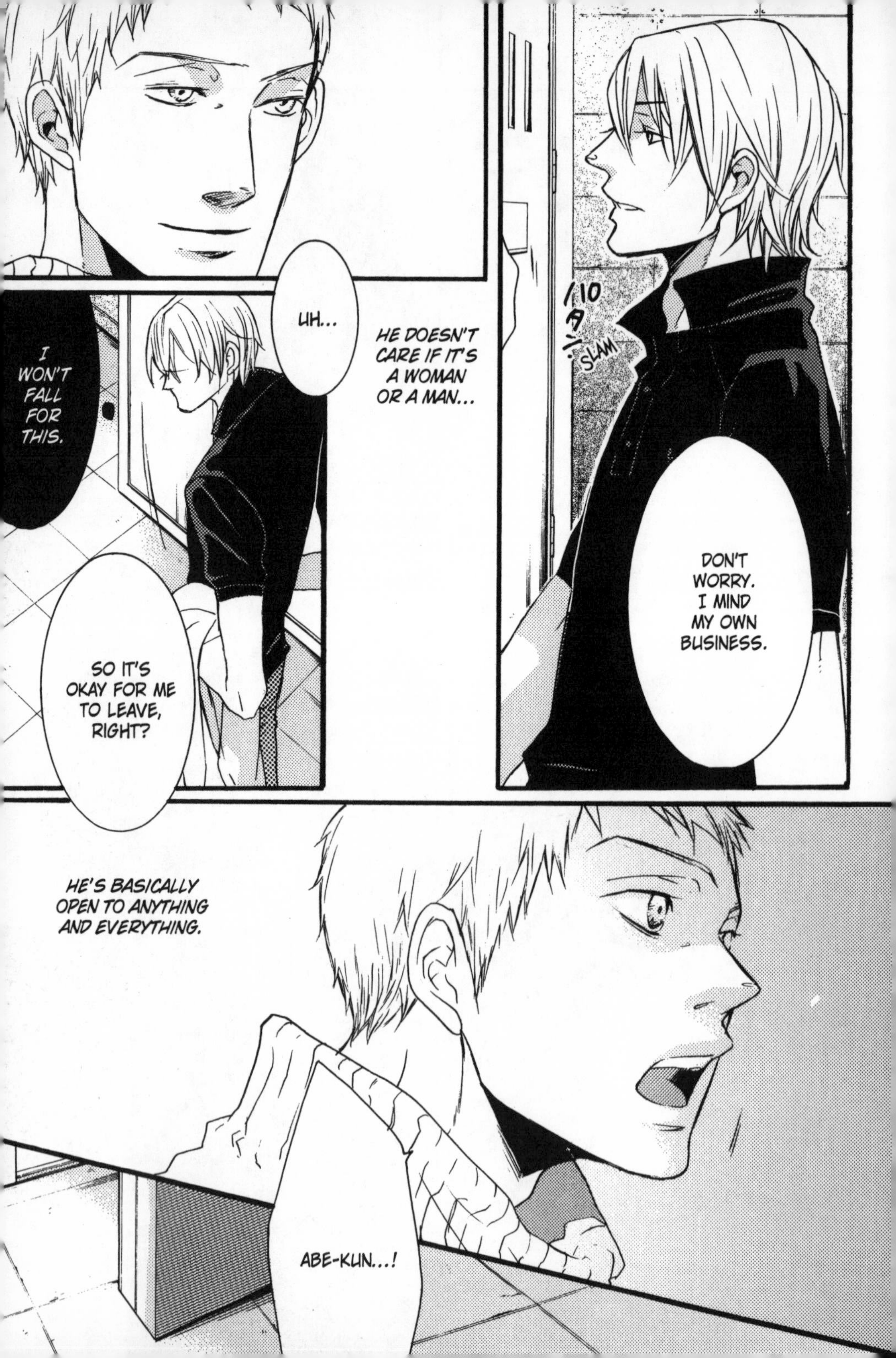
SLAM
DON'T WORRY. I MIND MY OWN BUSINESS.
UH...
HE DOESN'T CARE IF IT'S A WOMAN OR A MAN...
I WON'T FALL FOR THIS.
SO IT'S OKAY FOR ME TO LEAVE, RIGHT?
HE'S BASICALLY OPEN TO ANYTHING AND EVERYTHING.
ABE-KUN...!

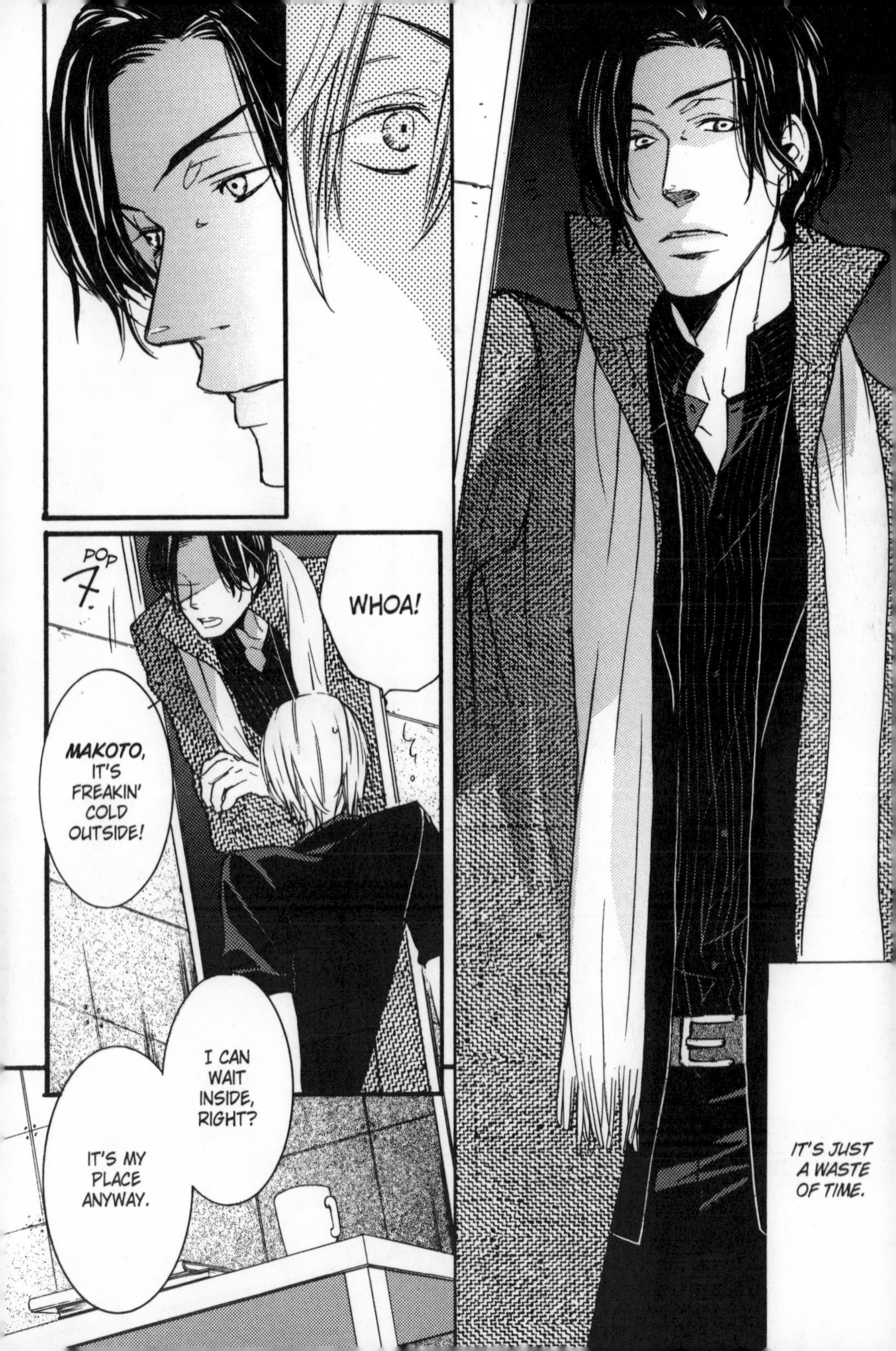
IT'S JUST A WASTE OF TIME.
POP
WHOA!
MAKOTO, IT'S FREAKIN' COLD OUTSIDE!
I CAN WAIT INSIDE, RIGHT?
IT'S MY PLACE ANYWAY.

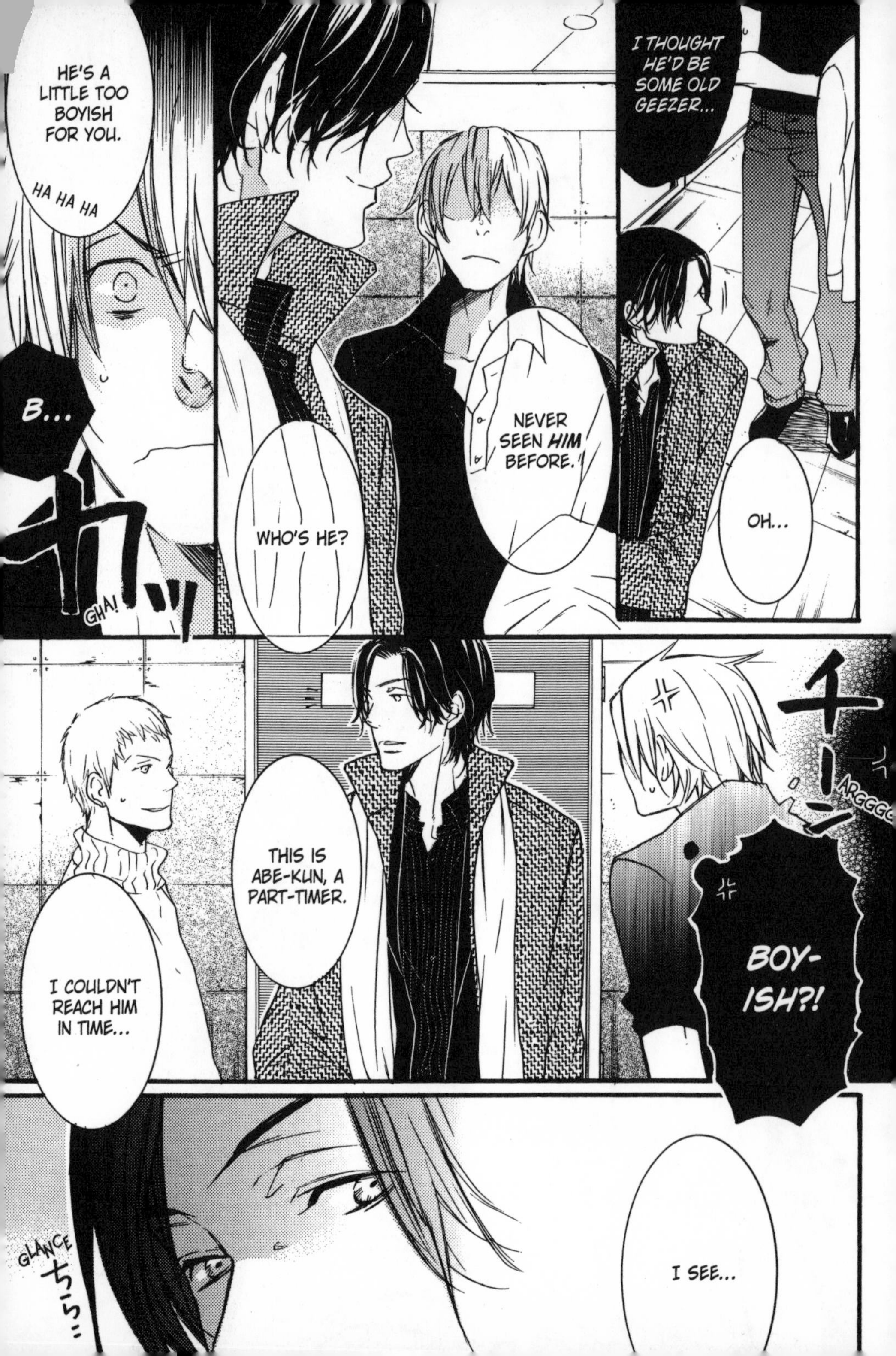
I THOUGHT HE'D BE SOME OLD GEEZER...
OH...
NEVER SEEN HIM BEFORE.
WHO'S HE?
HE'S A LITTLE TOO BOYISH FOR YOU.
HA HA HA
B...
GHA!
ARGGGG
BOY-ISH?!
THIS IS ABE-KUN, A PART-TIMER.
I COULDN'T REACH HIM IN TIME...
I SEE...
GLANCE

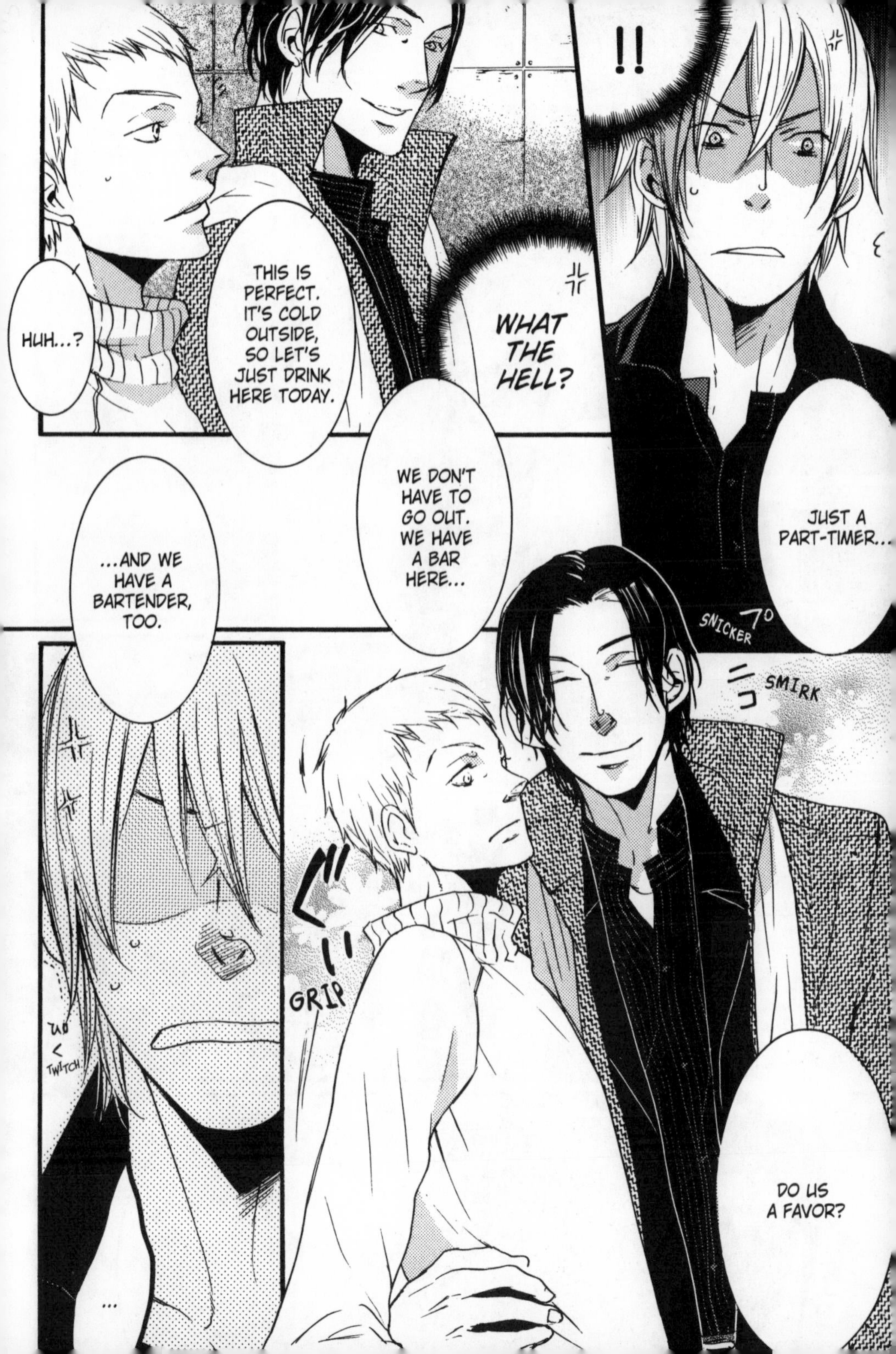

!!
WHAT THE HELL?
JUST A PART-TIMER...
THIS IS PERFECT. IT'S COLD OUTSIDE, SO LET'S JUST DRINK HERE TODAY.
HUH...?
WE DON'T HAVE TO GO OUT. WE HAVE A BAR HERE...
...AND WE HAVE A BARTENDER, TOO.
SNICKER
SMIRK
DO US A FAVOR?
GRIP
TWITCH
...

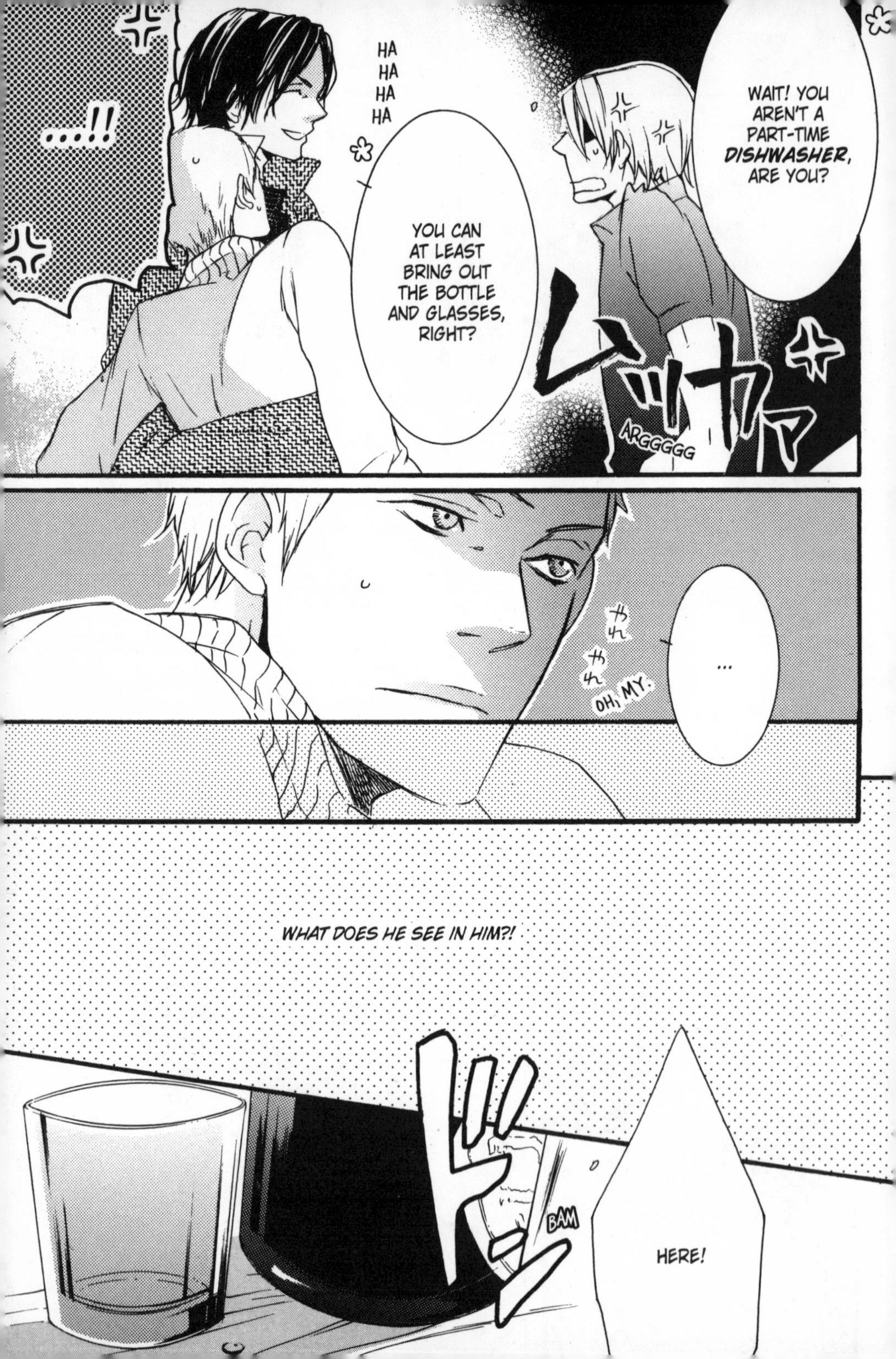
WAIT! YOU AREN'T A PART-TIME DISHWASHER, ARE YOU?
ムッカァ
ARGGGGG
HA HA HA HA
YOU CAN AT LEAST BRING OUT THE BOTTLE AND GLASSES, RIGHT?
...!!
...
やれやれ
OH, MY.
WHAT DOES HE SEE IN HIM?!
HERE!
BAM

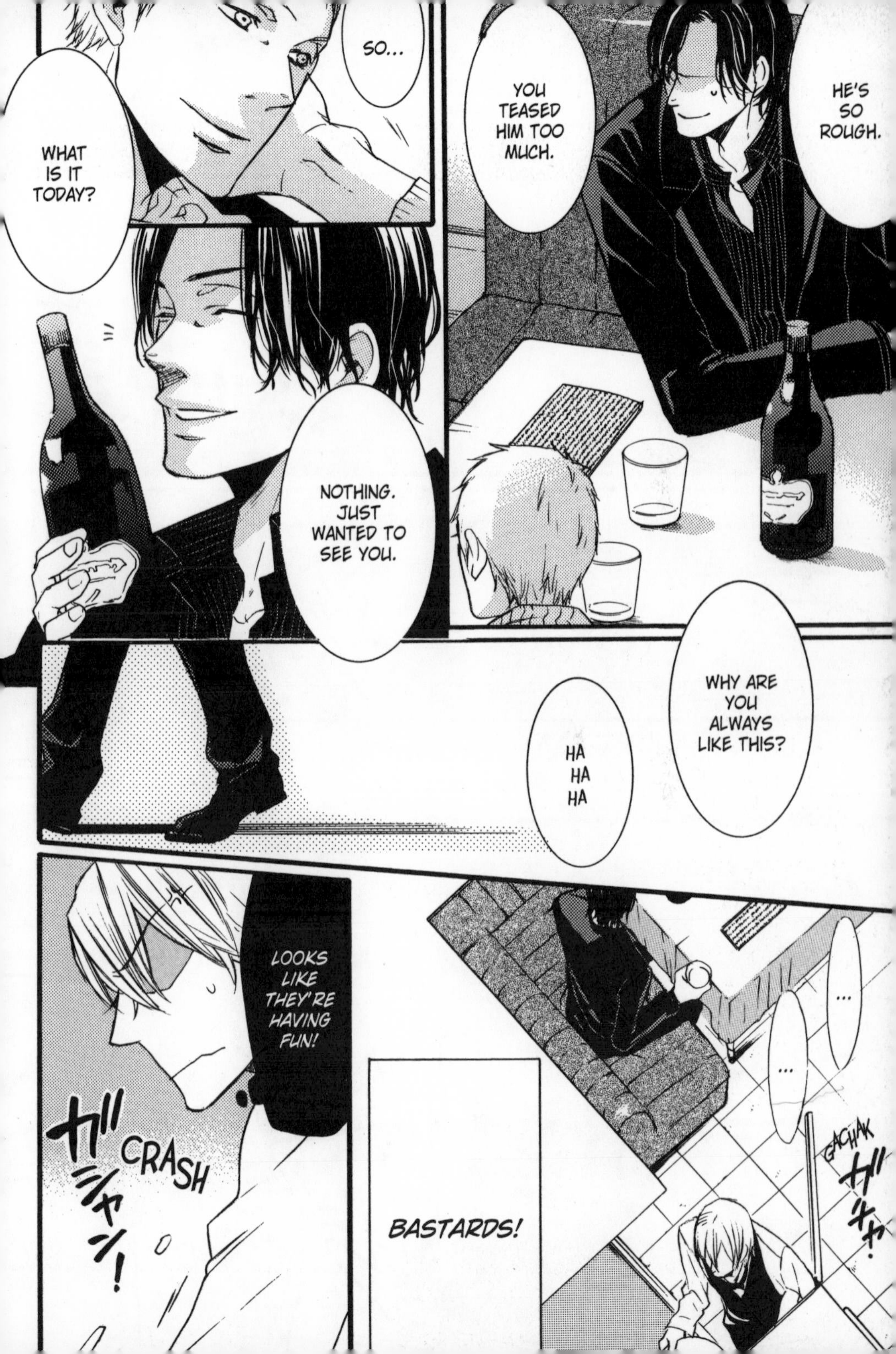
HE'S SO ROUGH.
YOU TEASED HIM TOO MUCH.
SO...
WHAT IS IT TODAY?
NOTHING. JUST WANTED TO SEE YOU.
WHY ARE YOU ALWAYS LIKE THIS?
HA HA HA
ガチャ
GACHAK
...
...
LOOKS LIKE THEY'RE HAVING FUN!
ガシャン!
CRASH
BASTARDS!

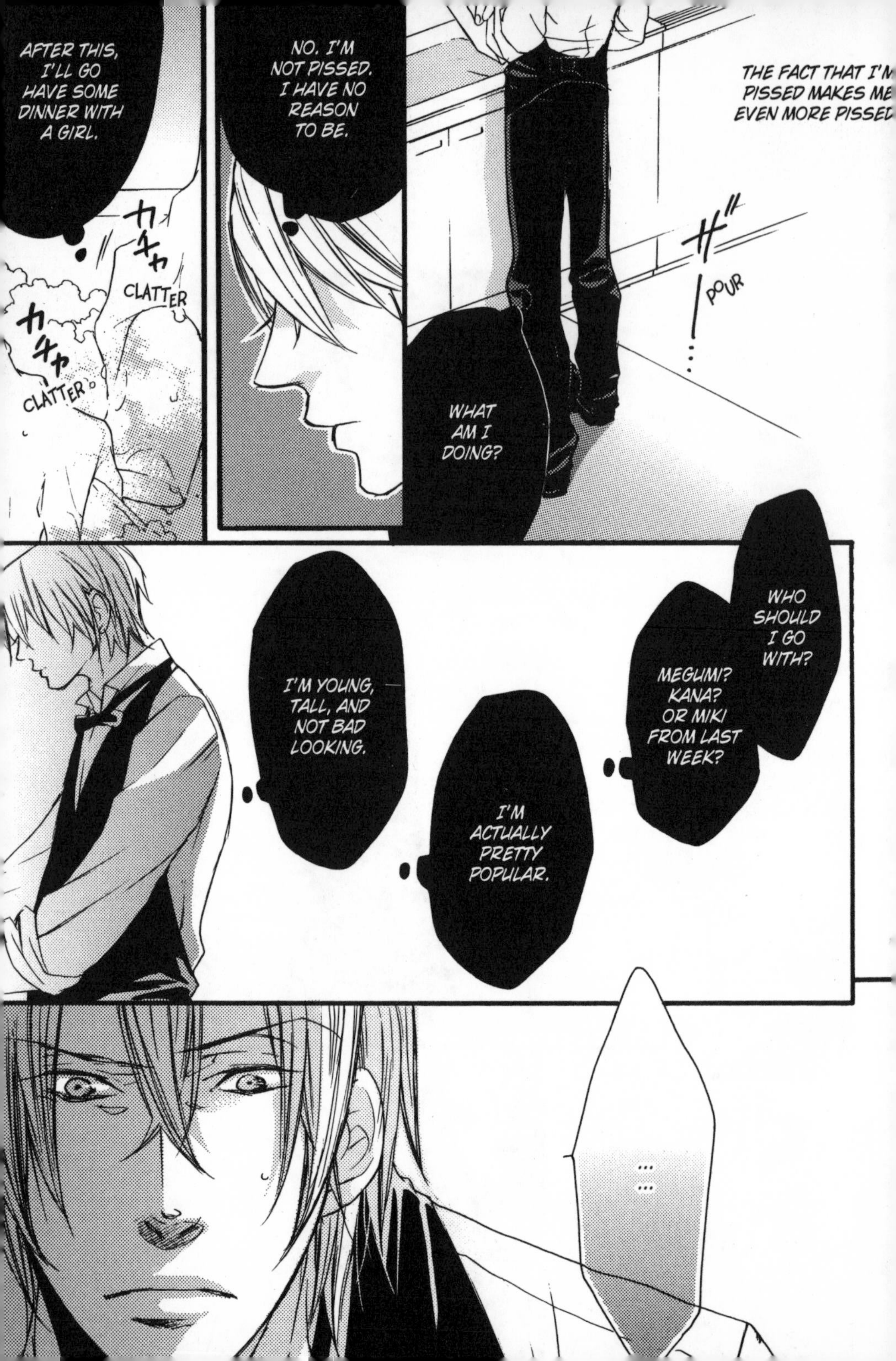
THE FACT THAT I'M PISSED MAKES ME EVEN MORE PISSED
ザ
POUR
WHAT AM I DOING?
NO. I'M NOT PISSED. I HAVE NO REASON TO BE.
AFTER THIS, I'LL GO HAVE SOME DINNER WITH A GIRL.
カチャ
CLATTER
カチャ
CLATTER
WHO SHOULD I GO WITH?
MEGUMI? KANA? OR MIKI FROM LAST WEEK?
I'M ACTUALLY PRETTY POPULAR.
I'M YOUNG, TALL, AND NOT BAD LOOKING.
…
…

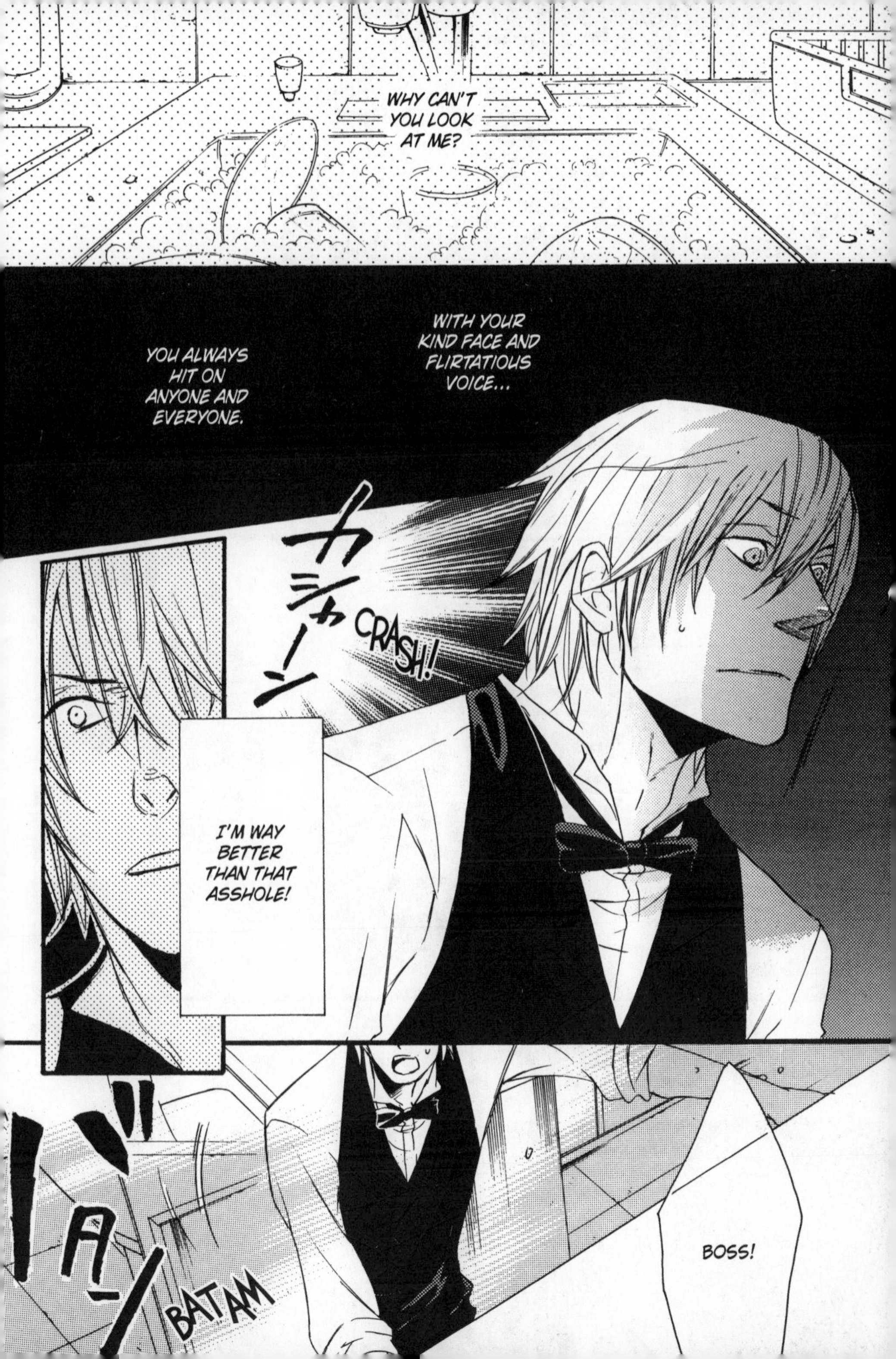

WHY CAN'T YOU LOOK AT ME?
WITH YOUR KIND FACE AND FLIRTATIOUS VOICE...
YOU ALWAYS HIT ON ANYONE AND EVERYONE.
カシャーン
CRASH!
I'M WAY BETTER THAN THAT ASSHOLE!
BOSS!
BATAM

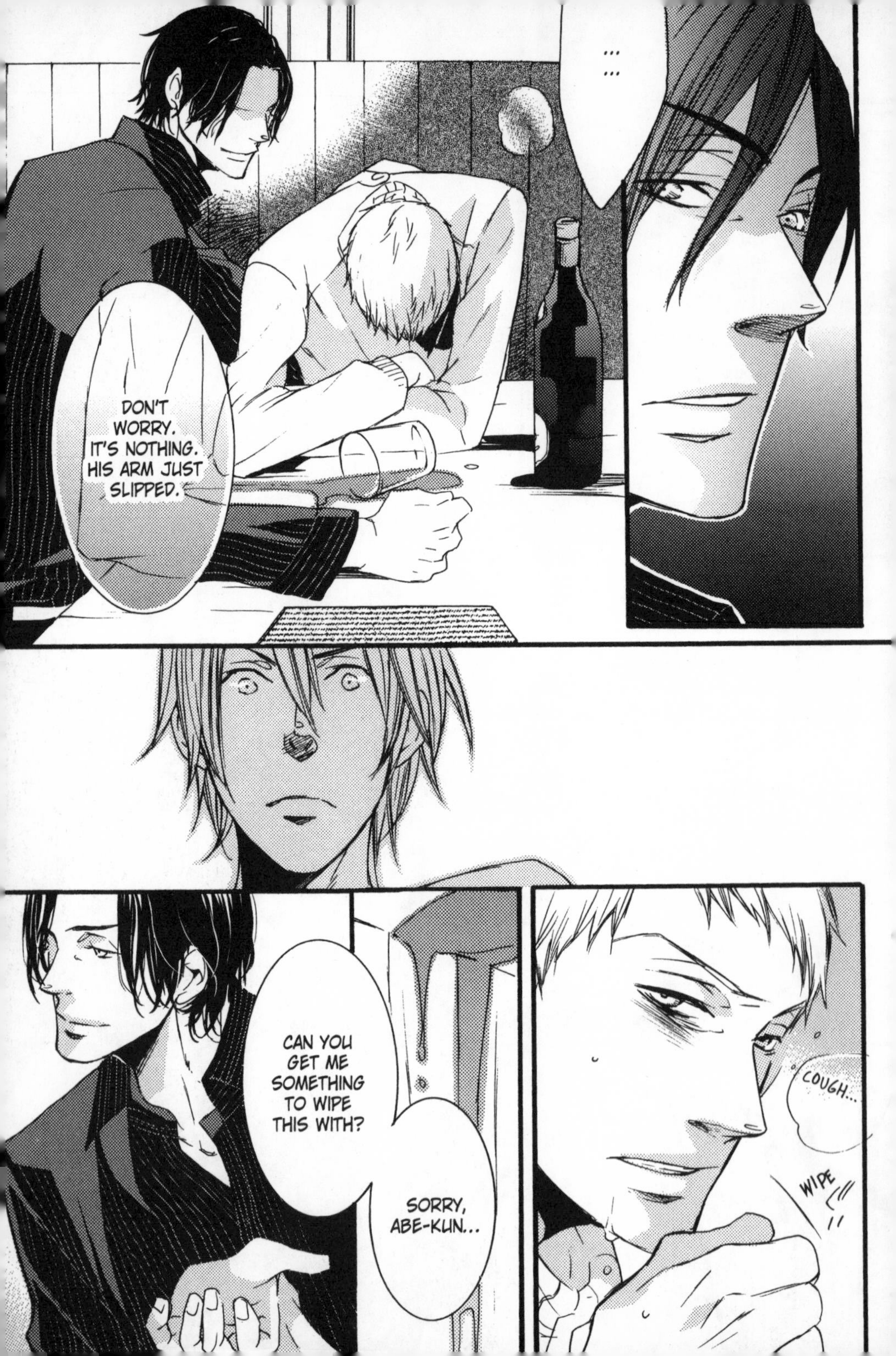
...
...
DON'T WORRY. IT'S NOTHING. HIS ARM JUST SLIPPED.
COUGH...
WIPE
CAN YOU GET ME SOMETHING TO WIPE THIS WITH?
SORRY, ABE-KUN...

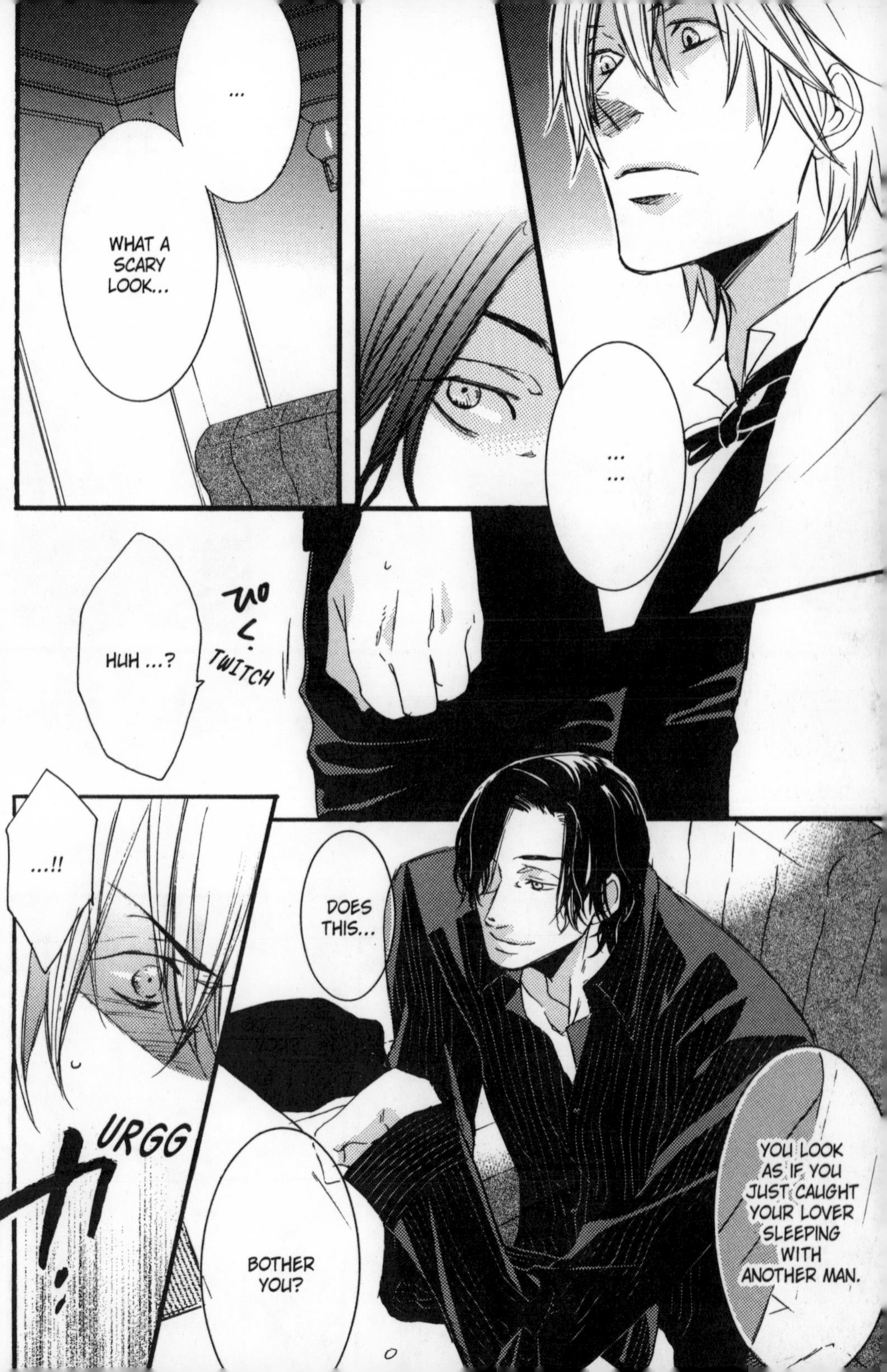
...
WHAT A SCARY LOOK...
... ...
TWITCH
HUH ...?
YOU LOOK AS IF YOU JUST CAUGHT YOUR LOVER SLEEPING WITH ANOTHER MAN.
DOES THIS...
BOTHER YOU?
...!!
URGG

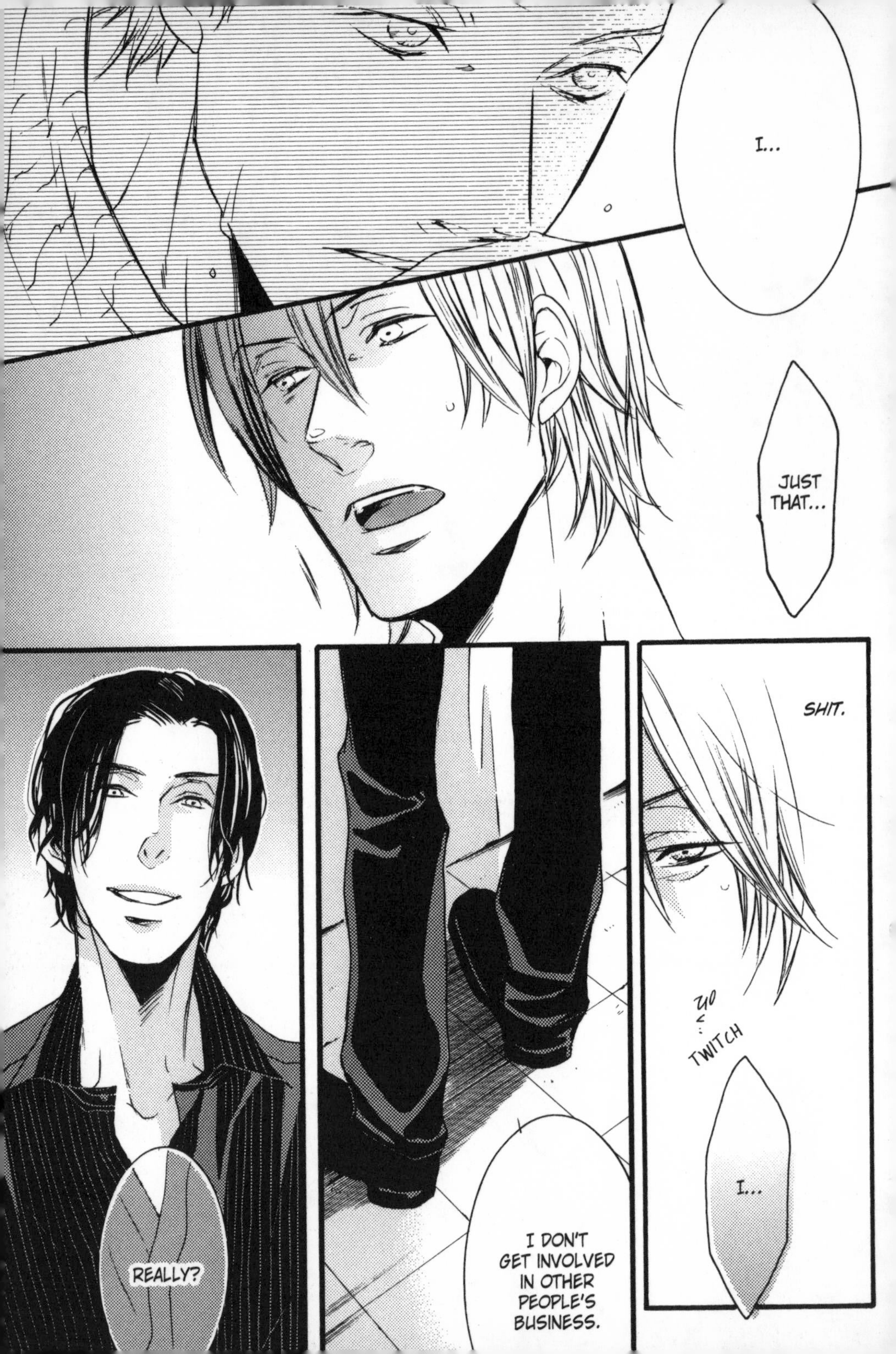
I...
JUST THAT...
SHIT.
TWITCH
I...
I DON'T GET INVOLVED IN OTHER PEOPLE'S BUSINESS.
REALLY?

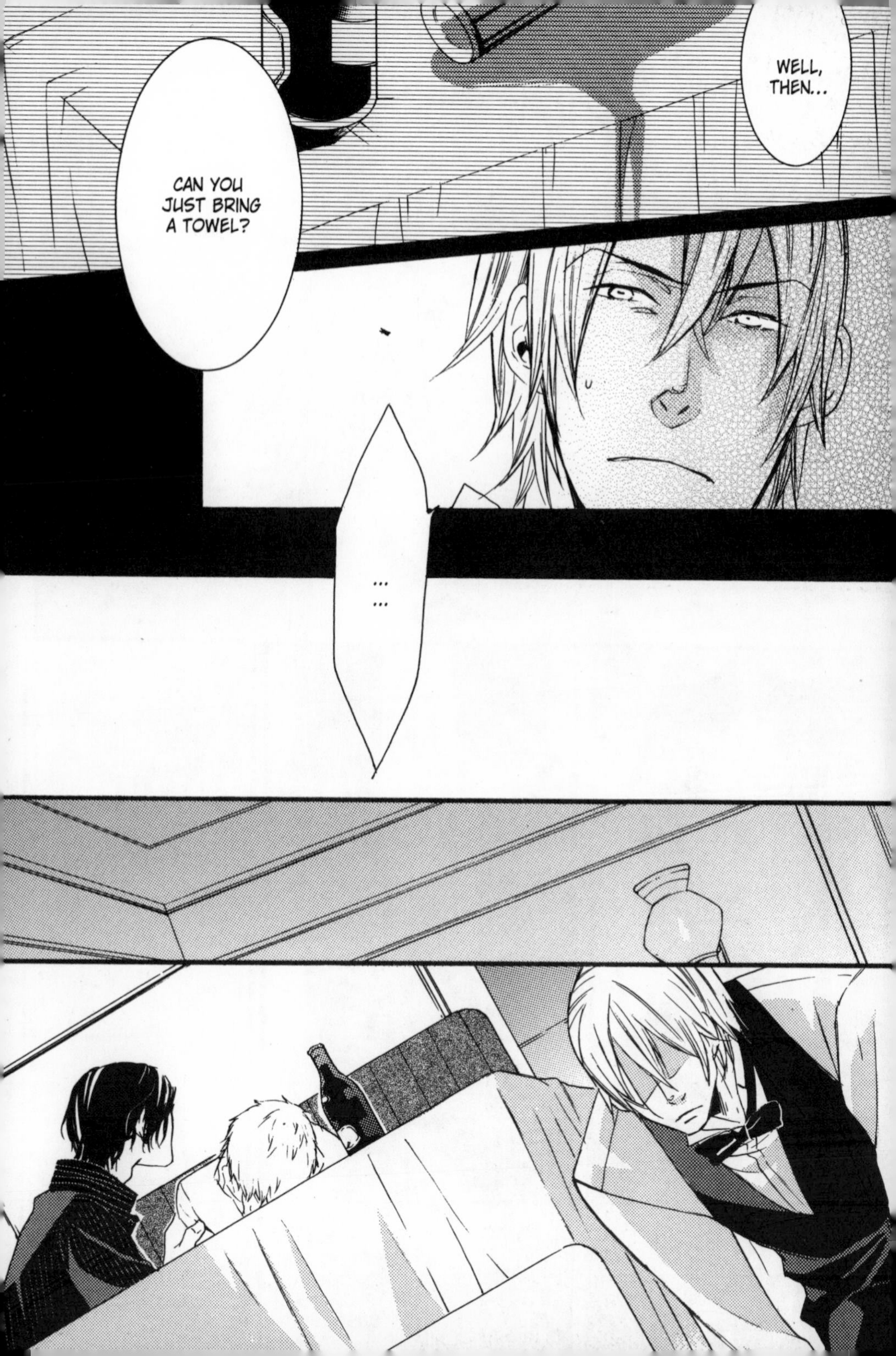
WELL, THEN...
CAN YOU JUST BRING A TOWEL?
... ...

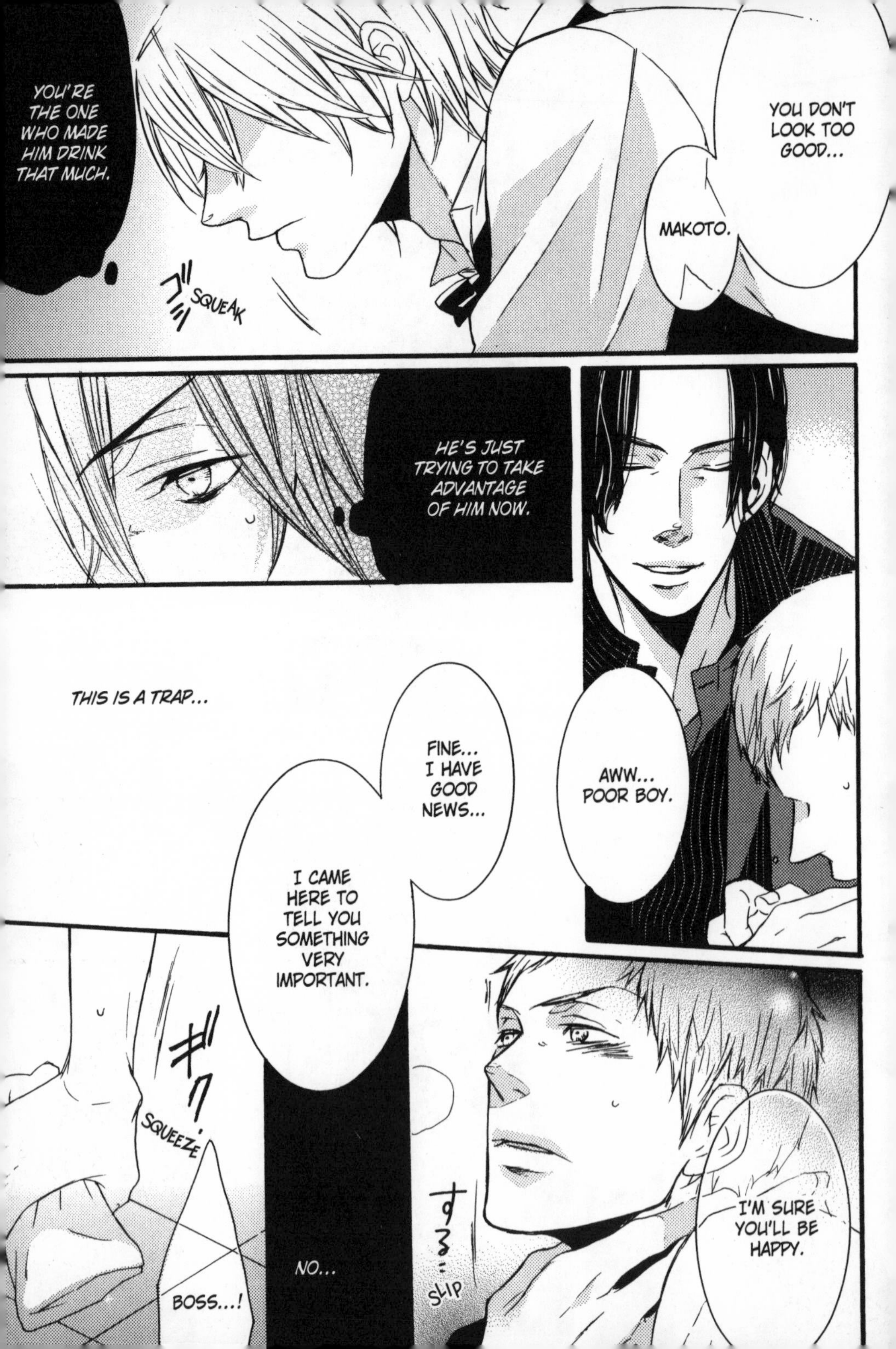

YOU DON'T LOOK TOO GOOD...
MAKOTO.
SQUEAK
YOU'RE THE ONE WHO MADE HIM DRINK THAT MUCH.
AWW... POOR BOY.
FINE... I HAVE GOOD NEWS...
I CAME HERE TO TELL YOU SOMETHING VERY IMPORTANT.
HE'S JUST TRYING TO TAKE ADVANTAGE OF HIM NOW.
THIS IS A TRAP...
I'M SURE YOU'LL BE HAPPY.
する
SLIP
NO...
SQUEEZE
BOSS...!

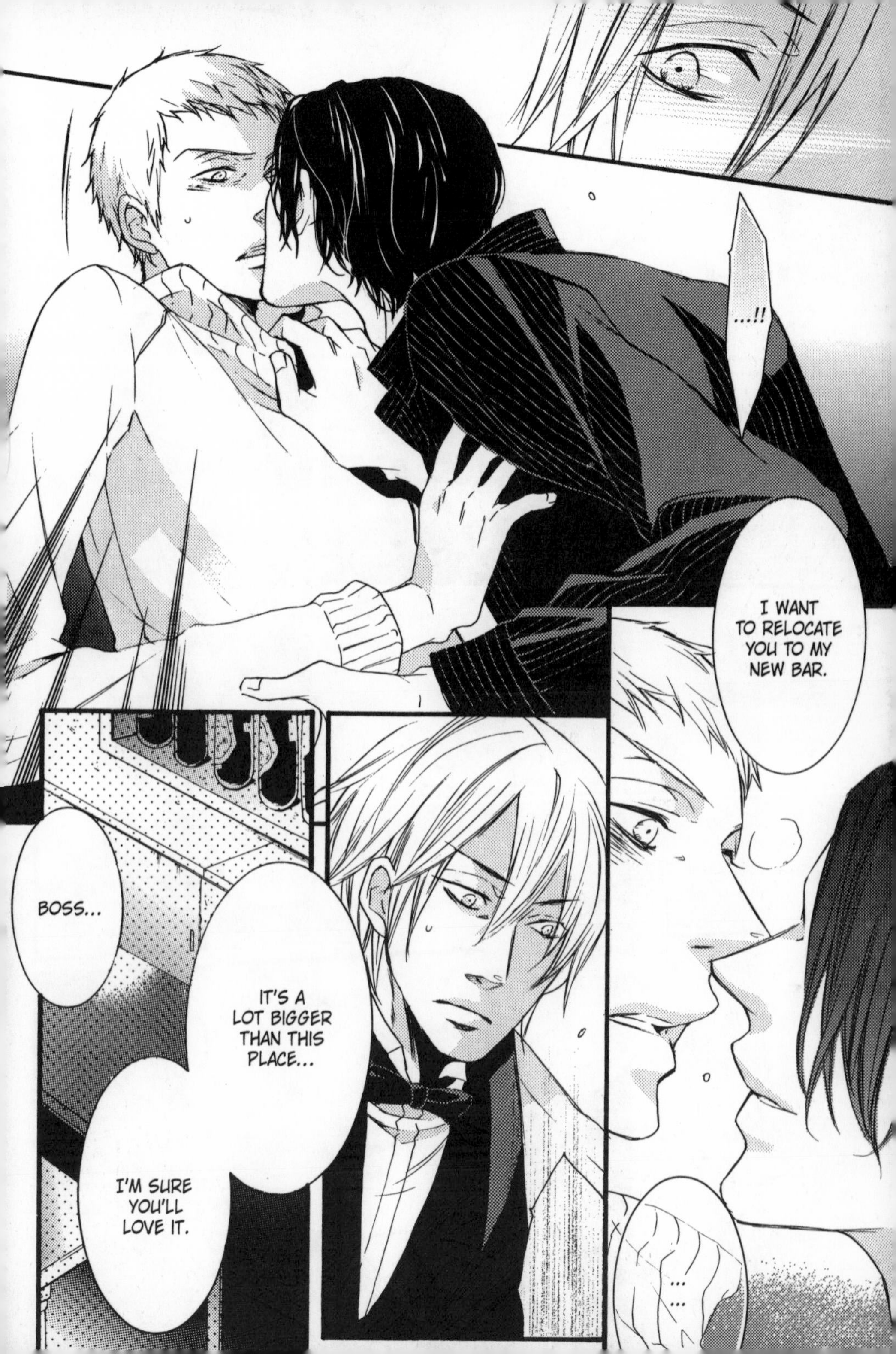
...!!
I WANT TO RELOCATE YOU TO MY NEW BAR.
IT'S A LOT BIGGER THAN THIS PLACE...
I'M SURE YOU'LL LOVE IT.
... ...
BOSS...

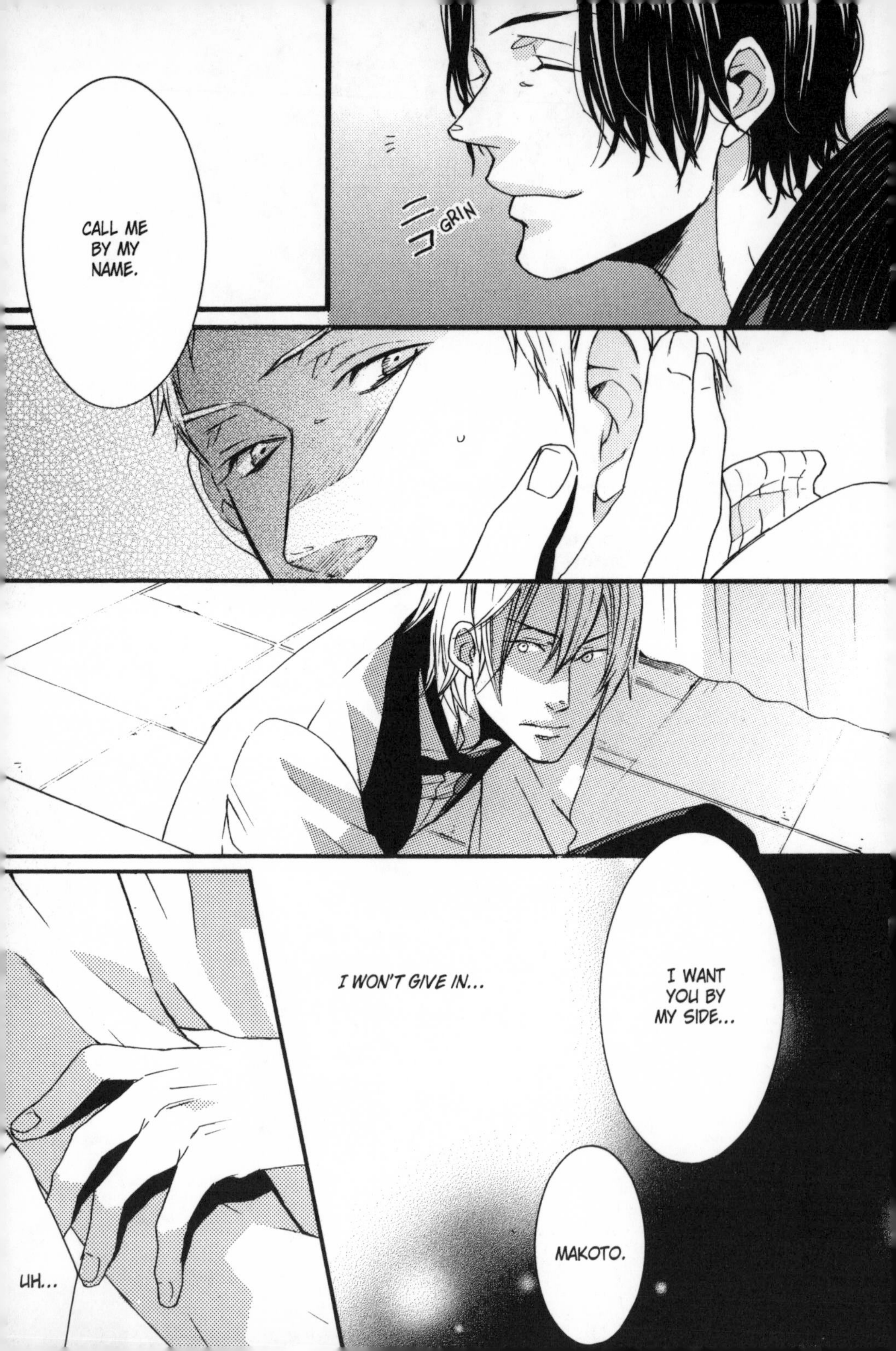
GRIN
CALL ME BY MY NAME.
I WANT YOU BY MY SIDE...
MAKOTO.
I WON'T GIVE IN...
UH...

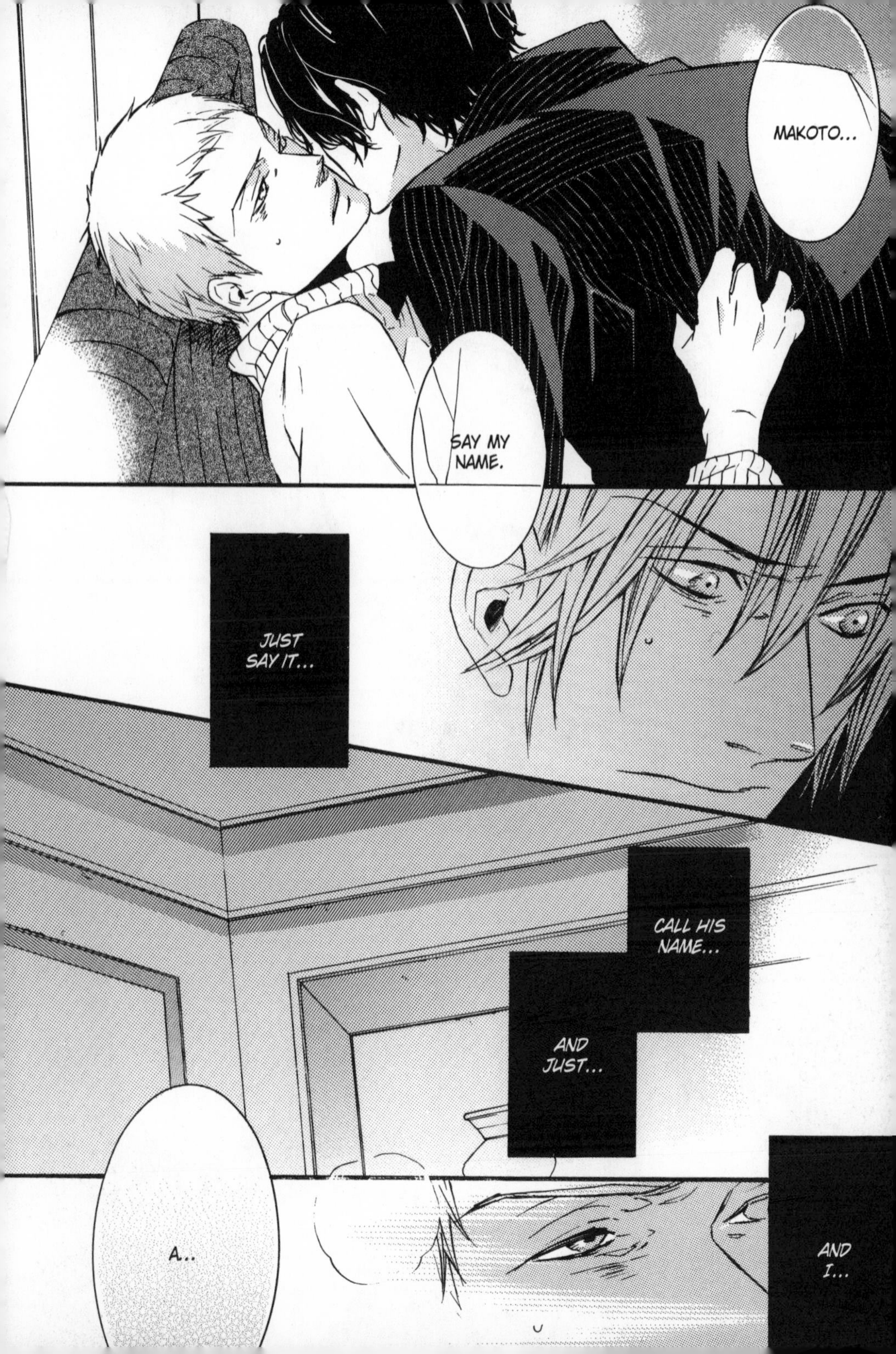
MAKOTO...
SAY MY NAME.
JUST SAY IT...
CALL HIS NAME...
AND JUST...
AND I...
A...

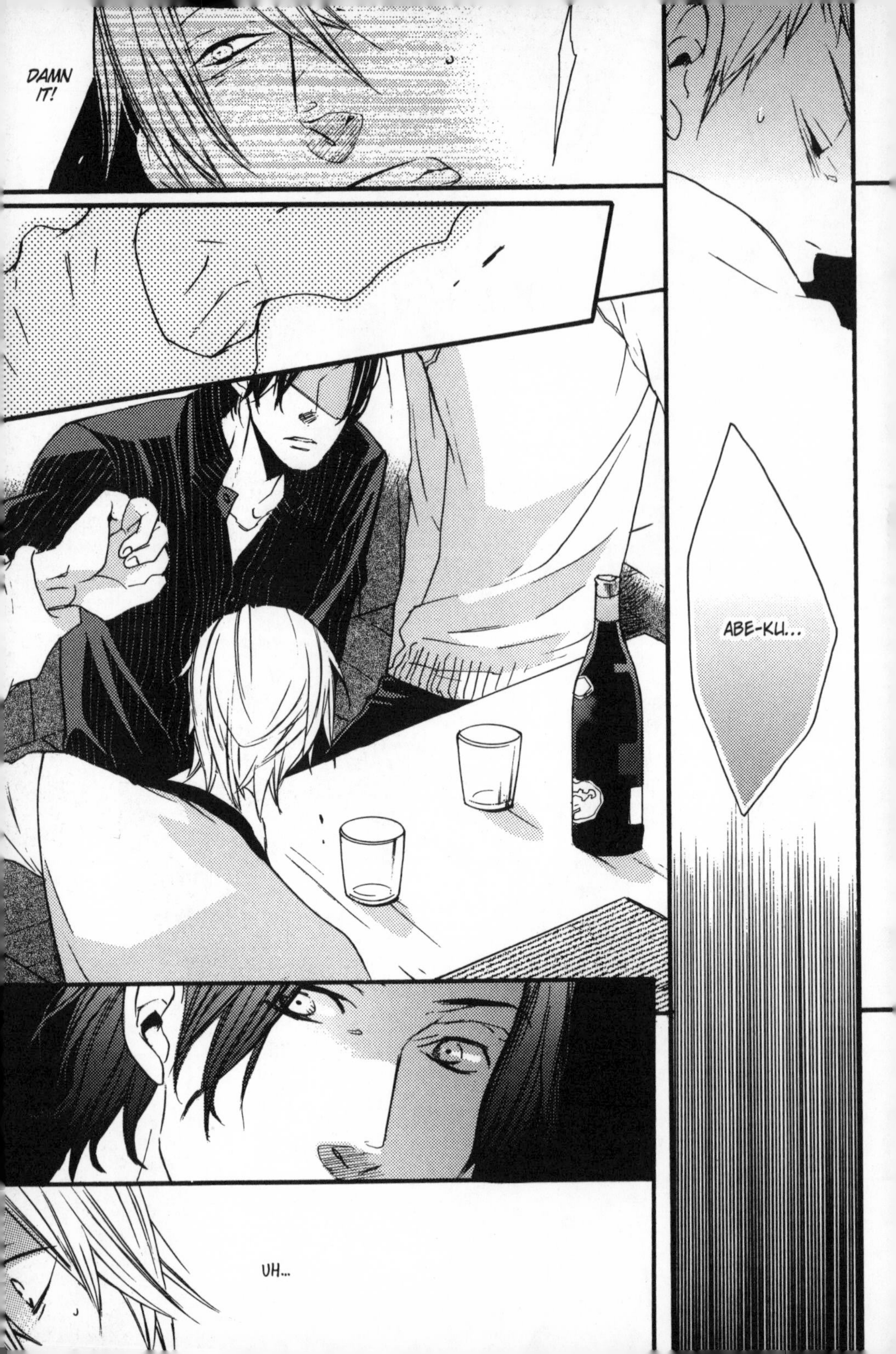
ABE-KU...
DAMN IT!
UH...

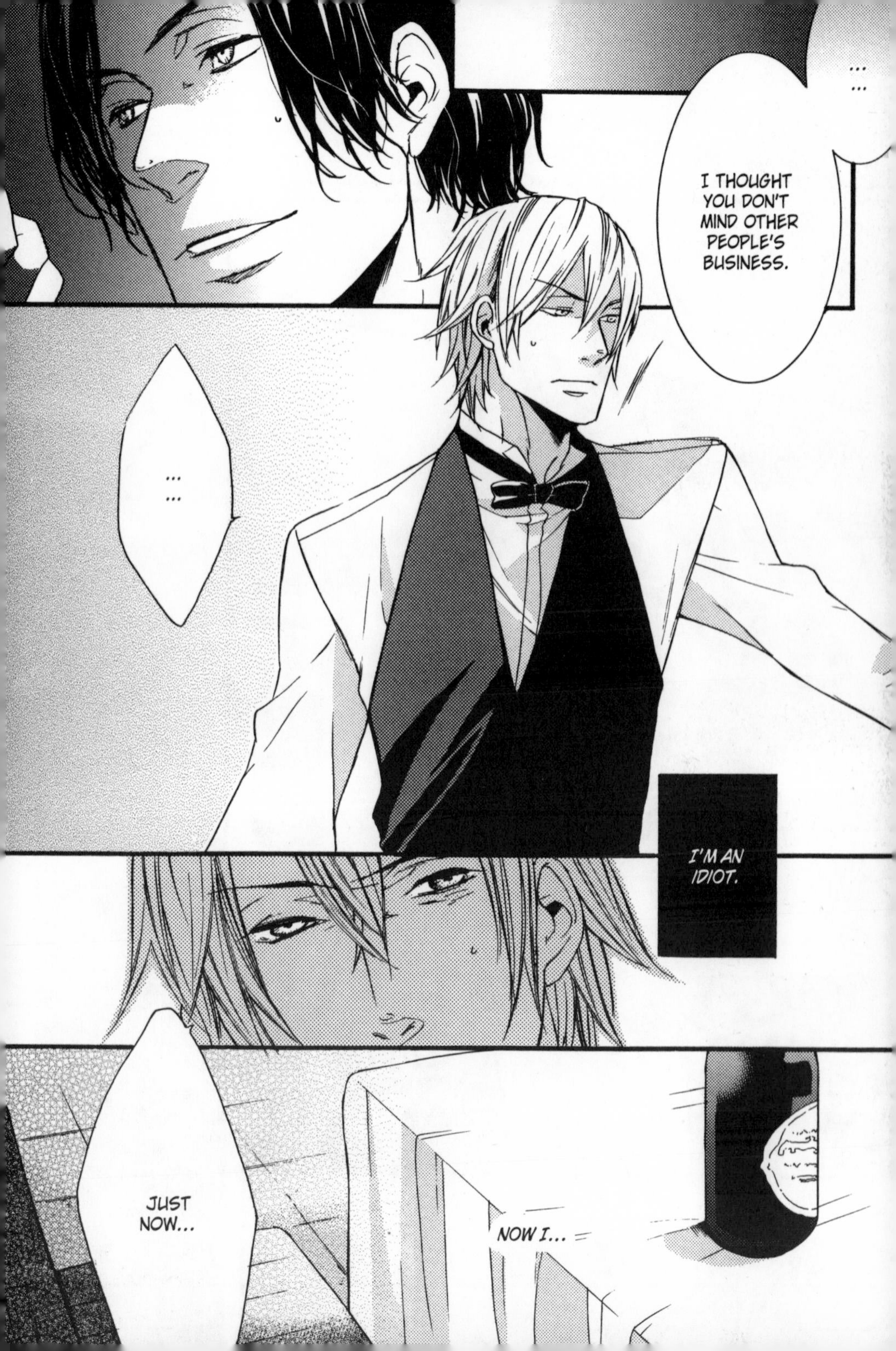
……
I THOUGHT YOU DON'T MIND OTHER PEOPLE'S BUSINESS.
……
I'M AN IDIOT.
JUST NOW...
NOW I...

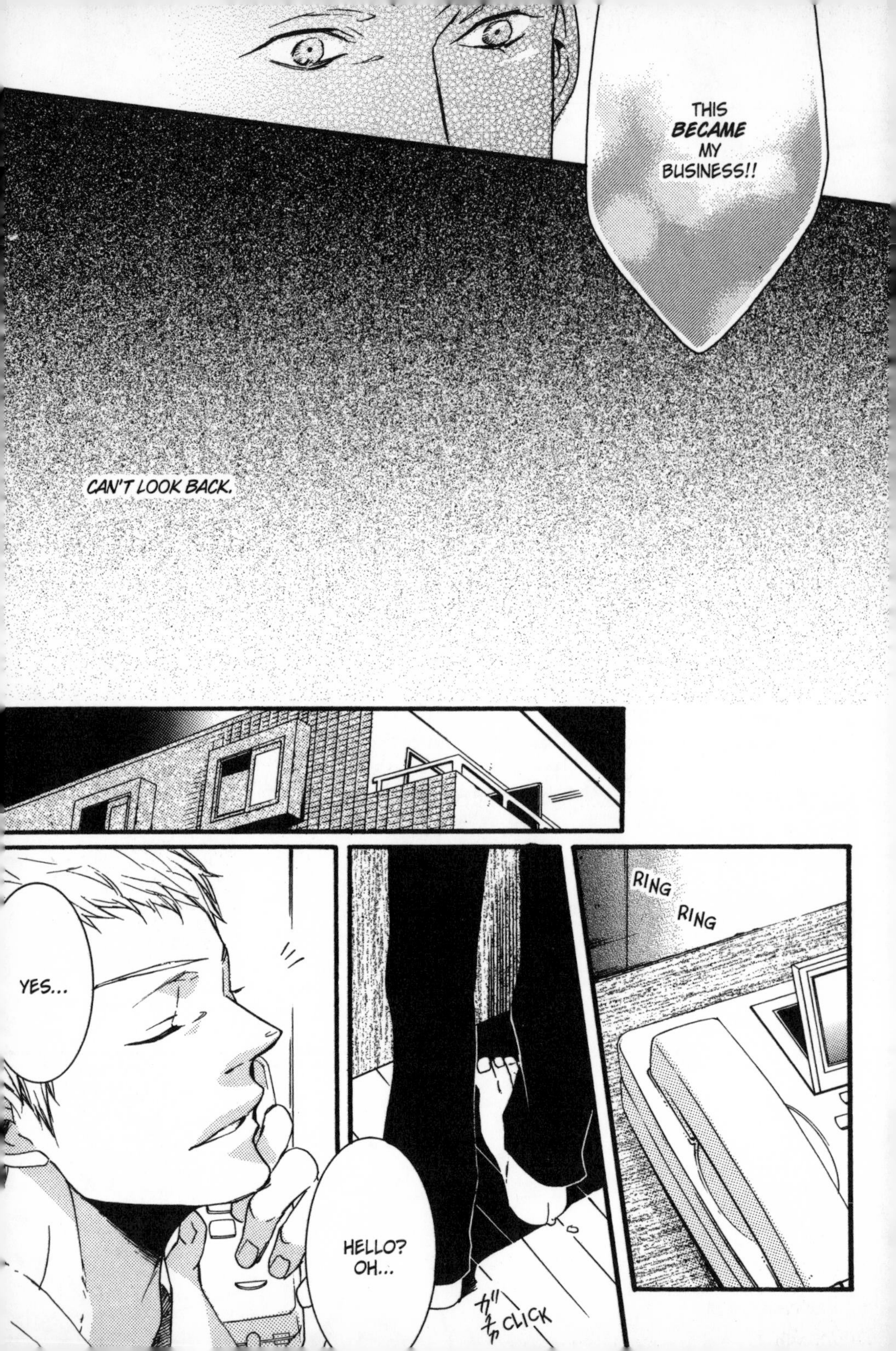

THIS BECAME MY BUSINESS!!
CAN'T LOOK BACK.
RING RING
HELLO? OH...
ガチャ CLICK
YES...

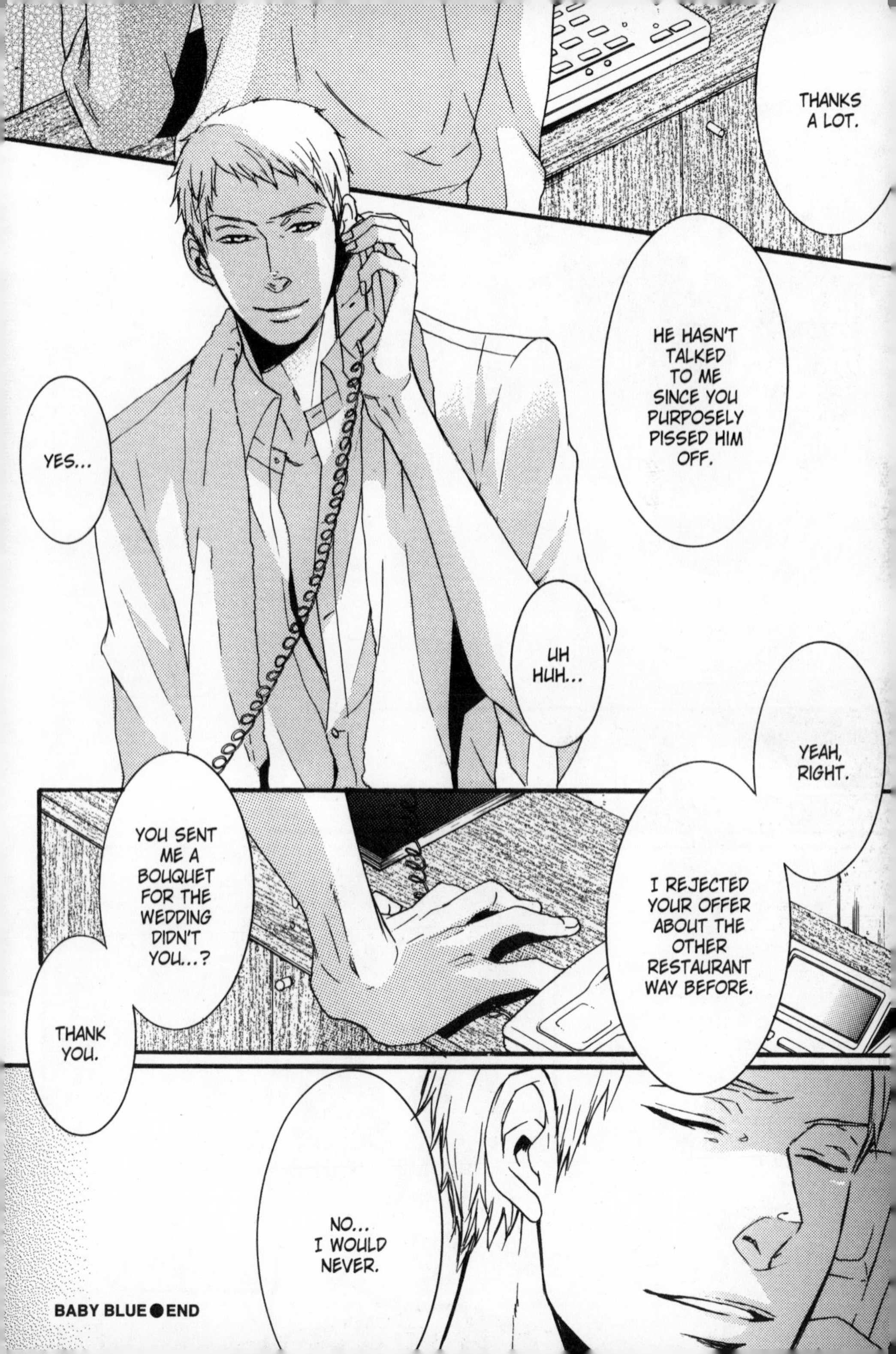
THANKS A LOT.
HE HASN'T TALKED TO ME SINCE YOU PURPOSELY PISSED HIM OFF.
YES...
UH HUH...
YEAH, RIGHT.
I REJECTED YOUR OFFER ABOUT THE OTHER RESTAURANT WAY BEFORE.
YOU SENT ME A BOUQUET FOR THE WEDDING DIDN'T YOU...?
THANK YOU.
NO... I WOULD NEVER.

BABY BLUE ● END

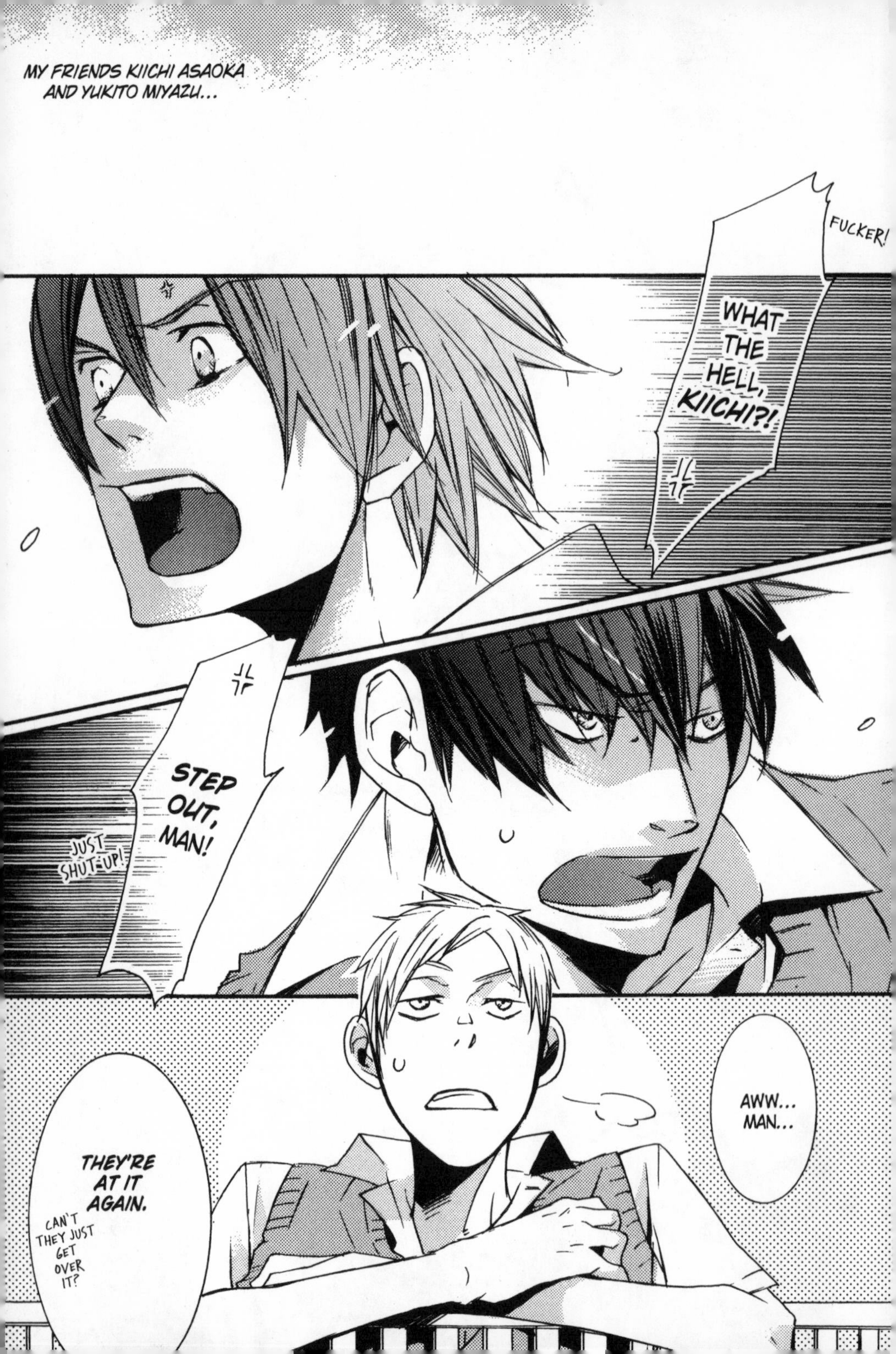
MY FRIENDS KIICHI ASAOKA AND YUKITO MIYAZU...
FUCKER!
WHAT THE HELL, KIICHI?!
STEP OUT, MAN!
JUST SHUT UP!
AWW... MAN...
THEY'RE AT IT AGAIN.
CAN'T THEY JUST GET OVER IT?

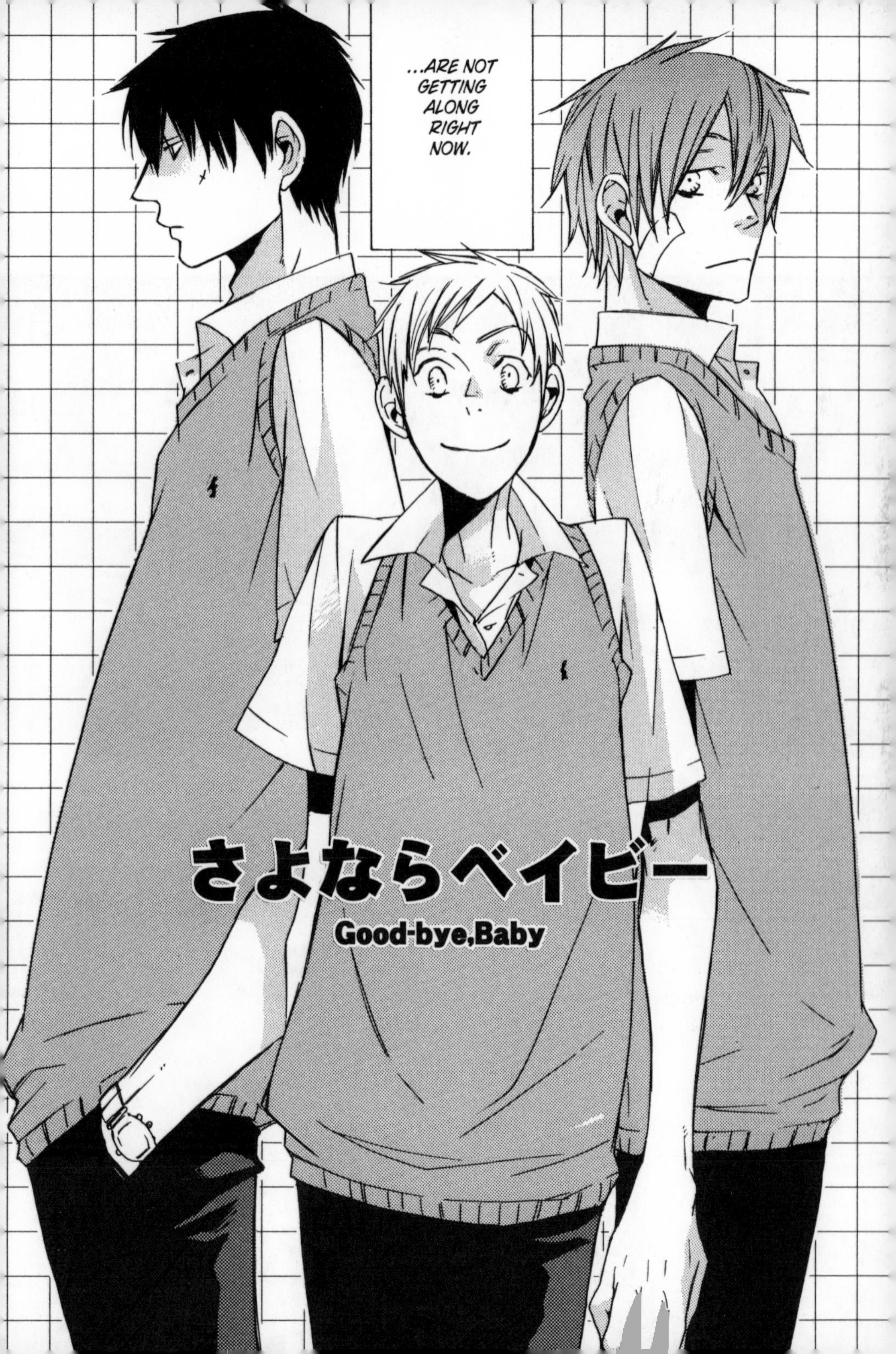
...ARE NOT GETTING ALONG RIGHT NOW.
さよならベイビー
Good-bye,Baby

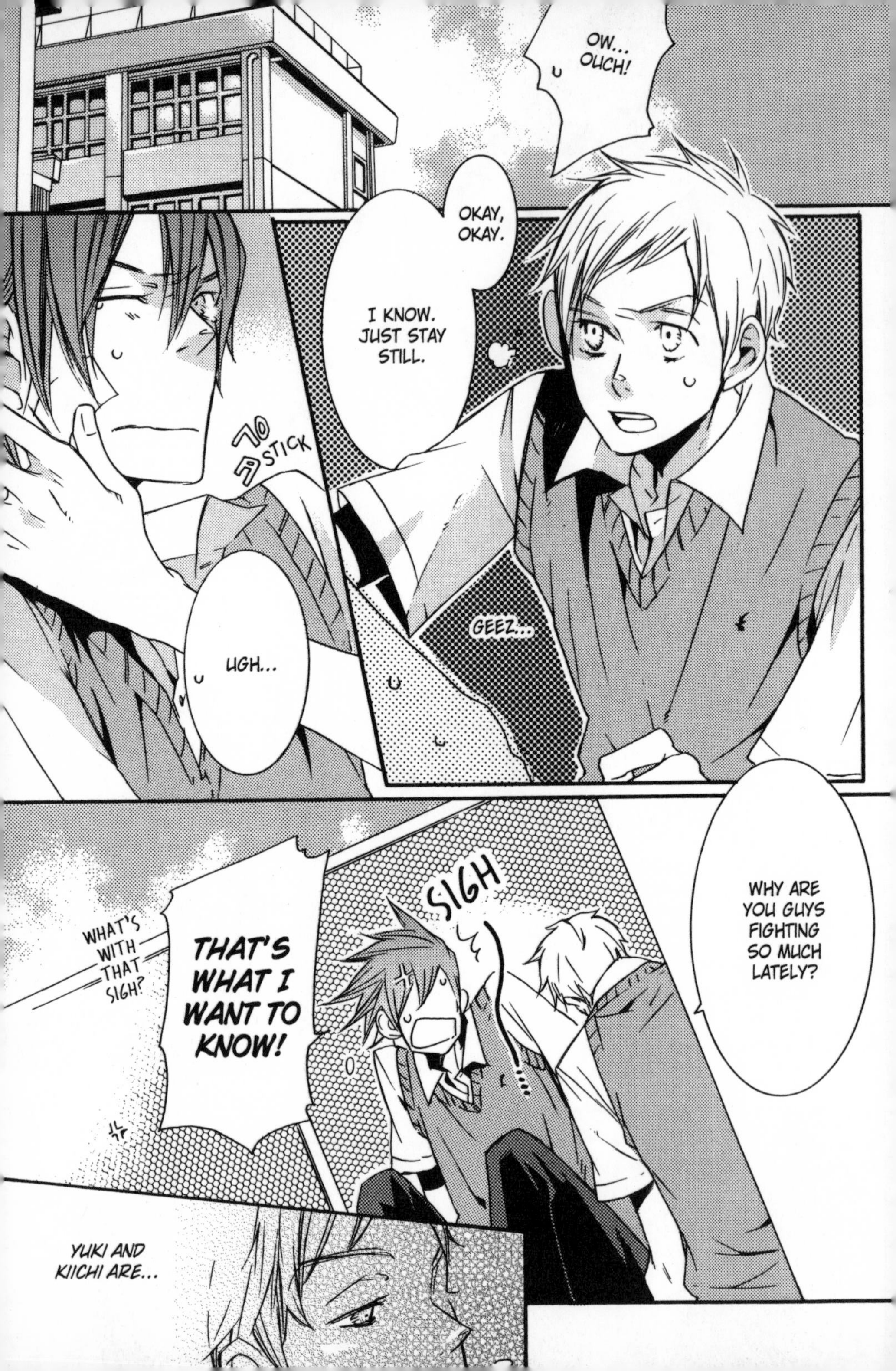
OW... OUCH!
OKAY, OKAY.
I KNOW. JUST STAY STILL.
GEEZ...
STICK
UGH...
WHY ARE YOU GUYS FIGHTING SO MUCH LATELY?
SIGH
THAT'S WHAT I WANT TO KNOW!
WHAT'S WITH THAT SIGH?
YUKI AND KIICHI ARE...

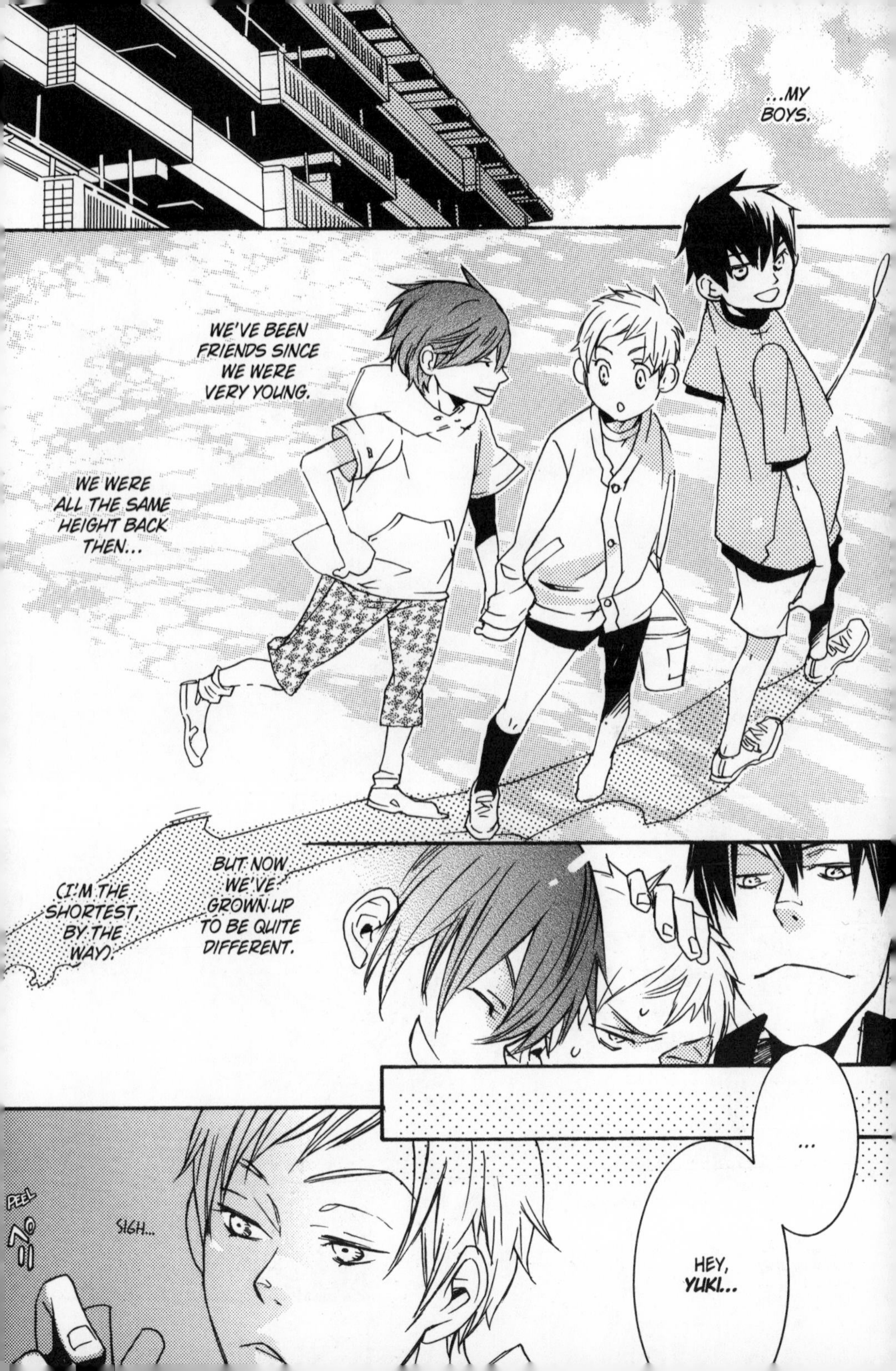
...MY BOYS.
WE'VE BEEN FRIENDS SINCE WE WERE VERY YOUNG.
WE WERE ALL THE SAME HEIGHT BACK THEN...
BUT NOW WE'VE GROWN UP TO BE QUITE DIFFERENT.
(I'M THE SHORTEST, BY THE WAY).
...
HEY, YUKI...
SIGH...
PEEL

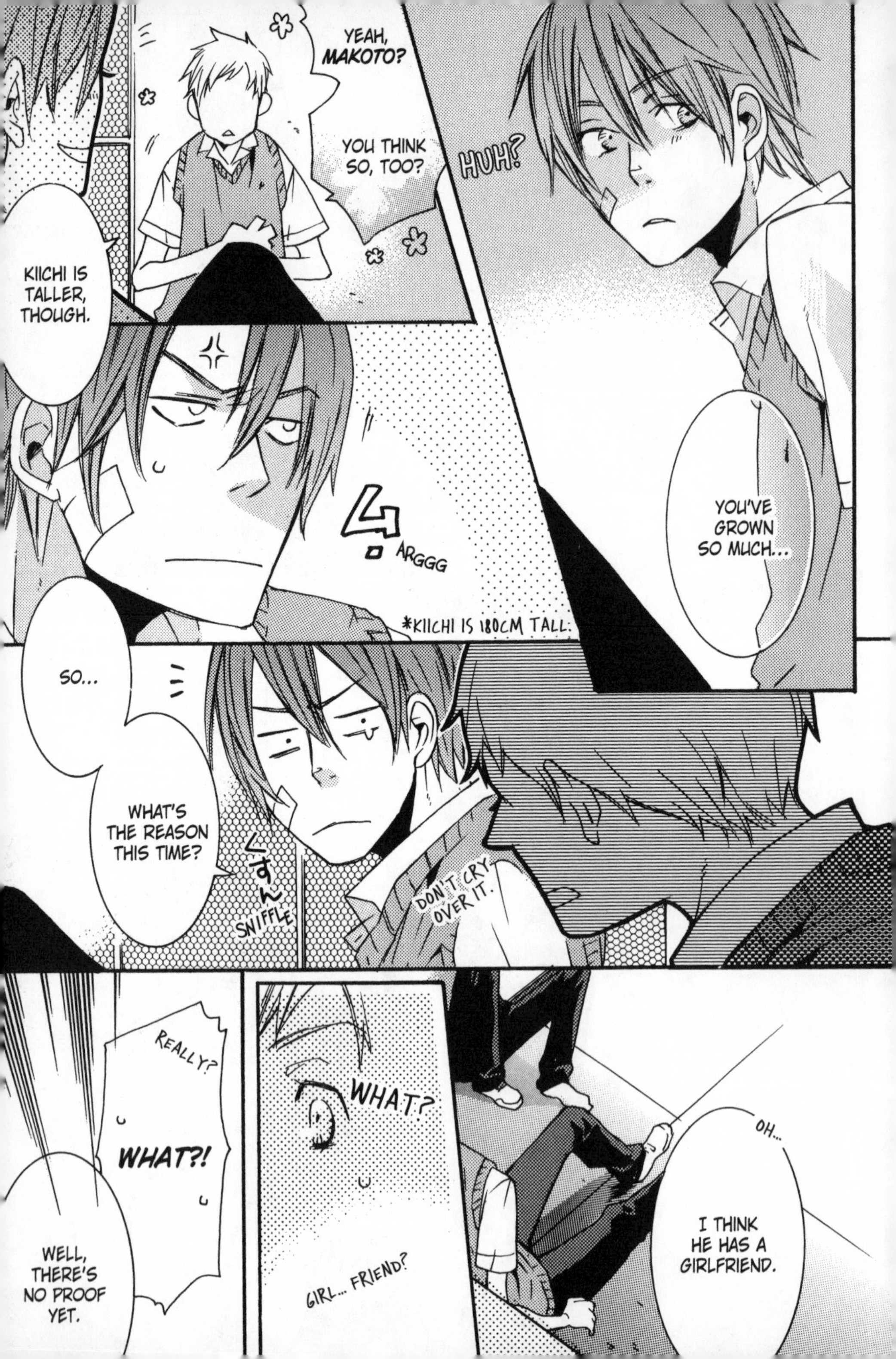
HUH?
YOU'VE GROWN SO MUCH...
YEAH, MAKOTO?
YOU THINK SO, TOO?
KIICHI IS TALLER, THOUGH.
ARGGG
*KIICHI IS 180CM TALL.
SO...
WHAT'S THE REASON THIS TIME?
くすん
SNIFFLE
DON'T CRY OVER IT.
OH...
I THINK HE HAS A GIRLFRIEND.
WHAT?
GIRL... FRIEND?
REALLY?
WHAT?!
WELL, THERE'S NO PROOF YET.

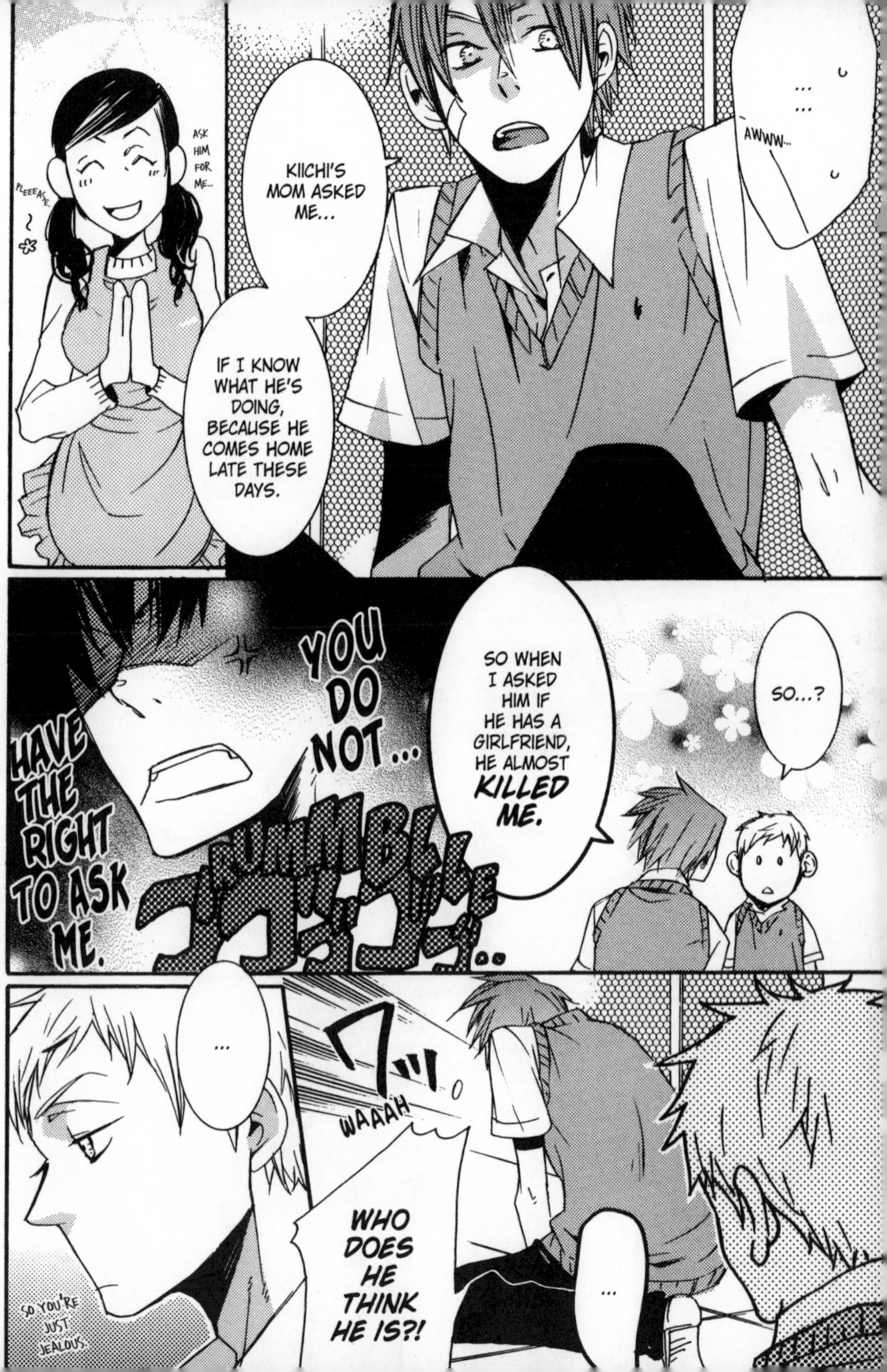
…
…
AWWW…
KIICHI'S MOM ASKED ME…
IF I KNOW WHAT HE'S DOING, BECAUSE HE COMES HOME LATE THESE DAYS.
ASK HIM FOR ME…
PLEEEASE.
SO…?
SO WHEN I ASKED HIM IF HE HAS A GIRLFRIEND, HE ALMOST KILLED ME.
YOU DO NOT…
HAVE THE RIGHT TO ASK ME.
…
WHO DOES HE THINK HE IS?!
WAAAH
…
SO YOU'RE JUST JEALOUS.

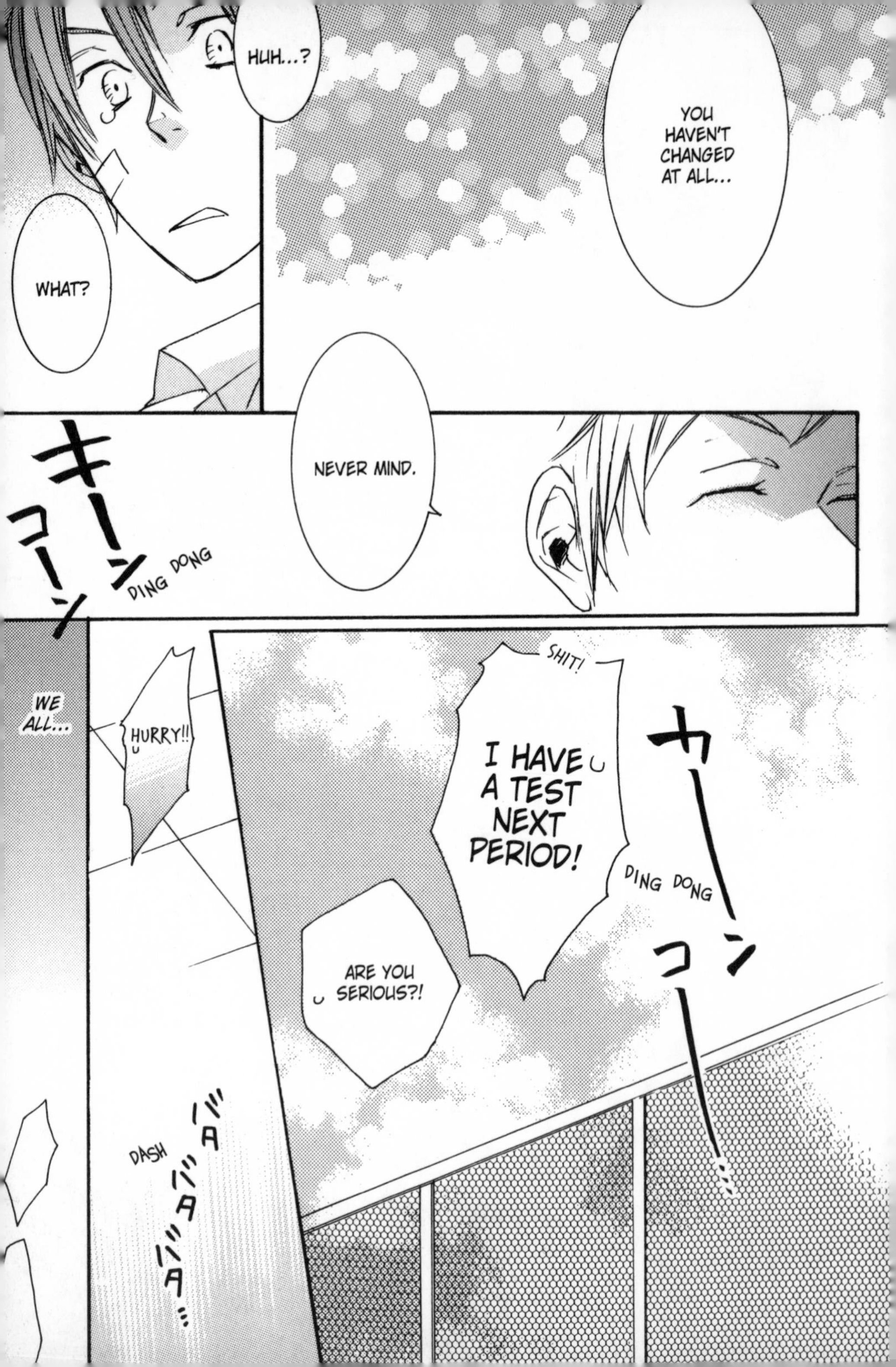
YOU HAVEN'T CHANGED AT ALL...
HUH...?
WHAT?
NEVER MIND.
キーンコーン
DING DONG
カーンコーン...
DING DONG
SHIT!
I HAVE A TEST NEXT PERIOD!
ARE YOU SERIOUS?!
HURRY!!
バタバタバタ...
DASH
WE ALL...

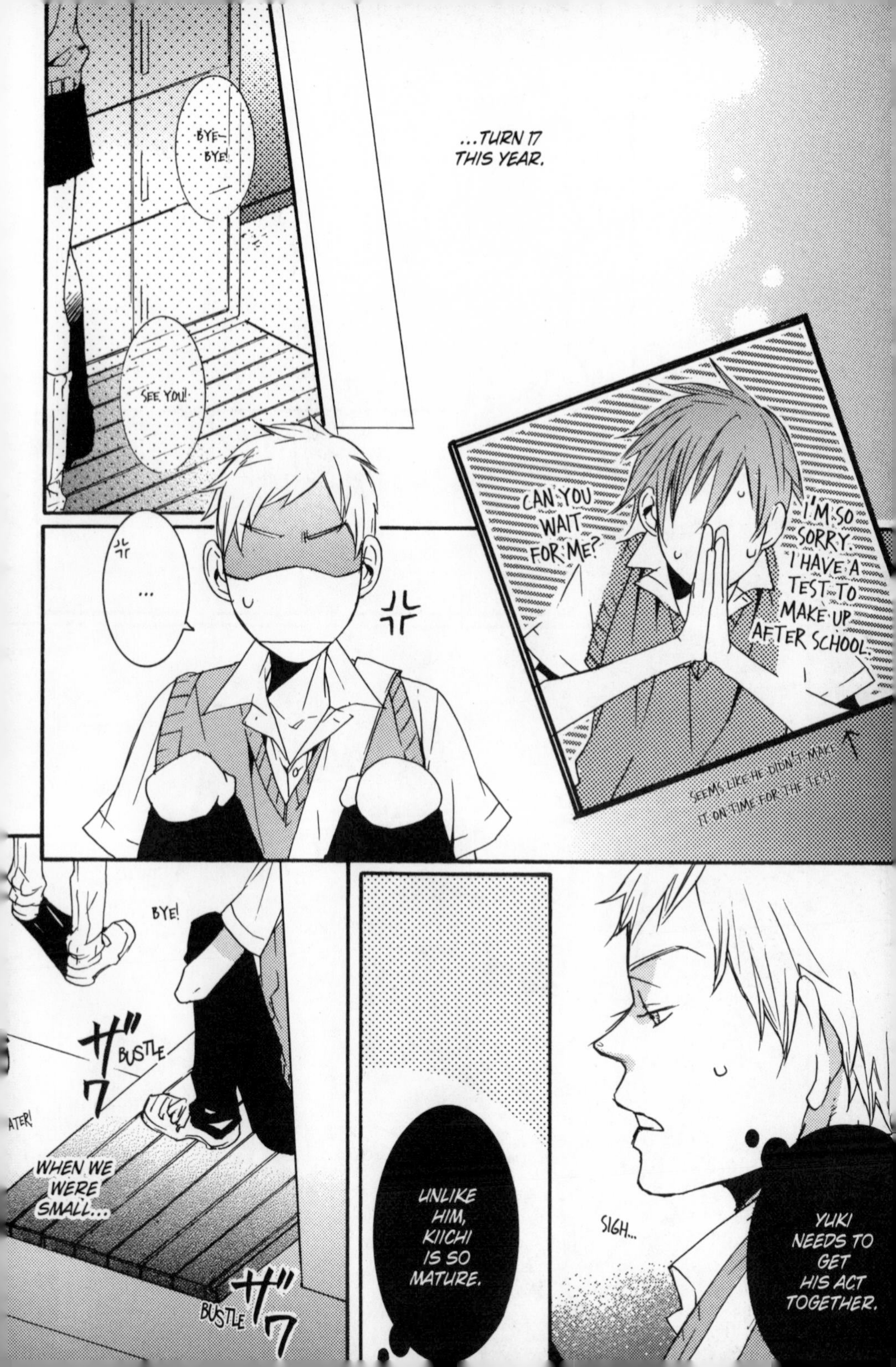
...TURN 17 THIS YEAR.
BYE-BYE!
SEE YOU!
I'M SO SORRY. I HAVE A TEST TO MAKE UP AFTER SCHOOL.
CAN YOU WAIT FOR ME?
SEEMS LIKE HE DIDN'T MAKE IT ON TIME FOR THE TEST.
...
YUKI NEEDS TO GET HIS ACT TOGETHER.
SIGH...
UNLIKE HIM, KIICHI IS SO MATURE.
BYE!
ザワ BUSTLE
ATER!
WHEN WE WERE SMALL...
BUSTLE ザワ

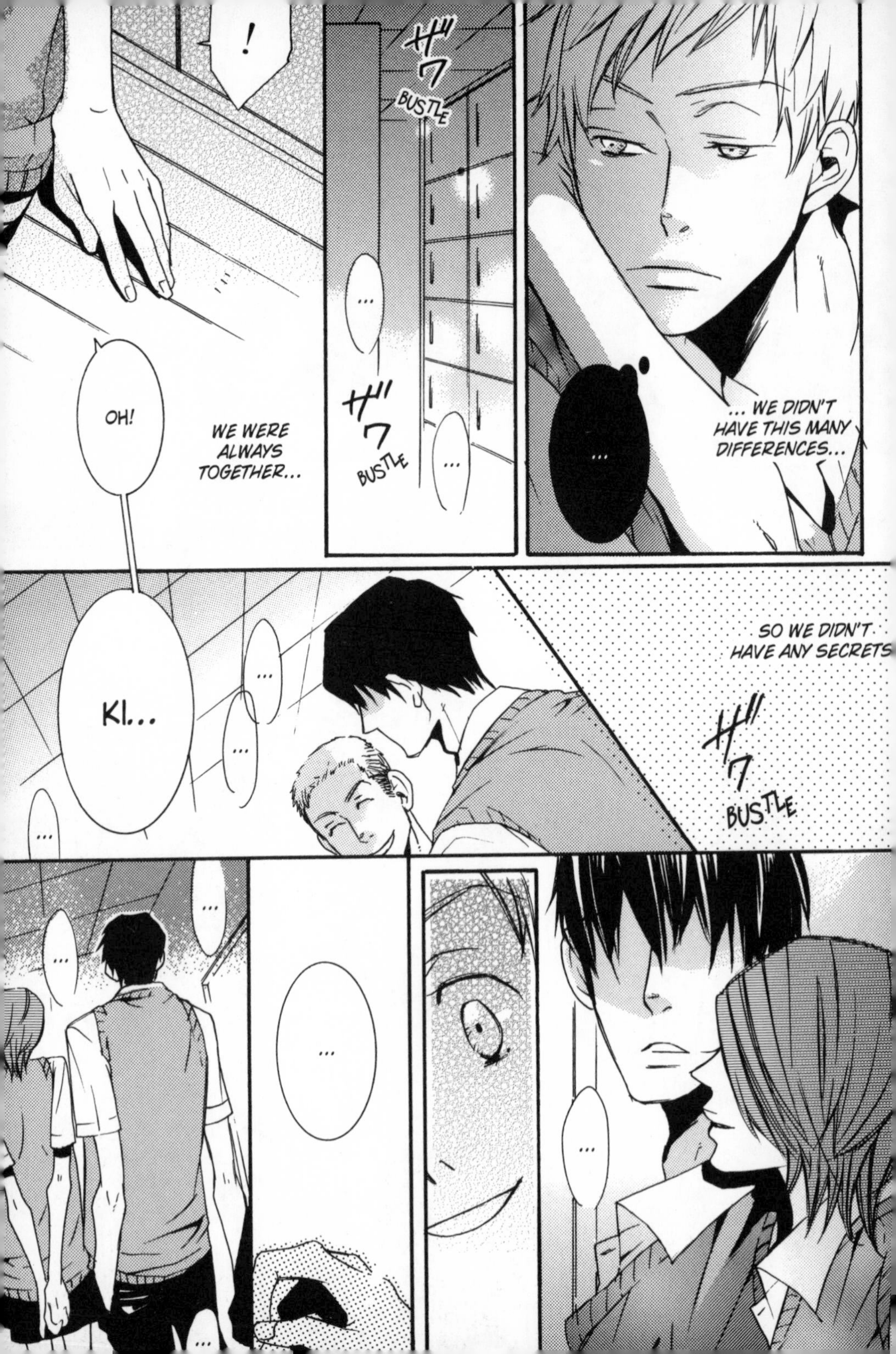

... WE DIDN'T HAVE THIS MANY DIFFERENCES...
...
ザワ
BUSTLE
...
ザワ
BUSTLE
...
!
WE WERE ALWAYS TOGETHER...
OH!
SO WE DIDN'T HAVE ANY SECRETS
ザワ
BUSTLE
...
...
KI...
...
...
...
...
...
...
...

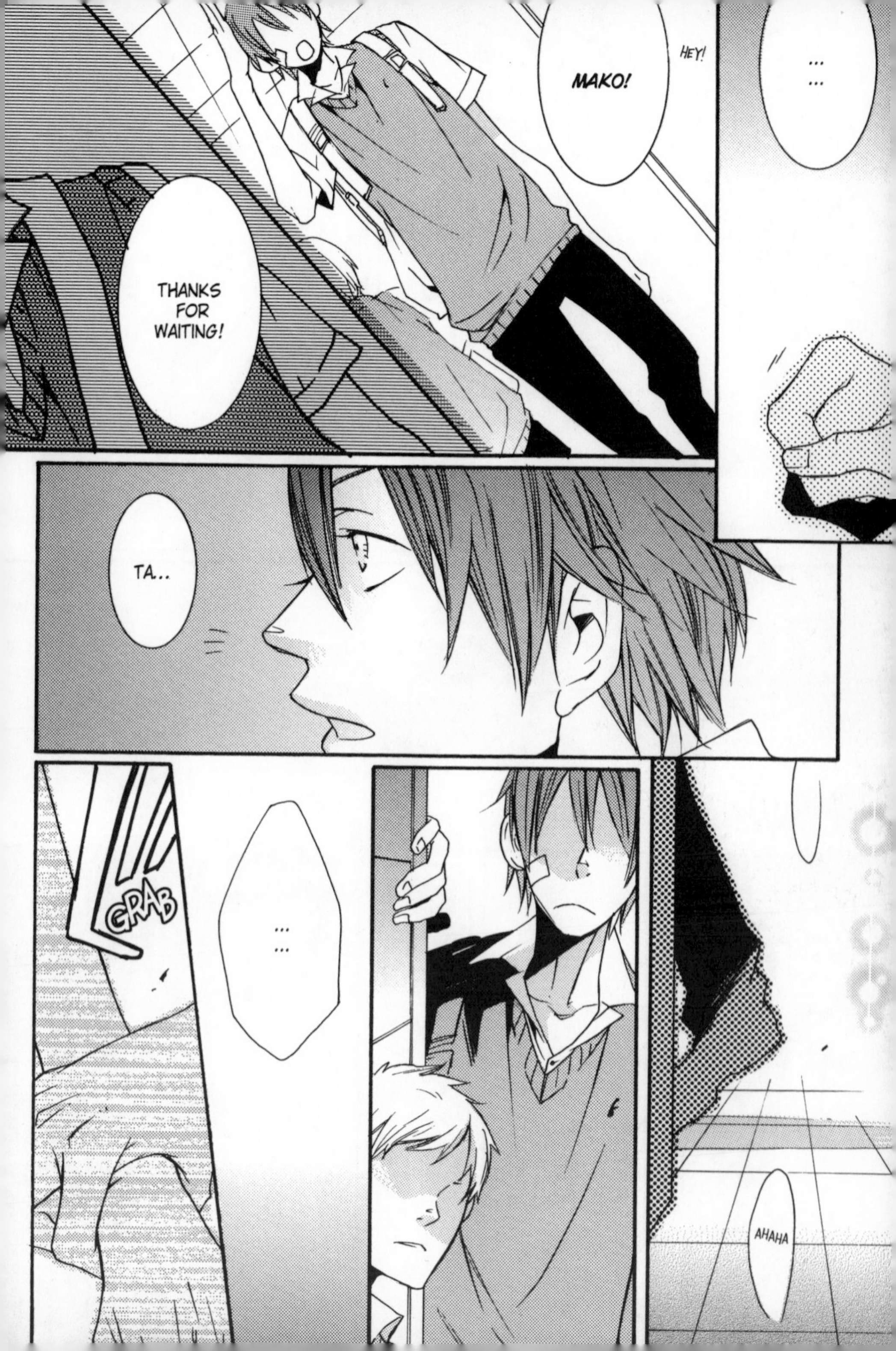
... ...
HEY!
MAKO!
THANKS FOR WAITING!
TA...
AHAHA
... ...
GRAB

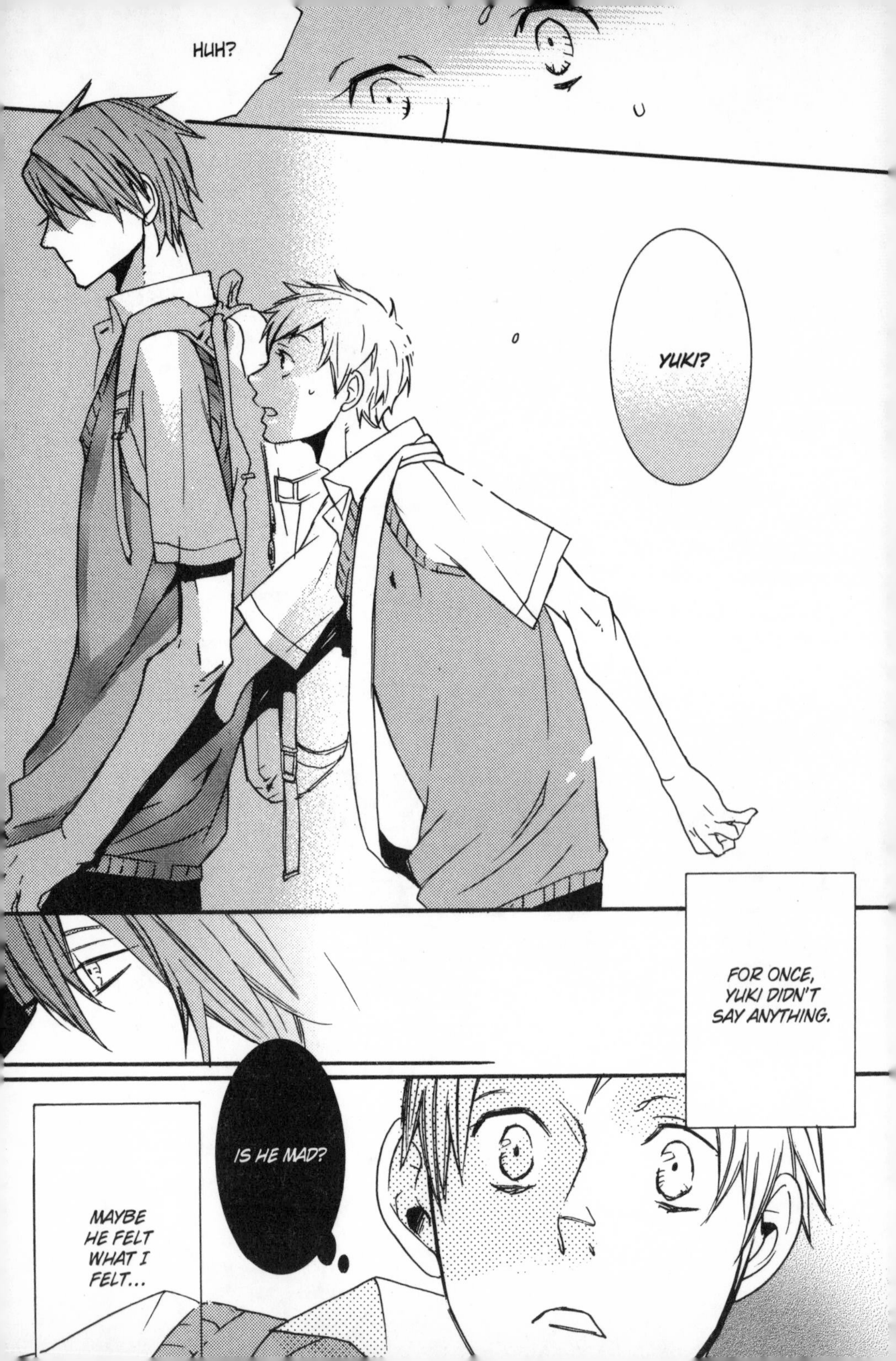
HUH?
YUKI?
FOR ONCE, YUKI DIDN'T SAY ANYTHING.
IS HE MAD?
MAYBE HE FELT WHAT I FELT...

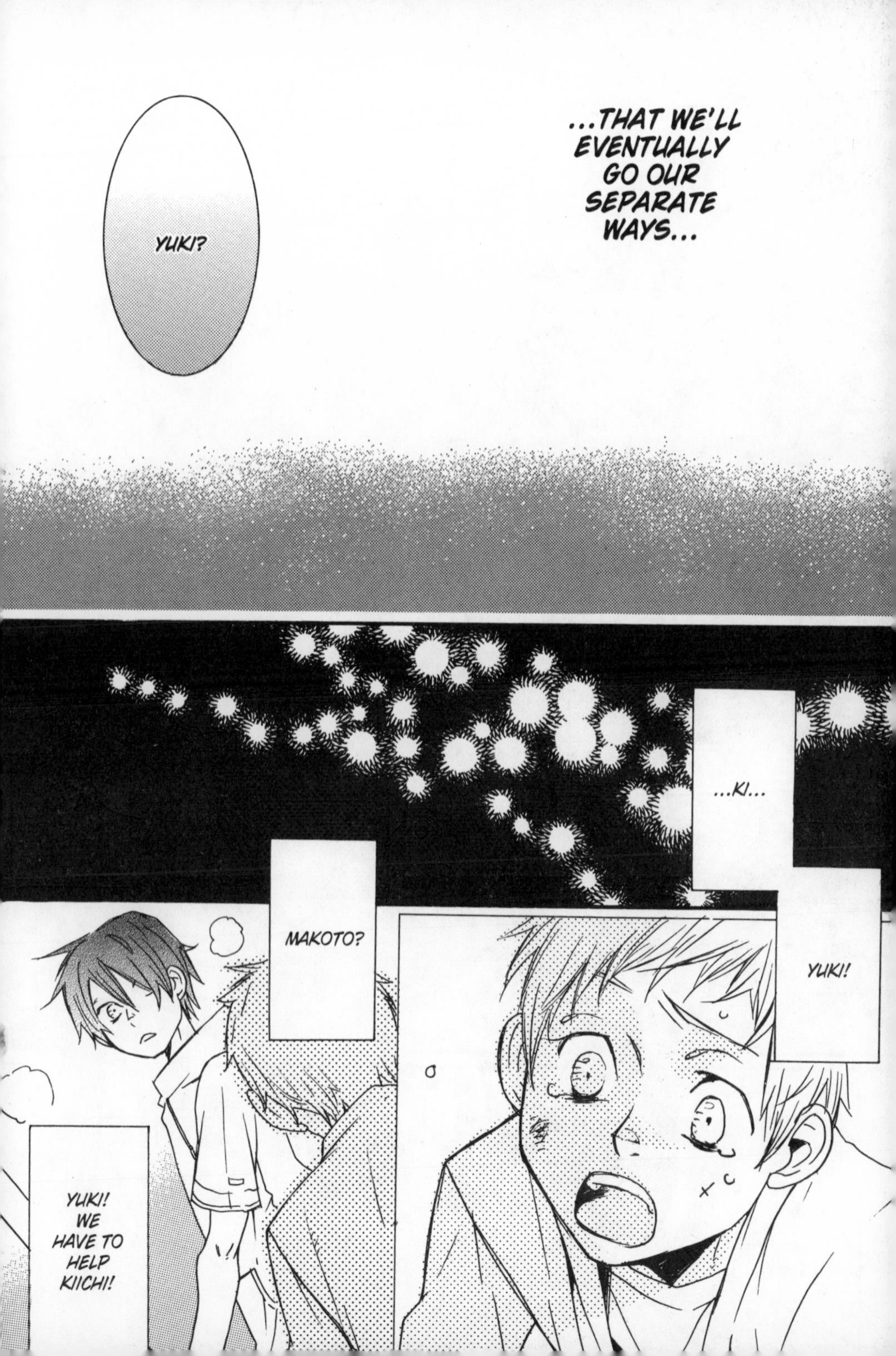
...THAT WE'LL EVENTUALLY GO OUR SEPARATE WAYS...
YUKI?
...KI...
YUKI!
MAKOTO?
YUKI! WE HAVE TO HELP KIICHI!

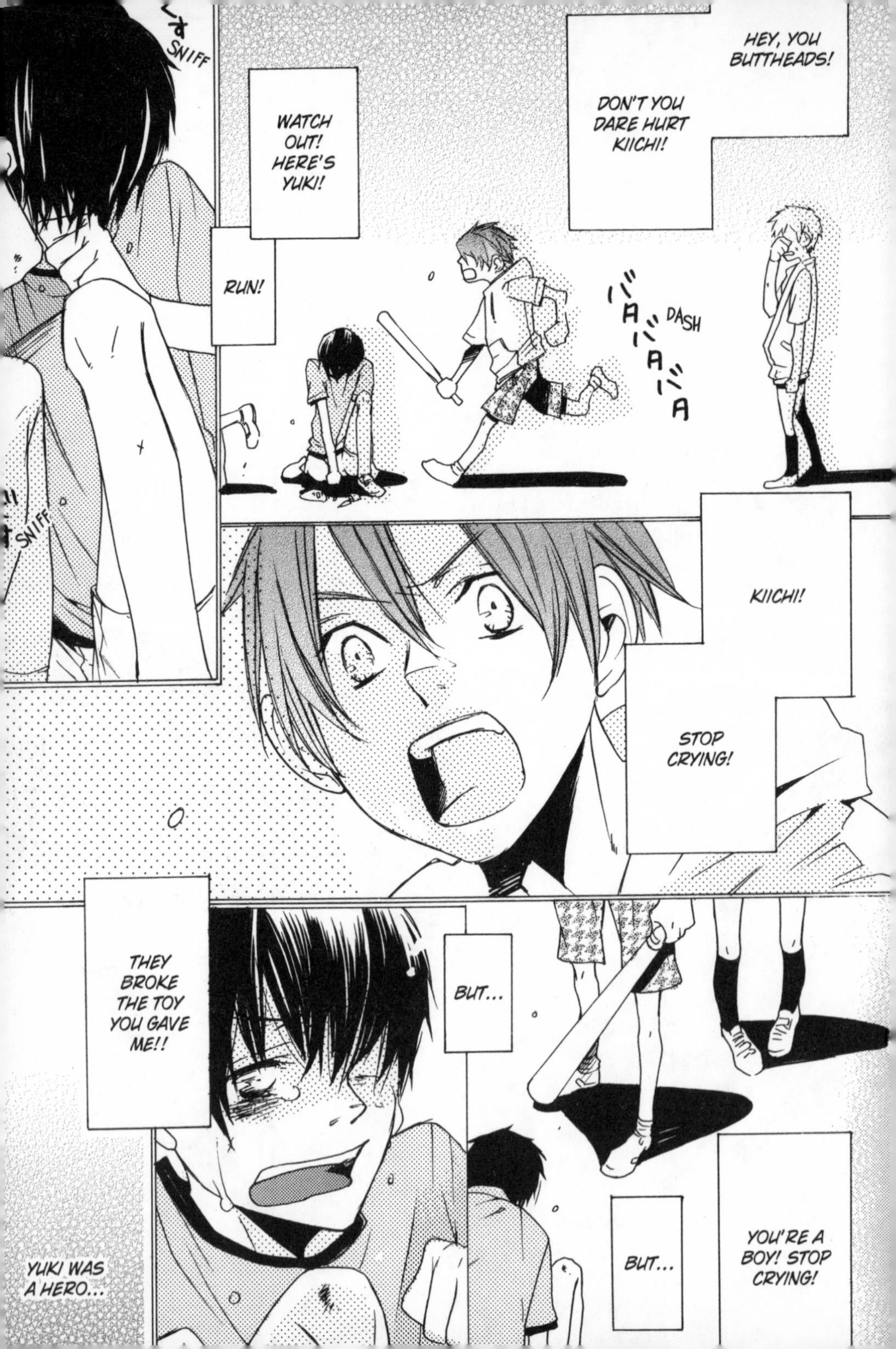
HEY, YOU BUTTHEADS!
DON'T YOU DARE HURT KIICHI!
WATCH OUT! HERE'S YUKI!
RUN!
DASH
KIICHI!
STOP CRYING!
SNIFF
SNIFF
YOU'RE A BOY! STOP CRYING!
BUT...
BUT...
THEY BROKE THE TOY YOU GAVE ME!!
YUKI WAS A HERO...

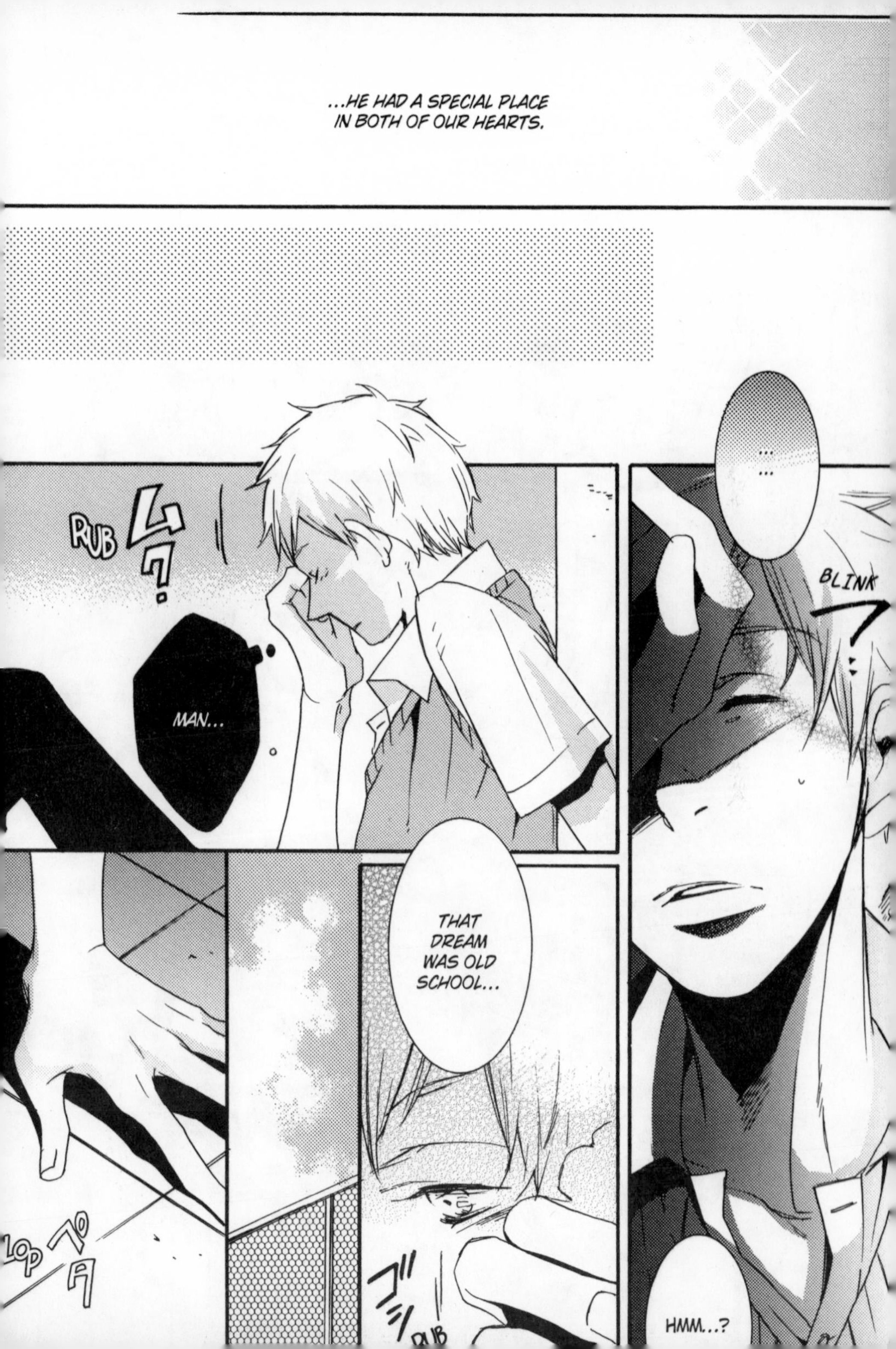
...HE HAD A SPECIAL PLACE IN BOTH OF OUR HEARTS.
......
BLINK
HMM...?
RUB
MAN...
THAT DREAM WAS OLD SCHOOL...
FLOP

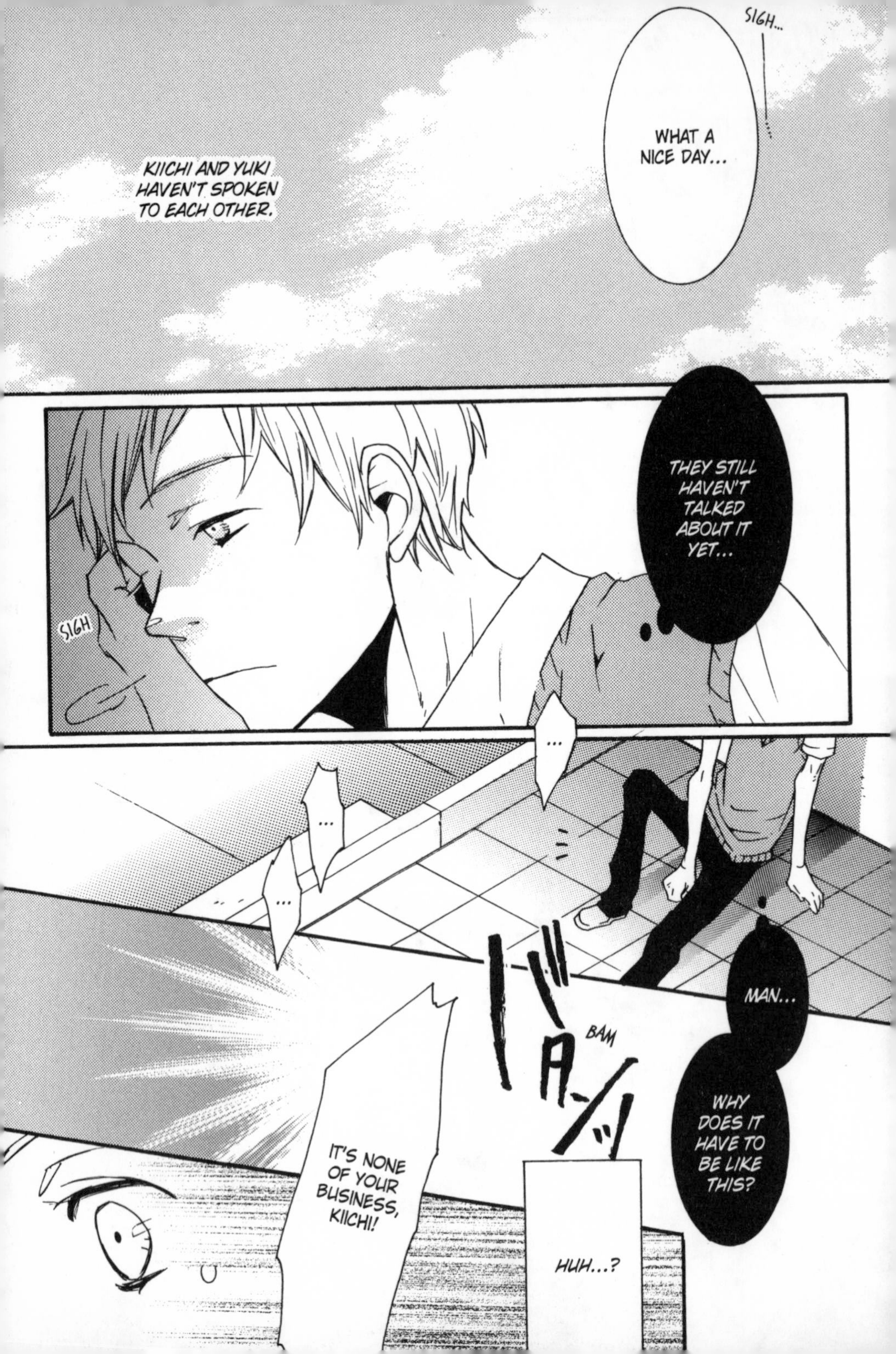

SIGH...
WHAT A NICE DAY...
KIICHI AND YUKI HAVEN'T SPOKEN TO EACH OTHER.
THEY STILL HAVEN'T TALKED ABOUT IT YET...
SIGH
...
...
...
MAN...
WHY DOES IT HAVE TO BE LIKE THIS?
BAM
IT'S NONE OF YOUR BUSINESS, KIICHI!
HUH...?

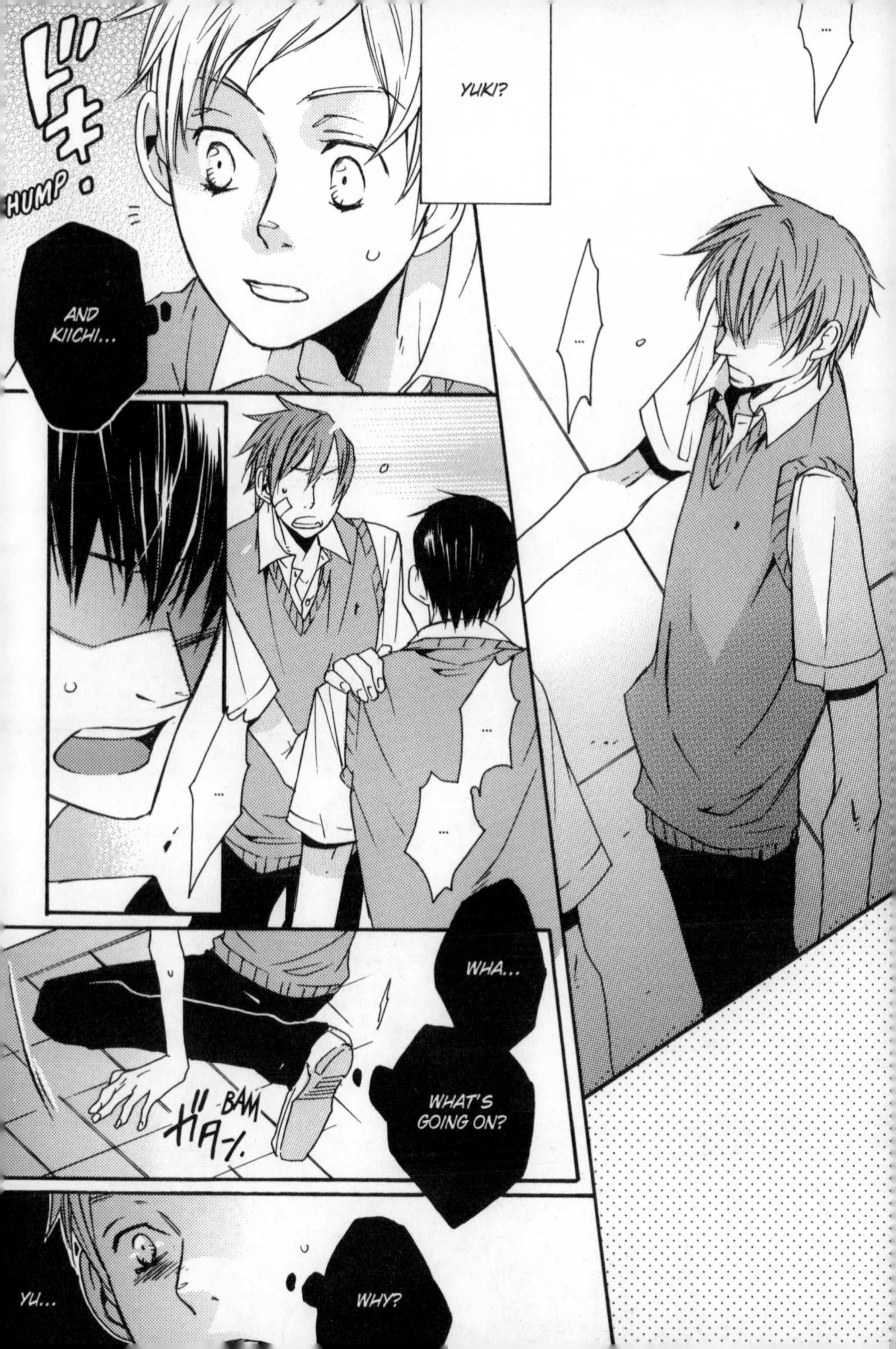...
YUKI?
...
ドキ
HUMP
AND KIICHI...
...
...
...
...
WHA...
WHAT'S GOING ON?
ガターン
BAM
WHY?
YU...

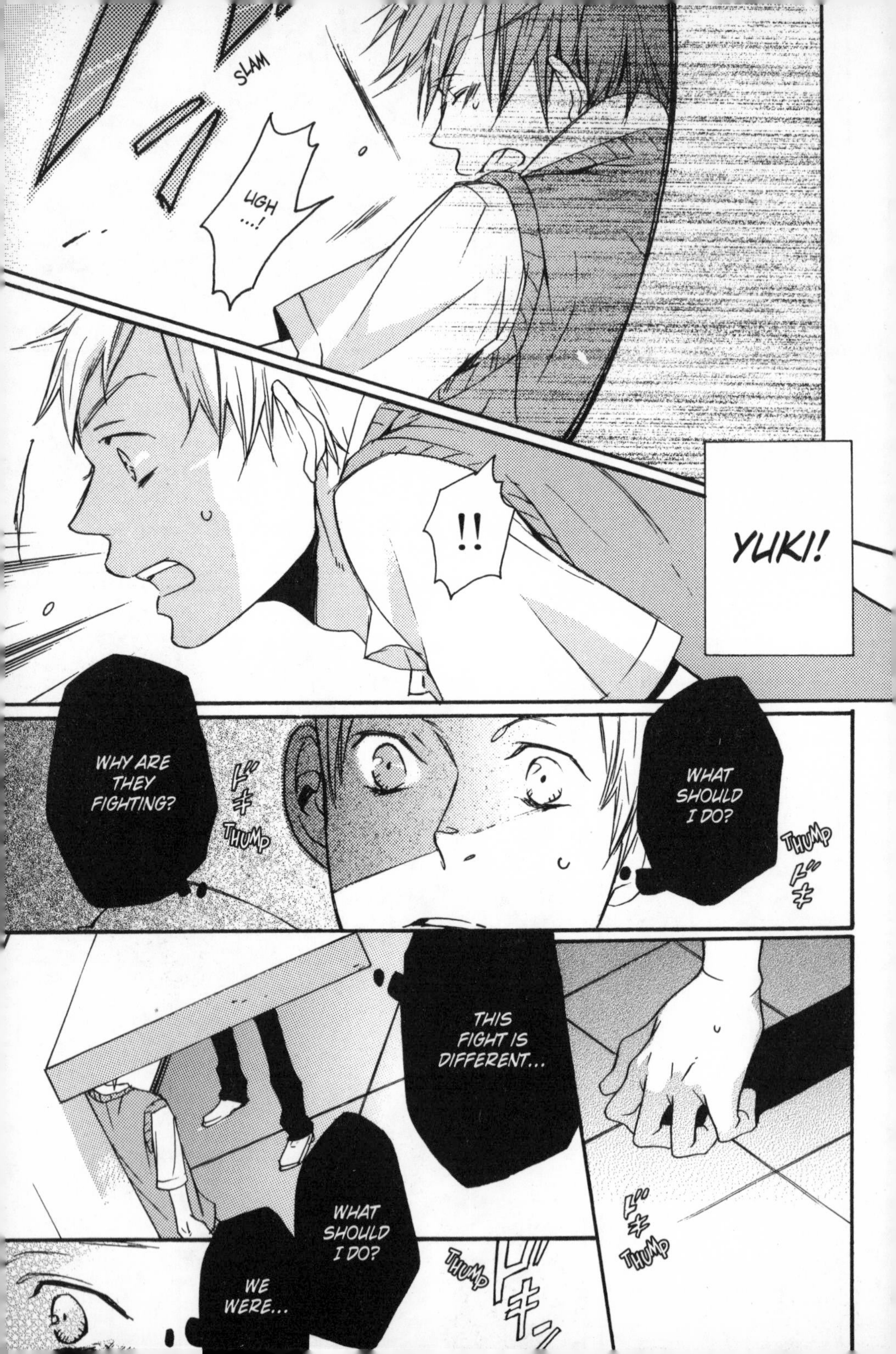

SLAM
UGH ...!
YUKI!
!!
WHAT SHOULD I DO?
THUMP
WHY ARE THEY FIGHTING?
THUMP
THUMP
THIS FIGHT IS DIFFERENT...
WHAT SHOULD I DO?
THUMP
WE WERE...

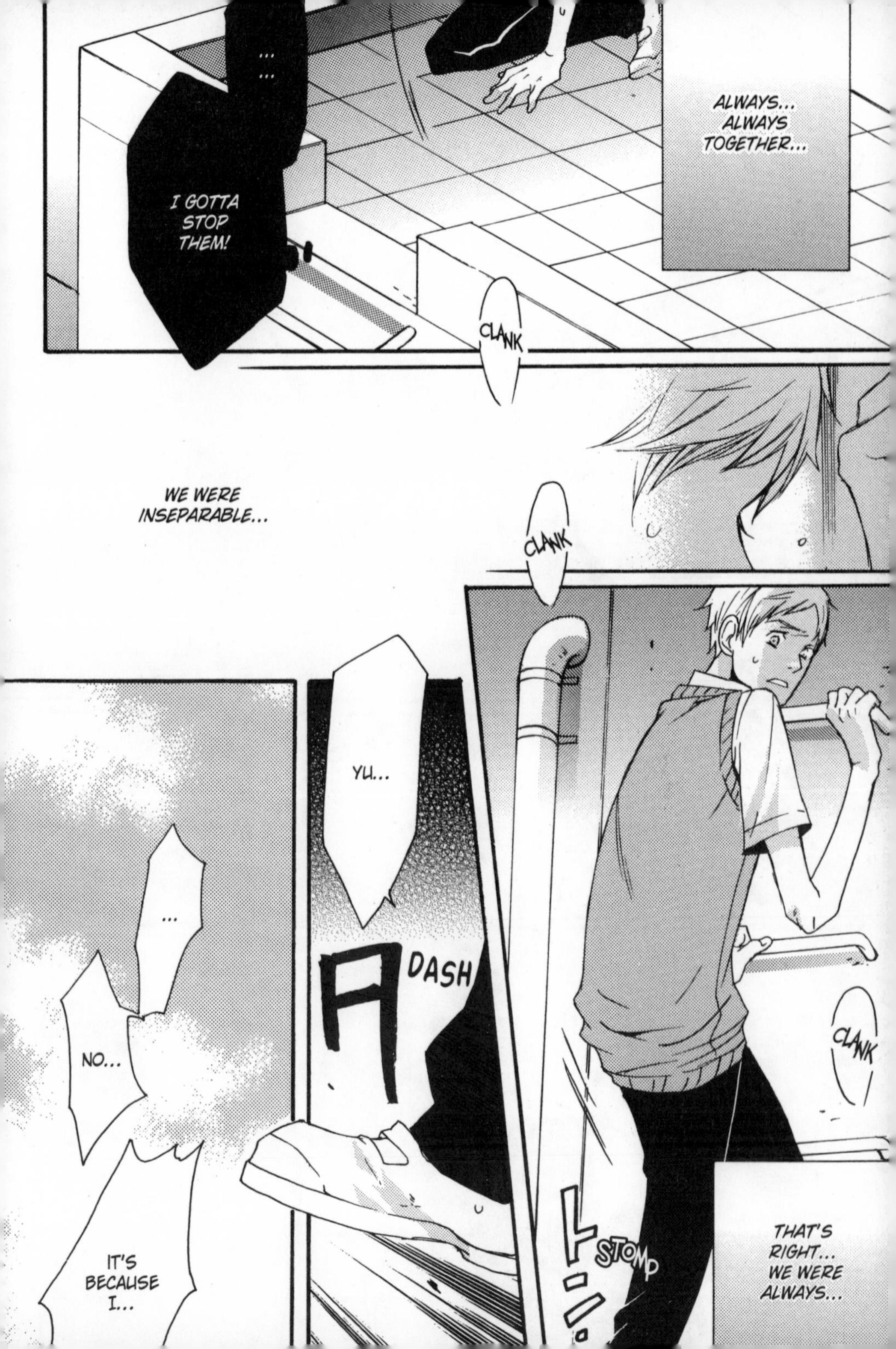
ALWAYS... ALWAYS TOGETHER...
... ...
I GOTTA STOP THEM!
CLANK
CLANK
WE WERE INSEPARABLE...
CLANK
THAT'S RIGHT... WE WERE ALWAYS...
STOMP
YU...
DASH
...
NO...
IT'S BECAUSE I...

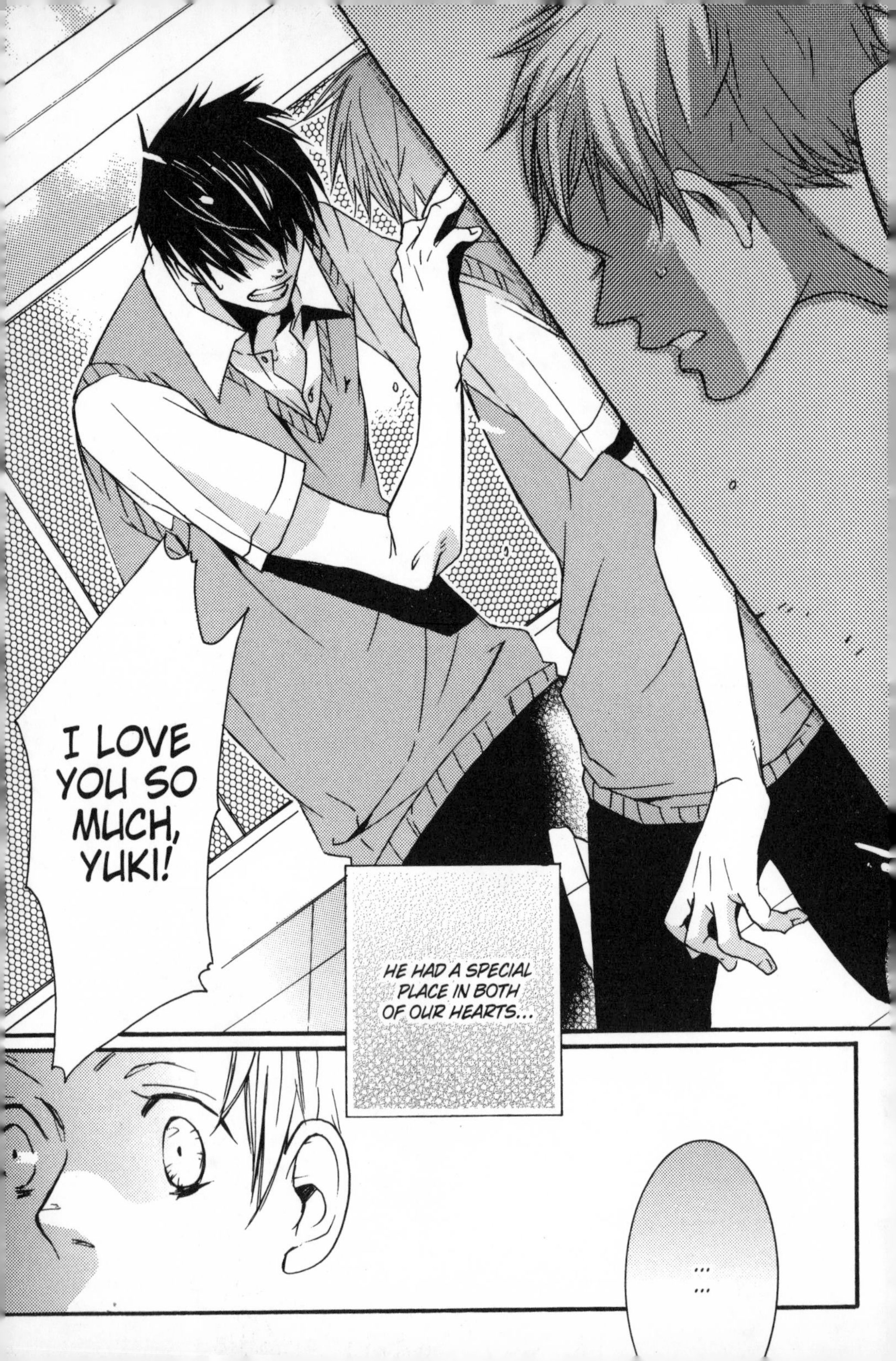
I LOVE YOU SO MUCH, YUKI!
HE HAD A SPECIAL PLACE IN BOTH OF OUR HEARTS...
... ...

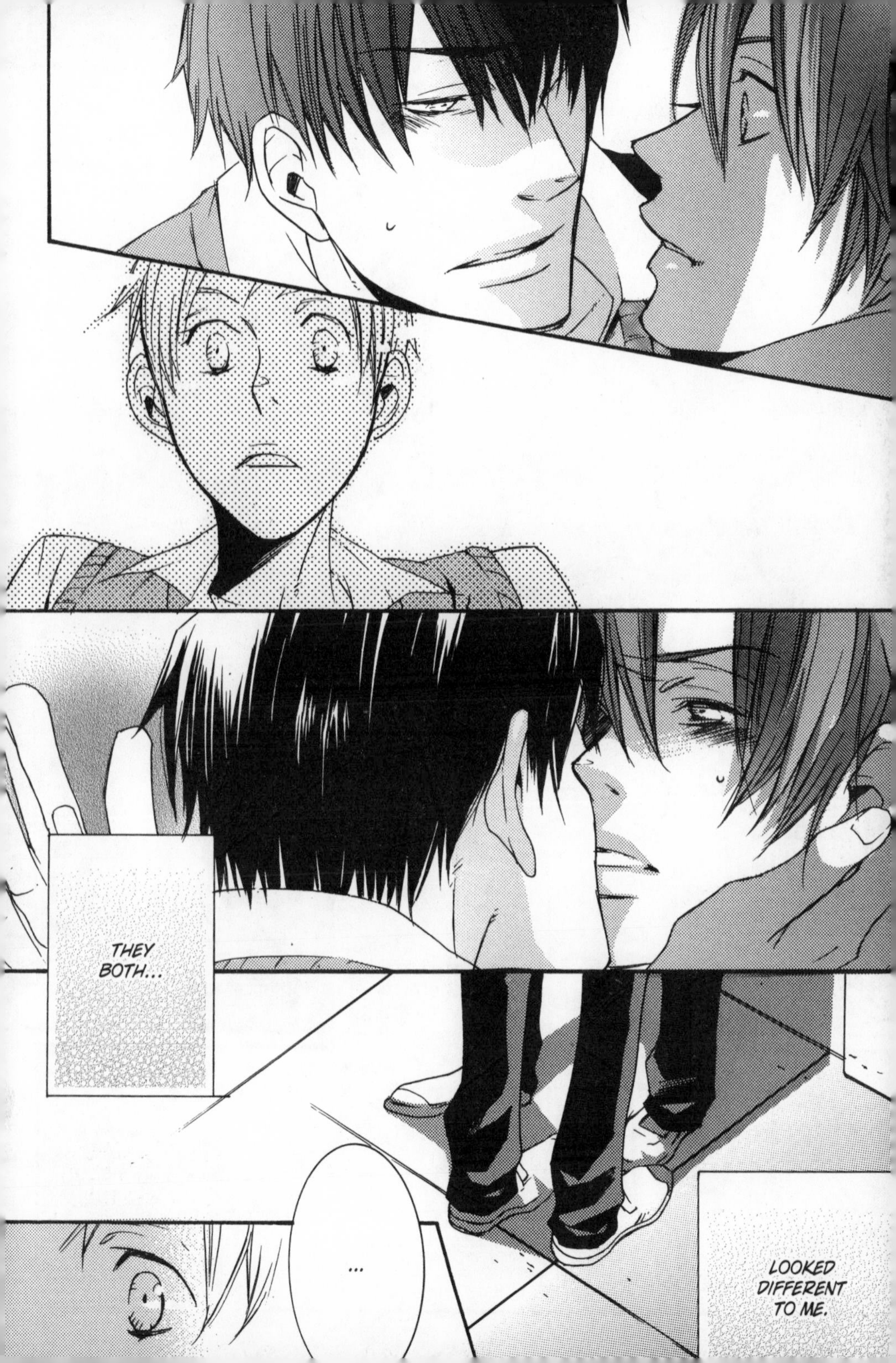
THEY BOTH...
LOOKED DIFFERENT TO ME.
...

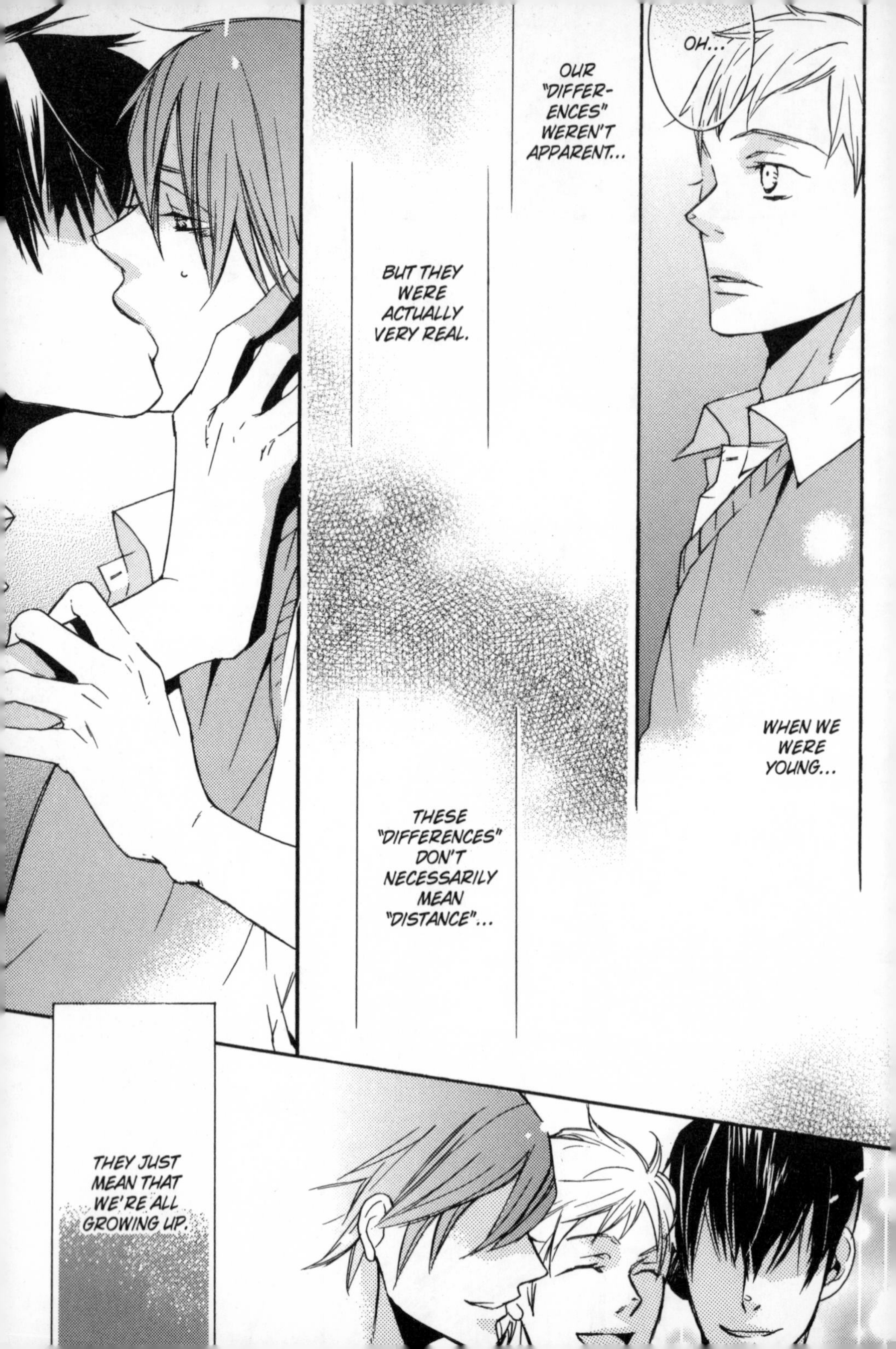
OH...
WHEN WE WERE YOUNG...
OUR "DIFFERENCES" WEREN'T APPARENT...
BUT THEY WERE ACTUALLY VERY REAL.
THESE "DIFFERENCES" DON'T NECESSARILY MEAN "DISTANCE"...
THEY JUST MEAN THAT WE'RE ALL GROWING UP.

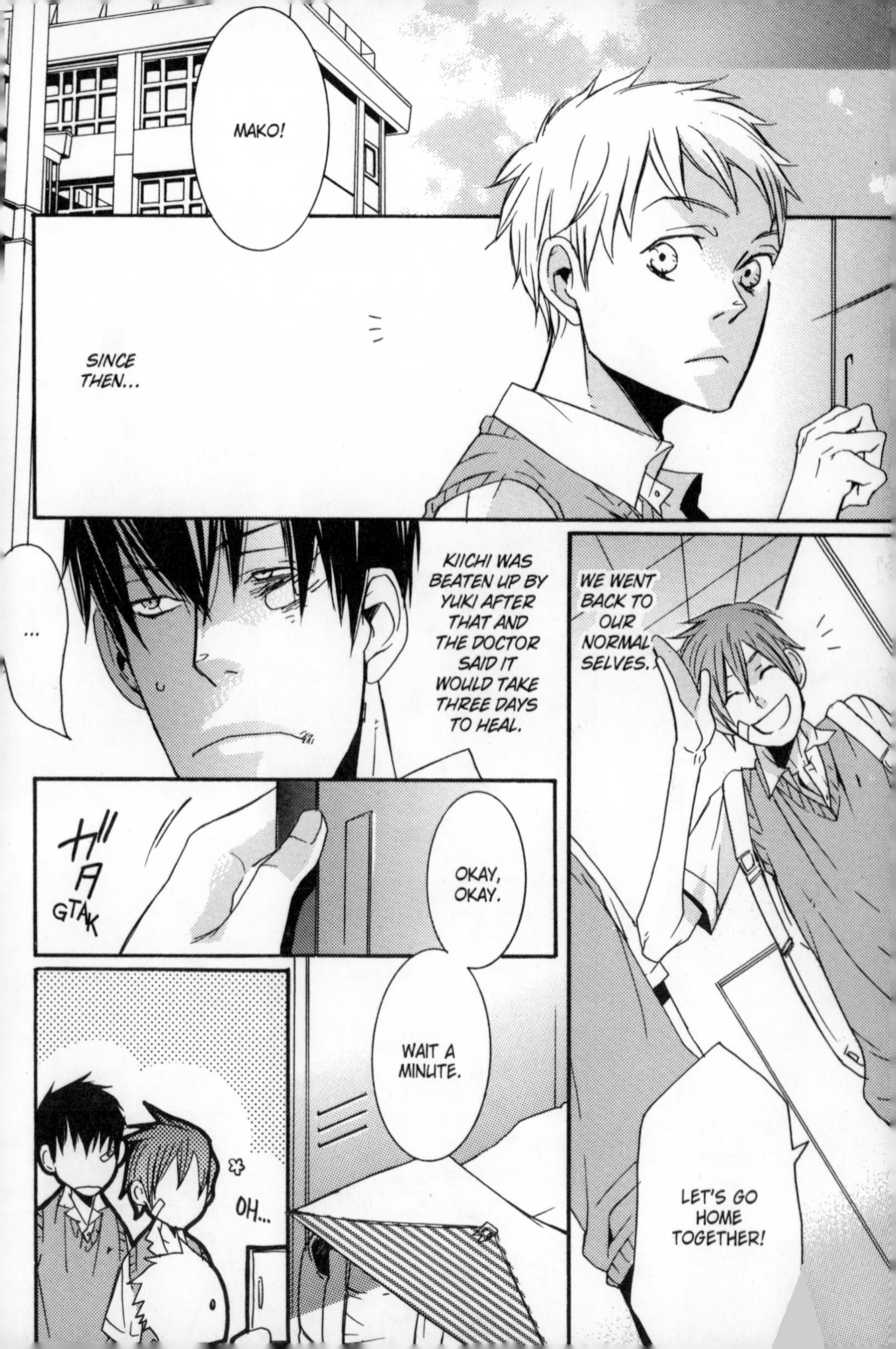
MAKO!
SINCE THEN...
WE WENT BACK TO OUR NORMAL SELVES...
LET'S GO HOME TOGETHER!
KIICHI WAS BEATEN UP BY YUKI AFTER THAT AND THE DOCTOR SAID IT WOULD TAKE THREE DAYS TO HEAL.
...
OKAY, OKAY.
GTAK
WAIT A MINUTE.
OH...

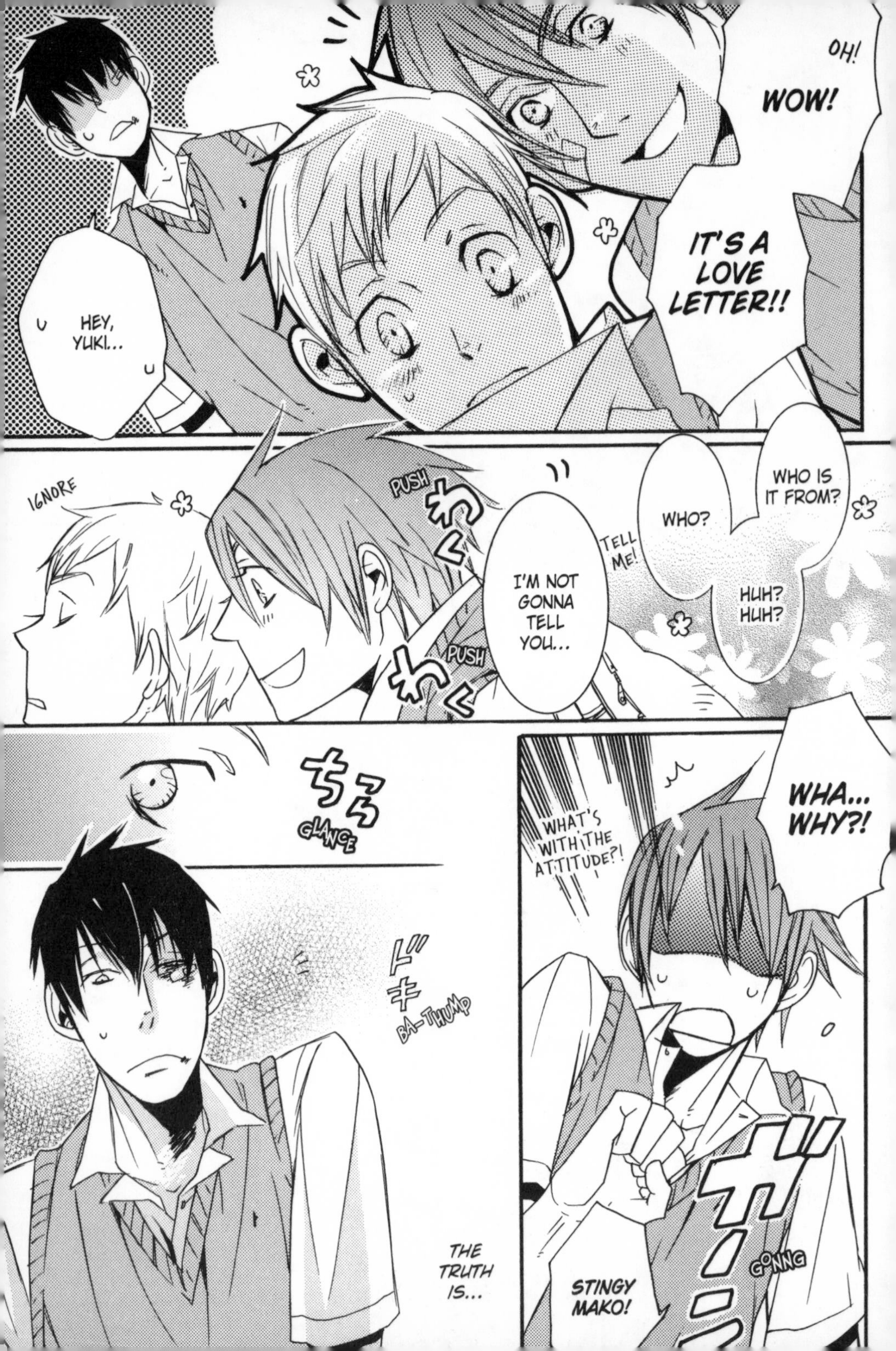
OH!
WOW!
IT'S A LOVE LETTER!!
HEY, YUKI...
WHO IS IT FROM?
WHO?
HUH? HUH?
TELL ME!
I'M NOT GONNA TELL YOU...
PUSH
PUSH
IGNORE
WHA... WHY?!
WHAT'S WITH THE ATTITUDE?!
GONNG
STINGY MAKO!
GLANCE
BA-THUMP
THE TRUTH IS...

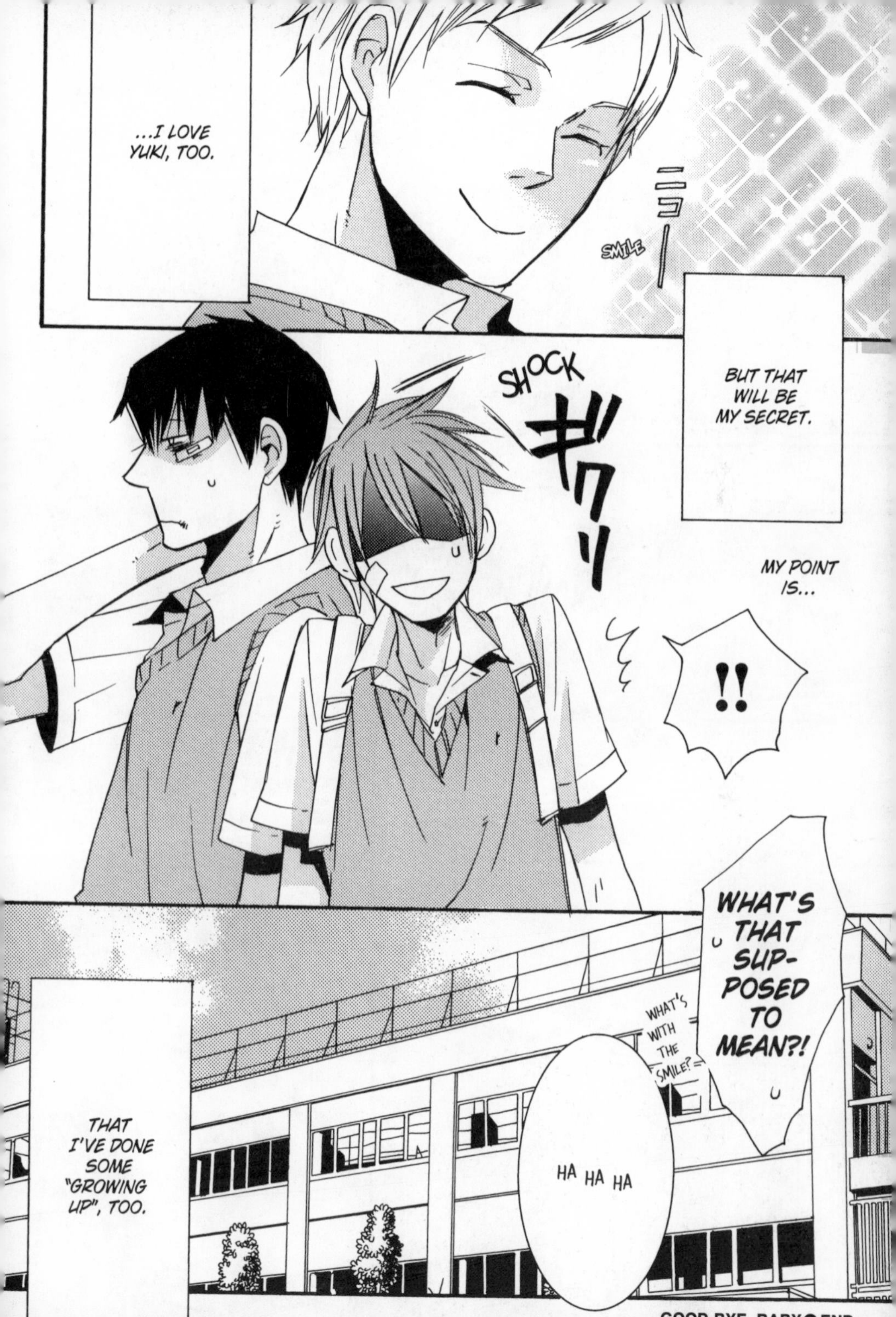
ニコー
SMILE
...I LOVE YUKI, TOO.
BUT THAT WILL BE MY SECRET.
ギクリ
SHOCK
MY POINT IS...
!!
WHAT'S THAT SUP-POSED TO MEAN?!
WHAT'S WITH THE SMILE?
HA HA HA
THAT I'VE DONE SOME "GROWING UP", TOO.

GOOD-BYE, BABY● END

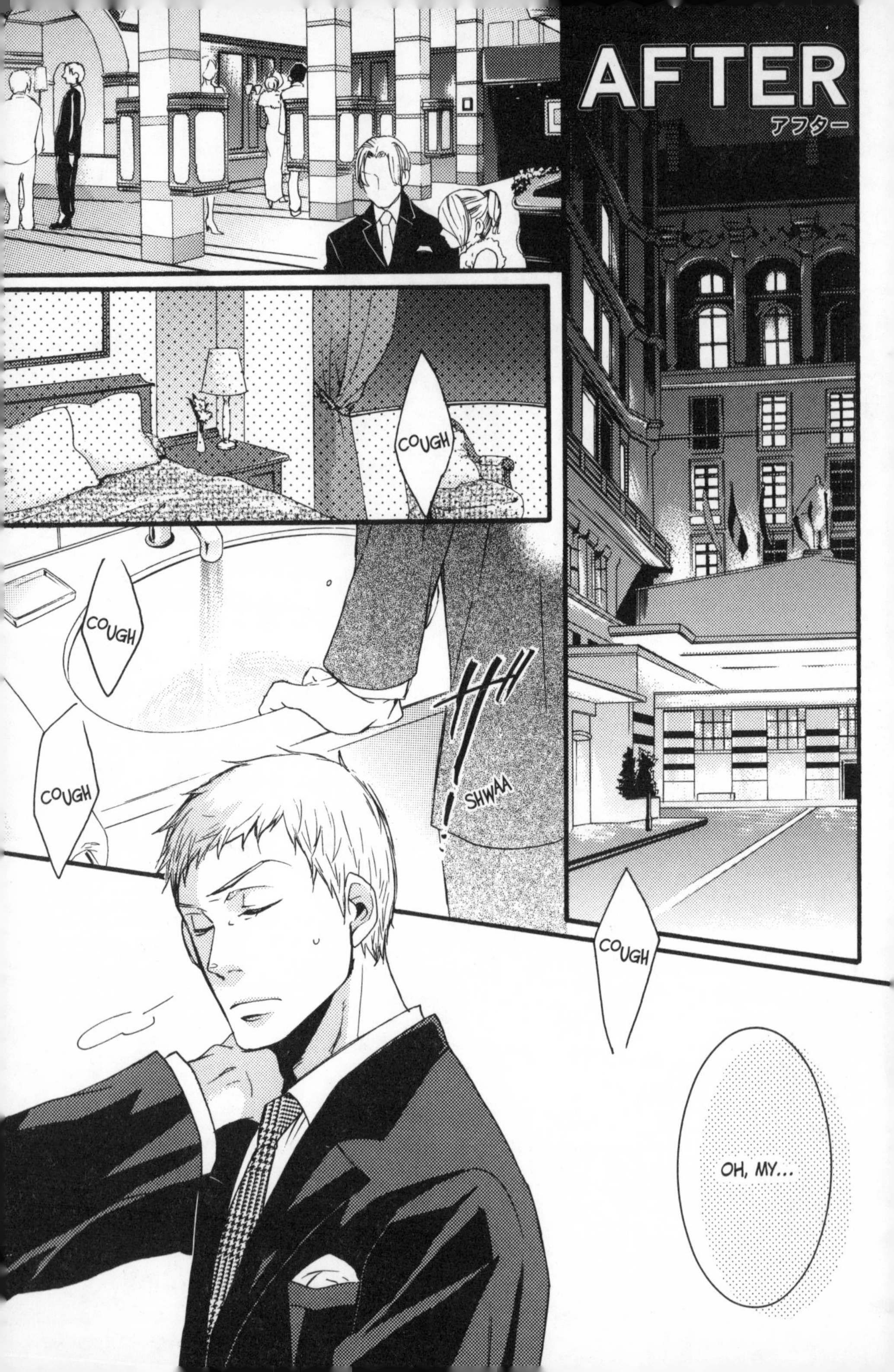

AFTER
アフター
COUGH
COUGH
COUGH
SHWAA
COUGH
OH, MY...

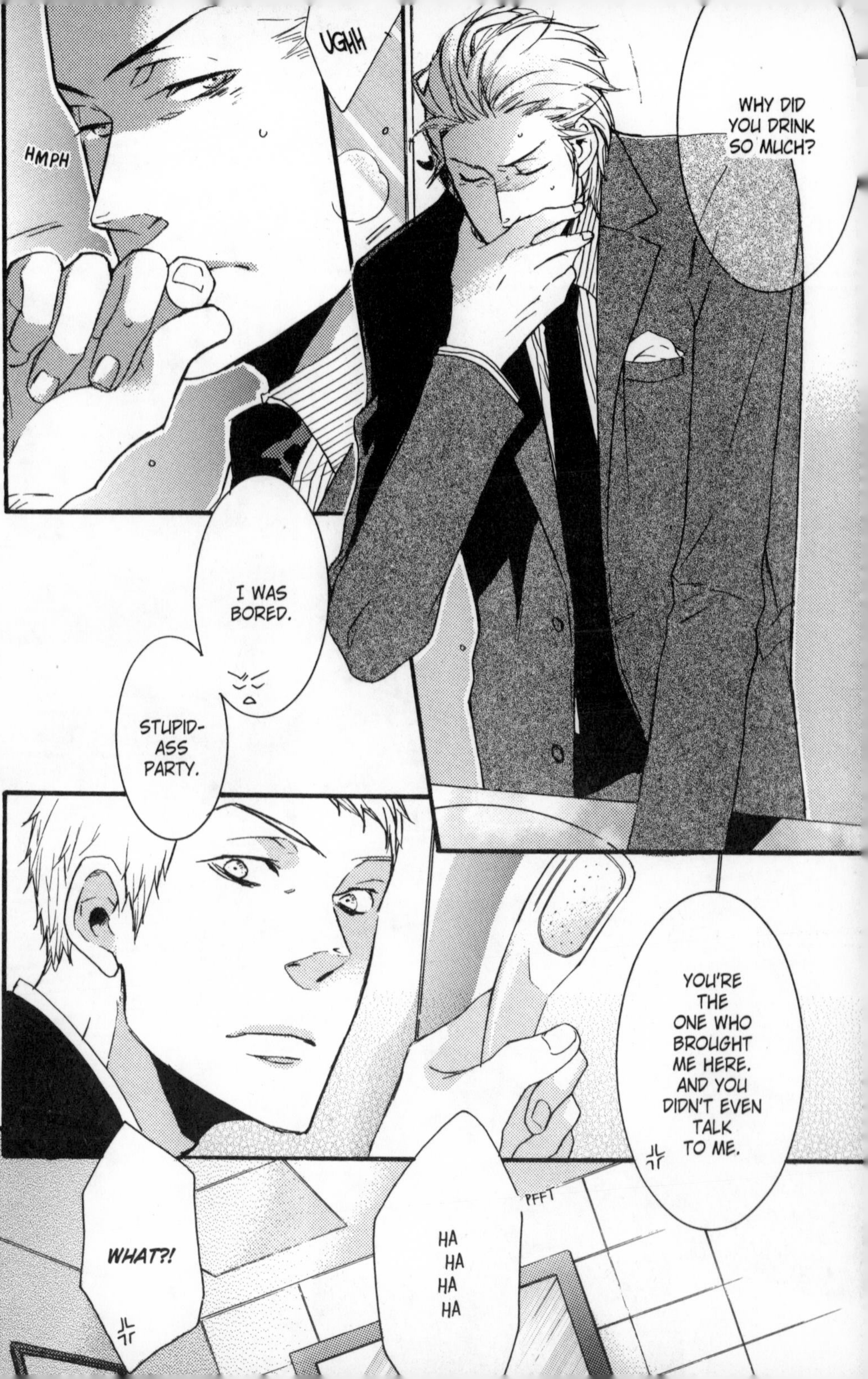
WHY DID YOU DRINK SO MUCH?
UGHH
HMPH
I WAS BORED.
STUPID-ASS PARTY.
YOU'RE THE ONE WHO BROUGHT ME HERE. AND YOU DIDN'T EVEN TALK TO ME.
PFFT
HA HA HA HA
WHAT?!

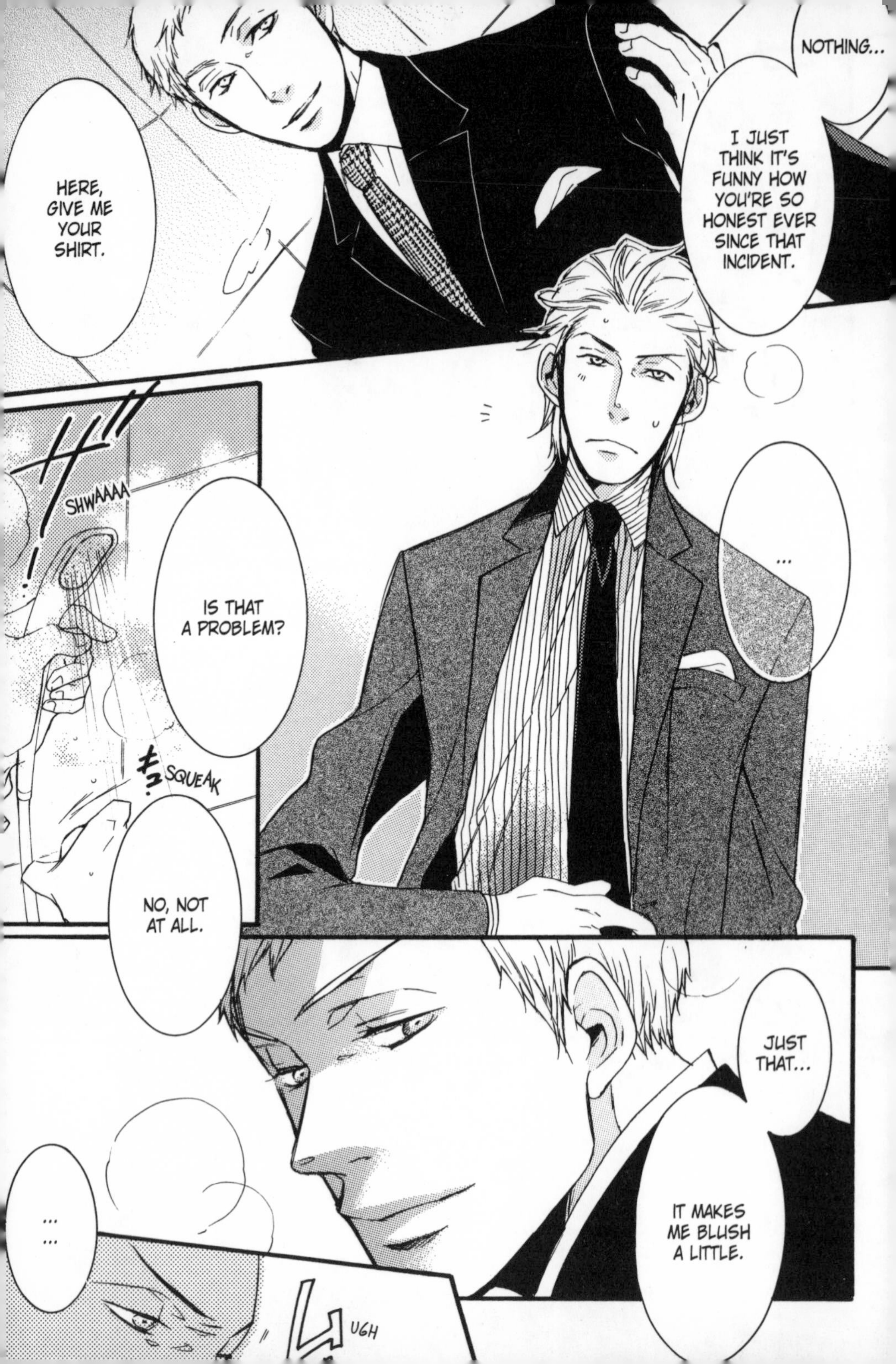
NOTHING...
I JUST THINK IT'S FUNNY HOW YOU'RE SO HONEST EVER SINCE THAT INCIDENT.
HERE, GIVE ME YOUR SHIRT.
...
IS THAT A PROBLEM?
SHWAAAA
SQUEAK
NO, NOT AT ALL.
JUST THAT...
IT MAKES ME BLUSH A LITTLE.
...
...
UGH

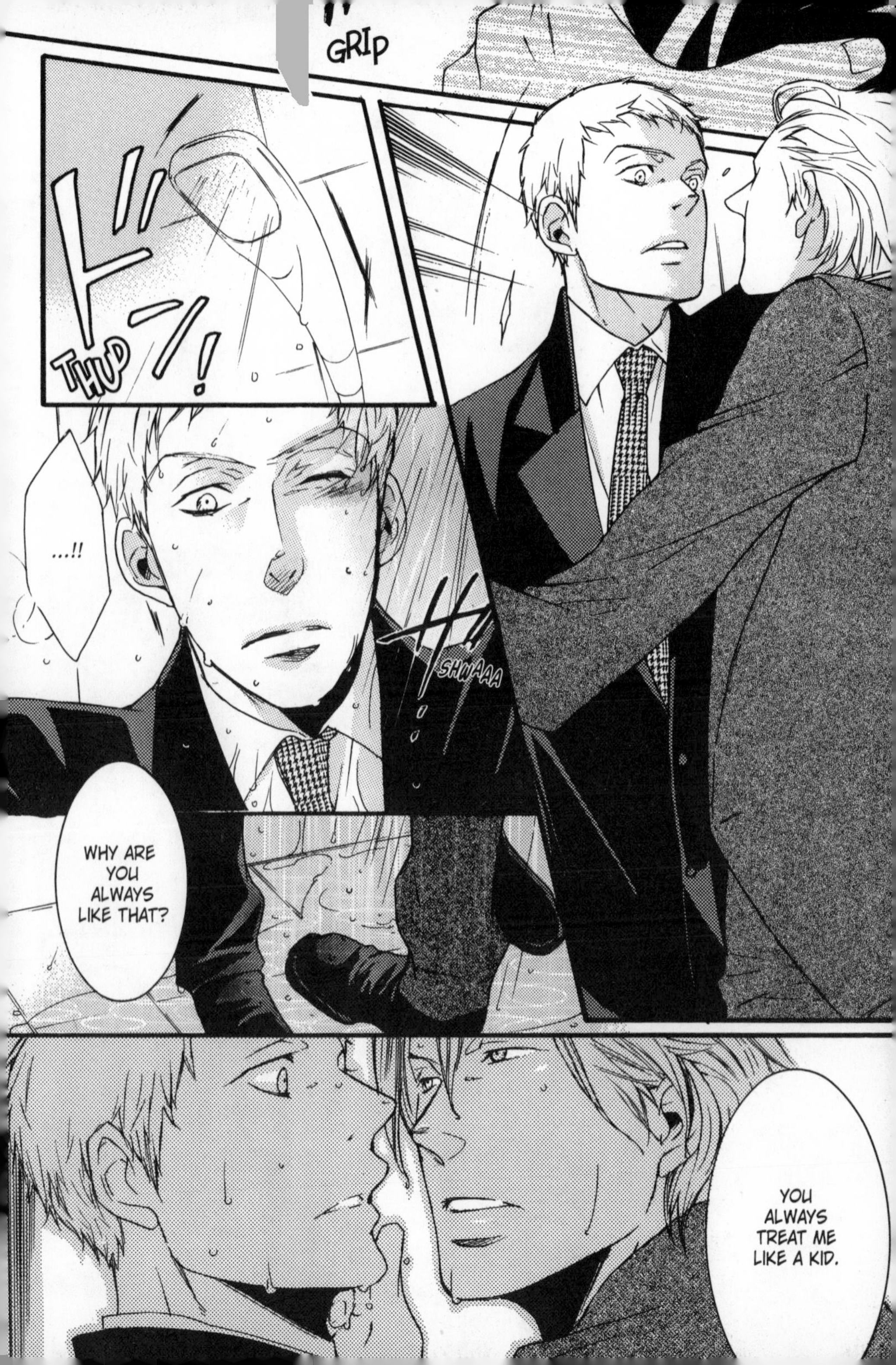
GRIP
SHWAAA
ドン!
THUP
...!!
WHY ARE YOU ALWAYS LIKE THAT?
YOU ALWAYS TREAT ME LIKE A KID.

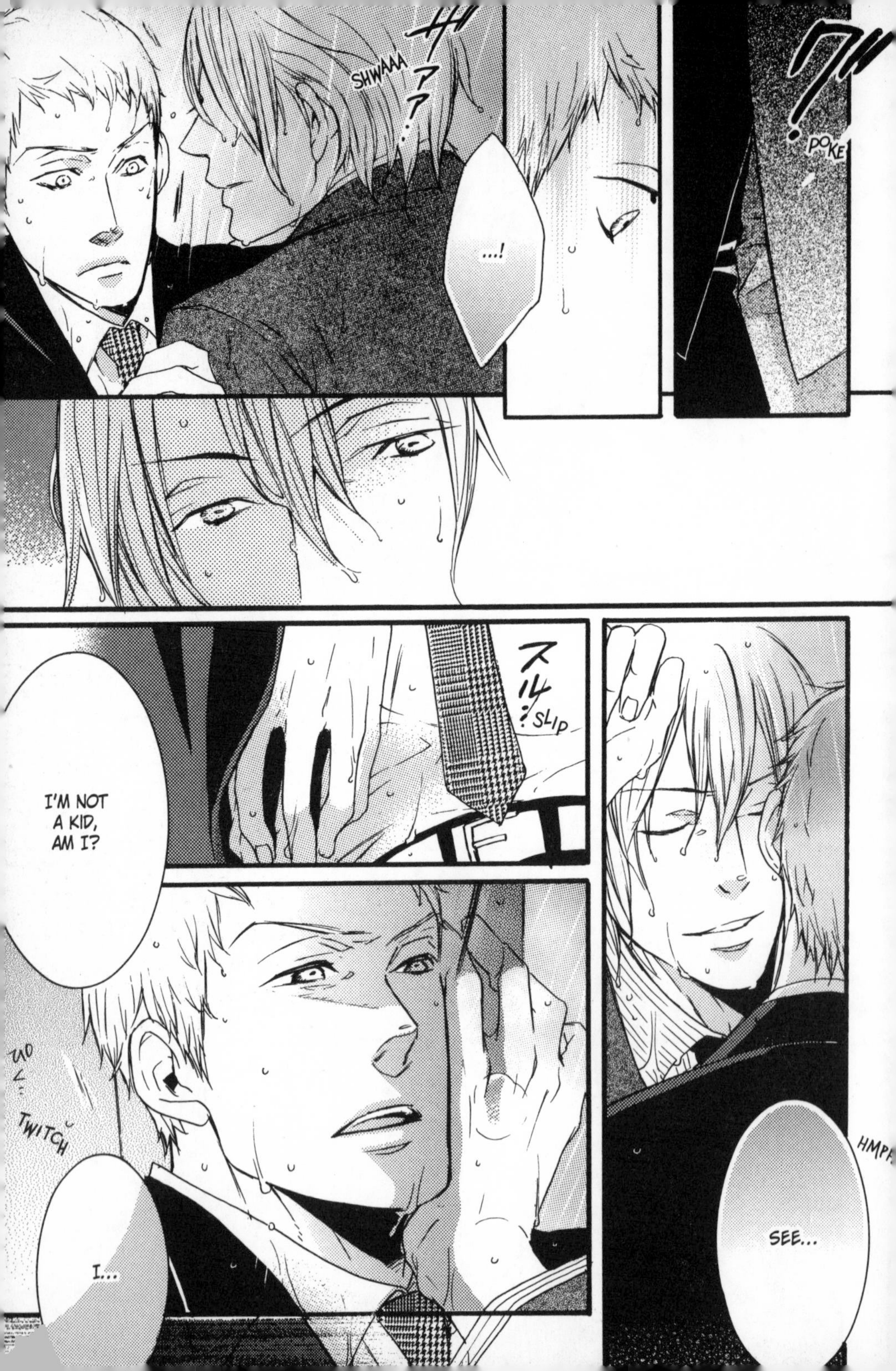

POKE
...!
SHWAAA
SEE...
SLIP
I'M NOT A KID, AM I?
TWITCH
I...

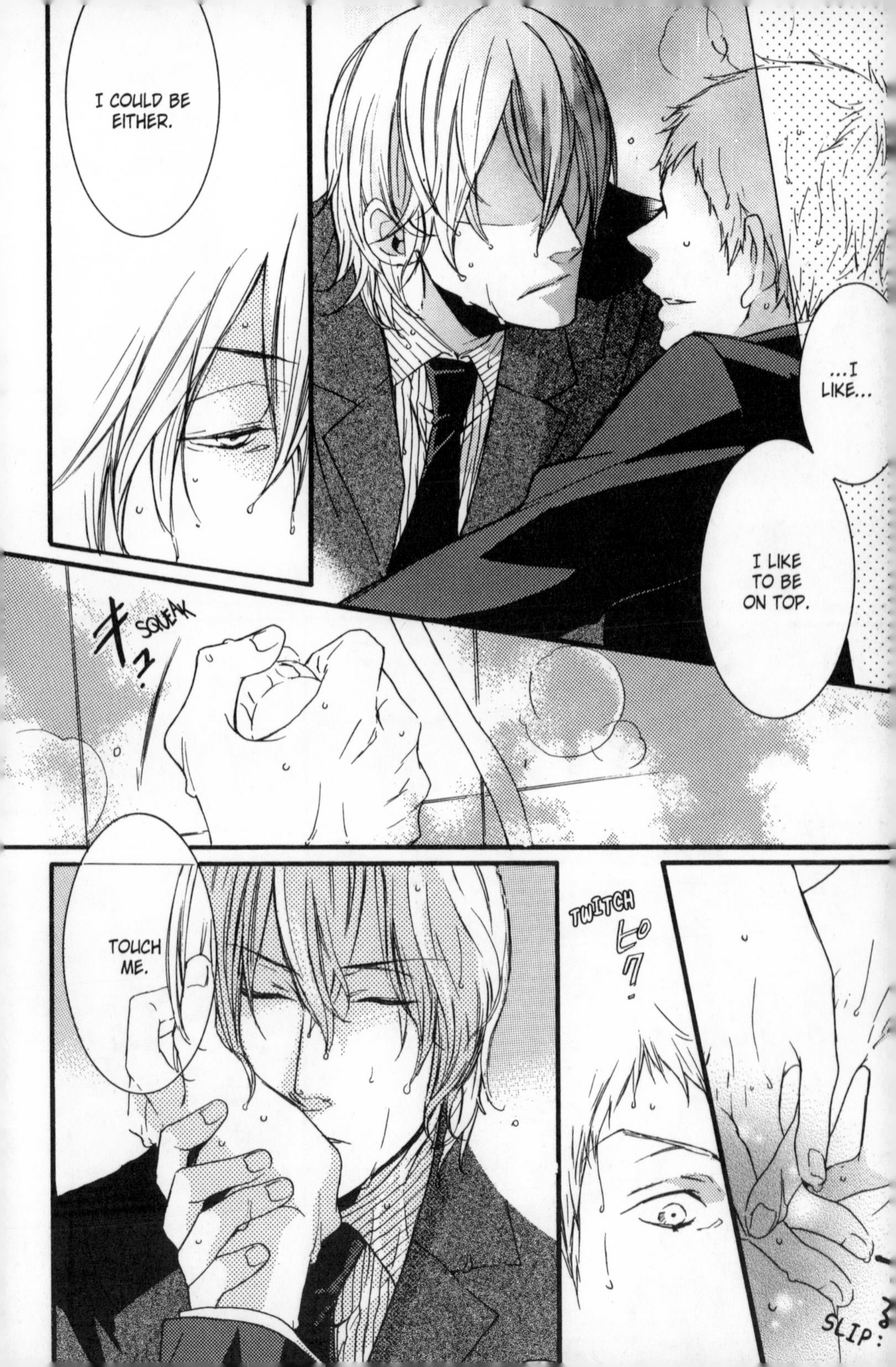

...I LIKE...
I LIKE TO BE ON TOP.
I COULD BE EITHER.
SQUEAK
TWITCH
SLIP
TOUCH ME.

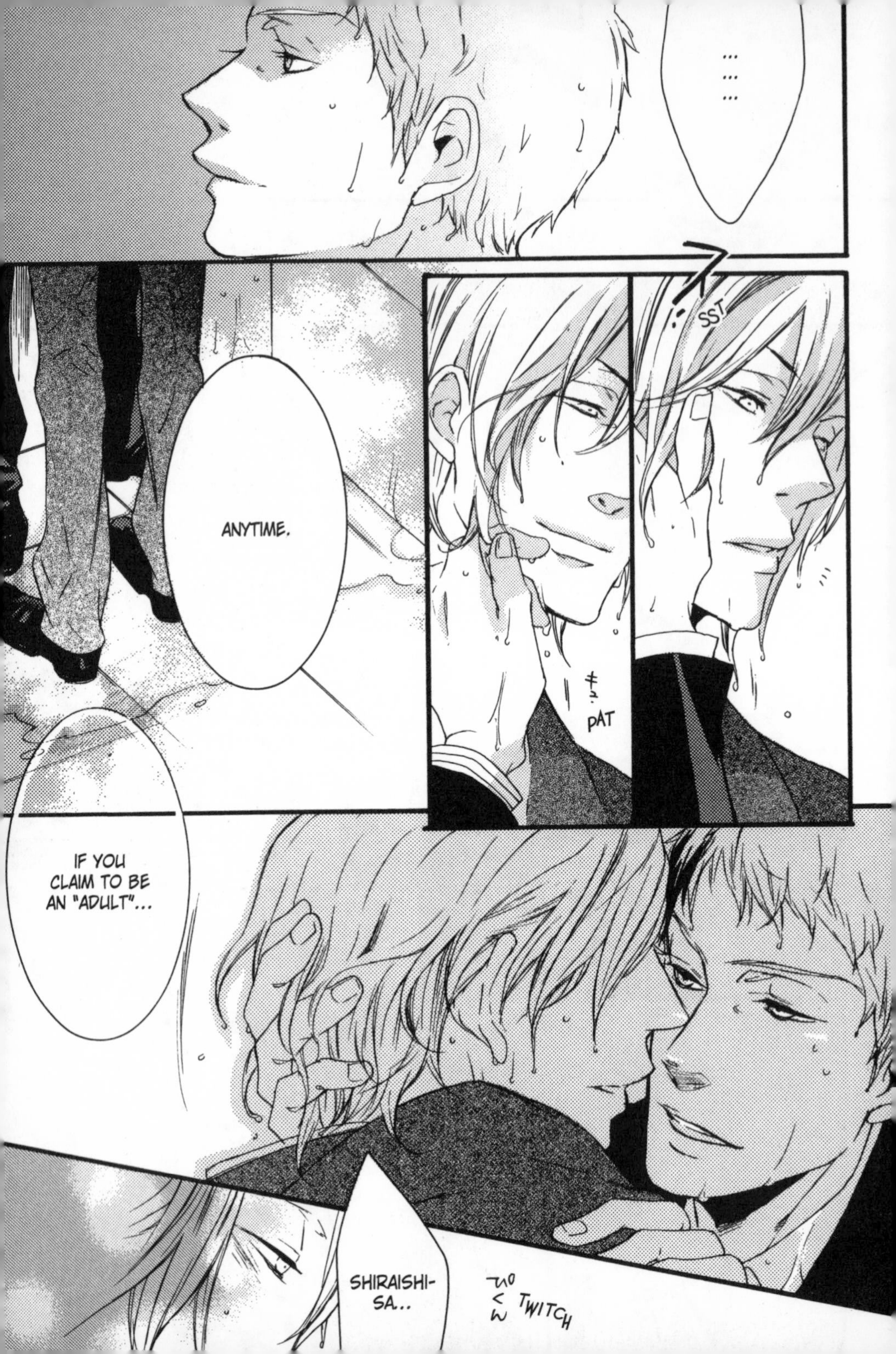

... ...
SST
PAT
ANYTIME.
IF YOU CLAIM TO BE AN "ADULT"...
SHIRAISHI-SA...
TWITCH

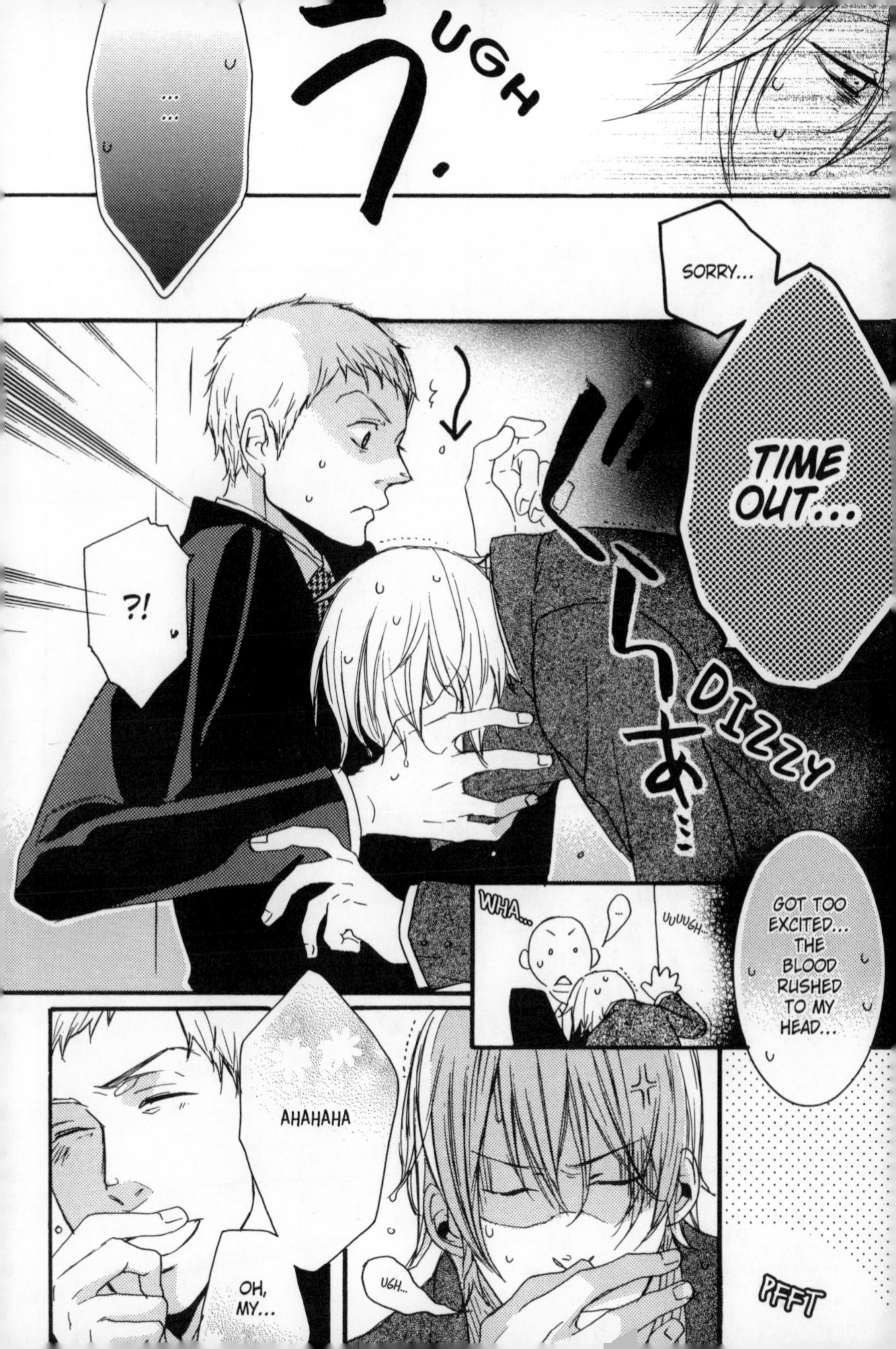
UGH
......
SORRY...
TIME OUT...
DIZZY
?!
GOT TOO EXCITED... THE BLOOD RUSHED TO MY HEAD...
UUUUGH...
...
WHA...
PFFT
UGH...
AHAHAHA
OH, MY...

WELL, WELL...

I GUESS *NEXT* TIME.

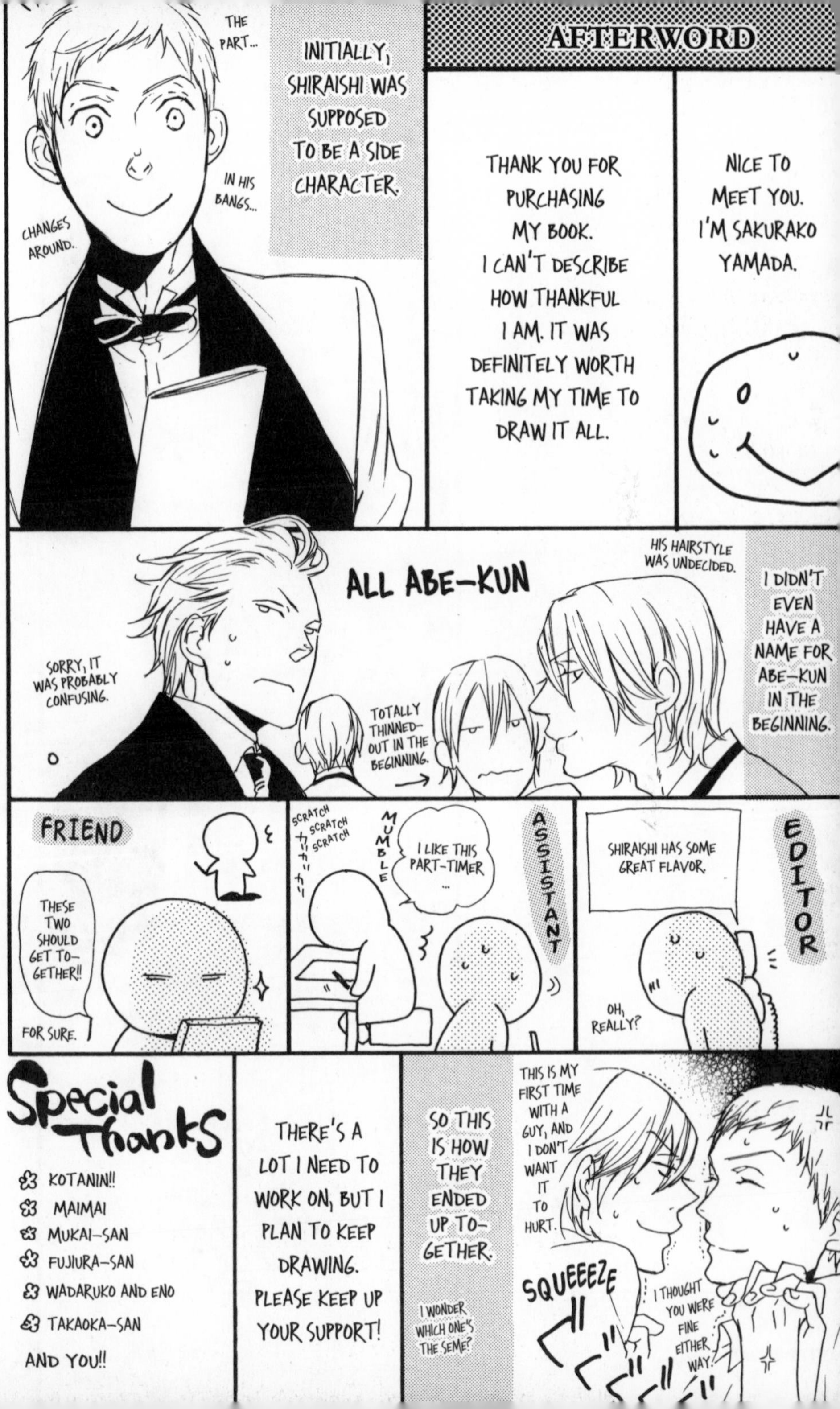
AFTERWORD
NICE TO MEET YOU. I'M SAKURAKO YAMADA.
THANK YOU FOR PURCHASING MY BOOK. I CAN'T DESCRIBE HOW THANKFUL I AM. IT WAS DEFINITELY WORTH TAKING MY TIME TO DRAW IT ALL.
INITIALLY, SHIRAISHI WAS SUPPOSED TO BE A SIDE CHARACTER.
THE PART...
IN HIS BANGS...
CHANGES AROUND.
I DIDN'T EVEN HAVE A NAME FOR ABE-KUN IN THE BEGINNING.
HIS HAIRSTYLE WAS UNDECIDED.
ALL ABE-KUN
TOTALLY THINNED-OUT IN THE BEGINNING.
SORRY, IT WAS PROBABLY CONFUSING.
EDITOR
SHIRAISHI HAS SOME GREAT FLAVOR.
OH, REALLY?
ASSISTANT
MUMBLE
I LIKE THIS PART-TIMER ...
SCRATCH SCRATCH SCRATCH
FRIEND
THESE TWO SHOULD GET TO-GETHER!!
FOR SURE.
THIS IS MY FIRST TIME WITH A GUY, AND I DON'T WANT IT TO HURT.
I THOUGHT YOU WERE FINE EITHER WAY.
SQUEEEZE
SO THIS IS HOW THEY ENDED UP TO-GETHER.
I WONDER WHICH ONE'S THE SEME?
THERE'S A LOT I NEED TO WORK ON, BUT I PLAN TO KEEP DRAWING. PLEASE KEEP UP YOUR SUPPORT!
Special Thanks
KOTANIN!!
MAIMAI
MUKAI-SAN
FUJIURA-SAN
WADARUKO AND ENO
TAKAOKA-SAN
AND YOU!!

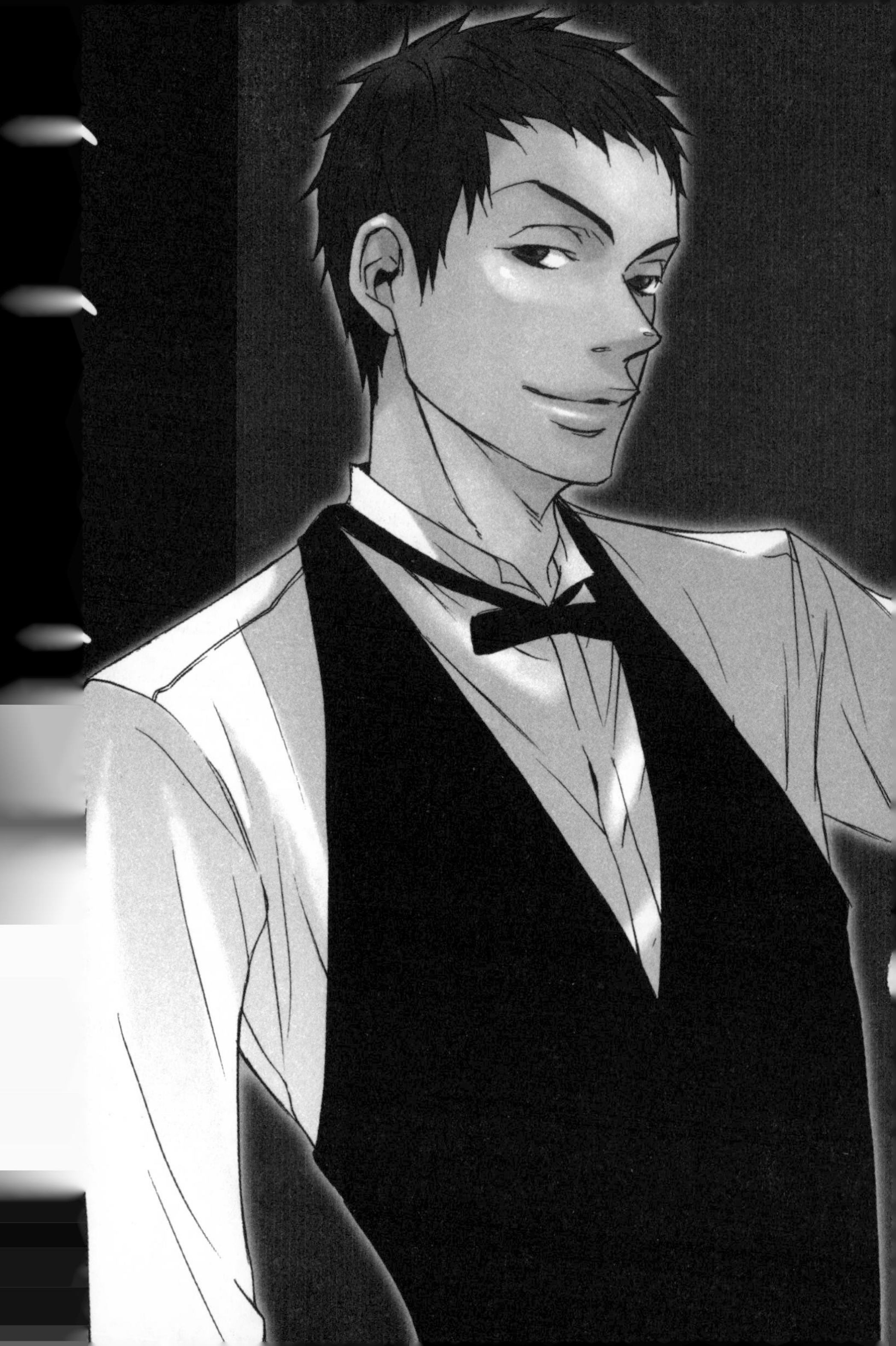

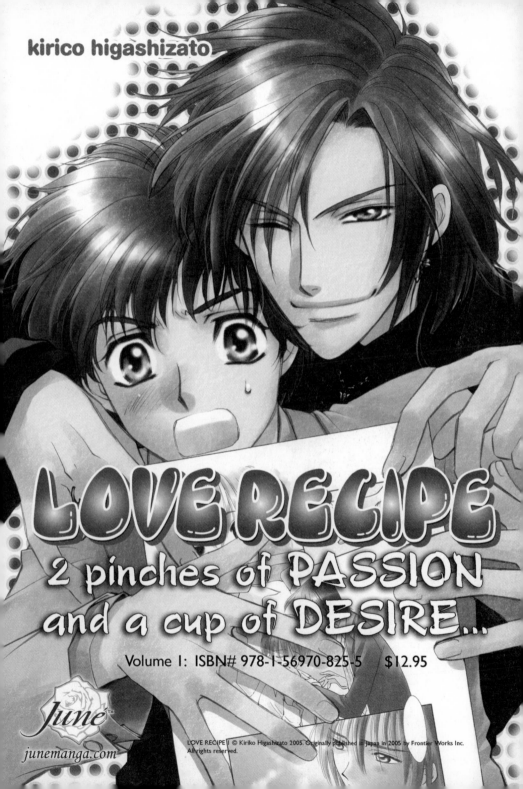

kirico higashizato

LOVE RECIPE
2 pinches of PASSION
and a cup of DESIRE...

Volume 1: ISBN# 978-1-56970-825-5 $12.95

june
junemanga.com

Love is like a Box of Chocolates

...Sweet and Full of Surprises!

Fake fur

Satomi Yamagata

SRP: $12.95

ISBN: 978-1-56970-826-2

June™

junemanga.com

Alcohol, Shirt & Kiss

A NEW DAY, A NEW LOVE

ISBN # 978-1-56970-840-8

$12.95

YUKO KUWABARA

巡査部長
Police Sergeant

june

junemanga.com

ALCOHOL SHIRT & KISS – Sake To Waishatsu To Kiss
© Yuko Kuwabara 2004. Originally published in Japan in 2004
by BIBLOS Co., Ltd.

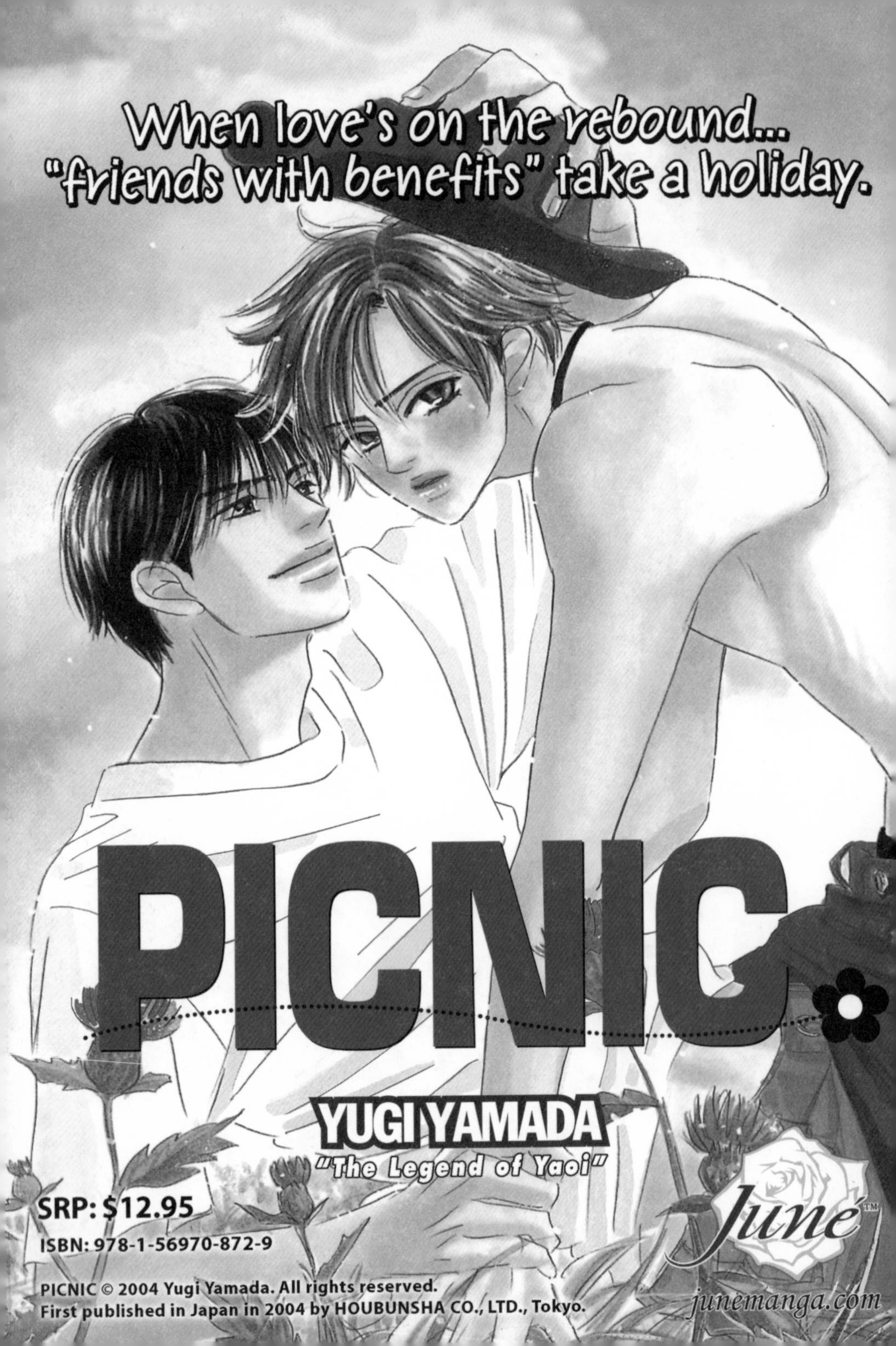
When love's on the rebound...
"friends with benefits" take a holiday.
PICNIC
YUGI YAMADA
"The Legend of Yaoi"
SRP: $12.95
ISBN: 978-1-56970-872-9
June™
PICNIC © 2004 Yugi Yamada. All rights reserved.
First published in Japan in 2004 by HOUBUNSHA CO., LTD., Tokyo.
junemanga.com

From the creator of
ANTIQUE BAKERY

A Duet Like No Other...

♪Solfege♪

Written & Illustrated by:
Fumi Yoshinaga

June™
junemanga.com

SRP: $12.95

ISBN: 978-1-56970-841-5

STOP

This is the back of the book! Start from the other side.

NATIVE MANGA readers read manga from *right to left*.

1
2
1
3
2
3
5
4
4
6
5
8
7
6

*If you run into our **Native Manga** logo on any of our books... you'll know that this manga is published in it's true original native Japanese right to left reading format, as it was intended. Turn to the other side of the book and start reading from right to left, top to bottom.*

Follow the diagram to see how its done.
Surf's Up!

NATIVE MANGA
READ RIGHT TO LEFT